MW00785748

First edition: January 2017
ISBN 978-0-692-81030-9

Written by
DINO STAMATOPOULOS

Illustrated by
LEAH TISCIONE

Consulting Editor
BRENDAN WRIGHT

Editor and President of Starburns Press
SIMON ORÉ

Published by Starburns Press
A division of Starburns Industries, Inc.
1700 W. Burbank Blvd.
Burbank, CA 91506

0 6 9 2 8 1 0 3 0 7
Printed in Canada

We proudly dedicate this book to _____ , whose unending love and support has not only inspired us throughout this entire project, but has also enriched each and every one of our goddamned lives. This is a person who makes every other human being on earth look like a complete and utter asshole. Seriously. Fuck everyone else. In hell.

foreword

BY Andy Richter

(SPOILER ALERT)

Way back in 1990, I was a young pimply improviser in Chicago. Which is to say that I lived in Chicago, I was paying various alcoholics who were slightly older than me to teach me improvisational comedy, and I had bad skin. The main point is that the only thing that differentiated me from any other loser on the street was that I had decided I was going to attempt to make it in comedy, but I didn't really have any idea how a person did that, or what "making it" even meant. I figured I'd just hang around where all the other funny people were and I'd eventually figure something out.

One of the places where the funny people were was the Annoyance Theater, which was located in a former drag show club on North Broadway in Boy's Town. The Annoyance was a group devoted to a more experimental brand of improv that was inspired by its leader, the wonderful Mick Napier. Mick was thrillingly funny and in possession of an inspiring magical genius, but he could also be terrifying, like some trickster from some old cautionary Kentucky folk tale. A wicked elf in banana yellow bike shorts with a pool cue in one hand and a cigarette/Miller Lite in the other, he might lead you on a life-changing journey of discovery, or become displeased and decide to fuck you and eat you. Or, worst of all, he could just decide you were boring.

The Annoyance was a great place to be if you were young and weird and wanted to have fun. The building had originally been a commercial carriage house and as such had never been intended for human habitation, so the rats from the alley came and went as freely as the collection of comedians, drugs-and-drink enthusiasts, and unchallenged hangers-on that made up the cast of the never-ending show that flowed from the stage back into the nooks and crannys of the house and then back onto the stage again.

The Annoyance shows reflected the libertine attitudes and non-existent behavioral barriers of the people who made them; the theater boasts the longest-running musical in Chicago theater history, Co-Ed Prison Sluts, which I think also boasts the most profanities of any play produced anywhere. The shows at the Annoyance were unlike what you would find at other theaters around town – lewd, loud, and loose. And very, very funny (well, most of them).

It was in this roster of shows that I first started seeing flyers on the wall for a show named "Trent", which quickly just started being referred to as "the dead baby musical". I didn't know anybody in the cast very well, but I had gone to Columbia College in the South Loop with the guy who wrote it, Dino Stamatopoulos. Although we were in different programs (Dino was in Theater, I was in Film) our paths had crossed a few times at the bar of the Blackstone hotel, which on Thursday nights became an odd mix of mostly under—age commuter art school kids attempting their best Robert Smith looks getting bombed before the drive back home to Mom and Dad, and slightly off—put travelling business folks who most likely decided to stay at the Hilton next time (Dino and I would get to know each other much better when we both got jobs on Late Night with Conan O'Brien).

"Trent" was exactly the kind of show that I'm sure my mother was afraid I'd be exposed to: a happy—go—lucky story of a young couple who decide to not let their newborn baby's death stop them from raising him. At the time, this kind of show was a revelation. I had probably only first heard the word "nihilism" a year or so before I saw "Trent", and now I was watching a show full of catchy hummable tunes in which the actors repeatedly picked up a doll by the head and shook it to see if it was alive or not. Except it wasn't a doll; it had transformed into a baby in the viewers mind as we all sat there laughing, realizing that laughter and horror and love and disgust were all floating around in some inter—connected muckiness in ourselves that we may not have even known about. And somehow, as pessimistic as "Trent" was, it still ended up hopeful, in its own sick way.

And now, a million years later, you hold in your hand the "Trent" graphic novel. Enjoy it, as the experience of reading it isn't far removed from what I saw way back in 1990 in the basement of the Annoyance. Dino, like the parents in the show, couldn't let go of that dead baby, either. Lucky you.

aol instant message
June 6, 2009

LOUIS CK: hey fuckface. you there?

LEAH TISCIONE: Heeeeey whats up??

LOUIS: hey I was just talking about you to my friend Dino
He has been writing some short stories and he's interested in developing them into graphic novels.
I told him about you and told him I woudl send him some links to some stuff of yours.
Will you please give me some links to what you would want him to see? somethign like the comic book you gave me, which was a good example of storyboarding and whatnot. and some other stuff in different styles.
Okay, fuckface?

LEAH: Fuck yes fucker!
Thank you for remembering my drawings!
did you send him to my website?

LOUIS: I don't think you'd make any money at the outset but if maybe you could do a sample for him on spec, like a page from one of his stories? I dunno. anyway he does get shit made so it could lead to somethign if he likes you, which he might not, because that's life. His name is Dino Stamatopolous. I still spell it wrong after knowing him for fifteen years.
I didn't send him anything. I'm contacting you so you can tell me what to send.

LEAH: Hot damn, well it depends, I'll definitely talk to him to see what he's all about, my wbsite is the best example of different styles and mediums. I also have the comic I could send him and story reels of storyboards, but thats if he likes my site first

LOUIS: okay well i'll give him your website and email and let him take it from there. DO not expect to hear from this person. He NEVER calls me back. He is an alcoholic and a total mess but a hilarious and gentle genius. so we'll just see what happens.
what email address should i give him?

LEAH: definitely [an email address], and it took me FOREVER to come up with leahtiscione.com for the site name. How creative
I won't expect anything. He's greek

LOUIS: yup

LEAH: I really appreciate the referral dude, thanks
he's gotta be awesome if he's your friend

LOUIS: no probablem dude

LEAH: bro

LOUIS: babe

LEAH: butt

LOUIS: pussy

LEAH: pube

LOUIS: cock

LEAH: cocknballs

LOUIS: okay that's it. you went too far.
i gotta go pal. have a good one.

LEAH: haha thanks again

The table of musical contents

THIS MUSICAL GRAPHIC NOVEL COMES WITH A FREE SOUNDTRACK RECORDING!
GO TO WWW.TRENTMUSICAL.COM TO DOWNLOAD IT

LOOK FOR THE TRACK BOX ON THE LEFT TO PLAY THE CORRESPONDING SONG

MUSIC PERFORMED BY JONNY POLONSKY

MUSIC ENGINEERED BY HAL CRAGIN

TRENT

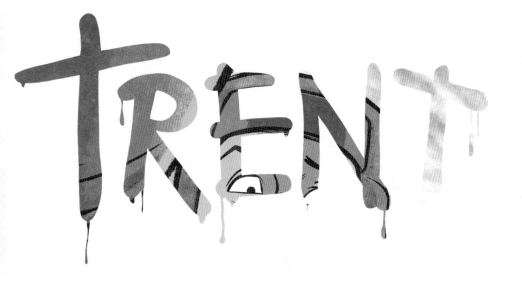

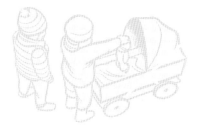

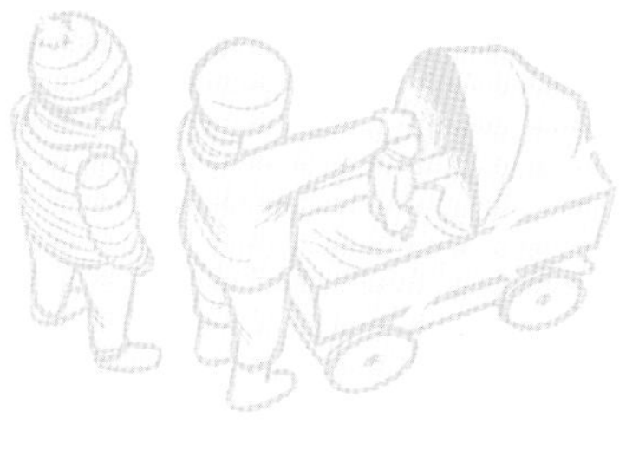

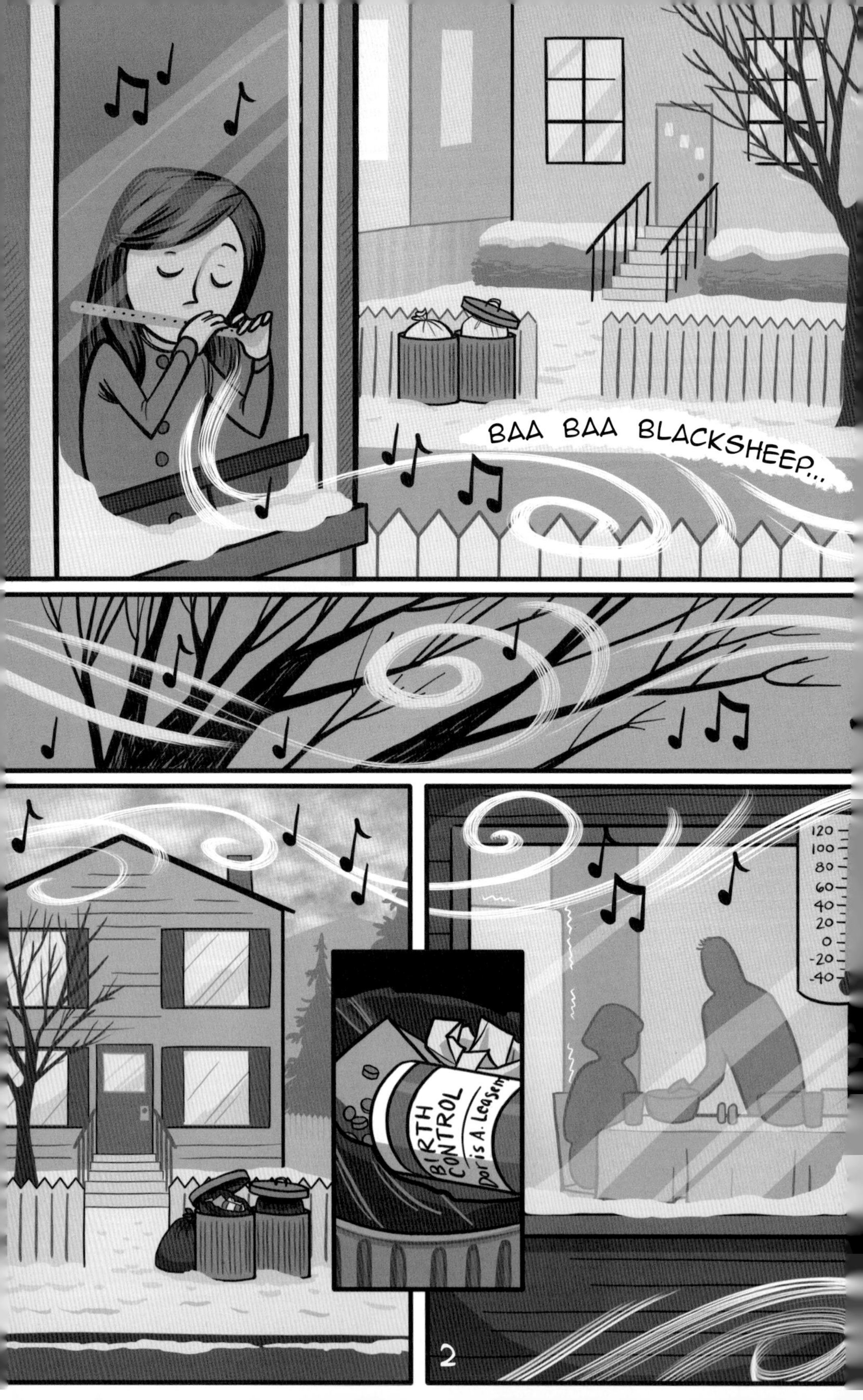
BAA BAA BLACKSHEEP...
120
100
80
60
40
20
0
-20
-40
BIRTH CONTROL
Doris A. Leasem

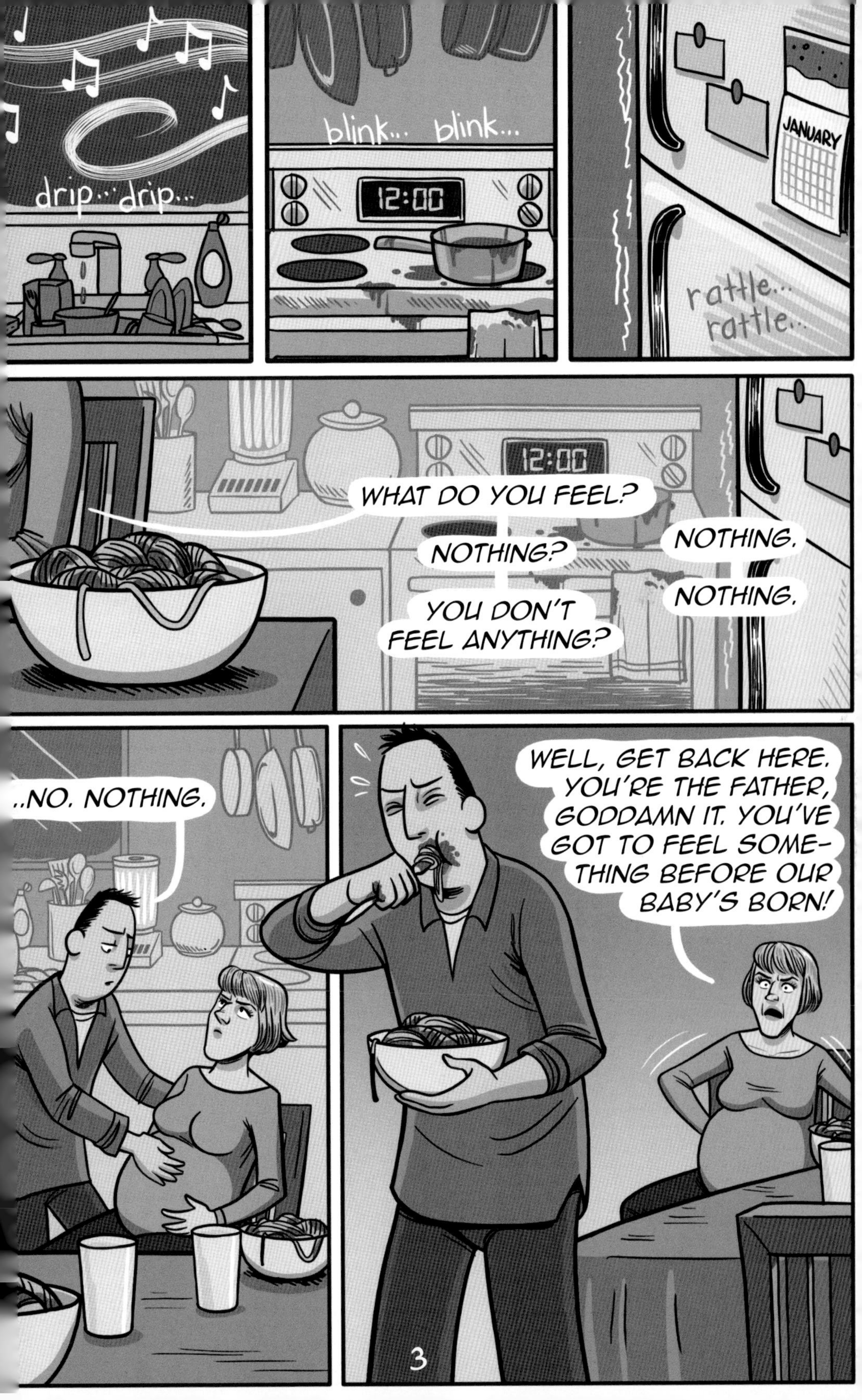
drip... drip...
blink... blink...
12:00
JANUARY
rattle... rattle...
12:00
WHAT DO YOU FEEL?
NOTHING?
YOU DON'T FEEL ANYTHING?
NOTHING.
NOTHING.
..NO. NOTHING.
WELL, GET BACK HERE. YOU'RE THE FATHER, GODDAMN IT. YOU'VE GOT TO FEEL SOME-THING BEFORE OUR BABY'S BORN!

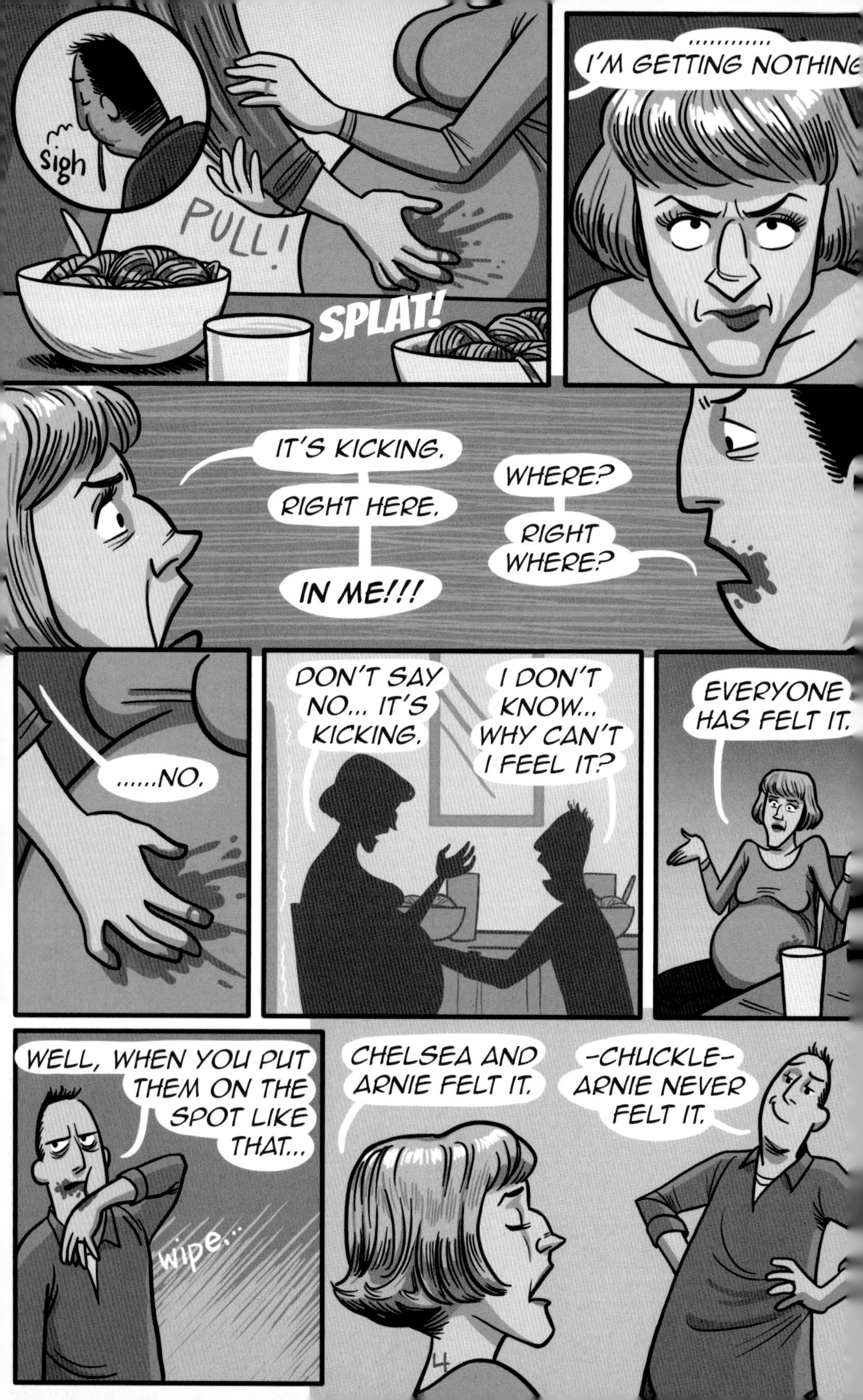

sigh
PULL!
SPLAT!
....
I'M GETTING NOTHING
IT'S KICKING.
RIGHT HERE.
IN ME!!!
WHERE?
RIGHT WHERE?
......NO.
DON'T SAY NO... IT'S KICKING.
I DON'T KNOW... WHY CAN'T I FEEL IT?
EVERYONE HAS FELT IT.
WELL, WHEN YOU PUT THEM ON THE SPOT LIKE THAT...
wipe...
CHELSEA AND ARNIE FELT IT.
-CHUCKLE- ARNIE NEVER FELT IT.

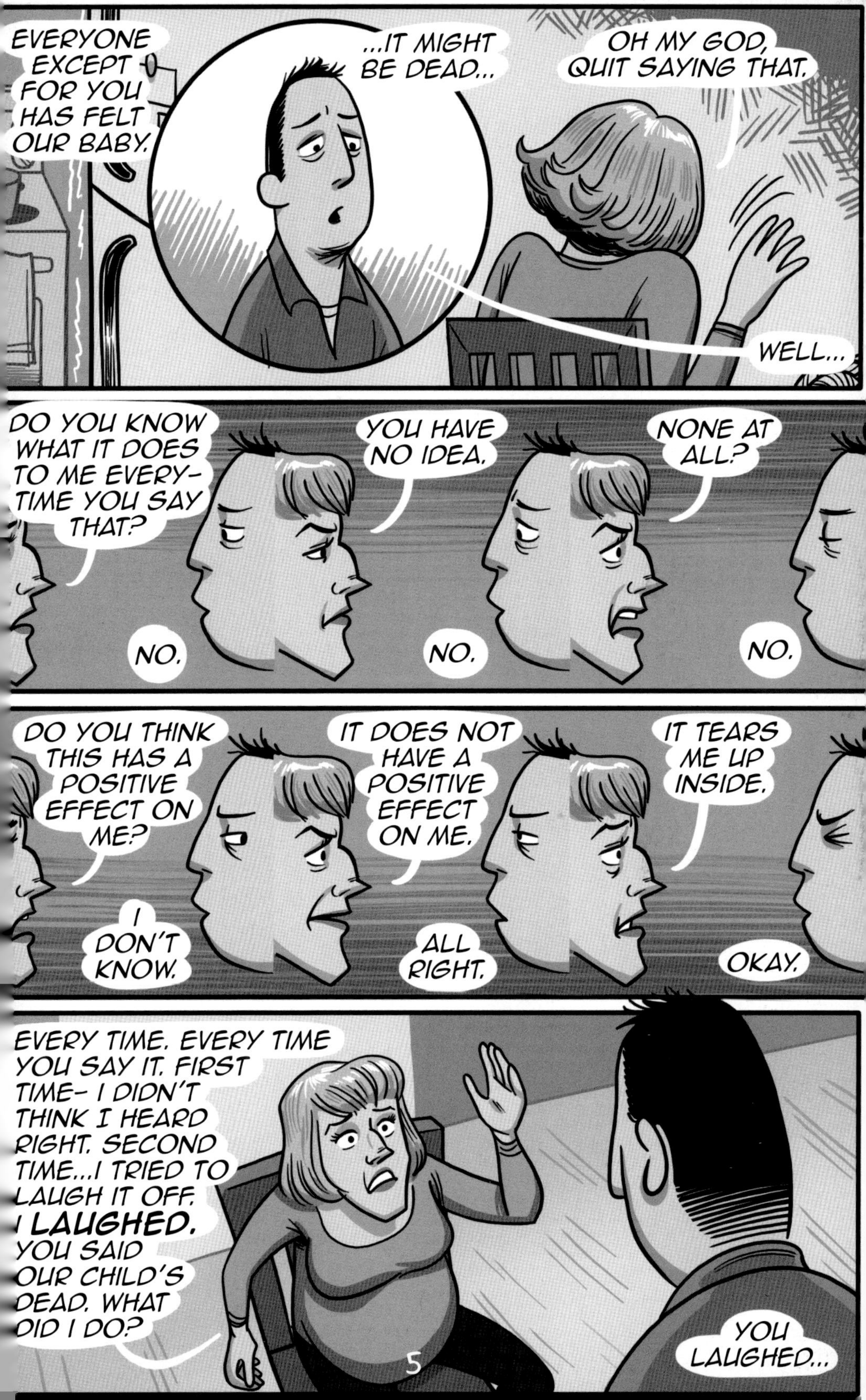
EVERYONE EXCEPT FOR YOU HAS FELT OUR BABY.
...IT MIGHT BE DEAD...
OH MY GOD, QUIT SAYING THAT.
WELL...
DO YOU KNOW WHAT IT DOES TO ME EVERY-TIME YOU SAY THAT?
NO.
YOU HAVE NO IDEA.
NO.
NONE AT ALL?
NO.
DO YOU THINK THIS HAS A POSITIVE EFFECT ON ME?
I DON'T KNOW.
IT DOES NOT HAVE A POSITIVE EFFECT ON ME.
ALL RIGHT.
IT TEARS ME UP INSIDE.
OKAY.
EVERY TIME. EVERY TIME YOU SAY IT. FIRST TIME- I DIDN'T THINK I HEARD RIGHT. SECOND TIME...I TRIED TO LAUGH IT OFF. I **LAUGHED.** YOU SAID OUR CHILD'S DEAD. WHAT DID I DO?
YOU LAUGHED...

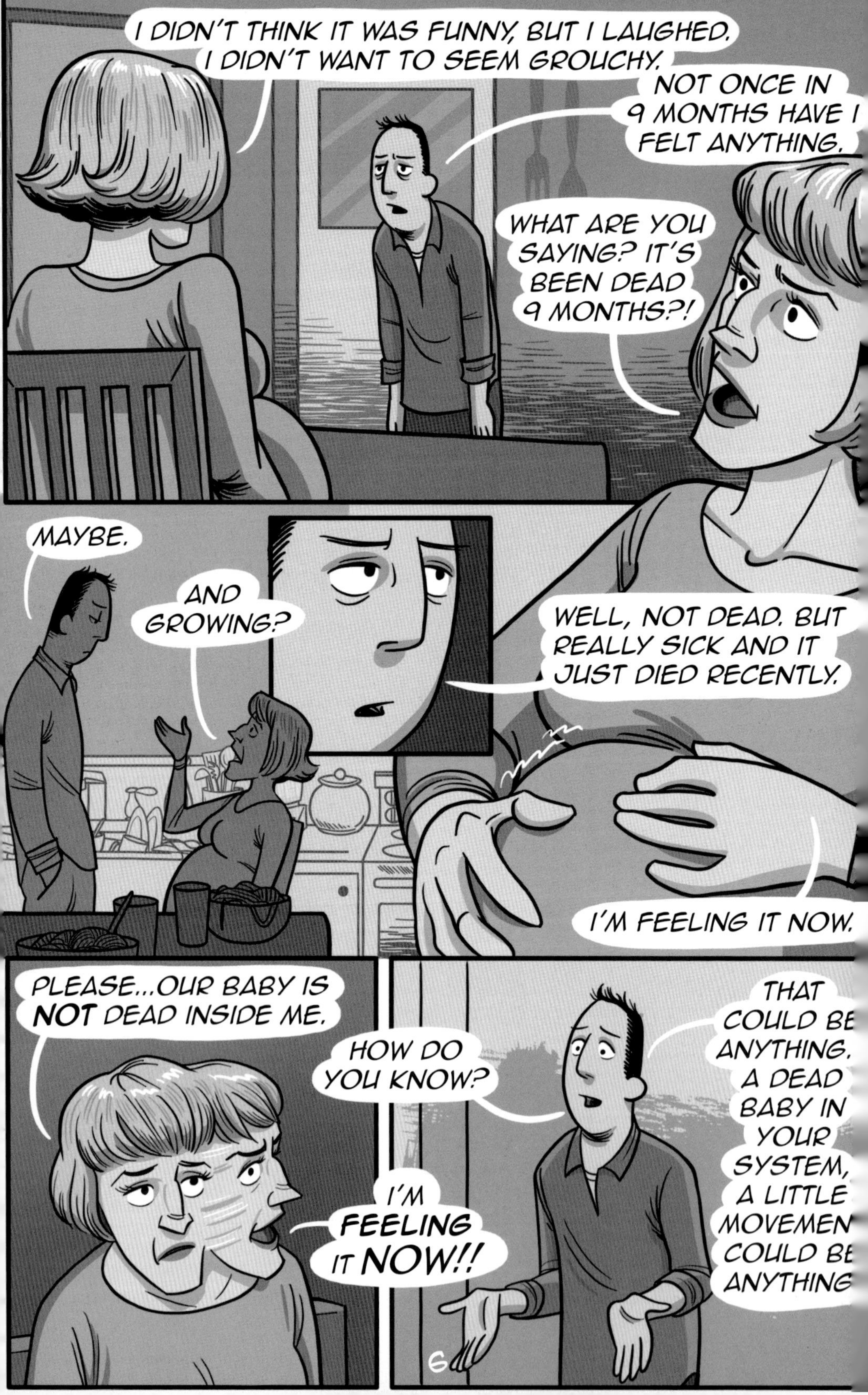
I DIDN'T THINK IT WAS FUNNY, BUT I LAUGHED. I DIDN'T WANT TO SEEM GROUCHY.
NOT ONCE IN 9 MONTHS HAVE I FELT ANYTHING.
WHAT ARE YOU SAYING? IT'S BEEN DEAD 9 MONTHS?!
MAYBE.
AND GROWING?
WELL, NOT DEAD. BUT REALLY SICK AND IT JUST DIED RECENTLY.
I'M FEELING IT NOW.
PLEASE...OUR BABY IS **NOT** DEAD INSIDE ME.
HOW DO YOU KNOW?
I'M **FEELING** IT **NOW!!**
THAT COULD BE ANYTHING. A DEAD BABY IN YOUR SYSTEM, A LITTLE MOVEMEN COULD BE ANYTHING

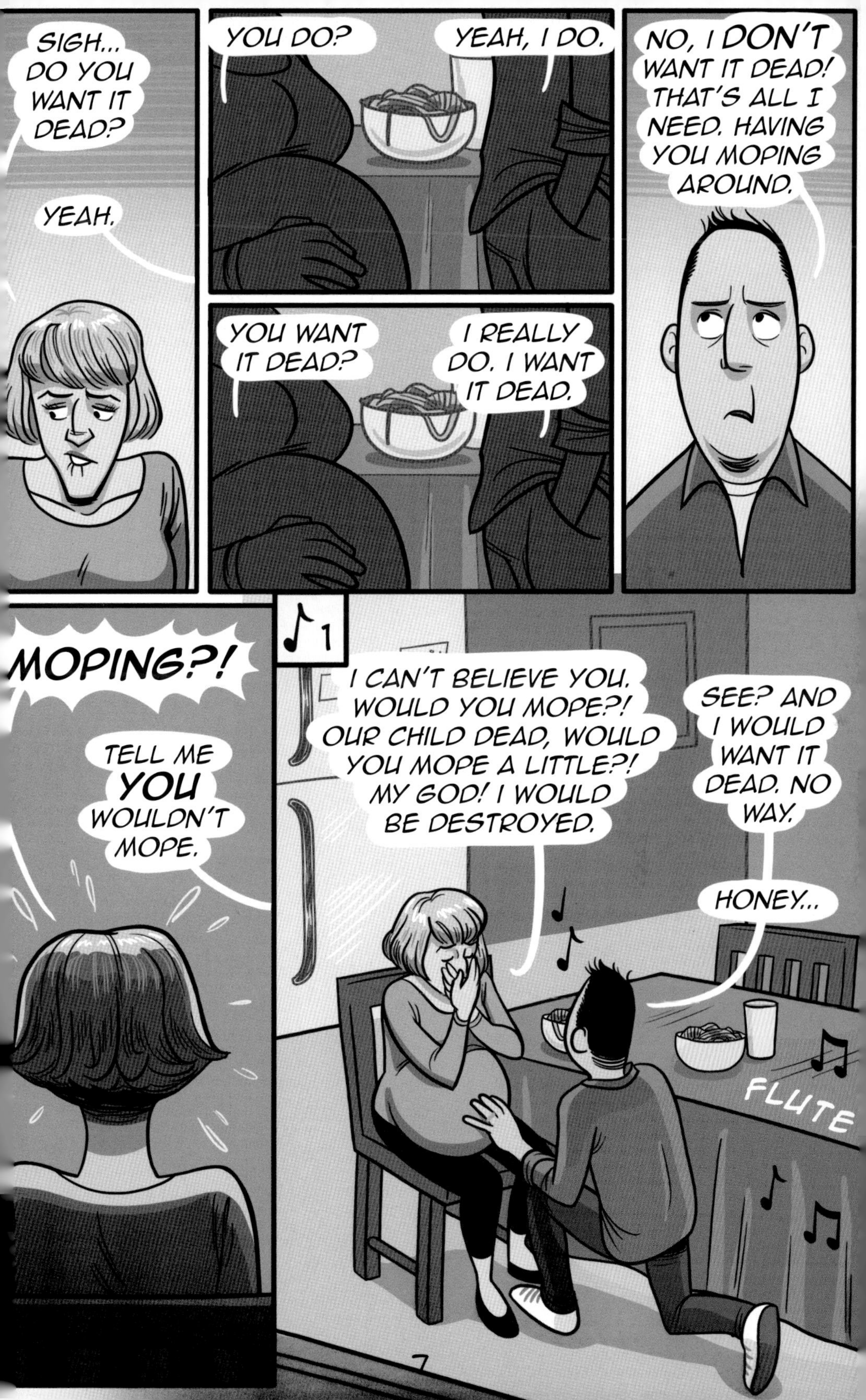
SIGH... DO YOU WANT IT DEAD?
YEAH.
YOU DO?
YEAH, I DO.
YOU WANT IT DEAD?
I REALLY DO. I WANT IT DEAD.
NO, I DON'T WANT IT DEAD! THAT'S ALL I NEED. HAVING YOU MOPING AROUND.
MOPING?!
TELL ME YOU WOULDN'T MOPE.
♪1
I CAN'T BELIEVE YOU. WOULD YOU MOPE?! OUR CHILD DEAD, WOULD YOU MOPE A LITTLE?! MY GOD! I WOULD BE DESTROYED.
SEE? AND I WOULD WANT IT DEAD. NO WAY.
HONEY...
FLUTE

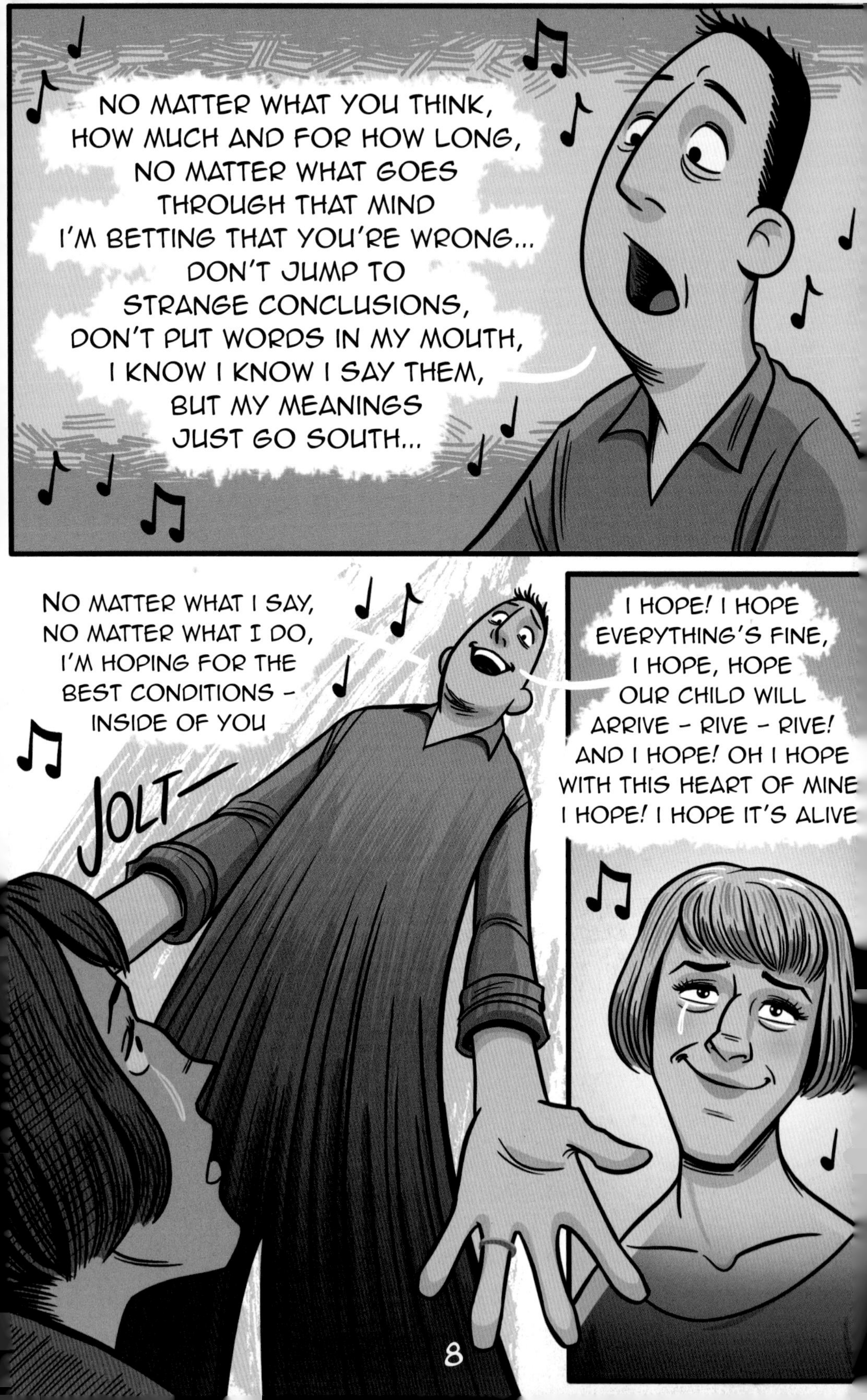
NO MATTER WHAT YOU THINK, HOW MUCH AND FOR HOW LONG, NO MATTER WHAT GOES THROUGH THAT MIND I'M BETTING THAT YOU'RE WRONG... DON'T JUMP TO STRANGE CONCLUSIONS, DON'T PUT WORDS IN MY MOUTH, I KNOW I KNOW I SAY THEM, BUT MY MEANINGS JUST GO SOUTH...
NO MATTER WHAT I SAY, NO MATTER WHAT I DO, I'M HOPING FOR THE BEST CONDITIONS - INSIDE OF YOU
JOLT—
I HOPE! I HOPE EVERYTHING'S FINE, I HOPE, HOPE OUR CHILD WILL ARRIVE - RIVE - RIVE! AND I HOPE! OH I HOPE WITH THIS HEART OF MINE I HOPE! I HOPE IT'S ALIVE

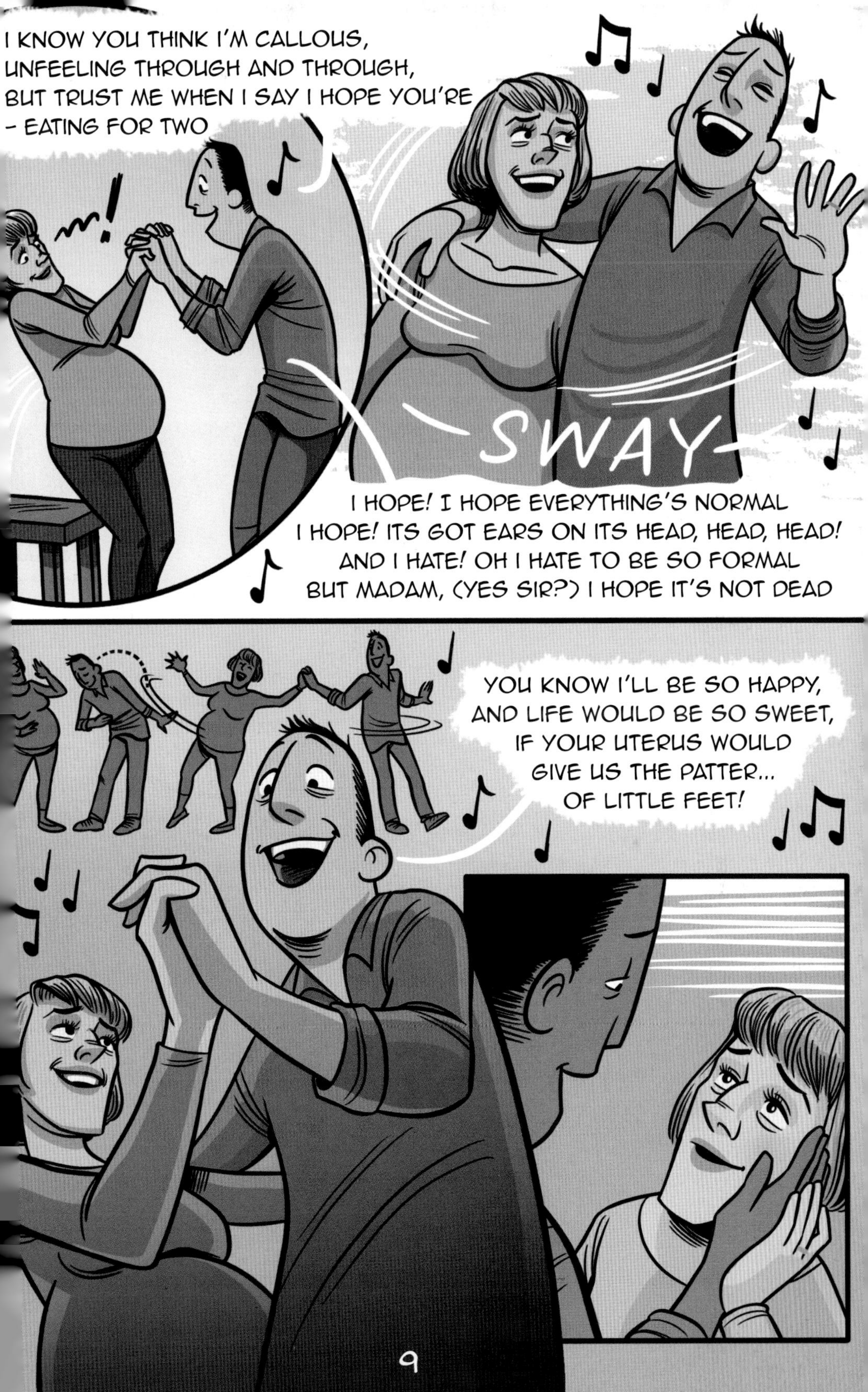

I KNOW YOU THINK I'M CALLOUS, UNFEELING THROUGH AND THROUGH, BUT TRUST ME WHEN I SAY I HOPE YOU'RE - EATING FOR TWO
SWAY
I HOPE! I HOPE EVERYTHING'S NORMAL
I HOPE! ITS GOT EARS ON ITS HEAD, HEAD, HEAD!
AND I HATE! OH I HATE TO BE SO FORMAL
BUT MADAM, (YES SIR?) I HOPE IT'S NOT DEAD
YOU KNOW I'LL BE SO HAPPY, AND LIFE WOULD BE SO SWEET, IF YOUR UTERUS WOULD GIVE US THE PATTER... OF LITTLE FEET!

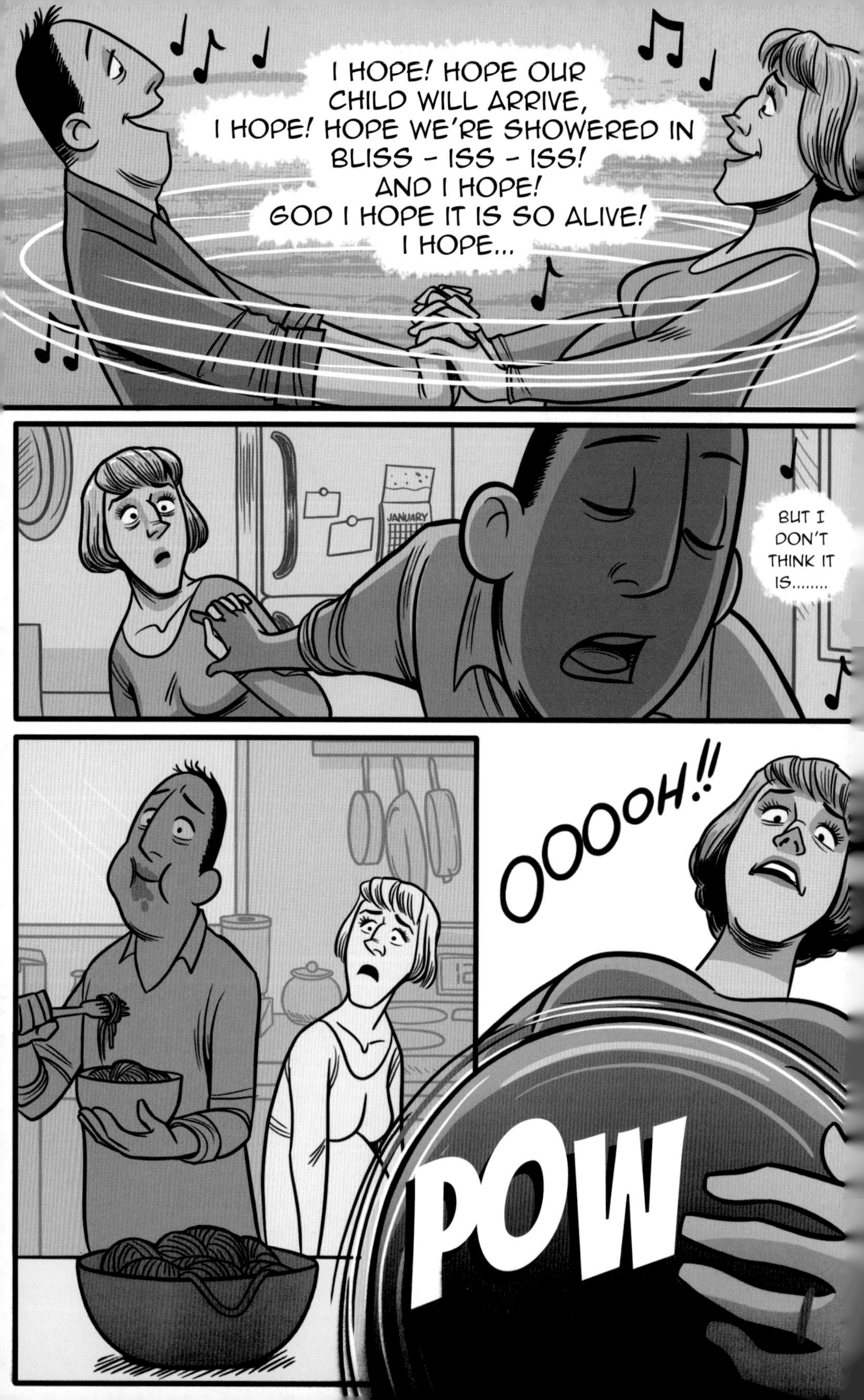
I HOPE! HOPE OUR CHILD WILL ARRIVE, I HOPE! HOPE WE'RE SHOWERED IN BLISS - ISS - ISS! AND I HOPE! GOD I HOPE IT IS SO ALIVE! I HOPE...
JANUARY
BUT I DON'T THINK IT IS........
OOOOH!!
POW

TRENT
IS
BORN

$\longrightarrow$

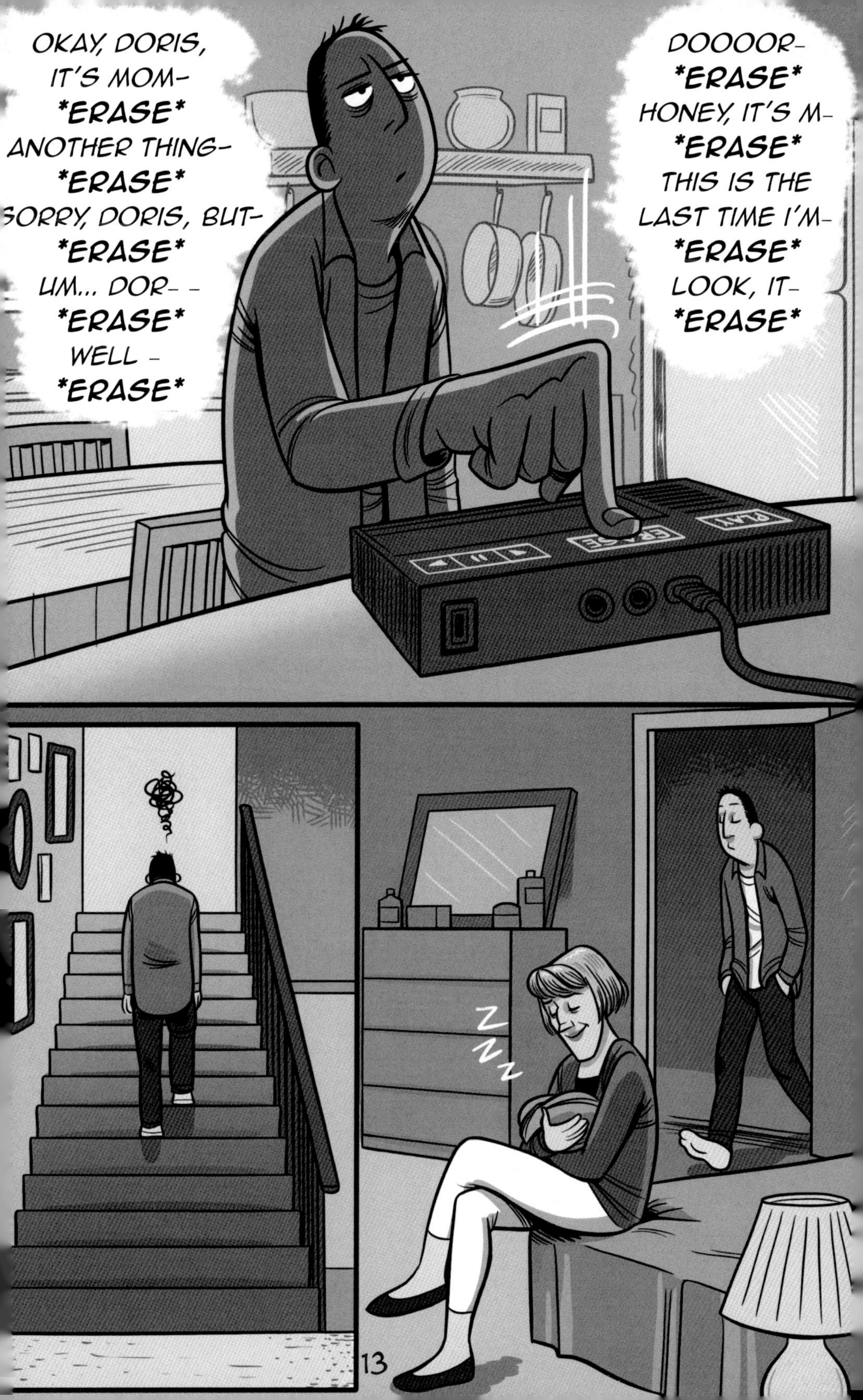
OKAY, DORIS, IT'S MOM- *ERASE* ANOTHER THING- *ERASE* SORRY, DORIS, BUT- *ERASE* UM... DOR- - *ERASE* WELL - *ERASE*
DOOOOR- *ERASE* HONEY, IT'S M- *ERASE* THIS IS THE LAST TIME I'M- *ERASE* LOOK, IT- *ERASE*
ERASE
PLAY
Z Z Z

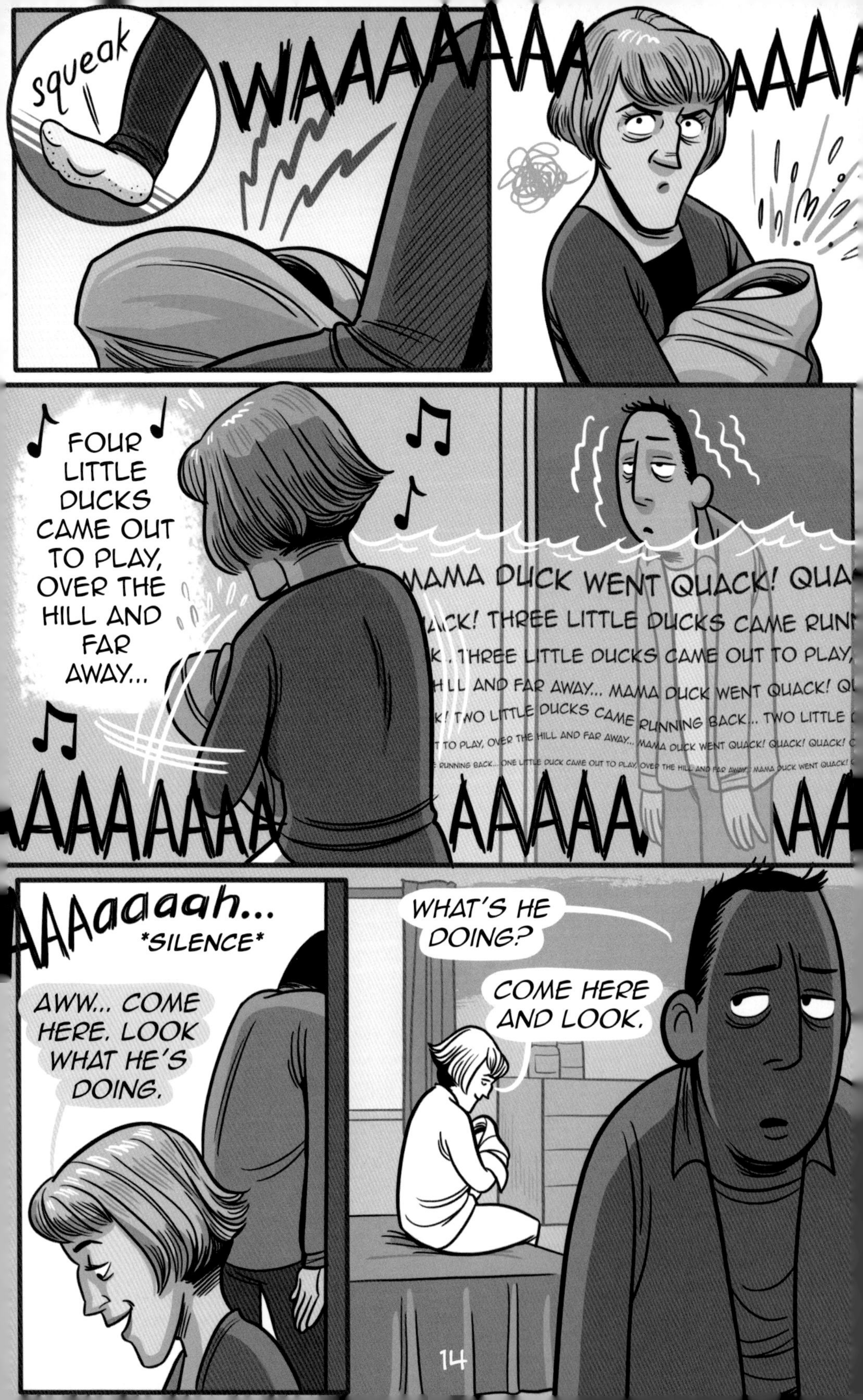

squeak
WAAAAAAAA AAAA
FOUR LITTLE DUCKS CAME OUT TO PLAY, OVER THE HILL AND FAR AWAY...
MAMA DUCK WENT QUACK! QUA
ACK! THREE LITTLE DUCKS CAME RUN
K... THREE LITTLE DUCKS CAME OUT TO PLAY,
HILL AND FAR AWAY... MAMA DUCK WENT QUACK! Q
K! TWO LITTLE DUCKS CAME RUNNING BACK... TWO LITTLE
T TO PLAY, OVER THE HILL AND FAR AWAY... MAMA DUCK WENT QUACK! QUACK! QUACK!
RUNNING BACK... ONE LITTLE DUCK CAME OUT TO PLAY, OVER THE HILL AND FAR AWAY... MAMA DUCK WENT QUACK!
AAAAAAAA AAAAA AA
AAAaaaah...
SILENCE
AWW... COME HERE. LOOK WHAT HE'S DOING.
WHAT'S HE DOING?
COME HERE AND LOOK.

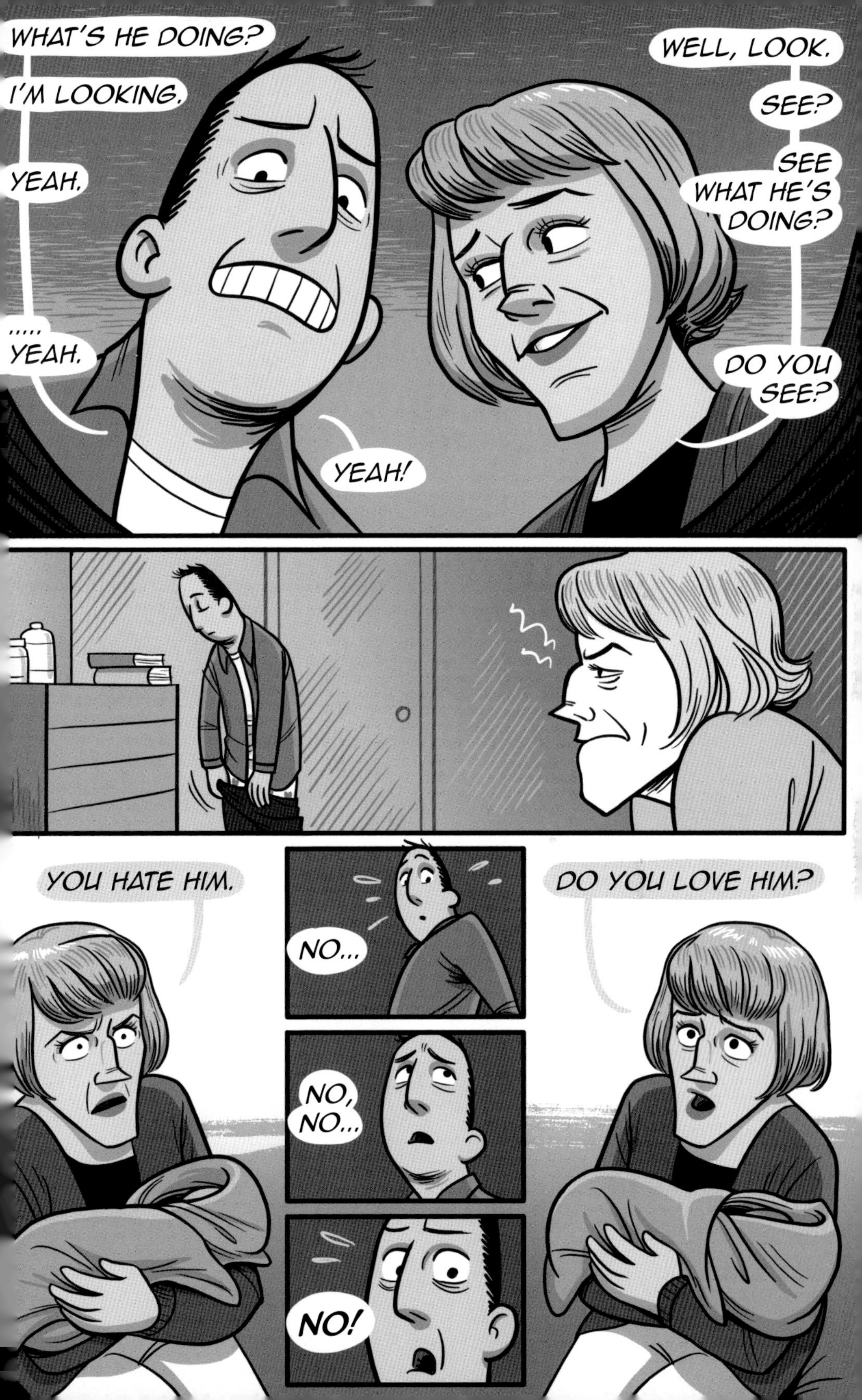
WHAT'S HE DOING?
WELL, LOOK.
I'M LOOKING.
SEE?
YEAH.
SEE WHAT HE'S DOING?
..... YEAH.
DO YOU SEE?
YEAH!
YOU HATE HIM.
NO...
NO, NO...
NO!
DO YOU LOVE HIM?

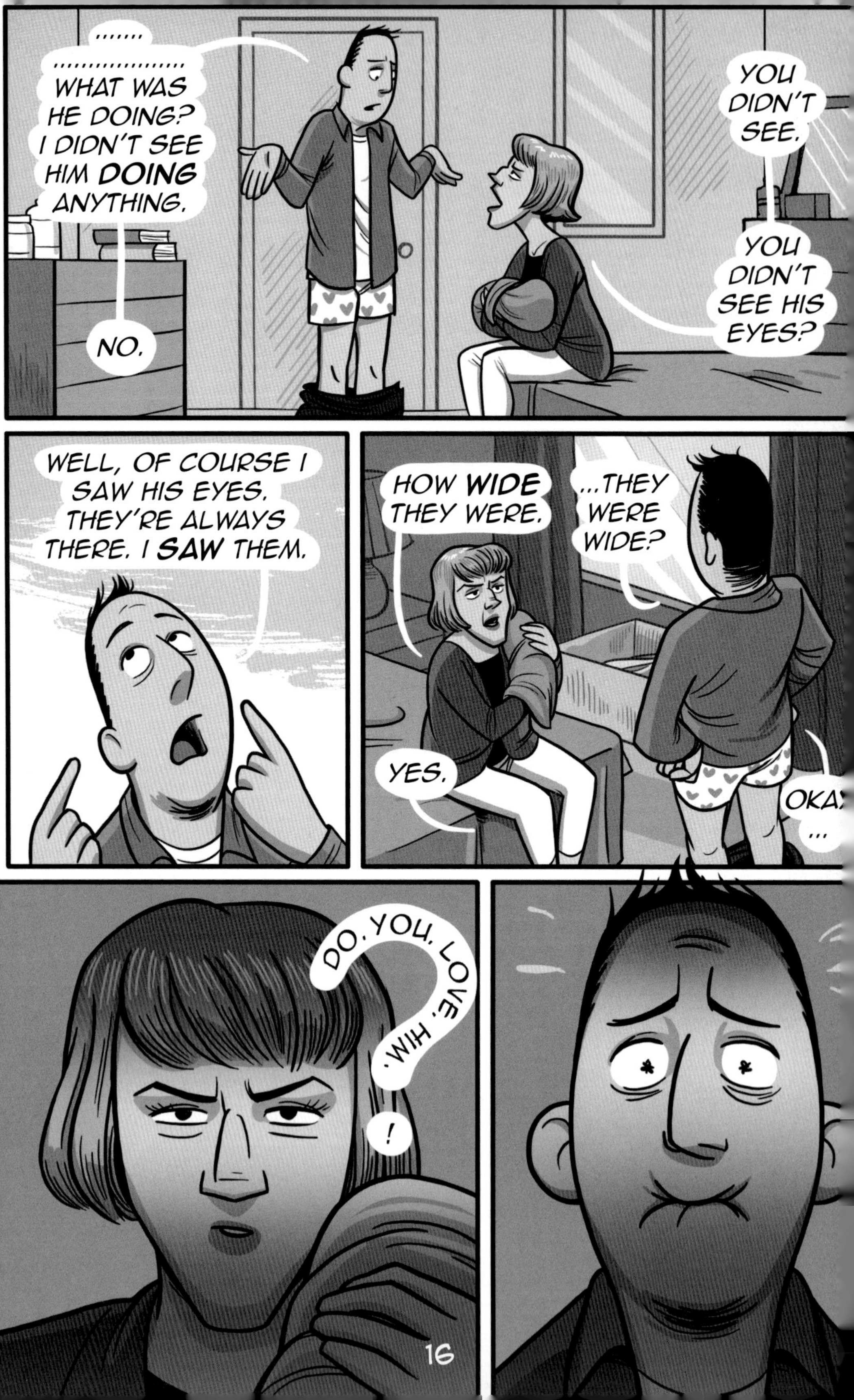
....
....
WHAT WAS HE DOING? I DIDN'T SEE HIM DOING ANYTHING.
NO.
YOU DIDN'T SEE.
YOU DIDN'T SEE HIS EYES?
WELL, OF COURSE I SAW HIS EYES. THEY'RE ALWAYS THERE. I SAW THEM.
HOW WIDE THEY WERE.
...THEY WERE WIDE?
YES.
OKA
...
DO. YOU. LOVE. HIM.
!

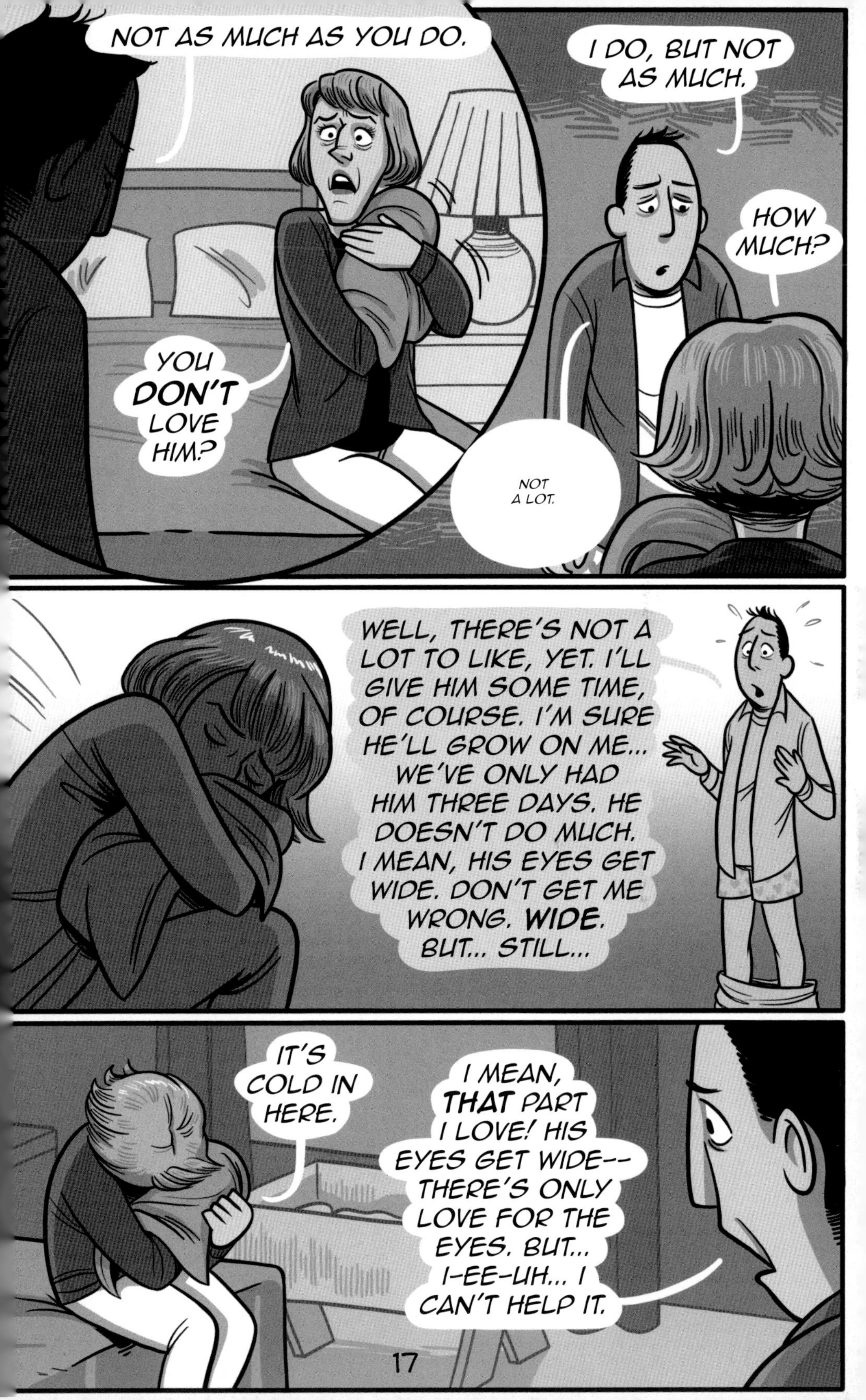
NOT AS MUCH AS YOU DO.
I DO, BUT NOT AS MUCH.
YOU DON'T LOVE HIM?
HOW MUCH?
NOT A LOT.
WELL, THERE'S NOT A LOT TO LIKE, YET. I'LL GIVE HIM SOME TIME, OF COURSE. I'M SURE HE'LL GROW ON ME... WE'VE ONLY HAD HIM THREE DAYS. HE DOESN'T DO MUCH. I MEAN, HIS EYES GET WIDE. DON'T GET ME WRONG. WIDE. BUT... STILL...
IT'S COLD IN HERE.
I MEAN, THAT PART I LOVE! HIS EYES GET WIDE-- THERE'S ONLY LOVE FOR THE EYES. BUT... I-EE-UH... I CAN'T HELP IT.

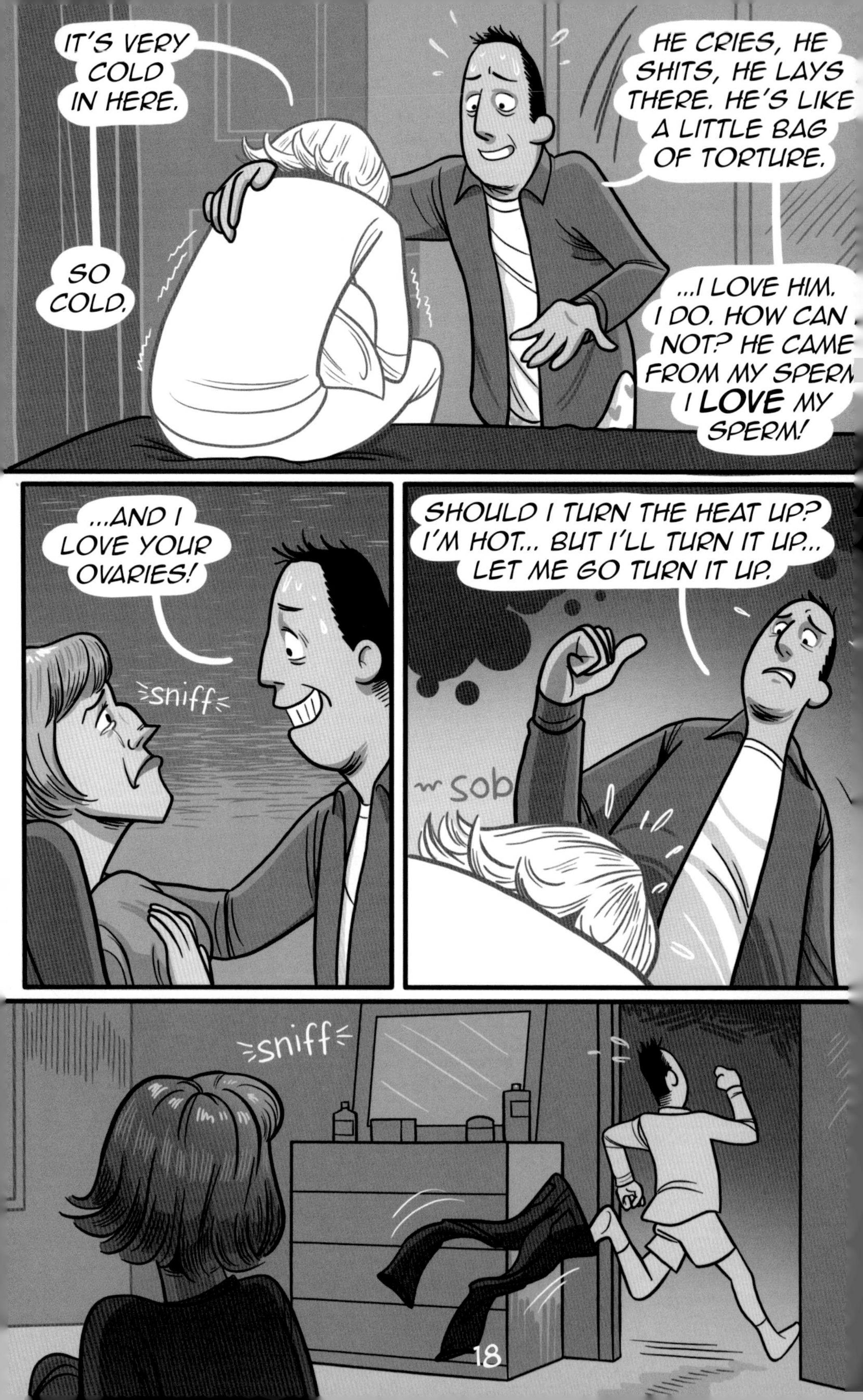

IT'S VERY COLD IN HERE.
SO COLD.
HE CRIES, HE SHITS, HE LAYS THERE. HE'S LIKE A LITTLE BAG OF TORTURE.
...I LOVE HIM. I DO. HOW CAN NOT? HE CAME FROM MY SPERM I **LOVE** MY SPERM!
...AND I LOVE YOUR OVARIES!
sniff
SHOULD I TURN THE HEAT UP? I'M HOT... BUT I'LL TURN IT UP... LET ME GO TURN IT UP.
sob
sniff

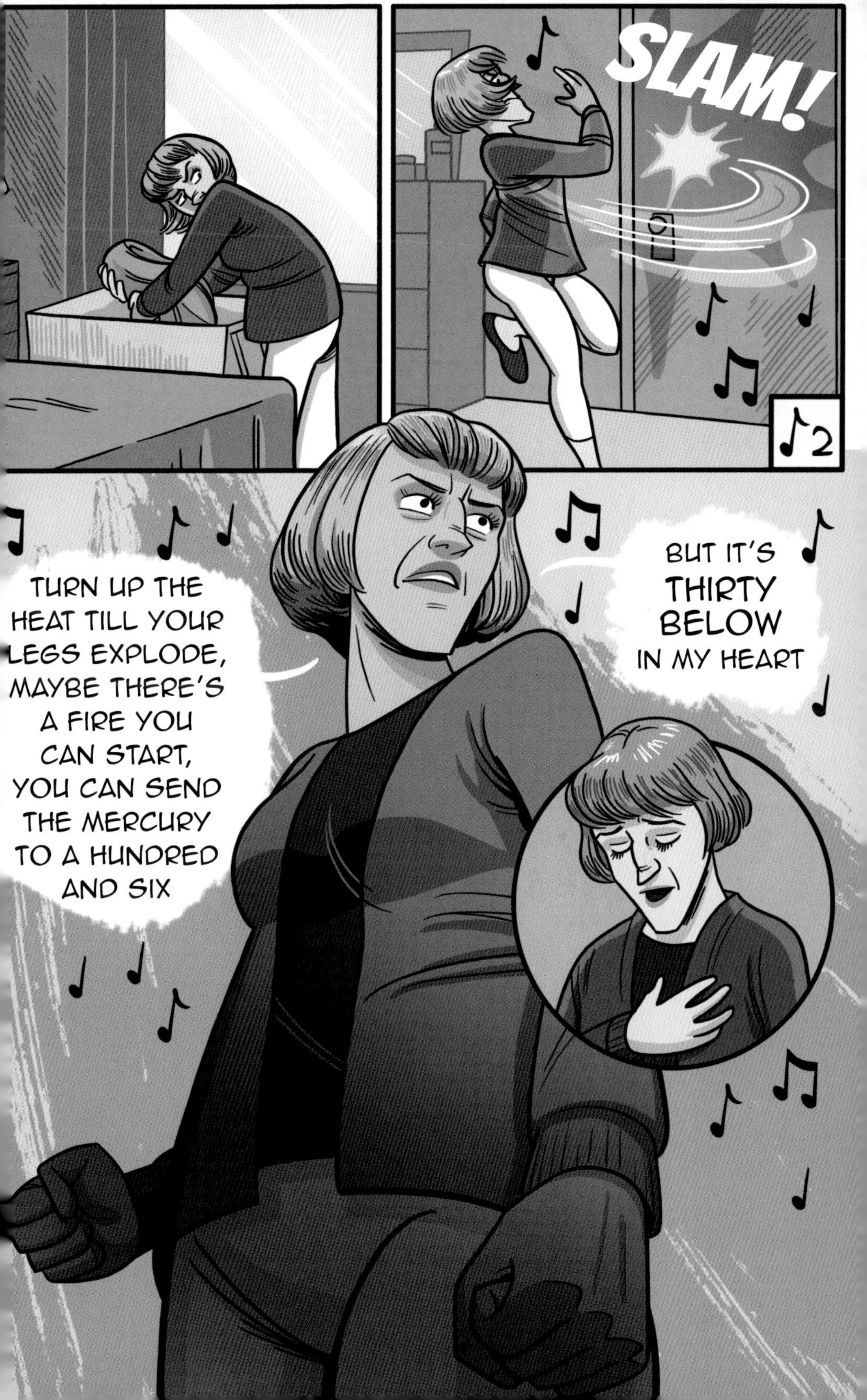
SLAM!
2
TURN UP THE HEAT TILL YOUR LEGS EXPLODE, MAYBE THERE'S A FIRE YOU CAN START, YOU CAN SEND THE MERCURY TO A HUNDRED AND SIX
BUT IT'S THIRTY BELOW IN MY HEART

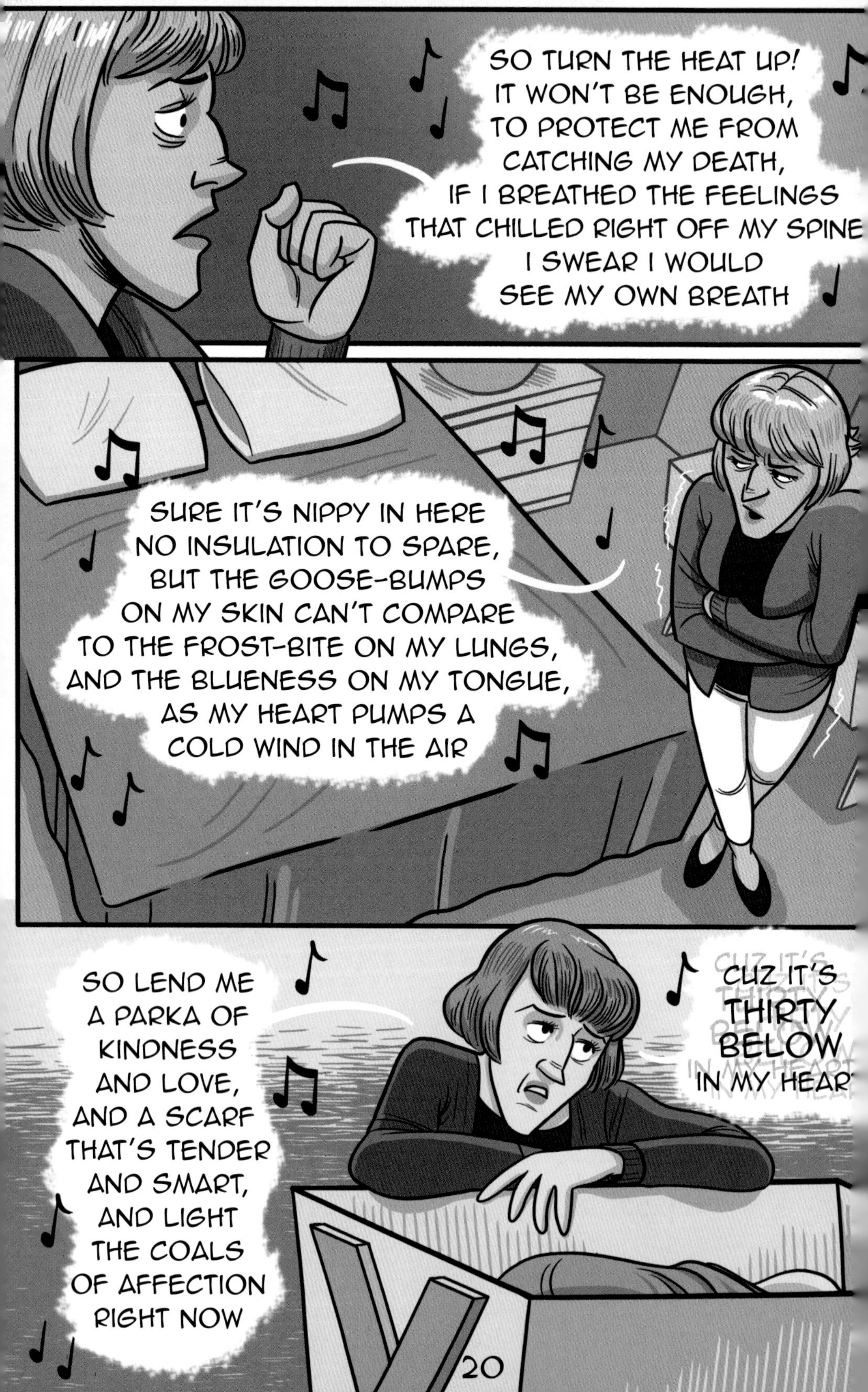
SO TURN THE HEAT UP! IT WON'T BE ENOUGH, TO PROTECT ME FROM CATCHING MY DEATH, IF I BREATHED THE FEELINGS THAT CHILLED RIGHT OFF MY SPINE I SWEAR I WOULD SEE MY OWN BREATH
SURE IT'S NIPPY IN HERE NO INSULATION TO SPARE, BUT THE GOOSE-BUMPS ON MY SKIN CAN'T COMPARE TO THE FROST-BITE ON MY LUNGS, AND THE BLUENESS ON MY TONGUE, AS MY HEART PUMPS A COLD WIND IN THE AIR
SO LEND ME A PARKA OF KINDNESS AND LOVE, AND A SCARF THAT'S TENDER AND SMART, AND LIGHT THE COALS OF AFFECTION RIGHT NOW
CUZ IT'S THIRTY BELOW IN MY HEAR

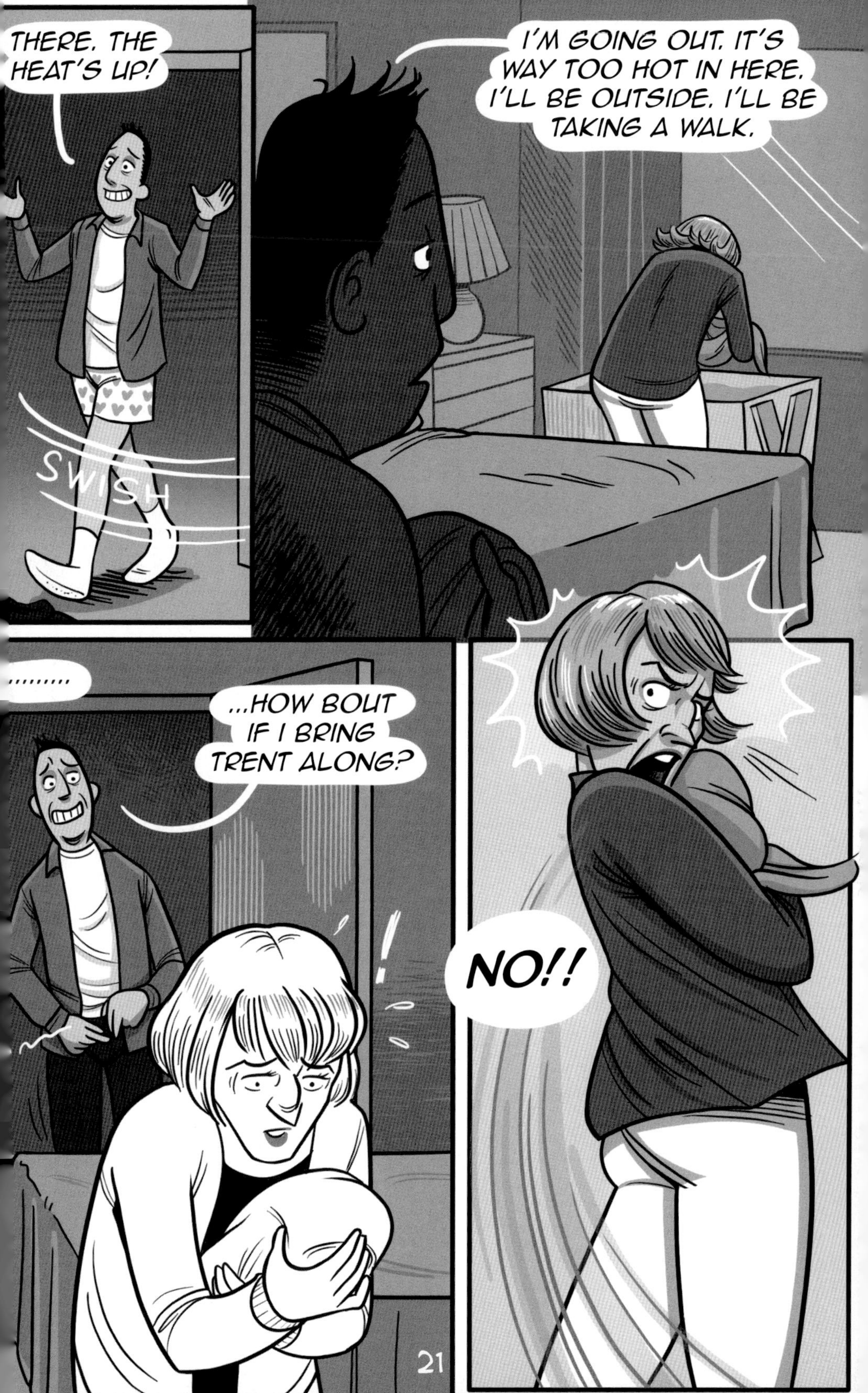
THERE. THE HEAT'S UP!
I'M GOING OUT. IT'S WAY TOO HOT IN HERE. I'LL BE OUTSIDE. I'LL BE TAKING A WALK.
SWISH
....
...HOW BOUT IF I BRING TRENT ALONG?
!
NO!!

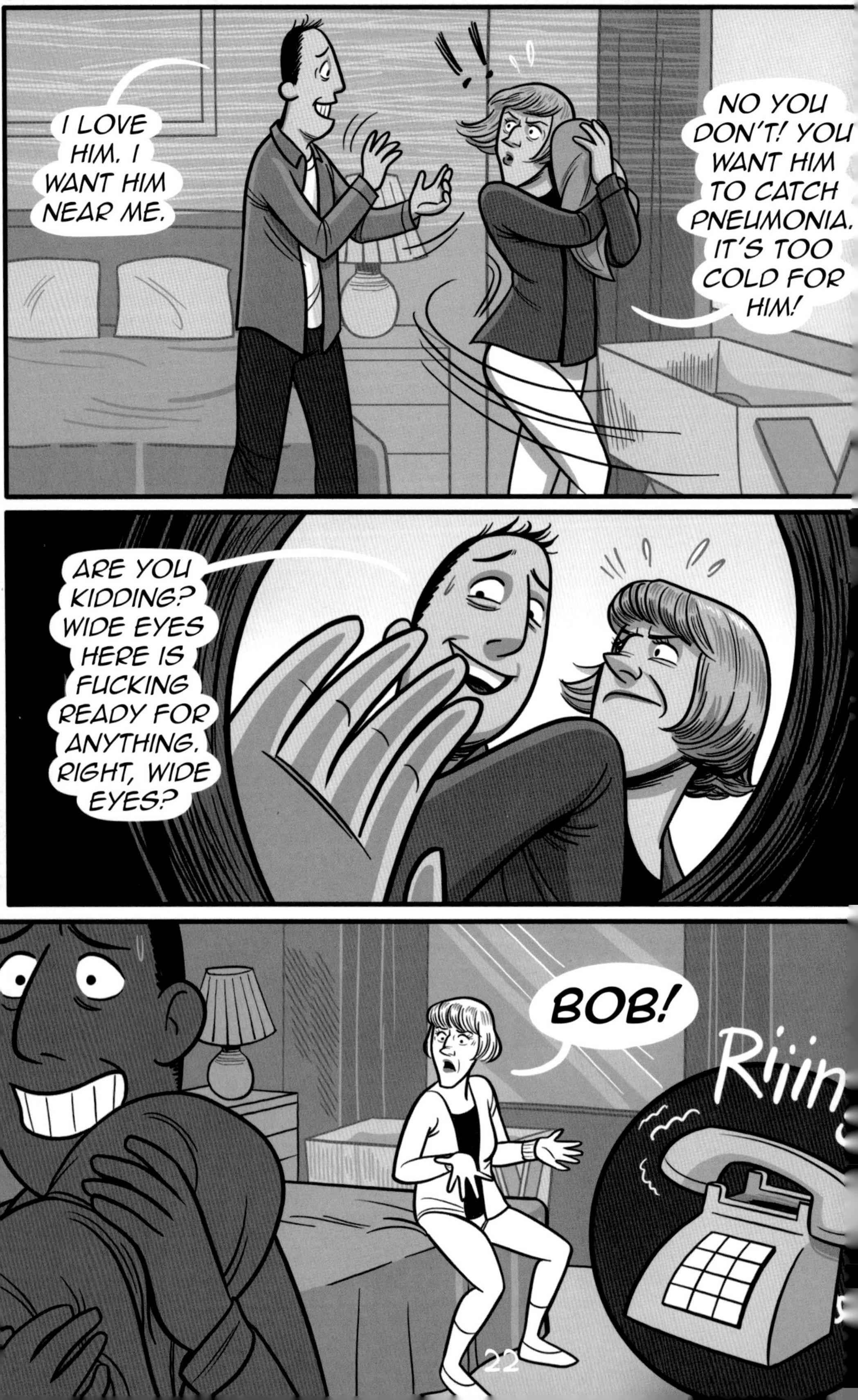
I LOVE HIM. I WANT HIM NEAR ME.
NO YOU DON'T! YOU WANT HIM TO CATCH PNEUMONIA. IT'S TOO COLD FOR HIM!
ARE YOU KIDDING? WIDE EYES HERE IS FUCKING READY FOR ANYTHING. RIGHT, WIDE EYES?
BOB!
Riiin

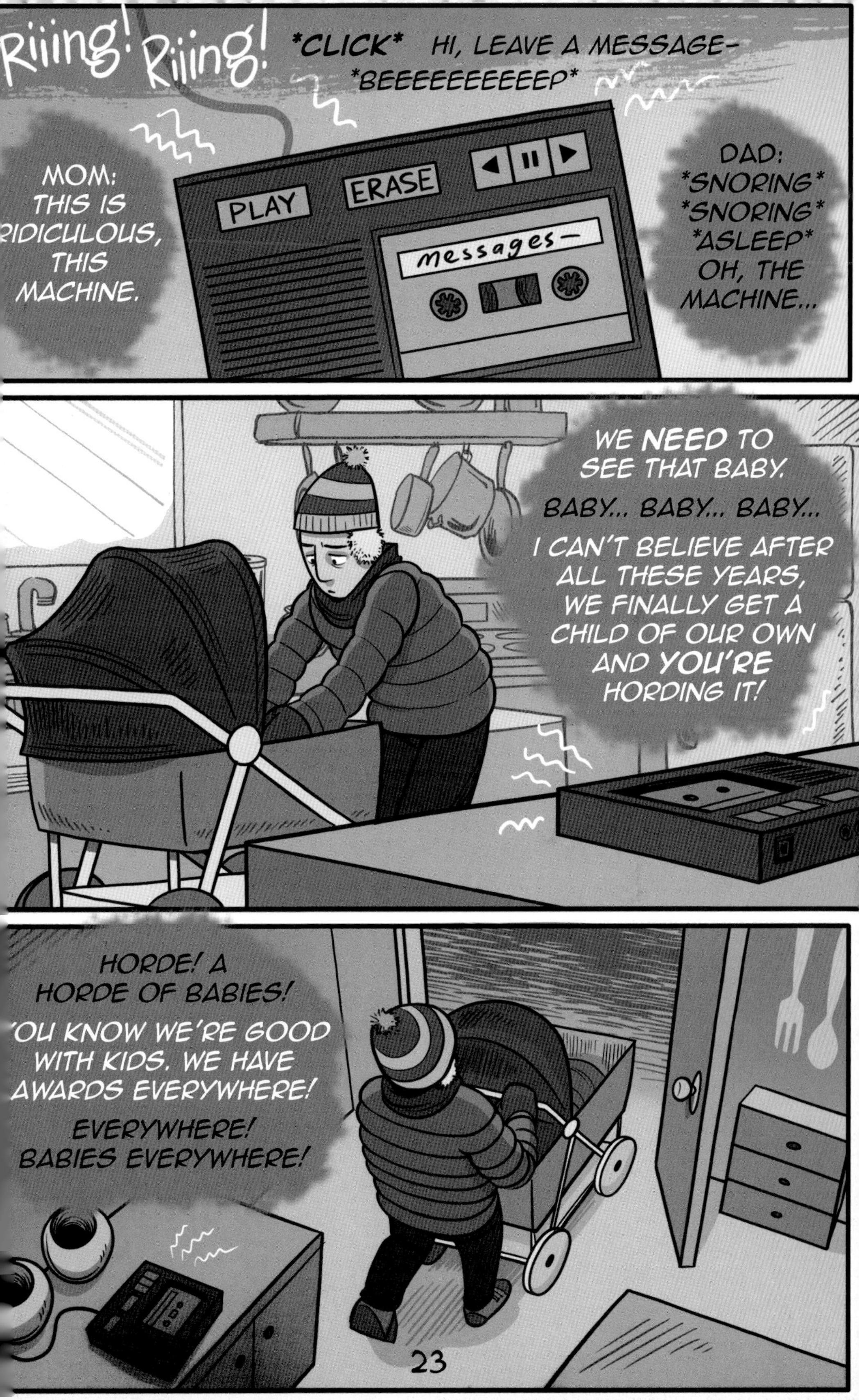
Riiing! Riiing!
CLICK HI, LEAVE A MESSAGE-
BEEEEEEEEEEEP
MOM: THIS IS RIDICULOUS, THIS MACHINE.
PLAY
ERASE
messages-
DAD: *SNORING* *SNORING* *ASLEEP* OH, THE MACHINE...
WE NEED TO SEE THAT BABY.
BABY... BABY... BABY...
I CAN'T BELIEVE AFTER ALL THESE YEARS, WE FINALLY GET A CHILD OF OUR OWN AND YOU'RE HORDING IT!
HORDE! A HORDE OF BABIES!
YOU KNOW WE'RE GOOD WITH KIDS. WE HAVE AWARDS EVERYWHERE!
EVERYWHERE! BABIES EVERYWHERE!

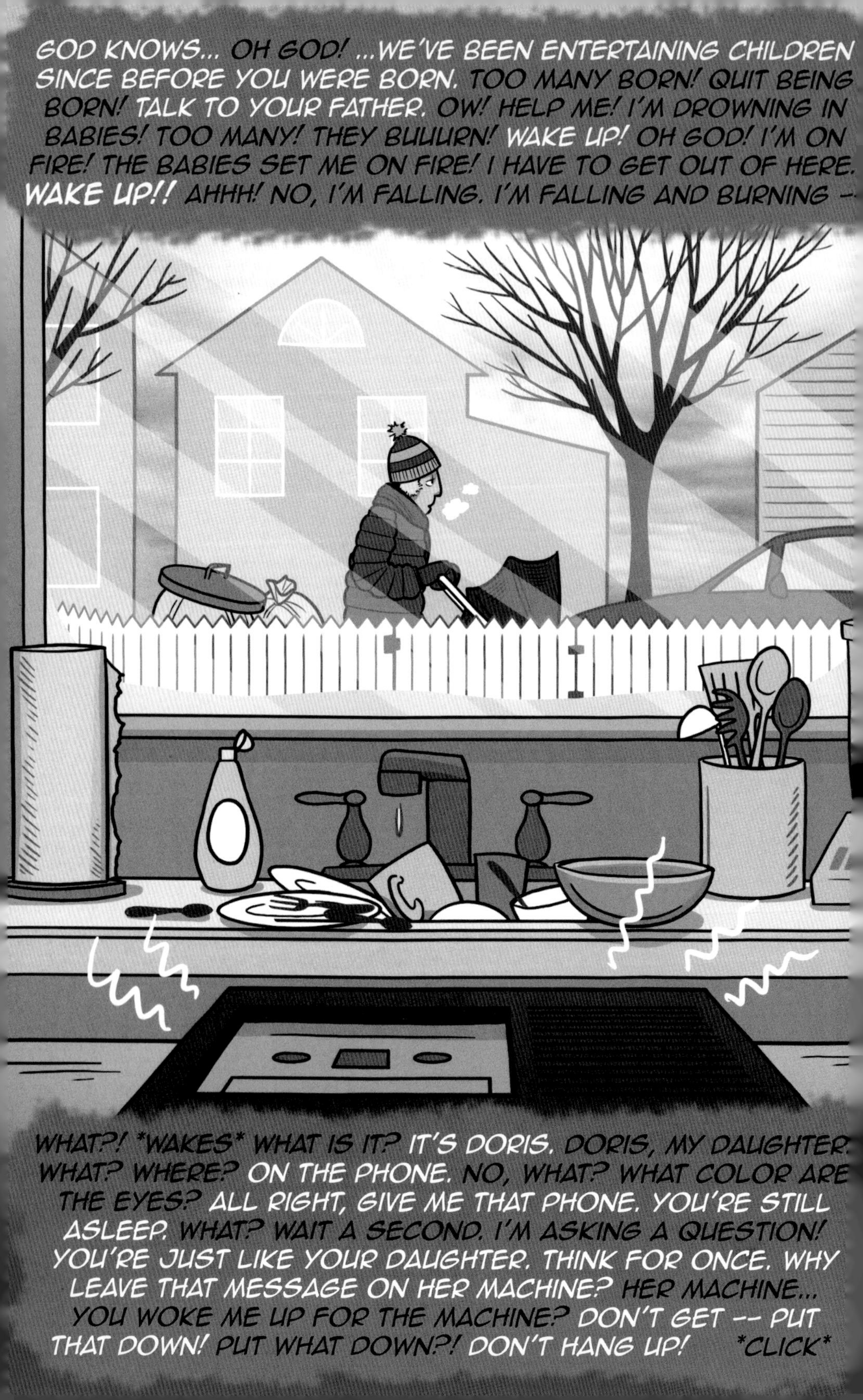
GOD KNOWS... OH GOD! ...WE'VE BEEN ENTERTAINING CHILDREN SINCE BEFORE YOU WERE BORN. TOO MANY BORN! QUIT BEING BORN! TALK TO YOUR FATHER. OW! HELP ME! I'M DROWNING IN BABIES! TOO MANY! THEY BUUURN! WAKE UP! OH GOD! I'M ON FIRE! THE BABIES SET ME ON FIRE! I HAVE TO GET OUT OF HERE. WAKE UP!! AHHH! NO, I'M FALLING. I'M FALLING AND BURNING --
WHAT?! *WAKES* WHAT IS IT? IT'S DORIS. DORIS, MY DAUGHTER. WHAT? WHERE? ON THE PHONE. NO, WHAT? WHAT COLOR ARE THE EYES? ALL RIGHT, GIVE ME THAT PHONE. YOU'RE STILL ASLEEP. WHAT? WAIT A SECOND. I'M ASKING A QUESTION! YOU'RE JUST LIKE YOUR DAUGHTER. THINK FOR ONCE. WHY LEAVE THAT MESSAGE ON HER MACHINE? HER MACHINE... YOU WOKE ME UP FOR THE MACHINE? DON'T GET -- PUT THAT DOWN! PUT WHAT DOWN?! DON'T HANG UP!
CLICK

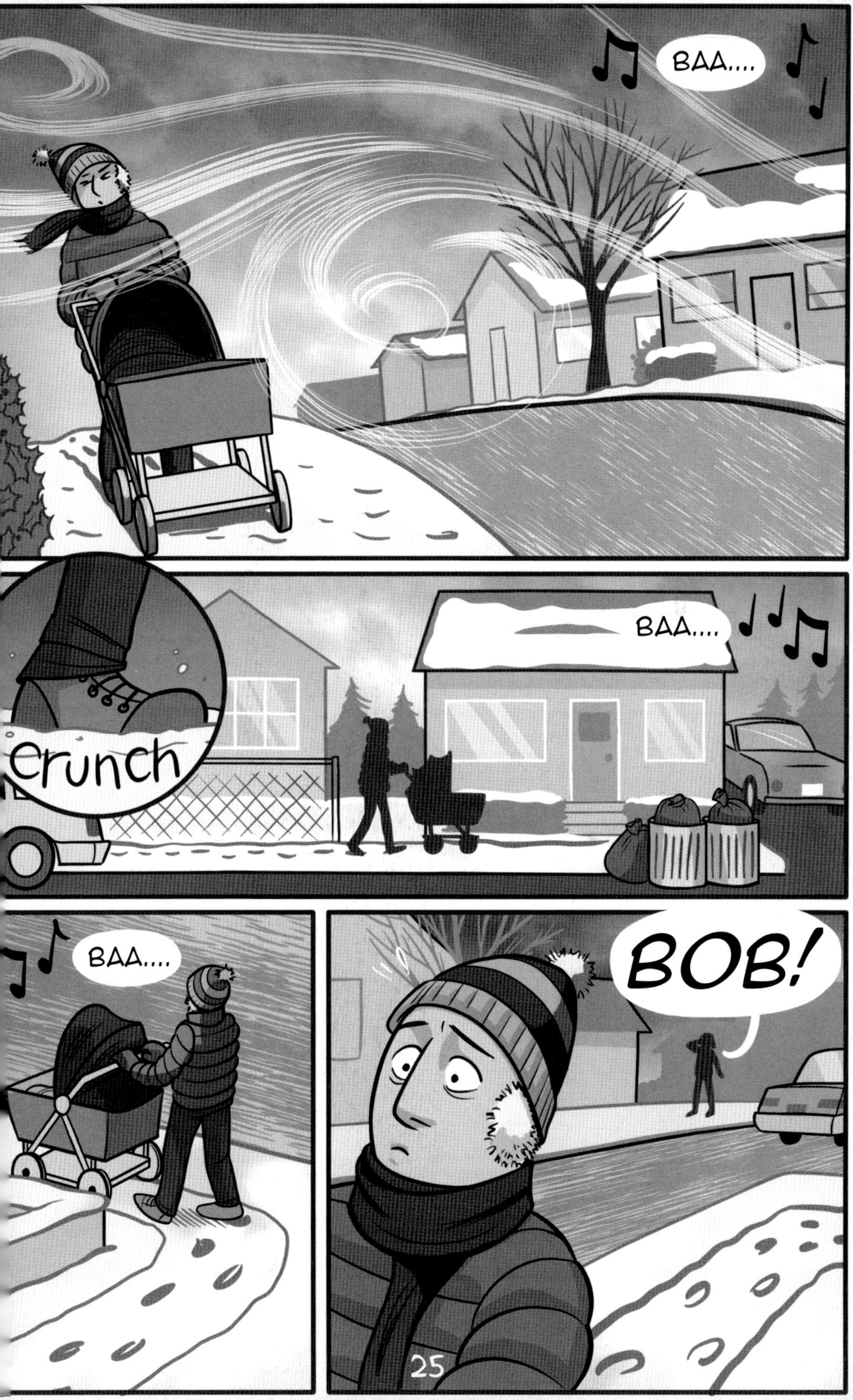
BAA....
crunch
BAA....
BAA....
BOB!

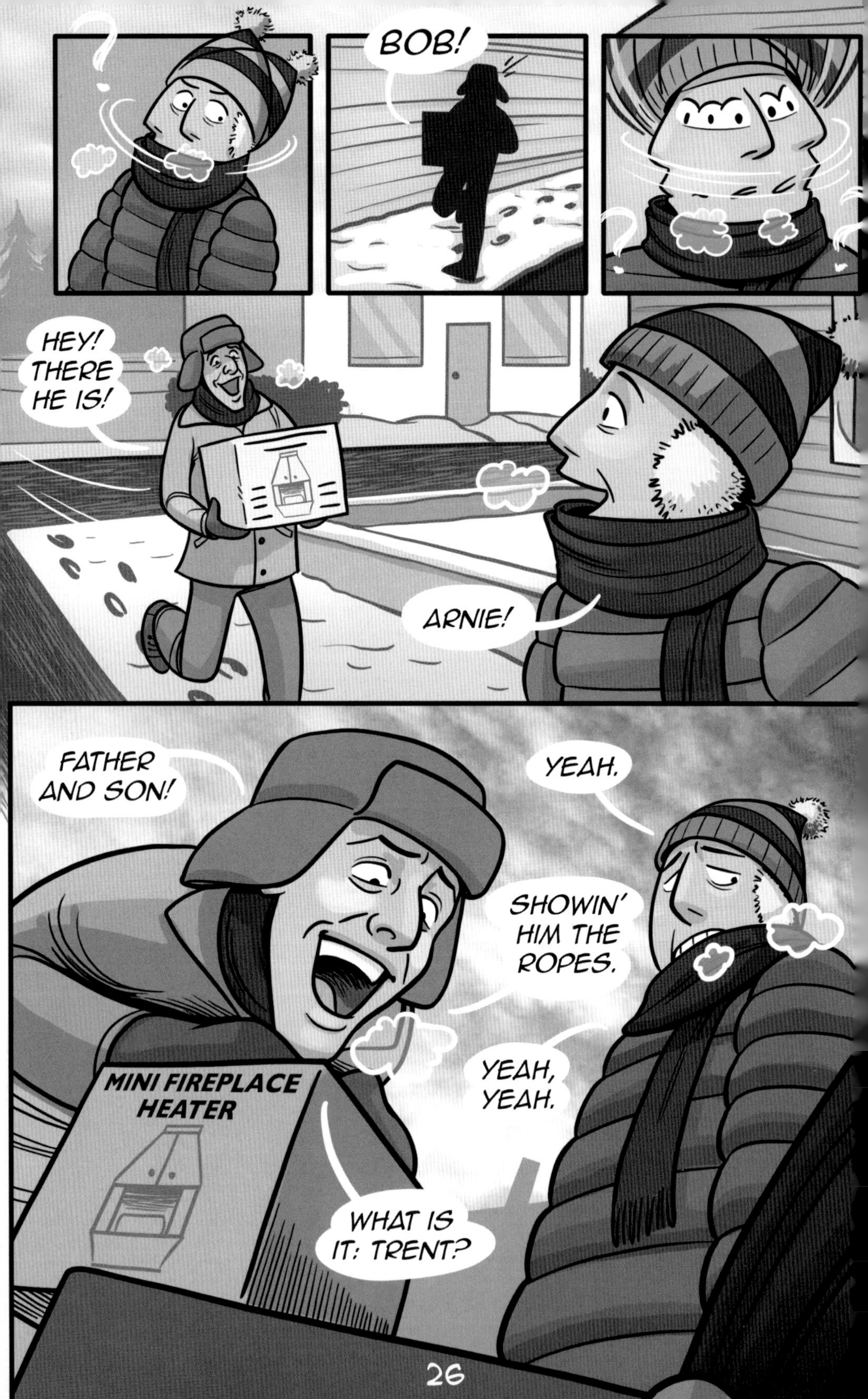
BOB!
HEY! THERE HE IS!
ARNIE!
FATHER AND SON!
YEAH.
SHOWIN' HIM THE ROPES.
YEAH, YEAH.
MINI FIREPLACE HEATER
WHAT IS IT: TRENT?

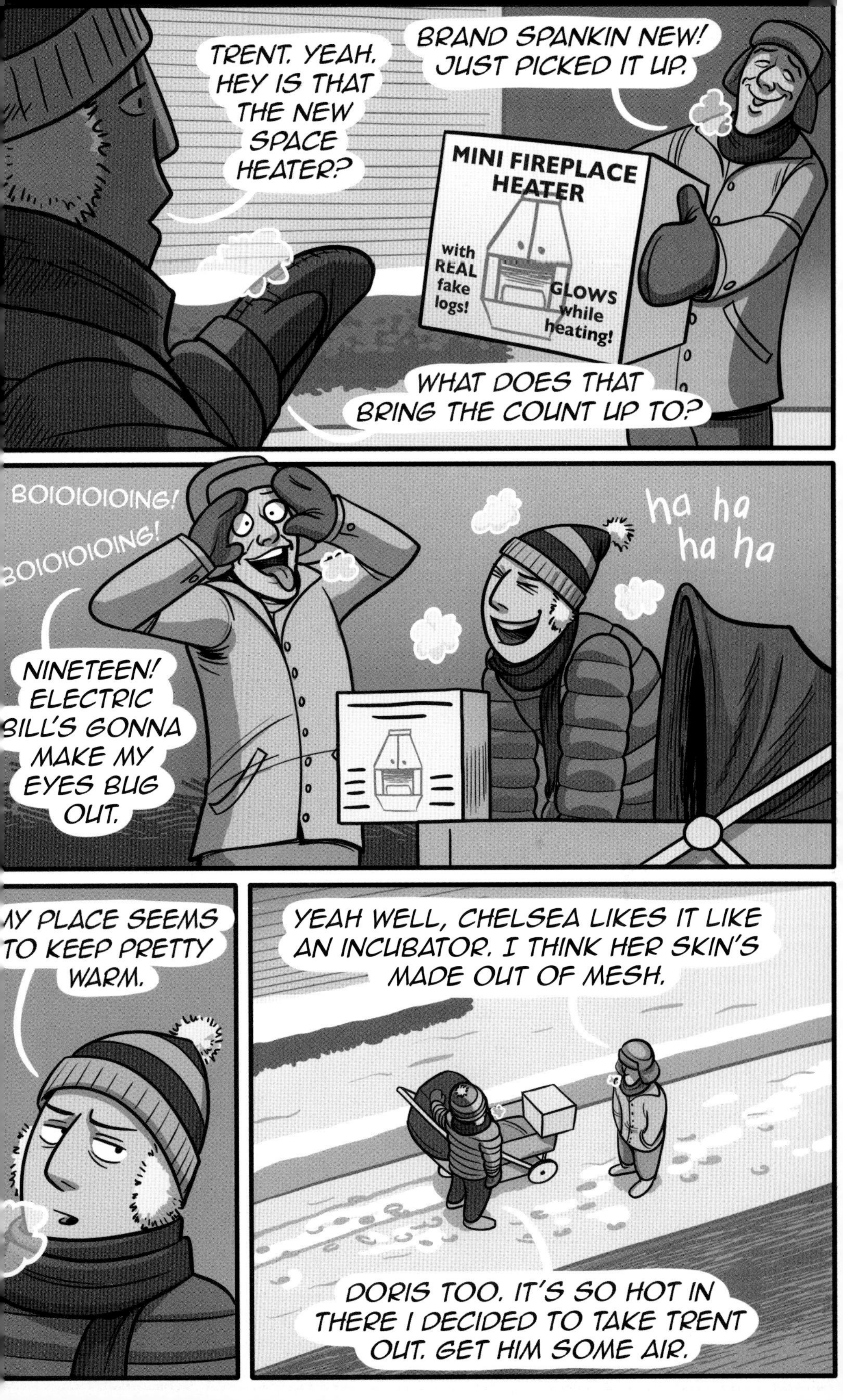
TRENT. YEAH. HEY IS THAT THE NEW SPACE HEATER?
BRAND SPANKIN NEW! JUST PICKED IT UP.
MINI FIREPLACE HEATER
with REAL fake logs!
GLOWS while heating!
WHAT DOES THAT BRING THE COUNT UP TO?
BOIOIOIOING!
BOIOIOIOING!
ha ha ha ha
NINETEEN! ELECTRIC BILL'S GONNA MAKE MY EYES BUG OUT.
MY PLACE SEEMS TO KEEP PRETTY WARM.
YEAH WELL, CHELSEA LIKES IT LIKE AN INCUBATOR. I THINK HER SKIN'S MADE OUT OF MESH.
DORIS TOO. IT'S SO HOT IN THERE I DECIDED TO TAKE TRENT OUT. GET HIM SOME AIR.

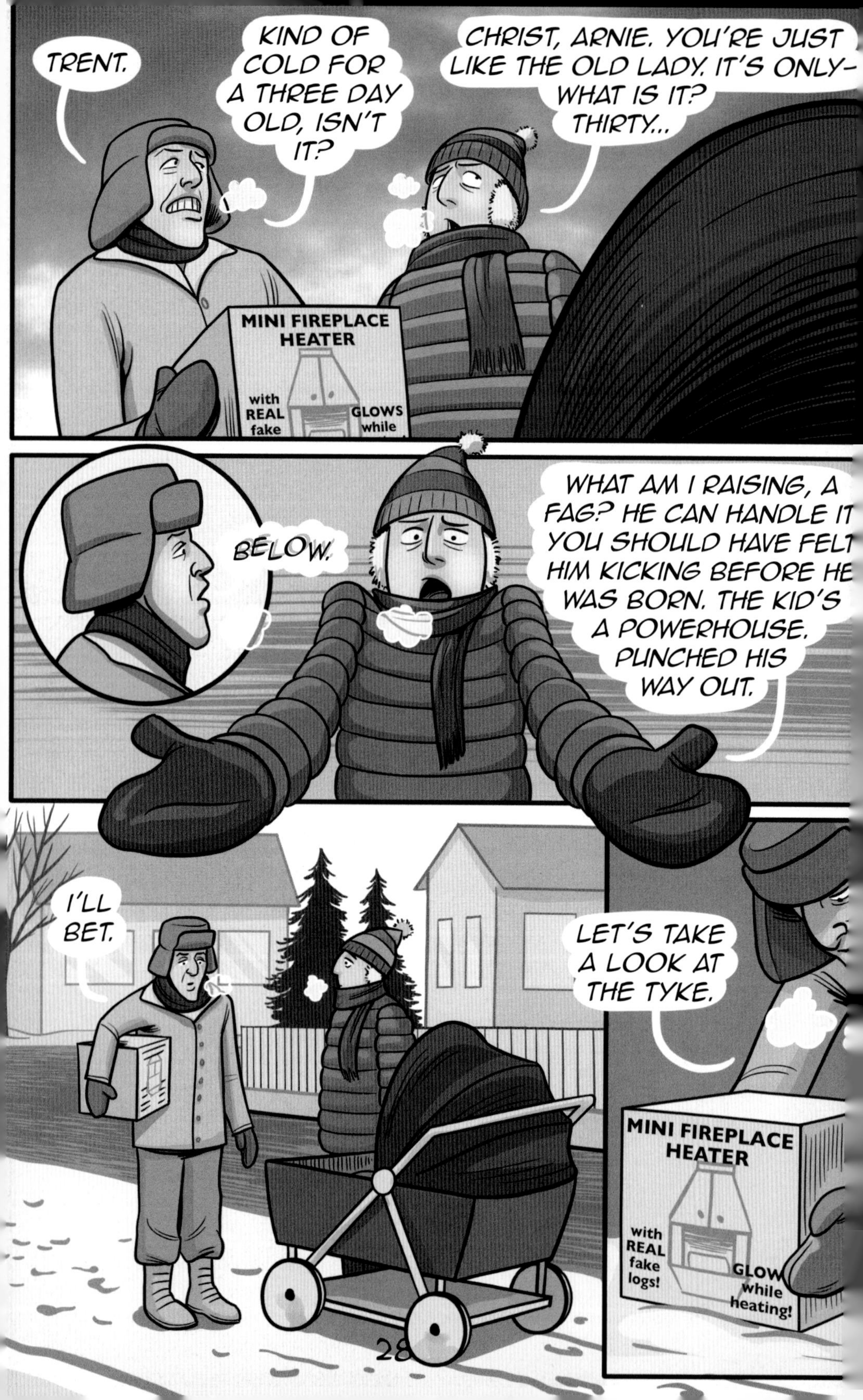
TRENT.
KIND OF COLD FOR A THREE DAY OLD, ISN'T IT?
CHRIST, ARNIE. YOU'RE JUST LIKE THE OLD LADY. IT'S ONLY- WHAT IS IT? THIRTY...
MINI FIREPLACE HEATER
with REAL fake
GLOWS while
BELOW.
WHAT AM I RAISING, A FAG? HE CAN HANDLE IT YOU SHOULD HAVE FELT HIM KICKING BEFORE HE WAS BORN. THE KID'S A POWERHOUSE. PUNCHED HIS WAY OUT.
I'LL BET.
LET'S TAKE A LOOK AT THE TYKE.
MINI FIREPLACE HEATER
with REAL fake logs!
GLOW while heating!

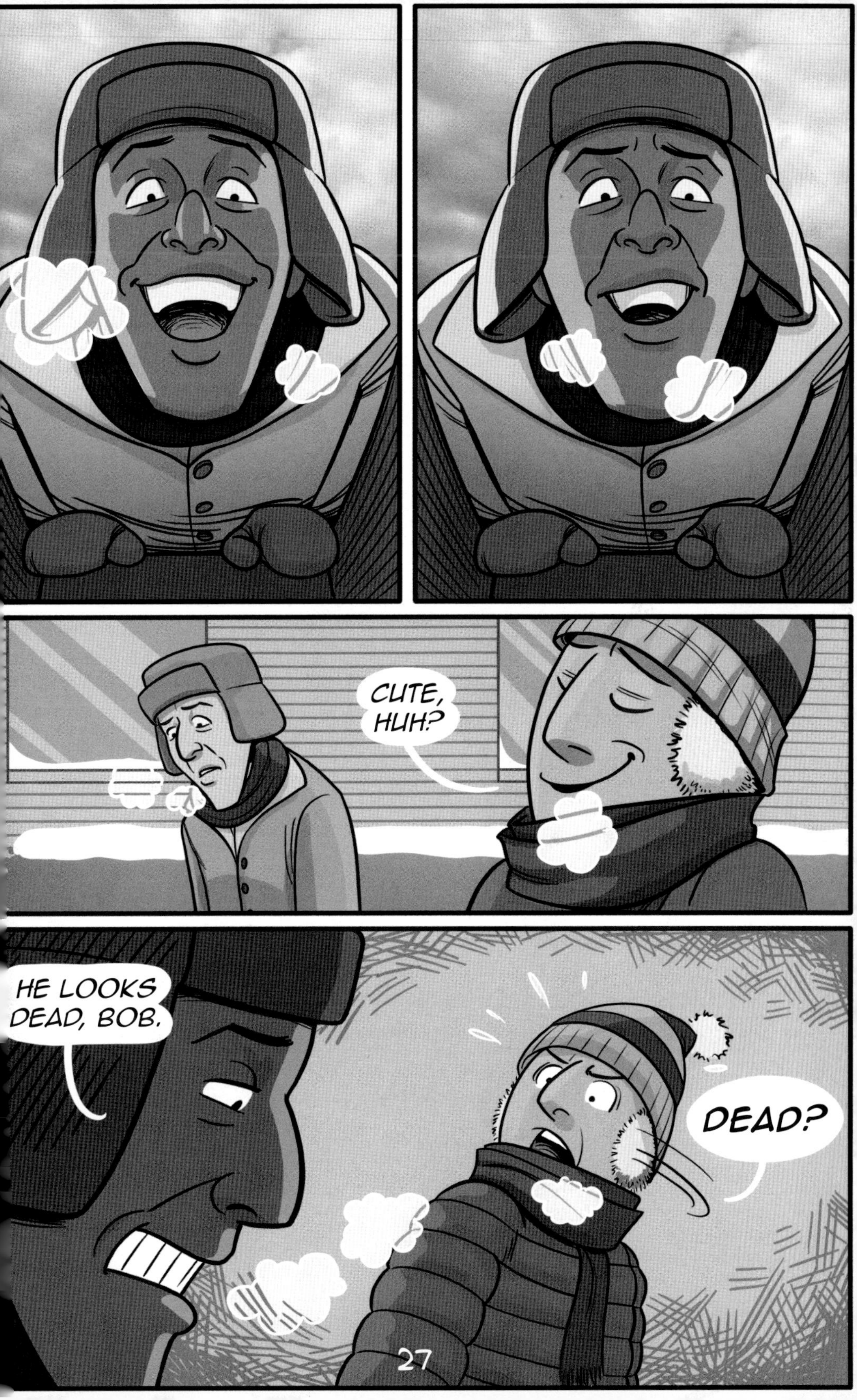
CUTE, HUH?
HE LOOKS DEAD, BOB.
DEAD?

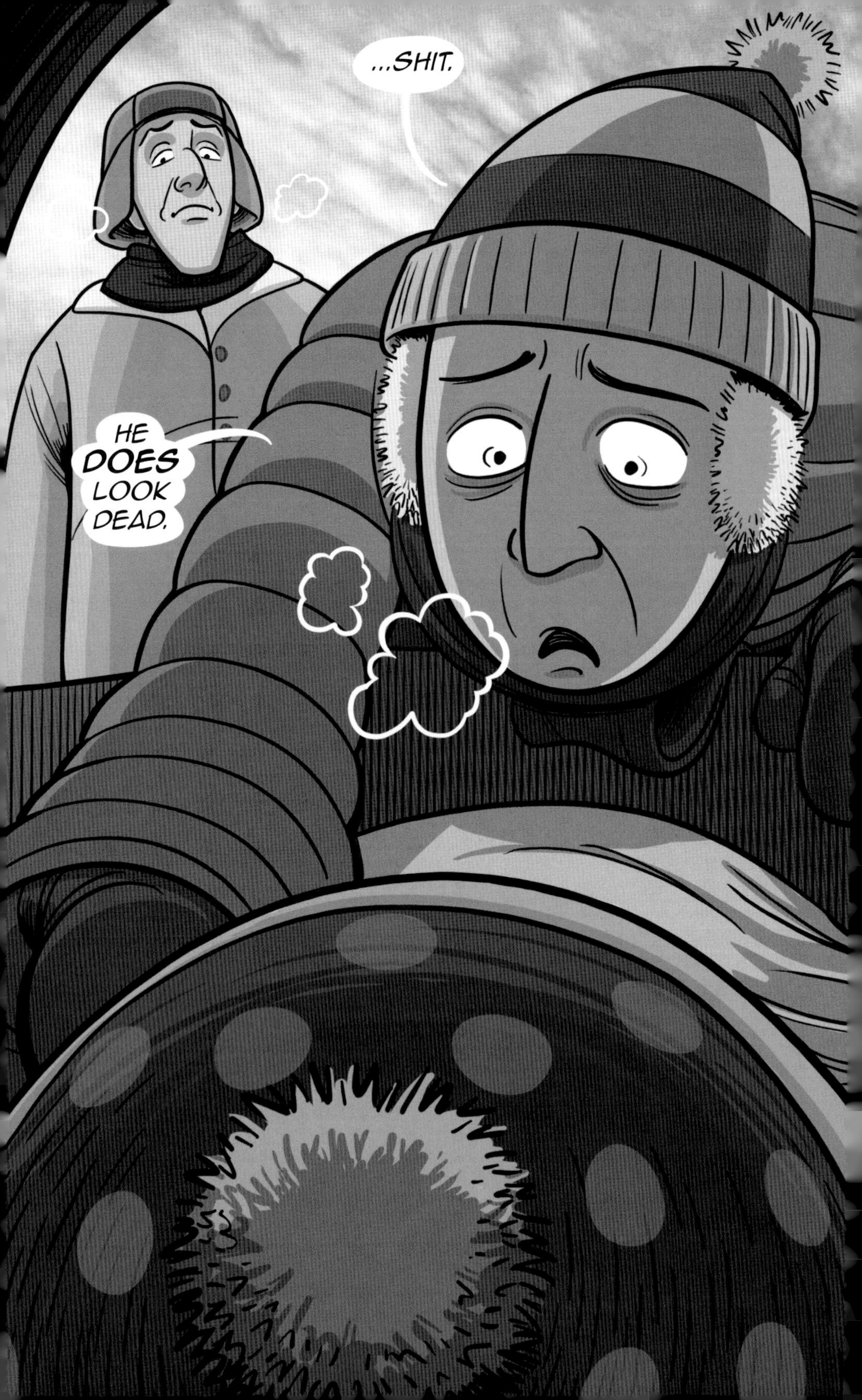
...SHIT.
HE **DOES** LOOK DEAD.

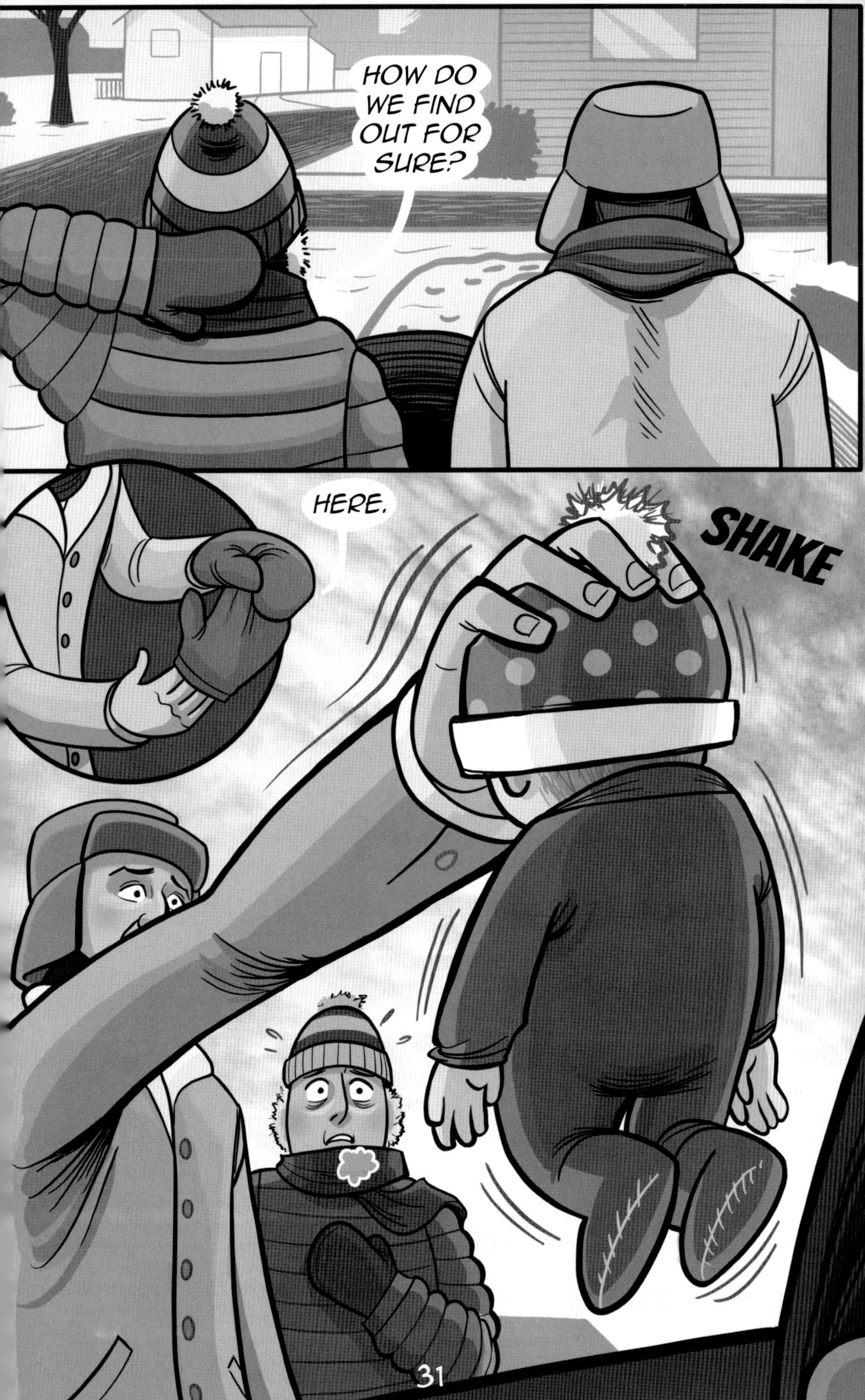
HOW DO WE FIND OUT FOR SURE?
HERE.
SHAKE

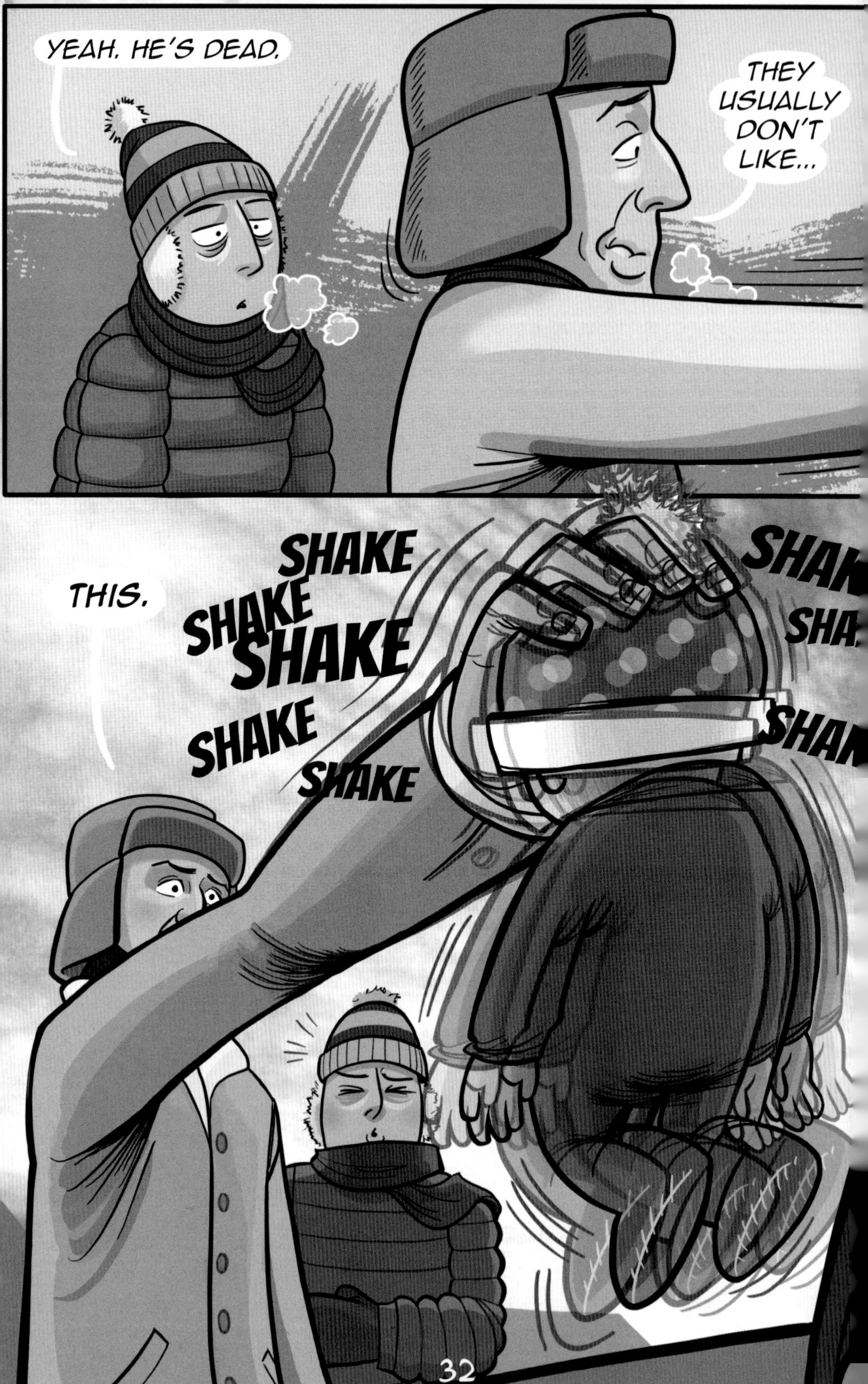
YEAH. HE'S DEAD.
THEY USUALLY DON'T LIKE...
THIS.
SHAKE
SHAKE
SHAKE
SHAKE
SHAKE

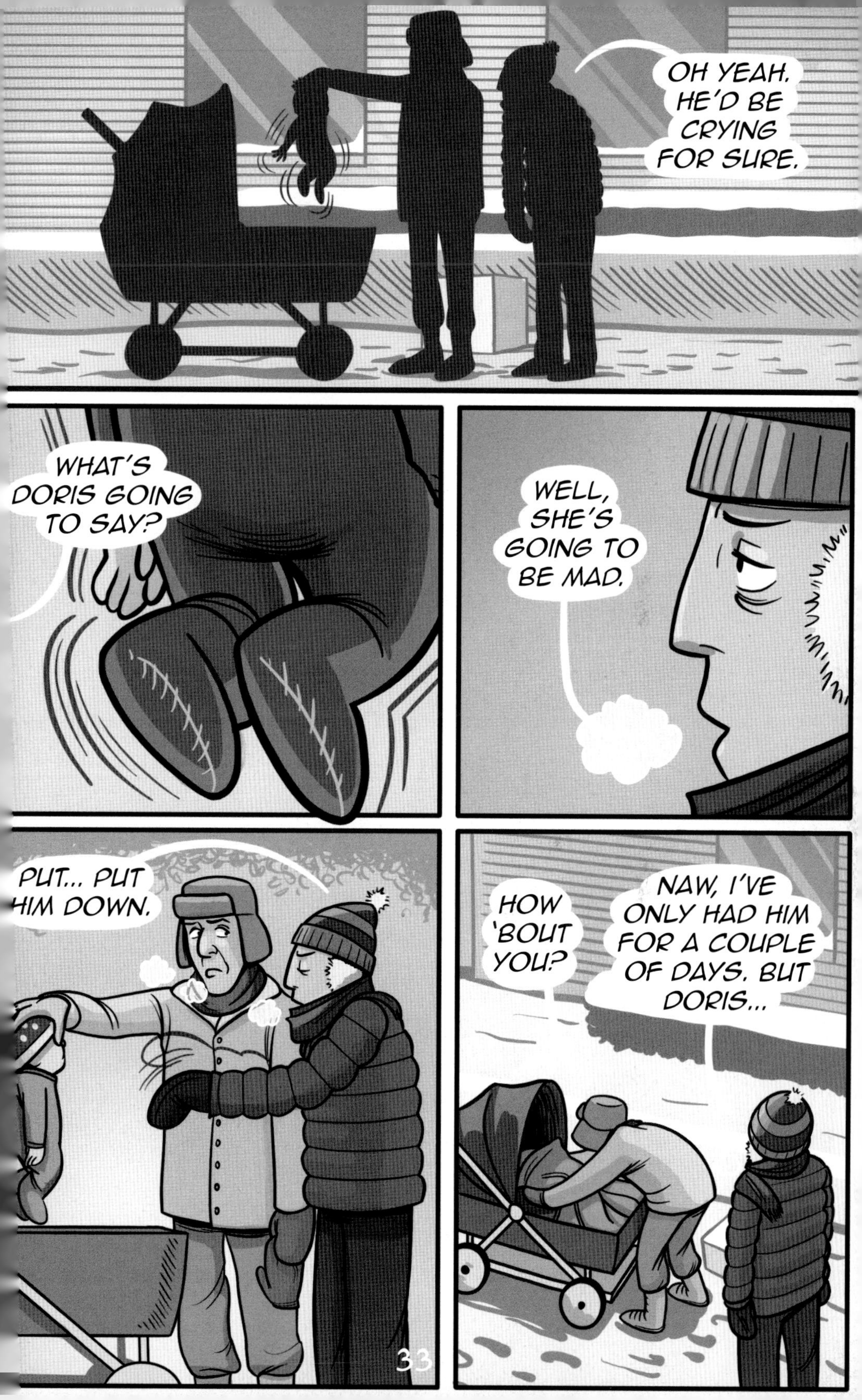
OH YEAH. HE'D BE CRYING FOR SURE.
WHAT'S DORIS GOING TO SAY?
WELL, SHE'S GOING TO BE MAD.
PUT... PUT HIM DOWN.
HOW 'BOUT YOU?
NAW, I'VE ONLY HAD HIM FOR A COUPLE OF DAYS. BUT DORIS...

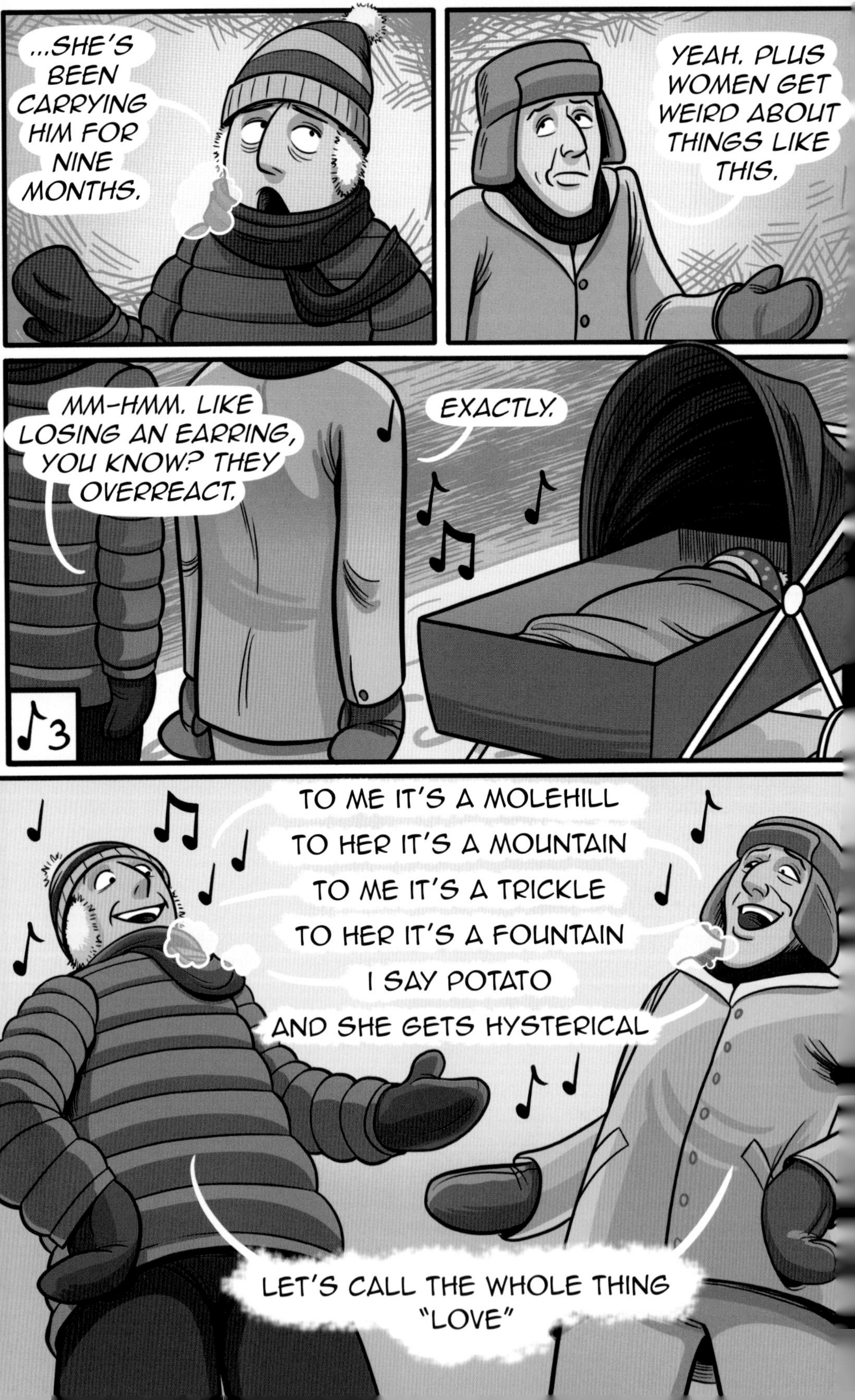
...SHE'S BEEN CARRYING HIM FOR NINE MONTHS.
YEAH. PLUS WOMEN GET WEIRD ABOUT THINGS LIKE THIS.
MM-HMM. LIKE LOSING AN EARRING, YOU KNOW? THEY OVERREACT.
EXACTLY.
♪3
TO ME IT'S A MOLEHILL
TO HER IT'S A MOUNTAIN
TO ME IT'S A TRICKLE
TO HER IT'S A FOUNTAIN
I SAY POTATO
AND SHE GETS HYSTERICAL
LET'S CALL THE WHOLE THING "LOVE"

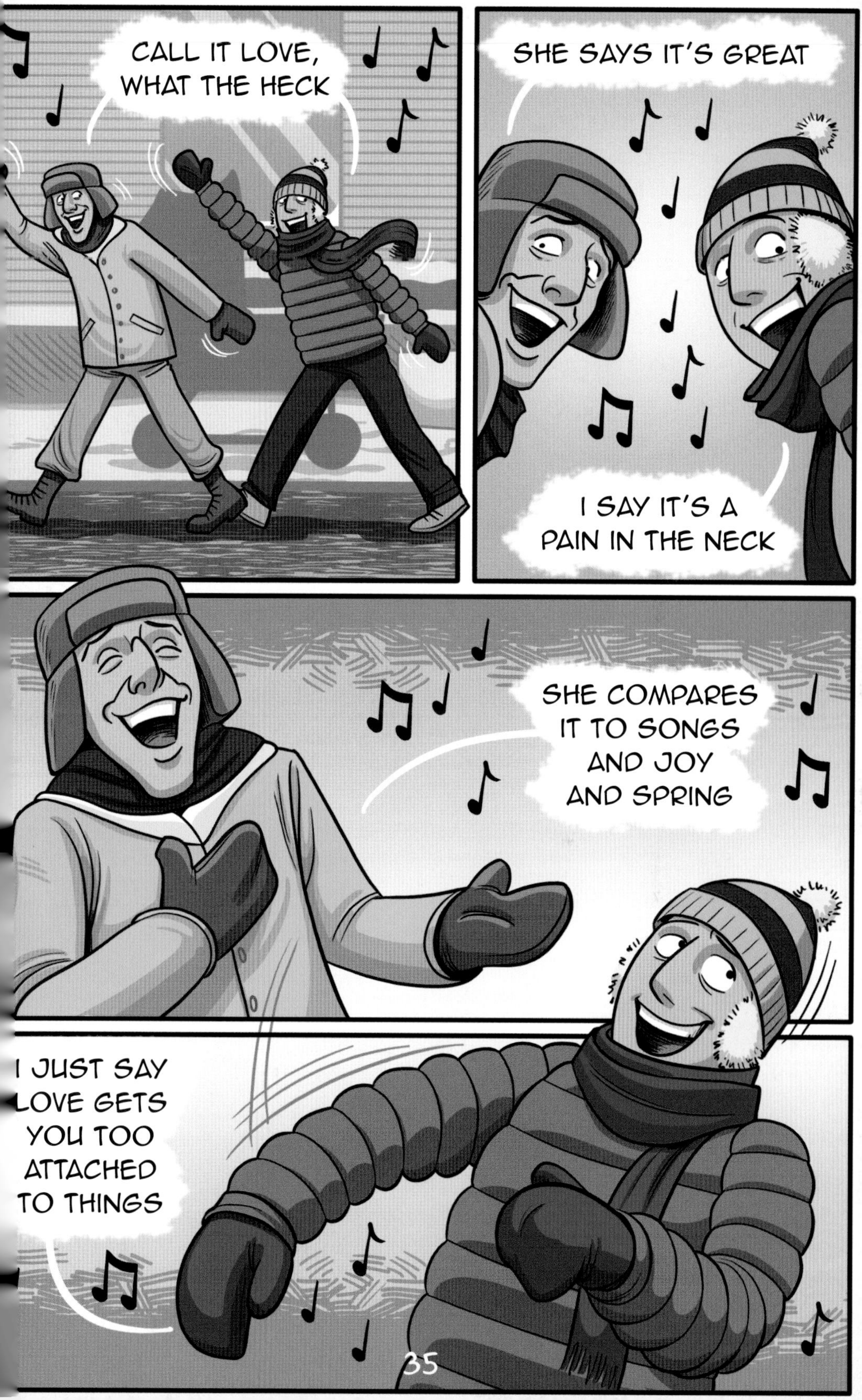
CALL IT LOVE, WHAT THE HECK
SHE SAYS IT'S GREAT
I SAY IT'S A PAIN IN THE NECK
SHE COMPARES IT TO SONGS AND JOY AND SPRING
I JUST SAY LOVE GETS YOU TOO ATTACHED TO THINGS

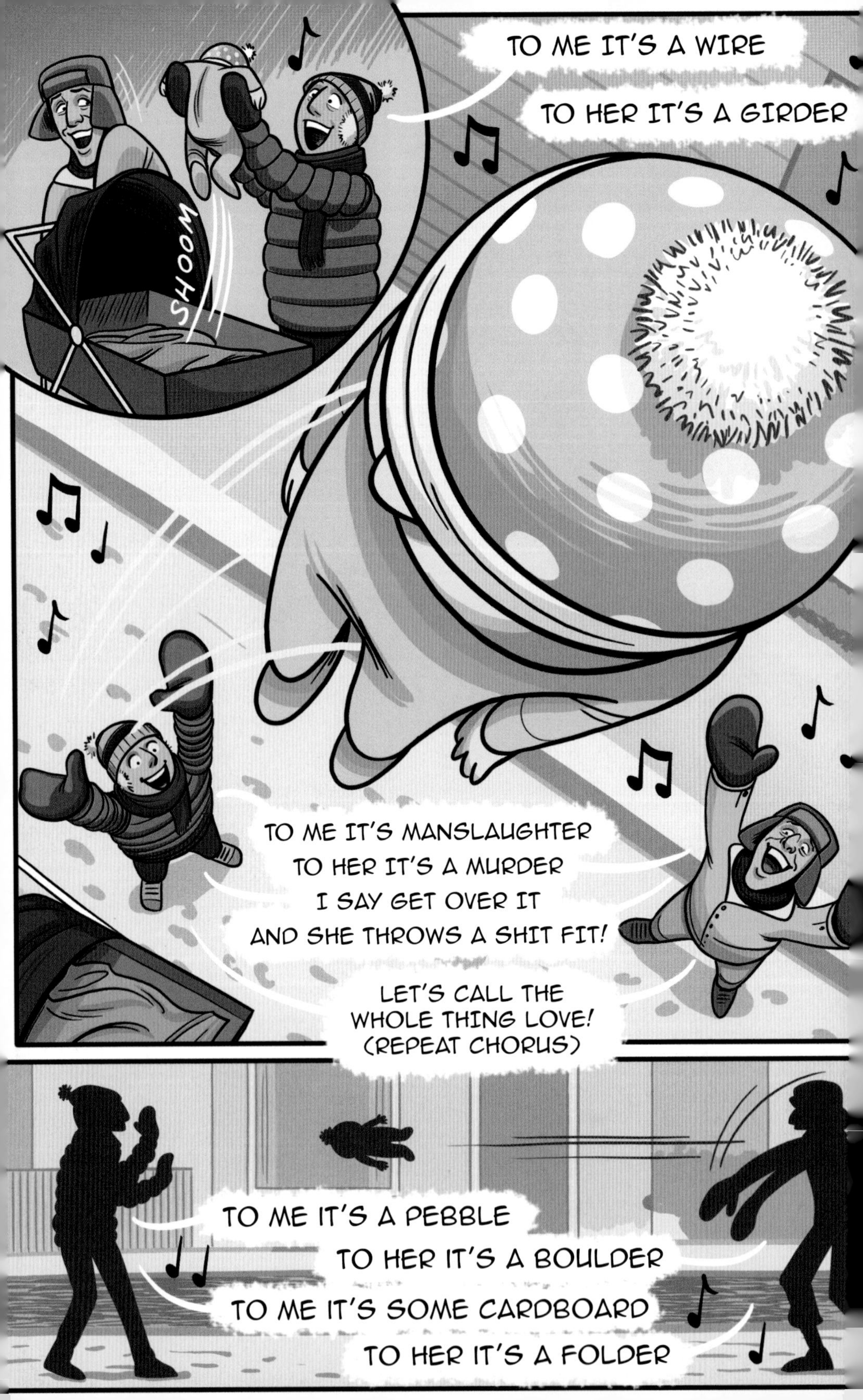
TO ME IT'S A WIRE
TO HER IT'S A GIRDER
SHOOM
TO ME IT'S MANSLAUGHTER
TO HER IT'S A MURDER
I SAY GET OVER IT
AND SHE THROWS A SHIT FIT!
LET'S CALL THE WHOLE THING LOVE! (REPEAT CHORUS)
TO ME IT'S A PEBBLE
TO HER IT'S A BOULDER
TO ME IT'S SOME CARDBOARD
TO HER IT'S A FOLDER

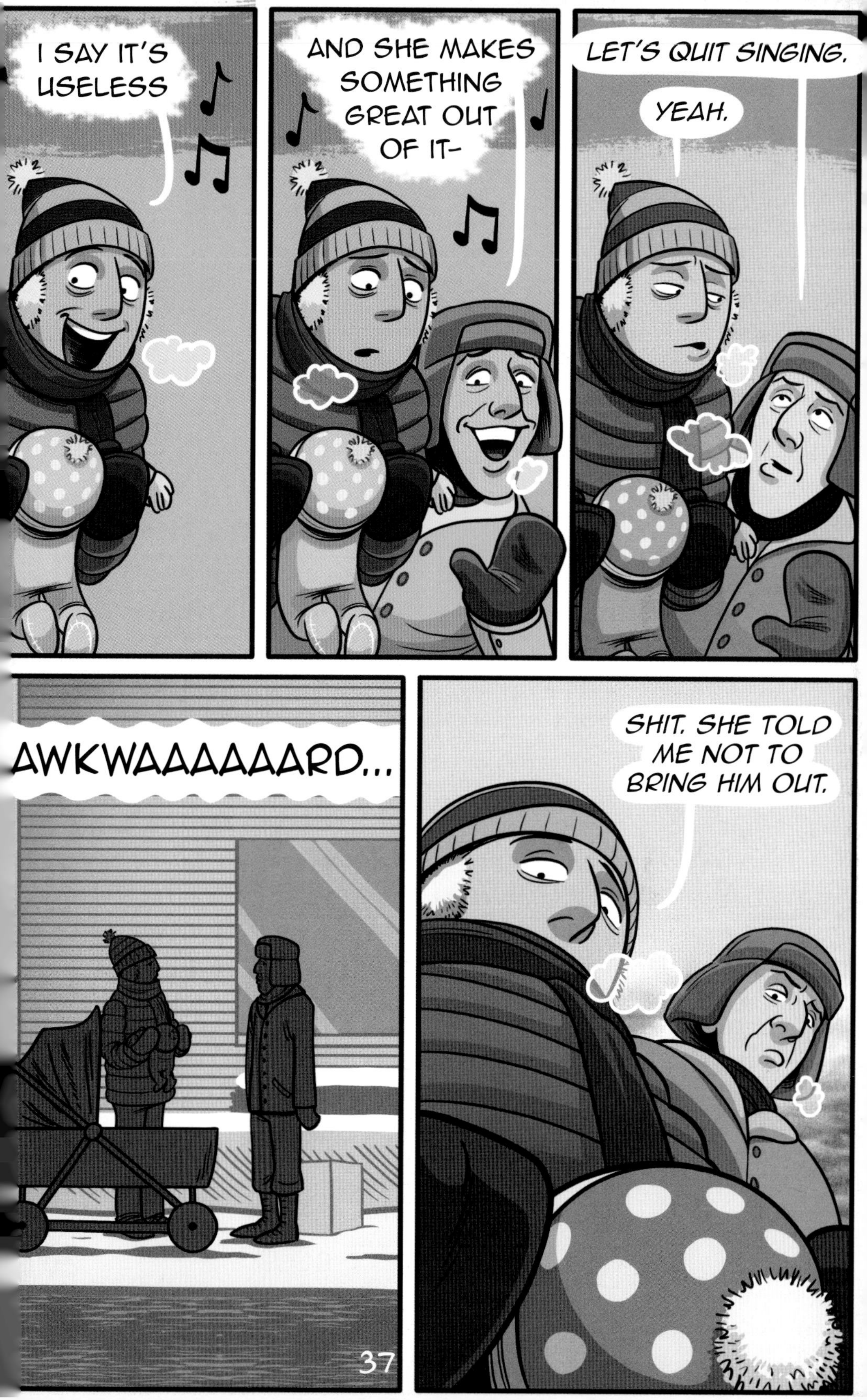

I SAY IT'S USELESS
AND SHE MAKES SOMETHING GREAT OUT OF IT-
LET'S QUIT SINGING.
YEAH.
AWKWAAAAAARD...
SHIT. SHE TOLD ME NOT TO BRING HIM OUT.

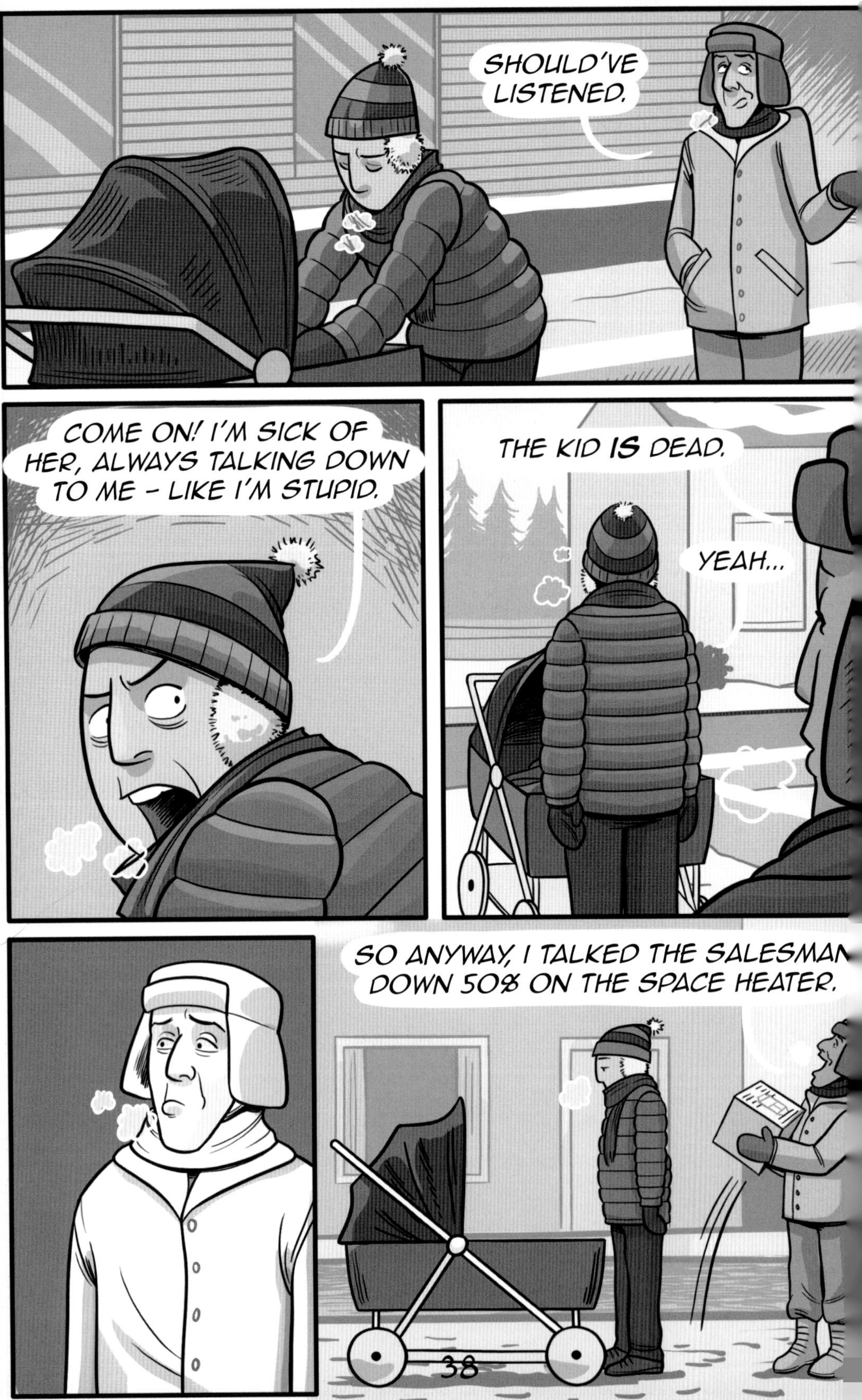
SHOULD'VE LISTENED.
COME ON! I'M SICK OF HER, ALWAYS TALKING DOWN TO ME - LIKE I'M STUPID.
THE KID IS DEAD.
YEAH...
SO ANYWAY, I TALKED THE SALESMAN DOWN 50% ON THE SPACE HEATER.

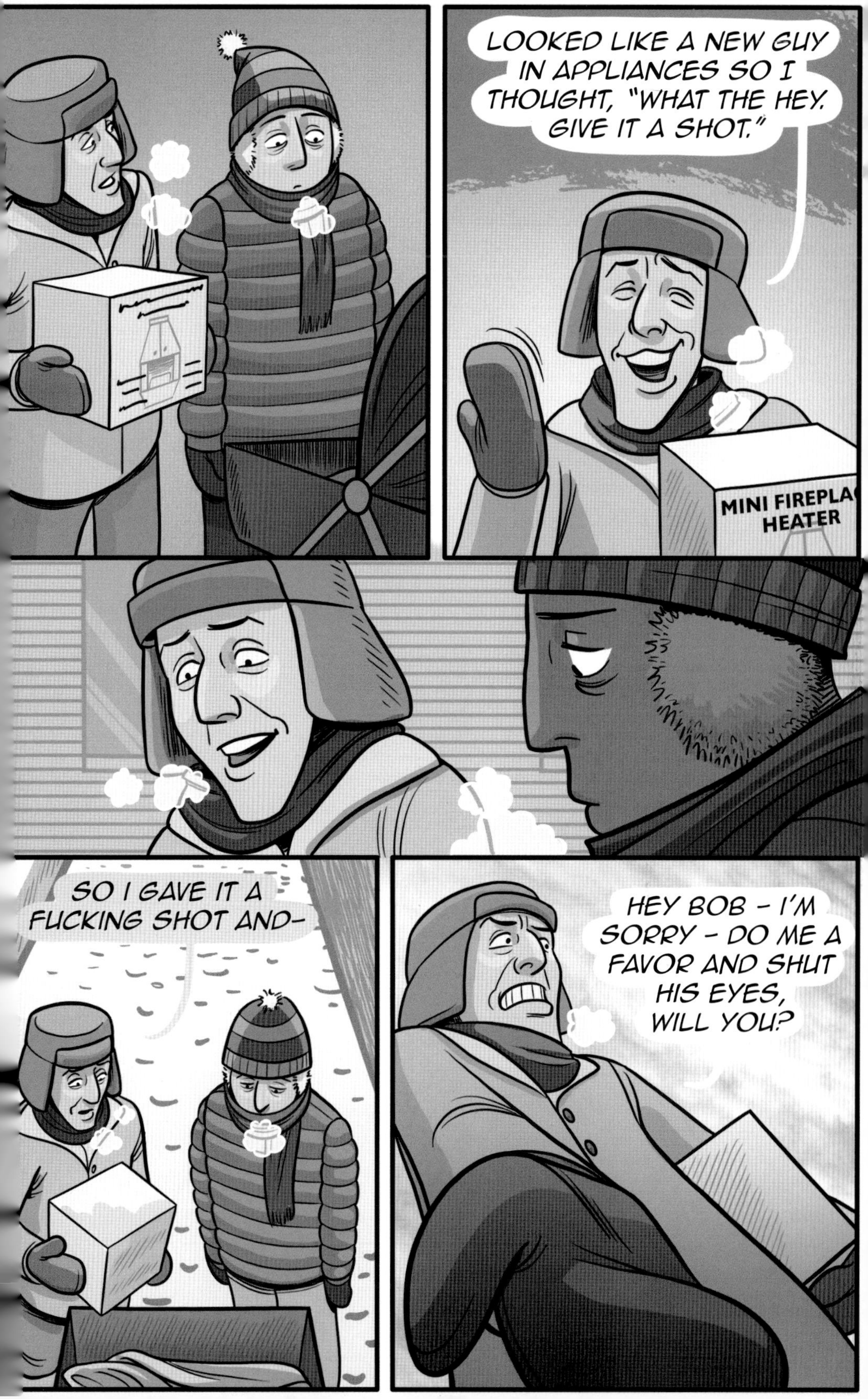
LOOKED LIKE A NEW GUY IN APPLIANCES SO I THOUGHT, "WHAT THE HEY. GIVE IT A SHOT."
MINI FIREPLA
HEATER
SO I GAVE IT A FUCKING SHOT AND-
HEY BOB - I'M SORRY - DO ME A FAVOR AND SHUT HIS EYES, WILL YOU?

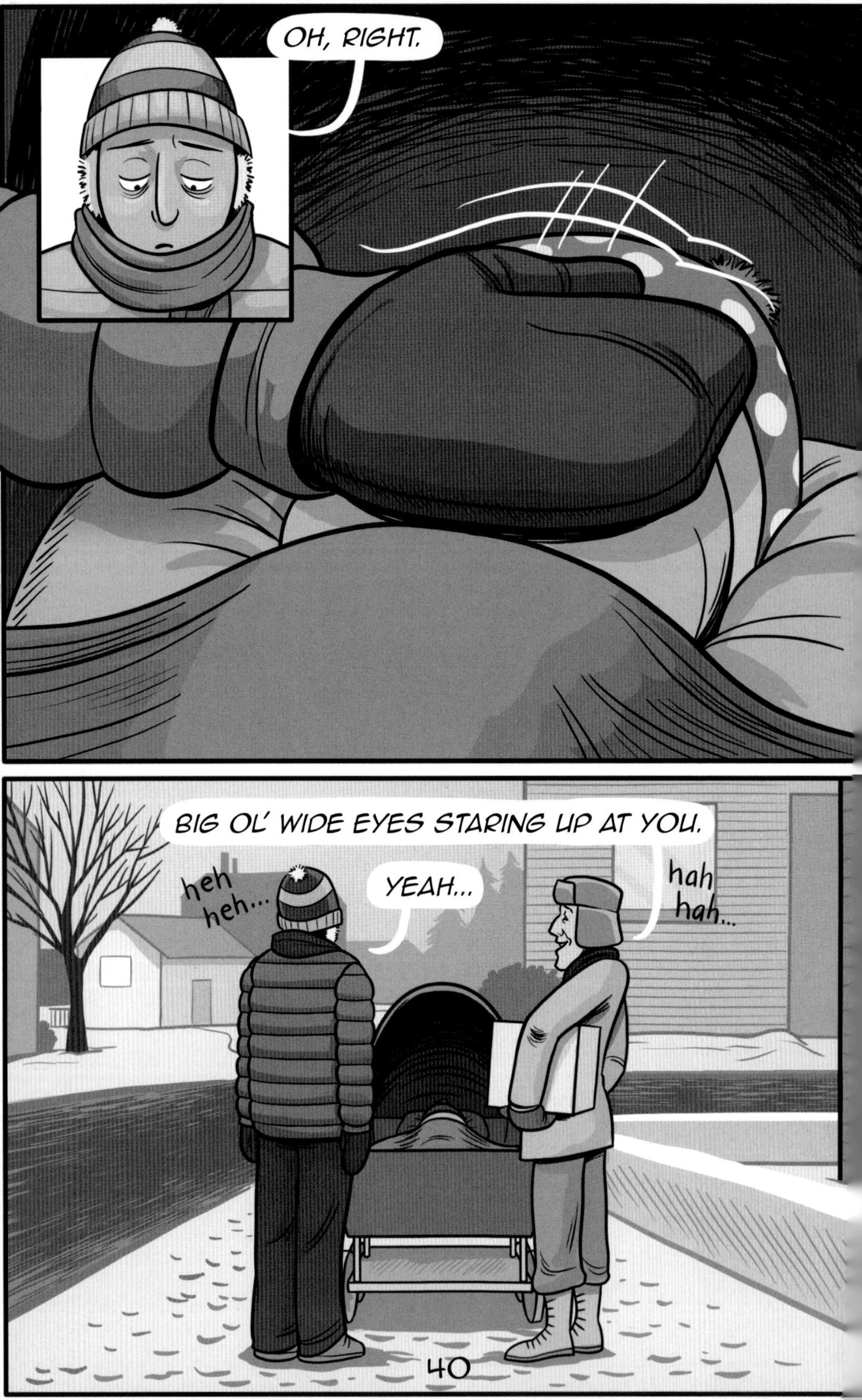
OH, RIGHT.
BIG OL' WIDE EYES STARING UP AT YOU.
heh heh...
YEAH...
hah hah...

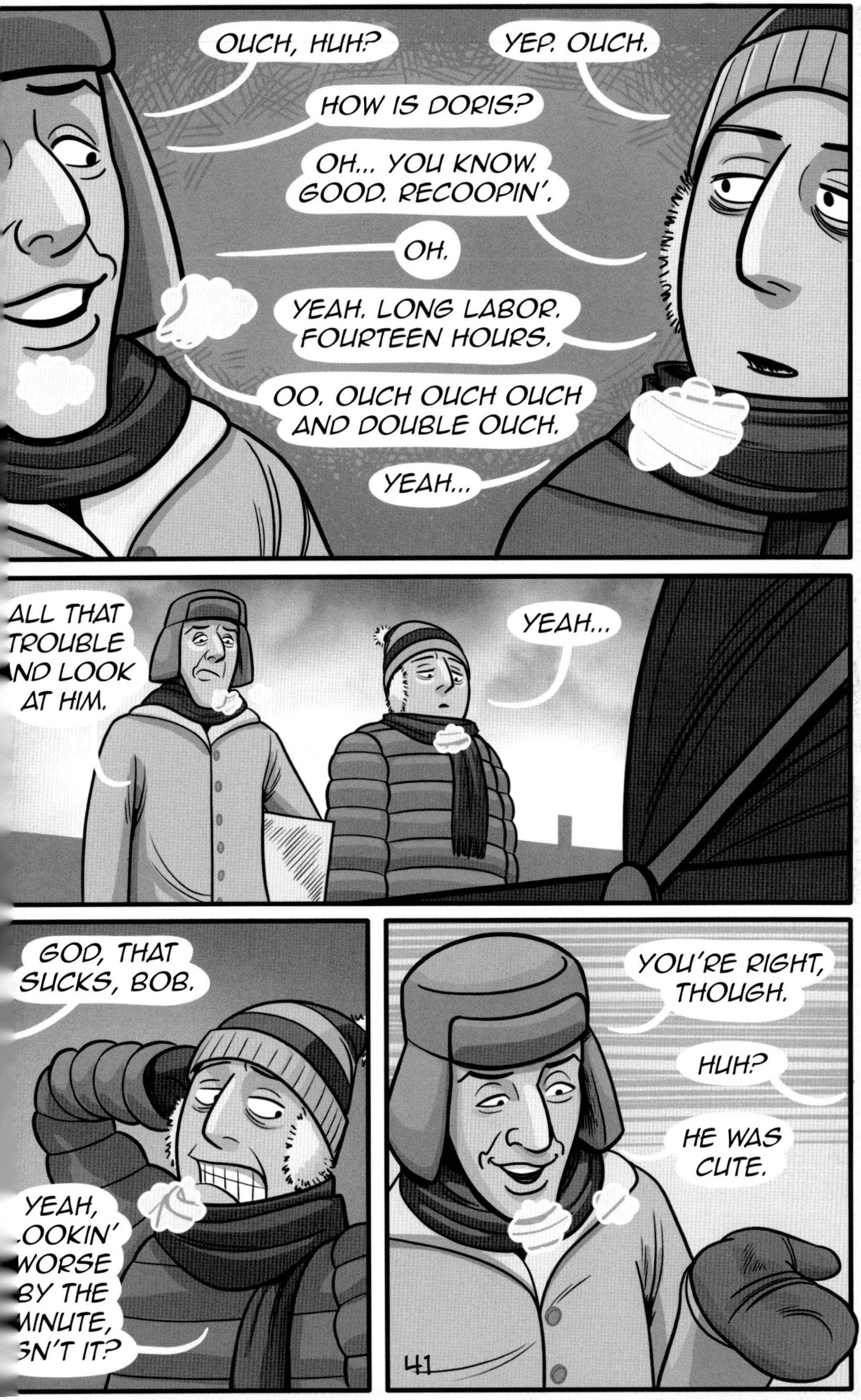
OUCH, HUH?
YEP. OUCH.
HOW IS DORIS?
OH... YOU KNOW. GOOD. RECOOPIN'.
OH.
YEAH. LONG LABOR. FOURTEEN HOURS.
OO. OUCH OUCH OUCH AND DOUBLE OUCH.
YEAH...
ALL THAT TROUBLE AND LOOK AT HIM.
YEAH...
GOD, THAT SUCKS, BOB.
YEAH, LOOKIN' WORSE BY THE MINUTE, ISN'T IT?
YOU'RE RIGHT, THOUGH.
HUH?
HE WAS CUTE.

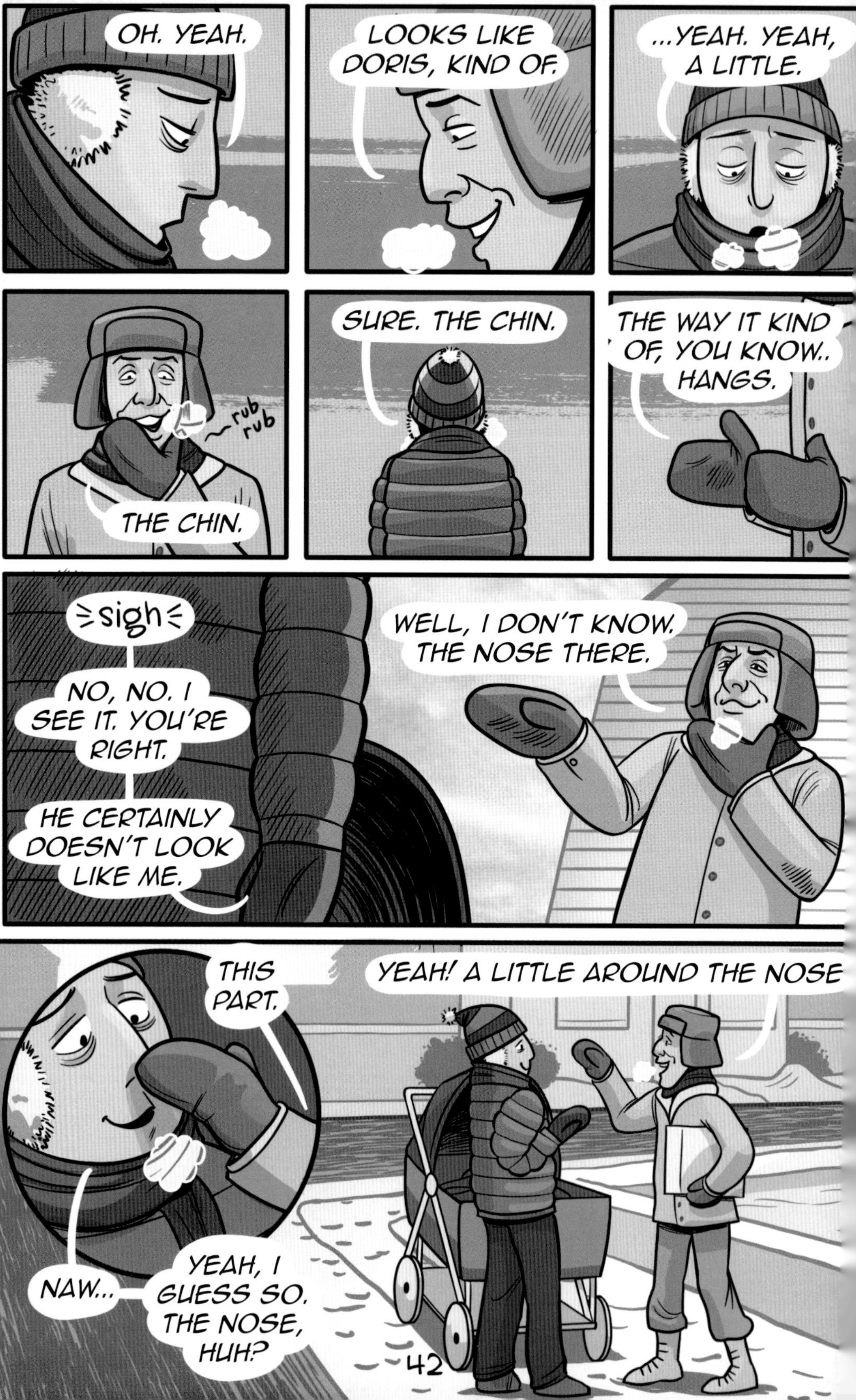
OH. YEAH.
LOOKS LIKE DORIS, KIND OF.
...YEAH. YEAH, A LITTLE.
THE CHIN.
rub rub
SURE. THE CHIN.
THE WAY IT KIND OF, YOU KNOW.. HANGS.
sigh
NO, NO. I SEE IT. YOU'RE RIGHT.
HE CERTAINLY DOESN'T LOOK LIKE ME.
WELL, I DON'T KNOW. THE NOSE THERE.
THIS PART.
YEAH! A LITTLE AROUND THE NOSE
NAW...
YEAH, I GUESS SO. THE NOSE, HUH?

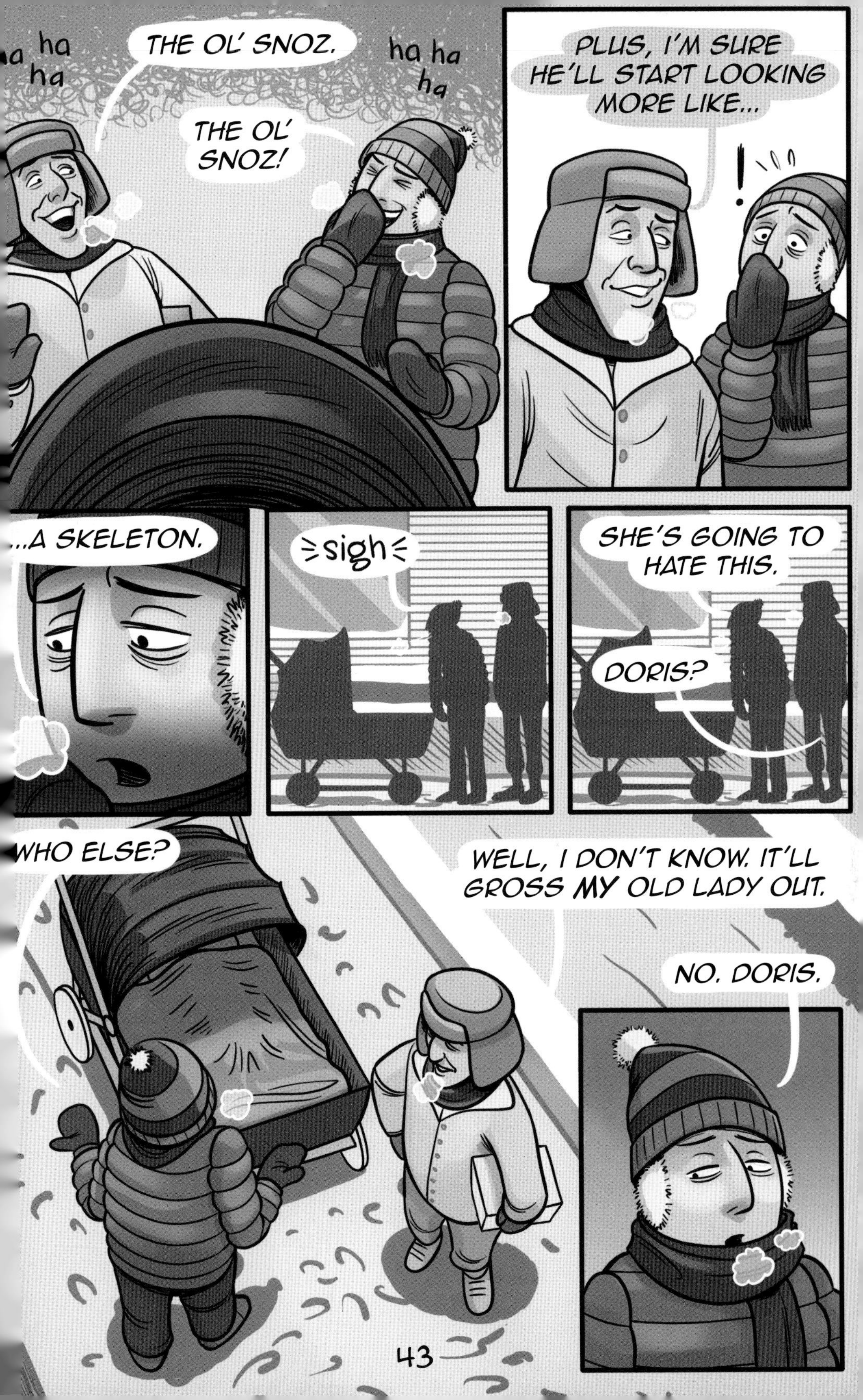
ha ha ha
THE OL' SNOZ.
ha ha ha
THE OL' SNOZ!
PLUS, I'M SURE HE'LL START LOOKING MORE LIKE...
!
...A SKELETON.
sigh
SHE'S GOING TO HATE THIS.
DORIS?
WHO ELSE?
WELL, I DON'T KNOW. IT'LL GROSS MY OLD LADY OUT.
NO. DORIS.

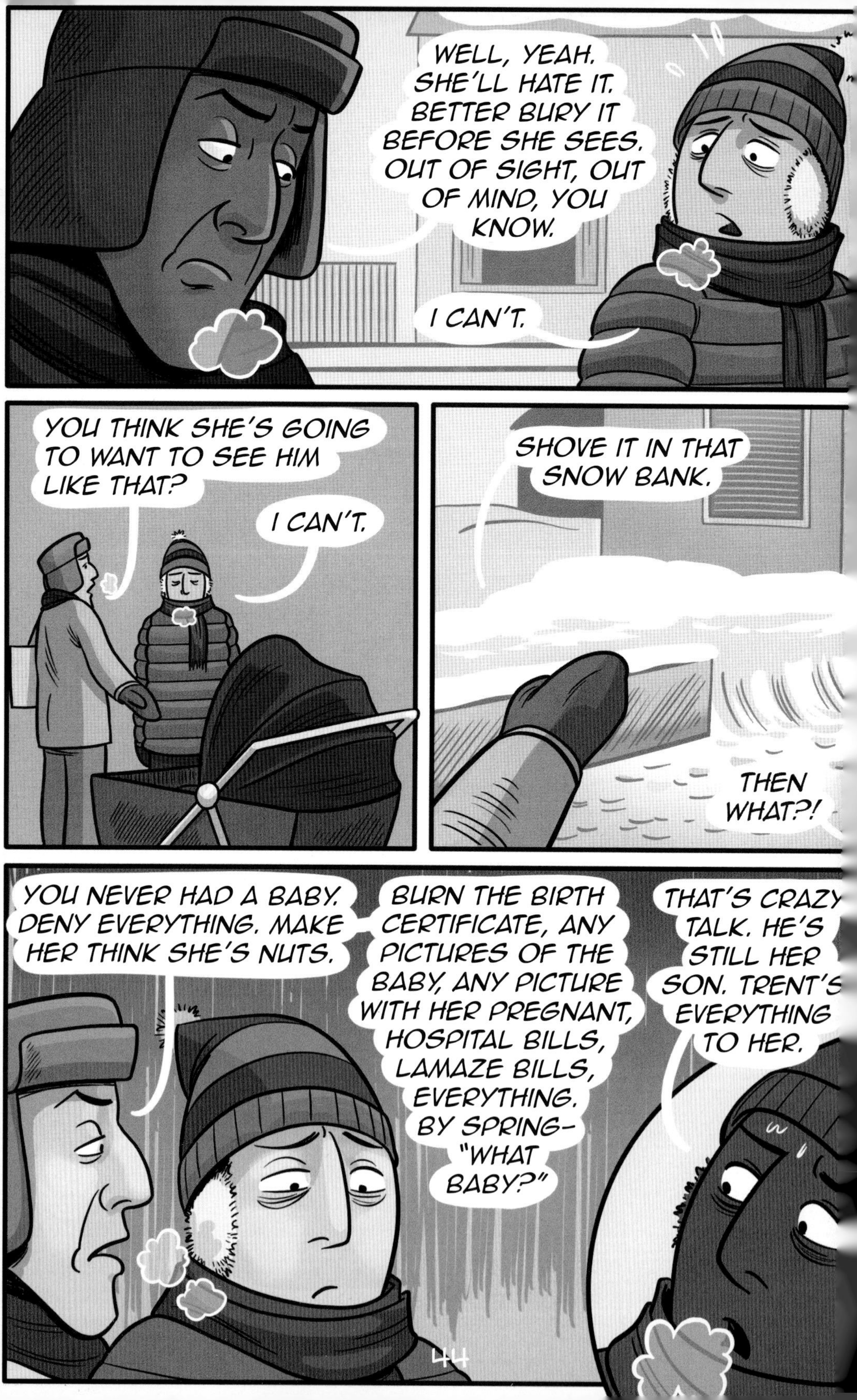
WELL, YEAH. SHE'LL HATE IT. BETTER BURY IT BEFORE SHE SEES. OUT OF SIGHT, OUT OF MIND, YOU KNOW.
I CAN'T.
YOU THINK SHE'S GOING TO WANT TO SEE HIM LIKE THAT?
I CAN'T.
SHOVE IT IN THAT SNOW BANK.
THEN WHAT?!
YOU NEVER HAD A BABY. DENY EVERYTHING. MAKE HER THINK SHE'S NUTS.
BURN THE BIRTH CERTIFICATE, ANY PICTURES OF THE BABY, ANY PICTURE WITH HER PREGNANT, HOSPITAL BILLS, LAMAZE BILLS, EVERYTHING. BY SPRING- "WHAT BABY?"
THAT'S CRAZY TALK. HE'S STILL HER SON. TRENT'S EVERYTHING TO HER.

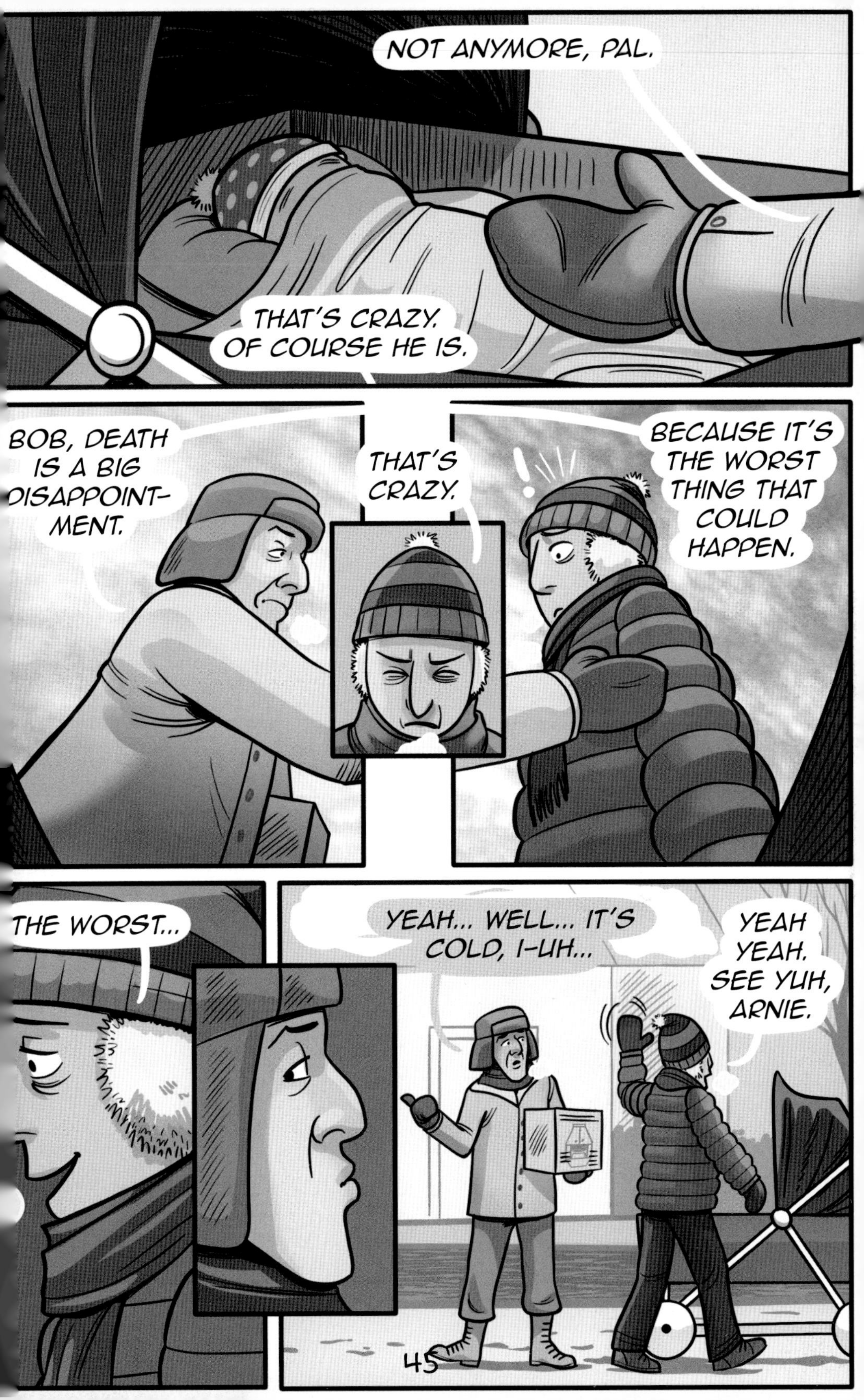
NOT ANYMORE, PAL.
THAT'S CRAZY. OF COURSE HE IS.
BOB, DEATH IS A BIG DISAPPOINT-MENT.
THAT'S CRAZY.
BECAUSE IT'S THE WORST THING THAT COULD HAPPEN.
THE WORST...
YEAH... WELL... IT'S COLD, I-UH...
YEAH YEAH. SEE YUH, ARNIE.

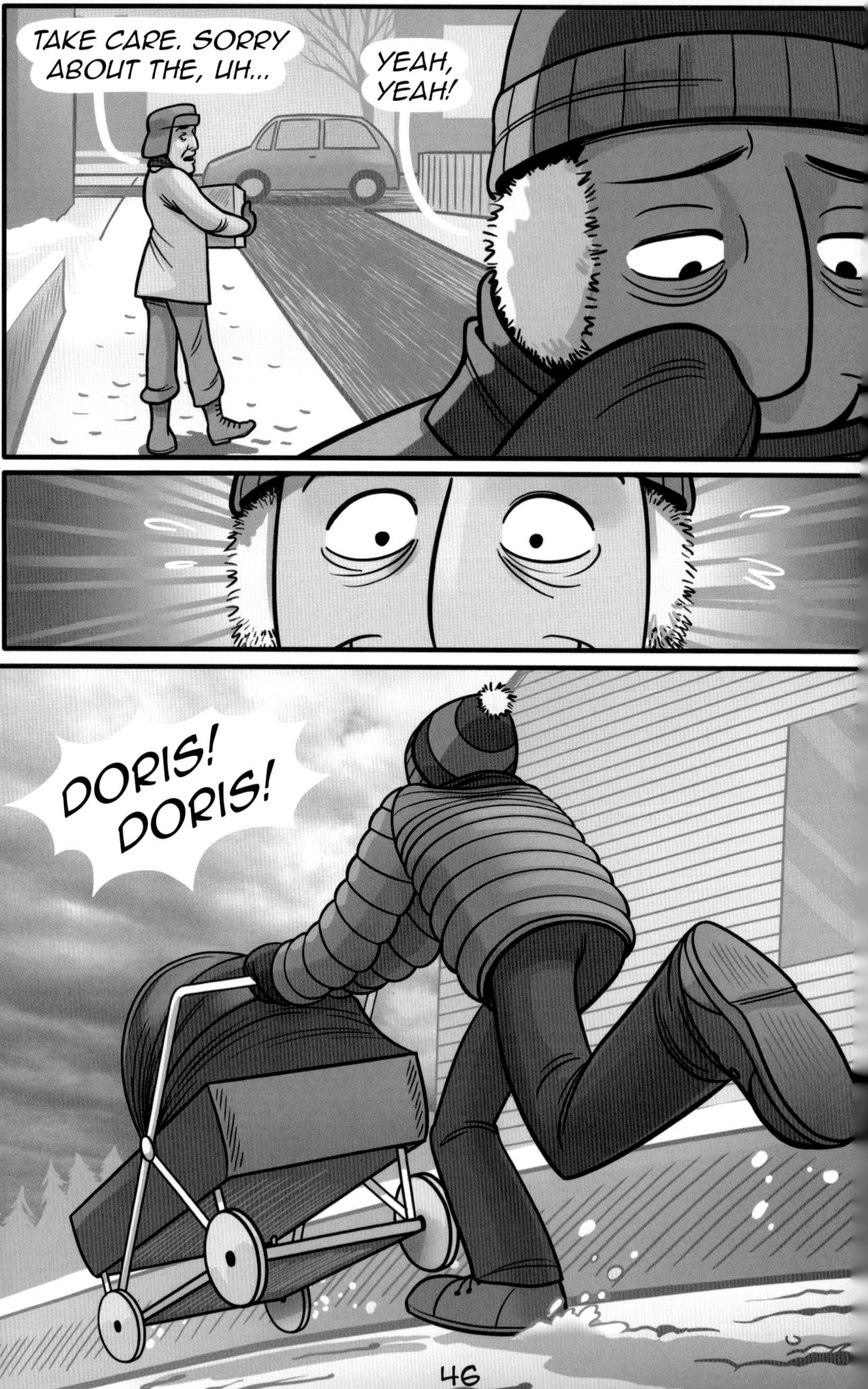
TAKE CARE. SORRY ABOUT THE, UH...
YEAH, YEAH!
DORIS! DORIS!

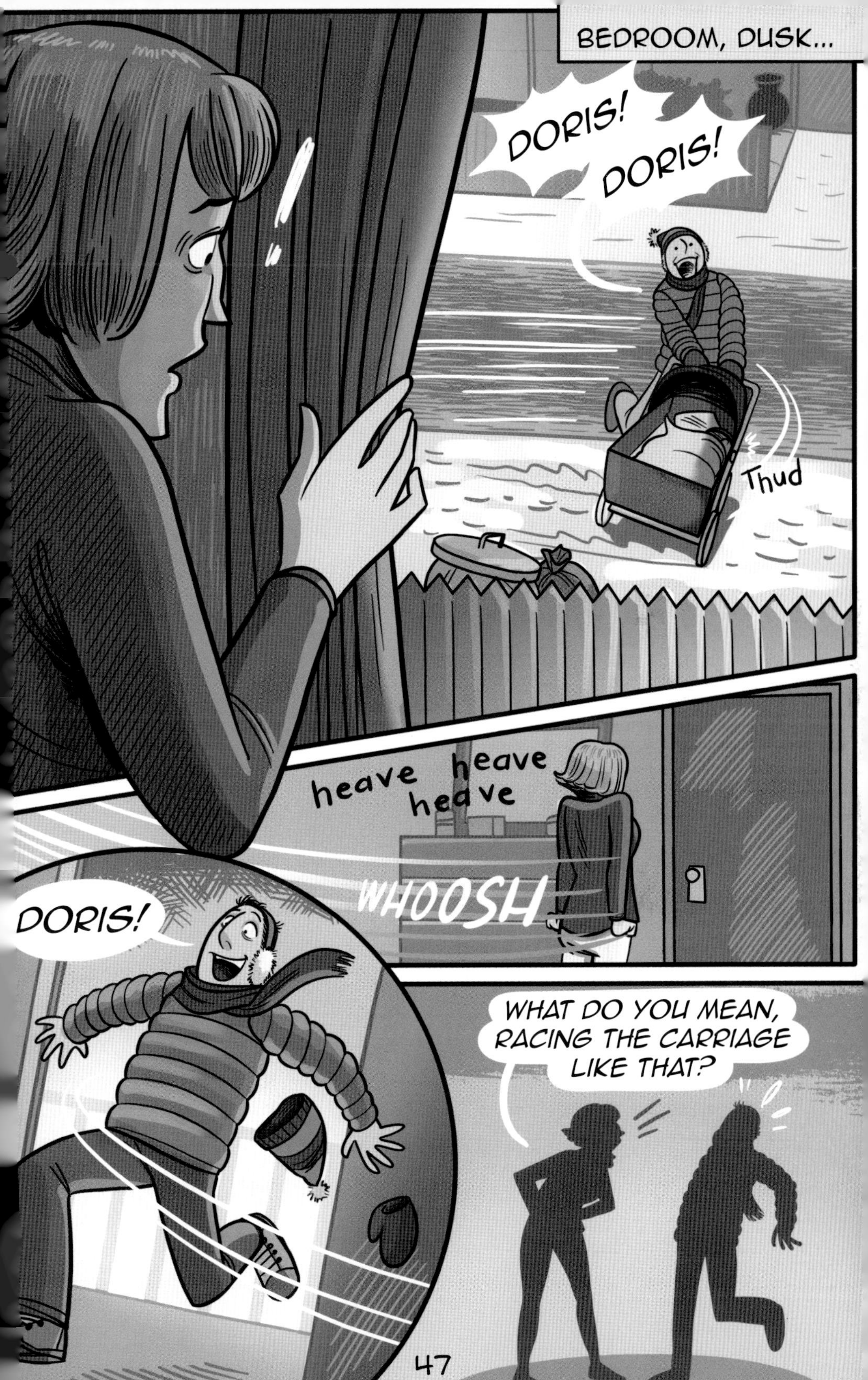
BEDROOM, DUSK...
DORIS!
DORIS!
Thud
heave heave
heave
WHOOSH
DORIS!
WHAT DO YOU MEAN, RACING THE CARRIAGE LIKE THAT?

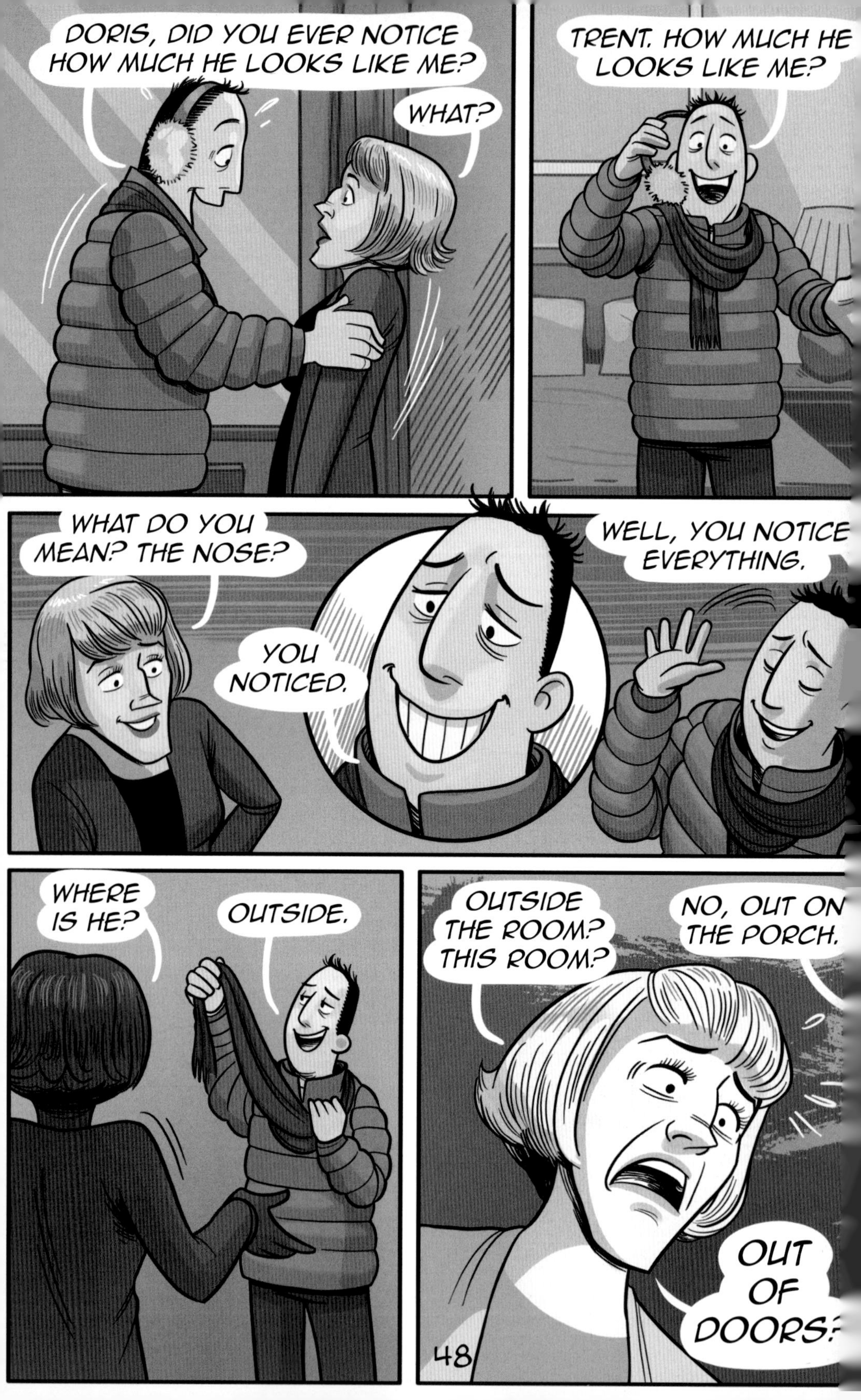
DORIS, DID YOU EVER NOTICE HOW MUCH HE LOOKS LIKE ME?
WHAT?
TRENT. HOW MUCH HE LOOKS LIKE ME?
WHAT DO YOU MEAN? THE NOSE?
YOU NOTICED.
WELL, YOU NOTICE EVERYTHING.
WHERE IS HE?
OUTSIDE.
OUTSIDE THE ROOM? THIS ROOM?
NO, OUT ON THE PORCH.
OUT OF DOORS?

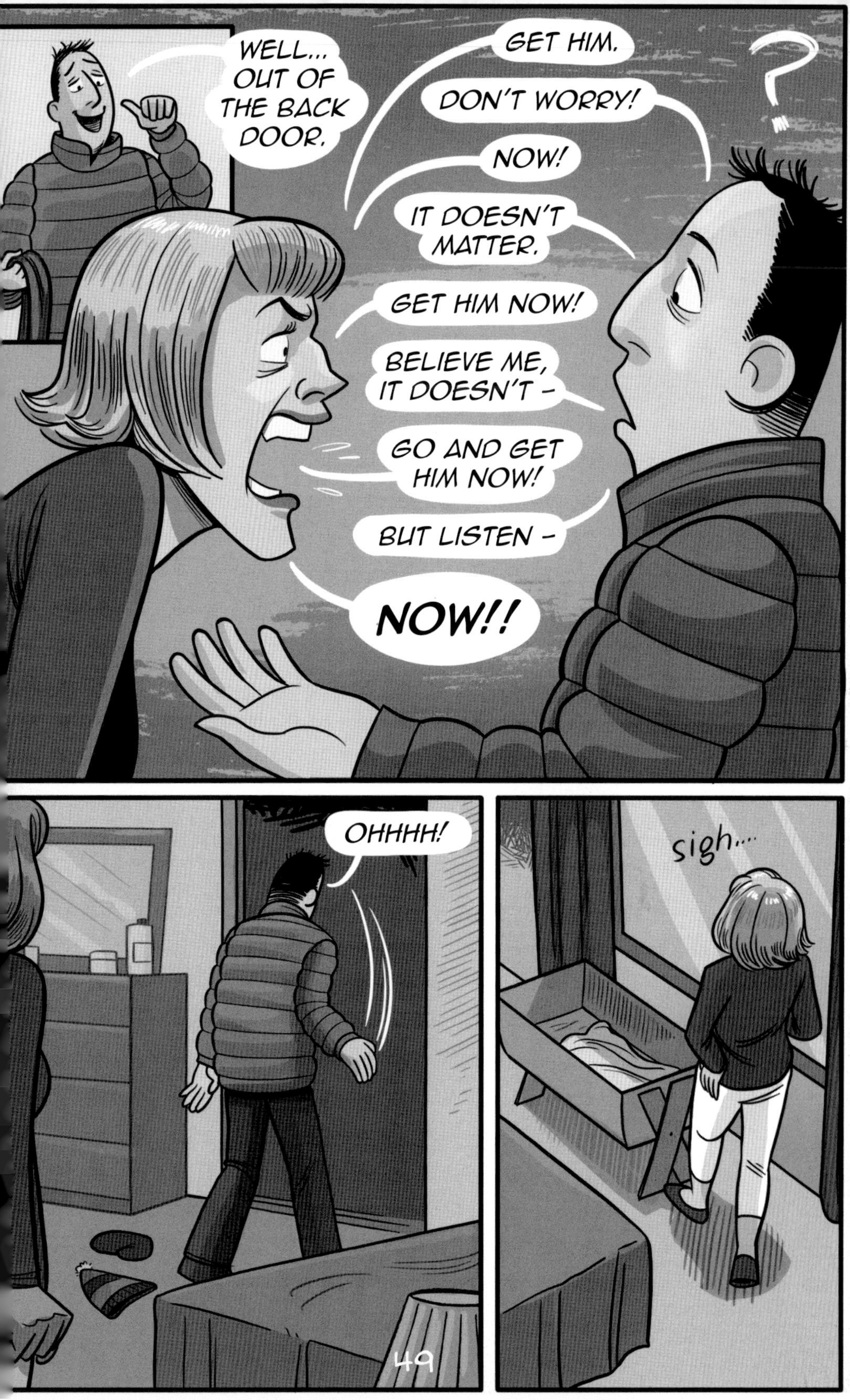
WELL... OUT OF THE BACK DOOR.
GET HIM.
DON'T WORRY!
NOW!
IT DOESN'T MATTER.
GET HIM NOW!
BELIEVE ME, IT DOESN'T -
GO AND GET HIM NOW!
BUT LISTEN -
NOW!!
OHHHH!
sigh....

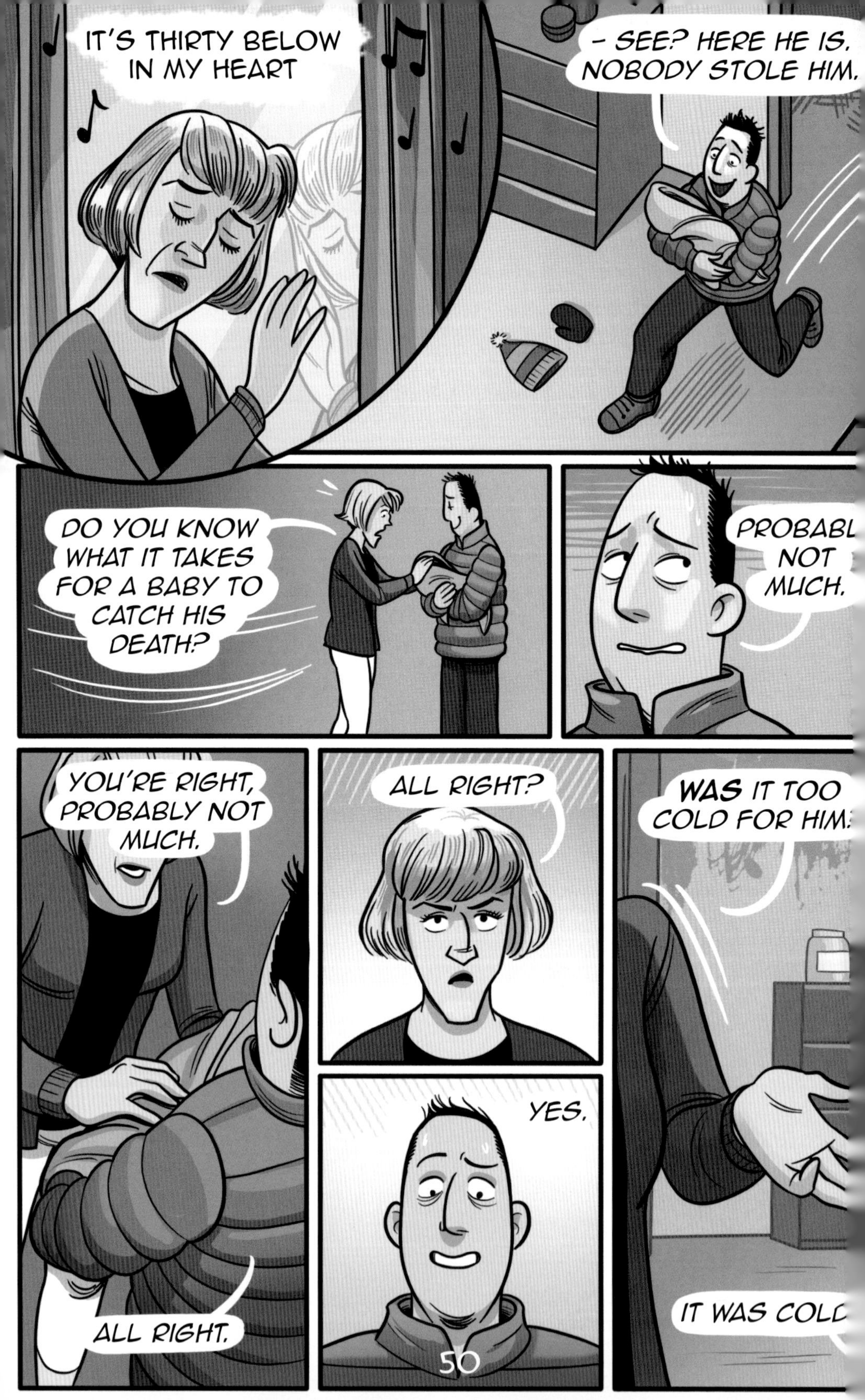
IT'S THIRTY BELOW
IN MY HEART
- SEE? HERE HE IS. NOBODY STOLE HIM.
DO YOU KNOW WHAT IT TAKES FOR A BABY TO CATCH HIS DEATH?
PROBABL NOT MUCH.
YOU'RE RIGHT, PROBABLY NOT MUCH.
ALL RIGHT.
ALL RIGHT?
YES.
WAS IT TOO COLD FOR HIM
IT WAS COLD

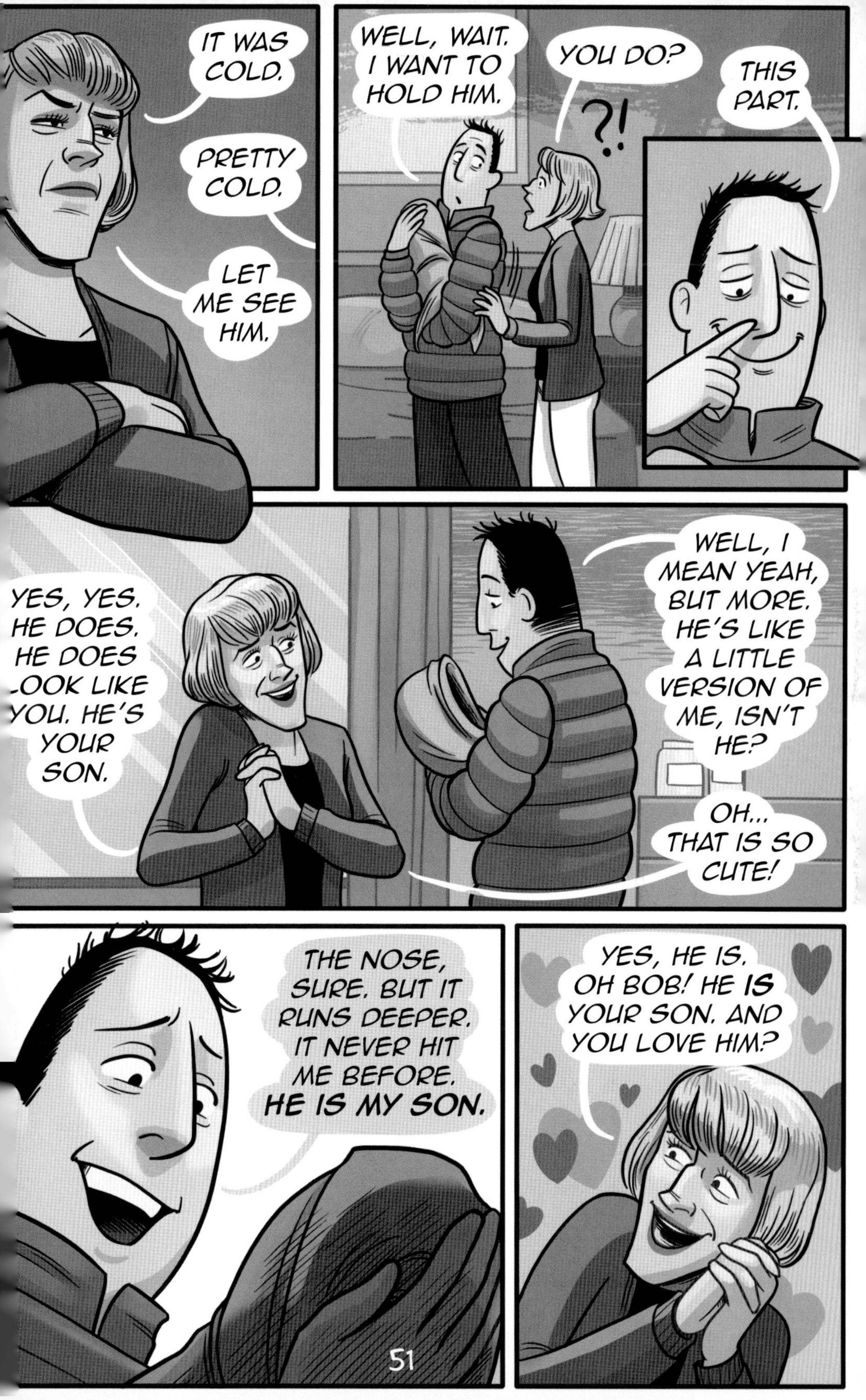
IT WAS COLD.
PRETTY COLD.
LET ME SEE HIM.
WELL, WAIT. I WANT TO HOLD HIM.
YOU DO?
?!
THIS PART.
WELL, I MEAN YEAH, BUT MORE. HE'S LIKE A LITTLE VERSION OF ME, ISN'T HE?
YES, YES. HE DOES. HE DOES LOOK LIKE YOU. HE'S YOUR SON.
OH... THAT IS SO CUTE!
THE NOSE, SURE. BUT IT RUNS DEEPER. IT NEVER HIT ME BEFORE. HE IS MY SON.
YES, HE IS. OH BOB! HE IS YOUR SON. AND YOU LOVE HIM?

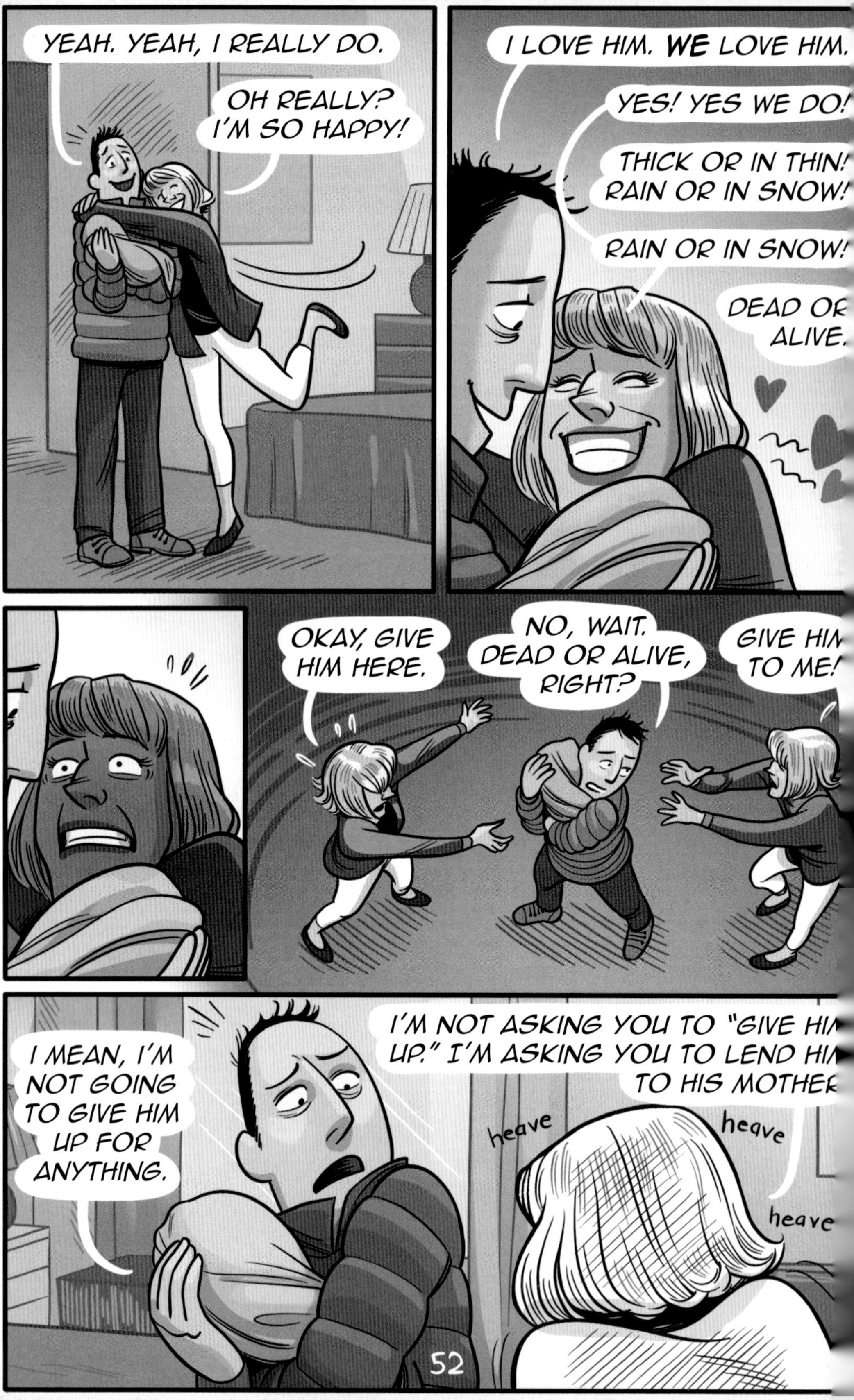
YEAH. YEAH, I REALLY DO.
OH REALLY? I'M SO HAPPY!
I LOVE HIM. **WE** LOVE HIM.
YES! YES WE DO!
THICK OR IN THIN! RAIN OR IN SNOW!
RAIN OR IN SNOW!
DEAD OR ALIVE.
OKAY, GIVE HIM HERE.
NO, WAIT. DEAD OR ALIVE, RIGHT?
GIVE HIM TO ME!
I MEAN, I'M NOT GOING TO GIVE HIM UP FOR ANYTHING.
I'M NOT ASKING YOU TO "GIVE HIM UP." I'M ASKING YOU TO LEND HIM TO HIS MOTHER
heave
heave
heave

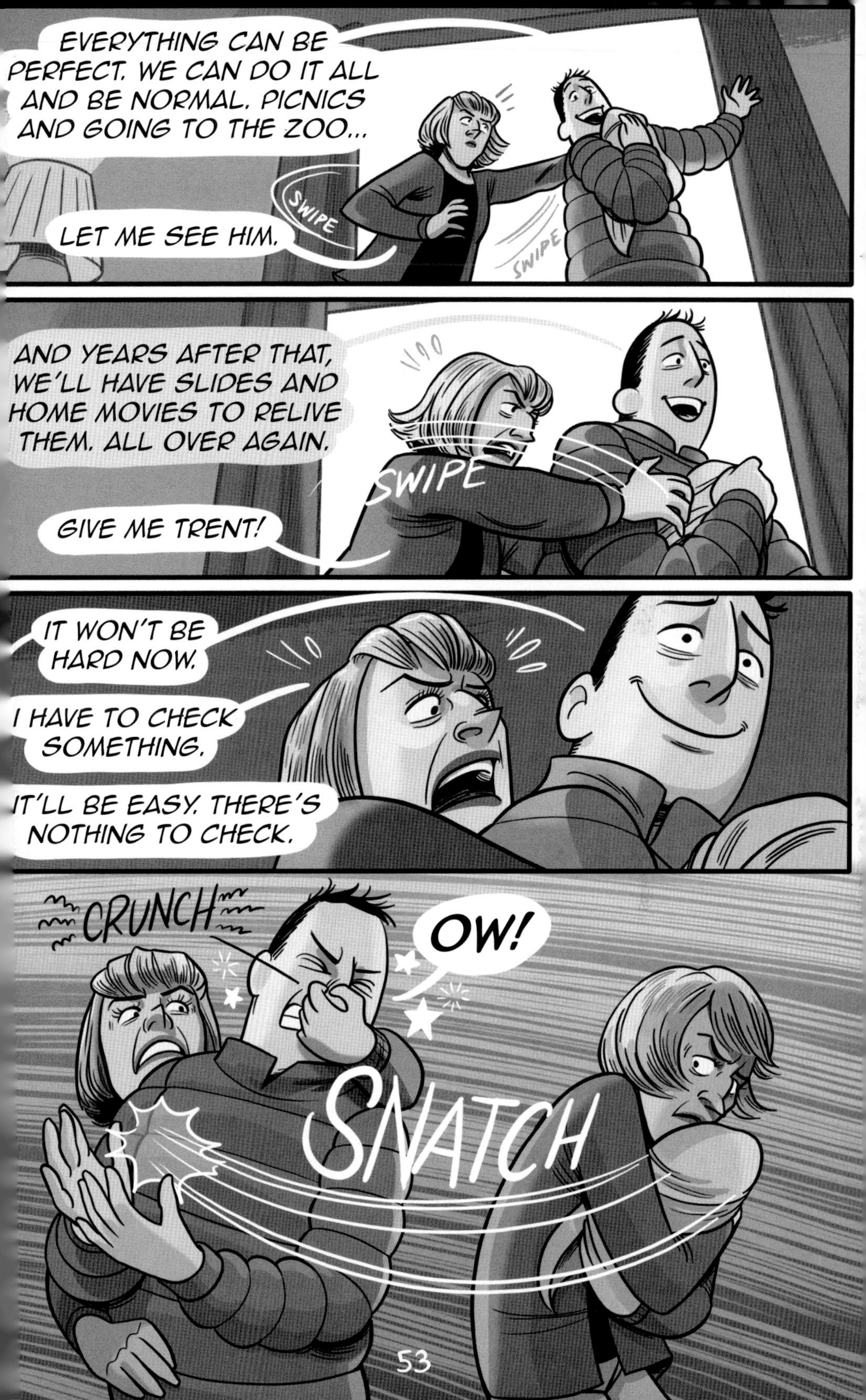
EVERYTHING CAN BE PERFECT. WE CAN DO IT ALL AND BE NORMAL. PICNICS AND GOING TO THE ZOO...
SWIPE
LET ME SEE HIM.
SWIPE
AND YEARS AFTER THAT, WE'LL HAVE SLIDES AND HOME MOVIES TO RELIVE THEM. ALL OVER AGAIN.
SWIPE
GIVE ME TRENT!
IT WON'T BE HARD NOW.
I HAVE TO CHECK SOMETHING.
IT'LL BE EASY. THERE'S NOTHING TO CHECK.
CRUNCH
OW!
SNATCH

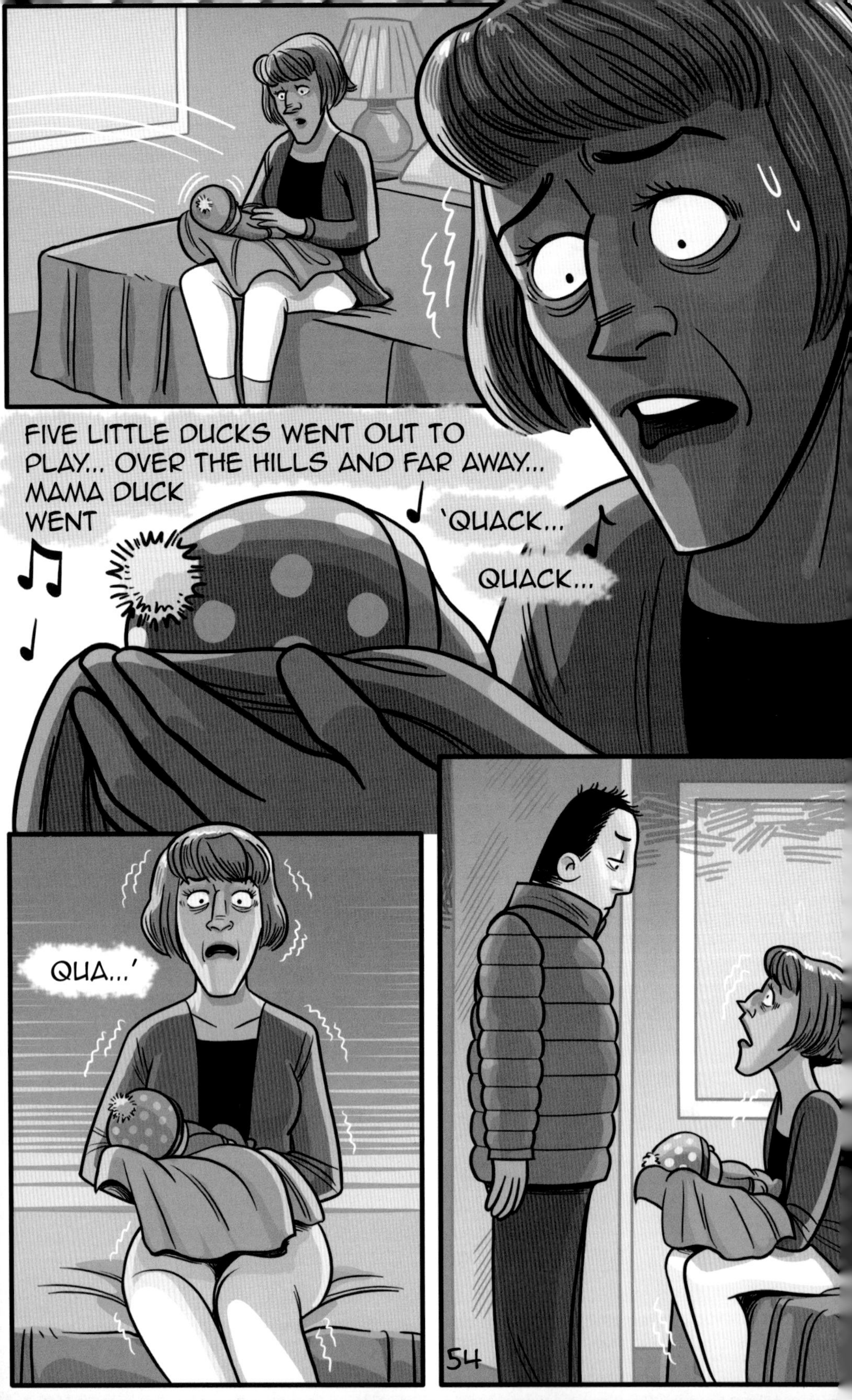
FIVE LITTLE DUCKS WENT OUT TO PLAY... OVER THE HILLS AND FAR AWAY... MAMA DUCK WENT
'QUACK...
QUACK...
QUA...'

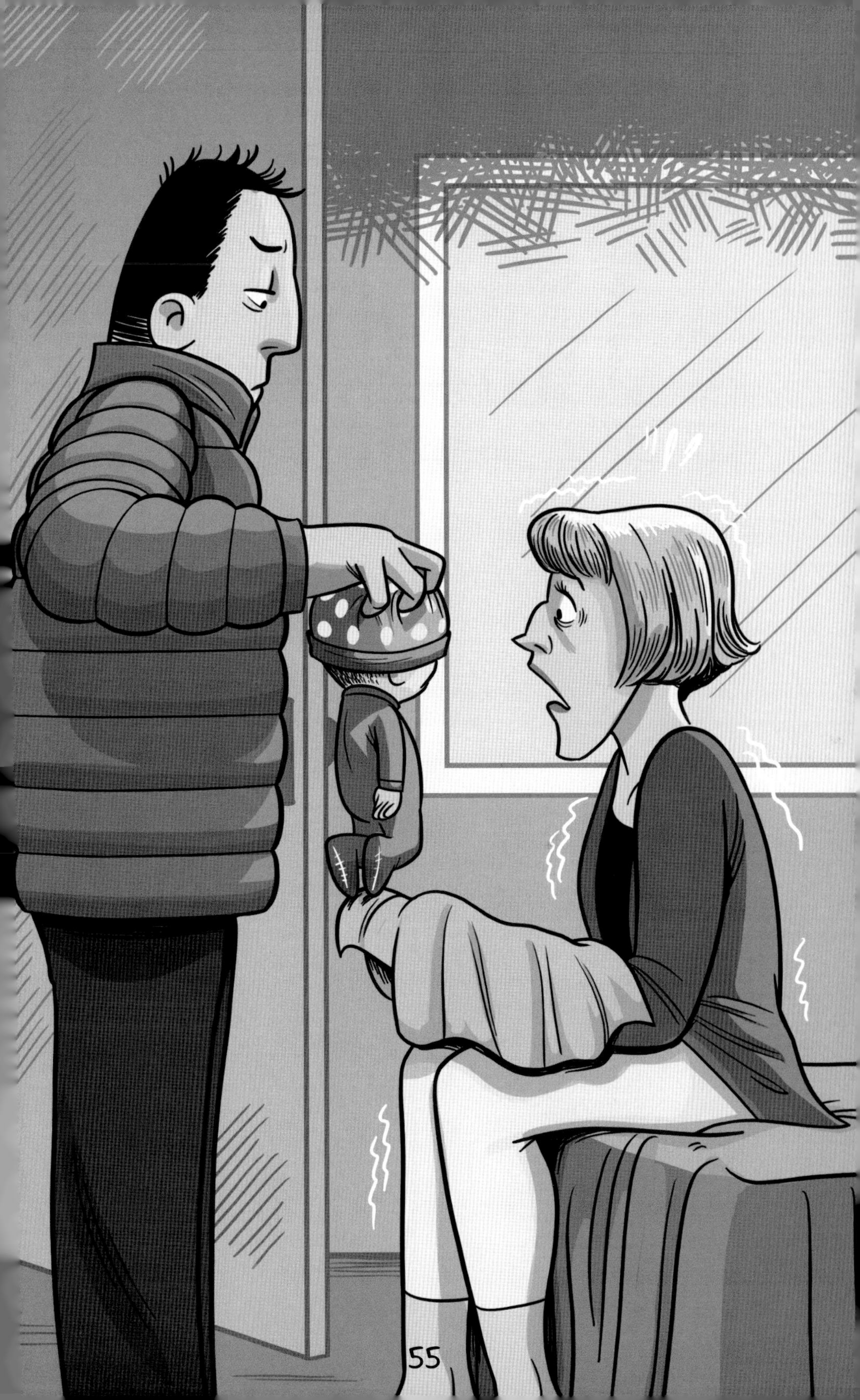

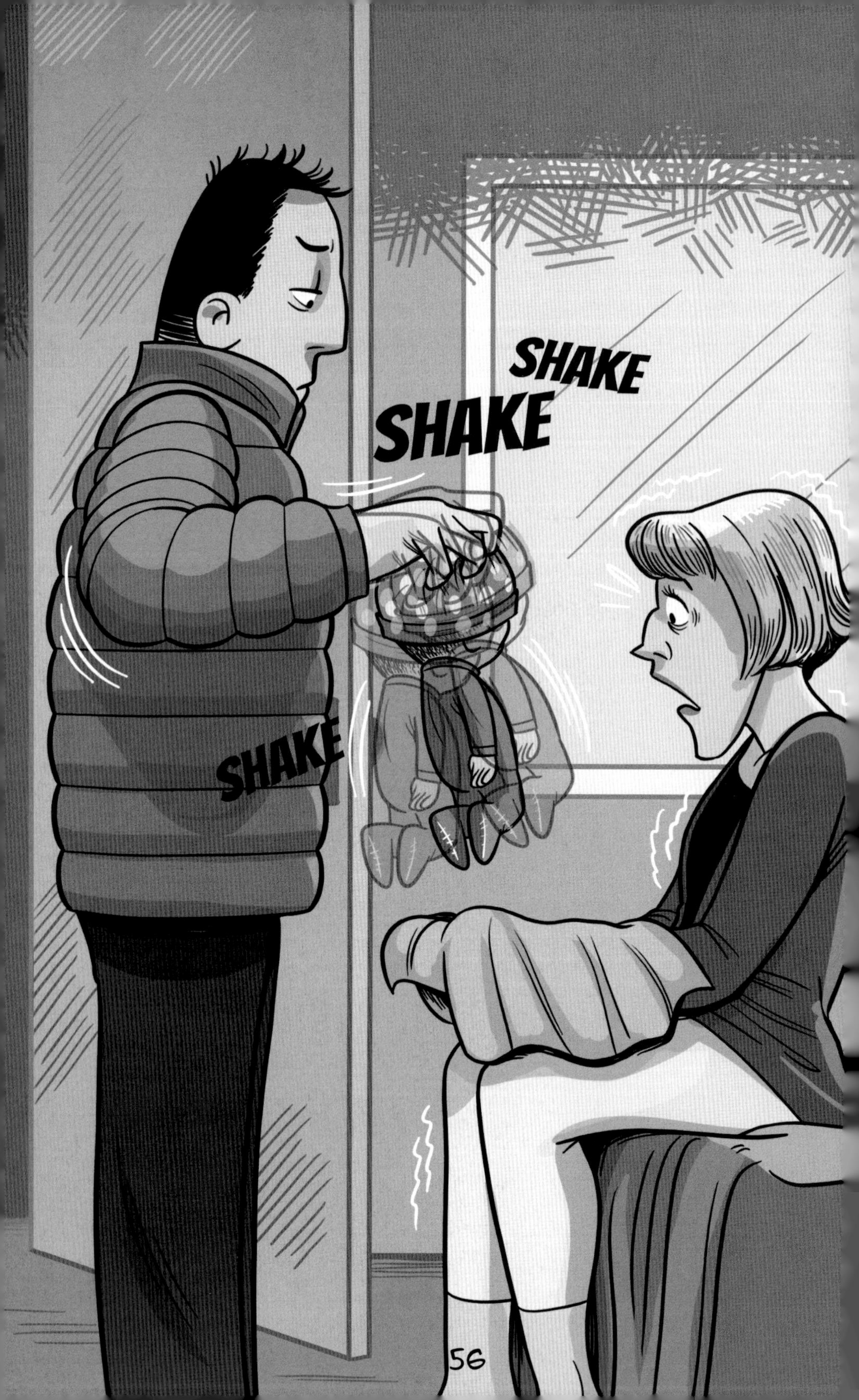
SHAKE
SHAKE
SHAKE

WHAT DO YOU FEEL?

NOTHING.

NOTHING?

NOTHING.

YOU DON'T FEEL ANYTHING?

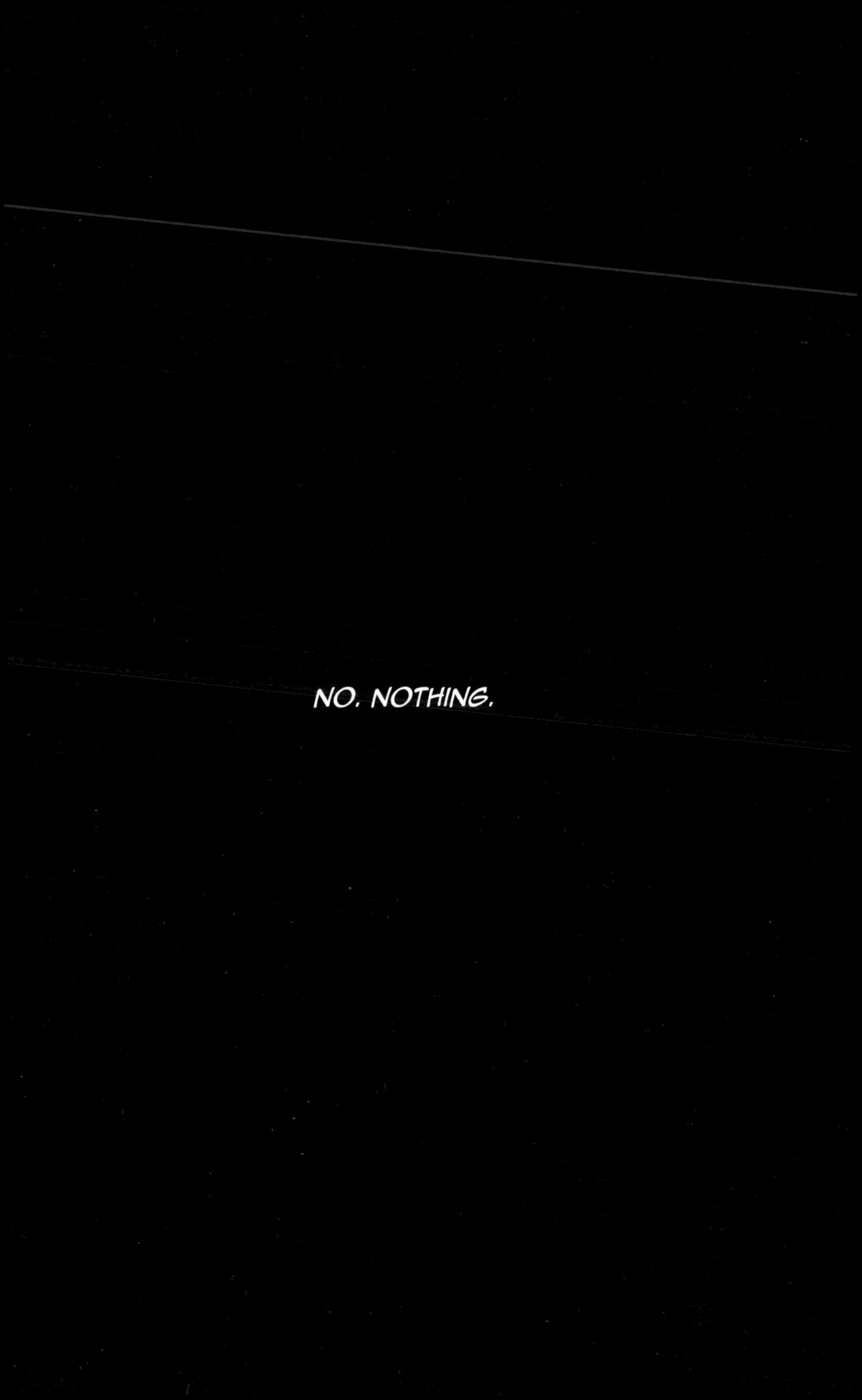
NO. NOTHING.

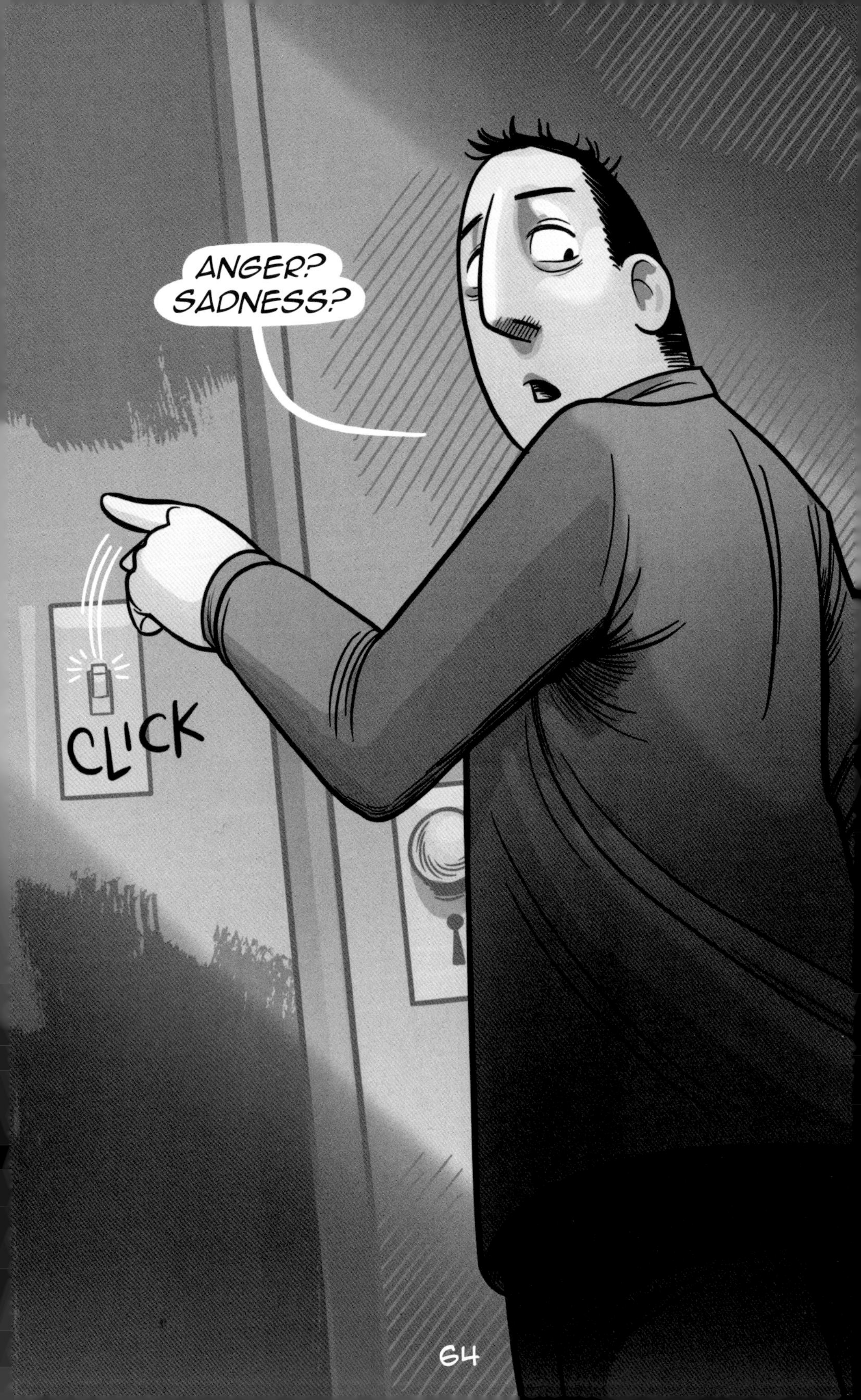
ANGER?
SADNESS?
CLICK

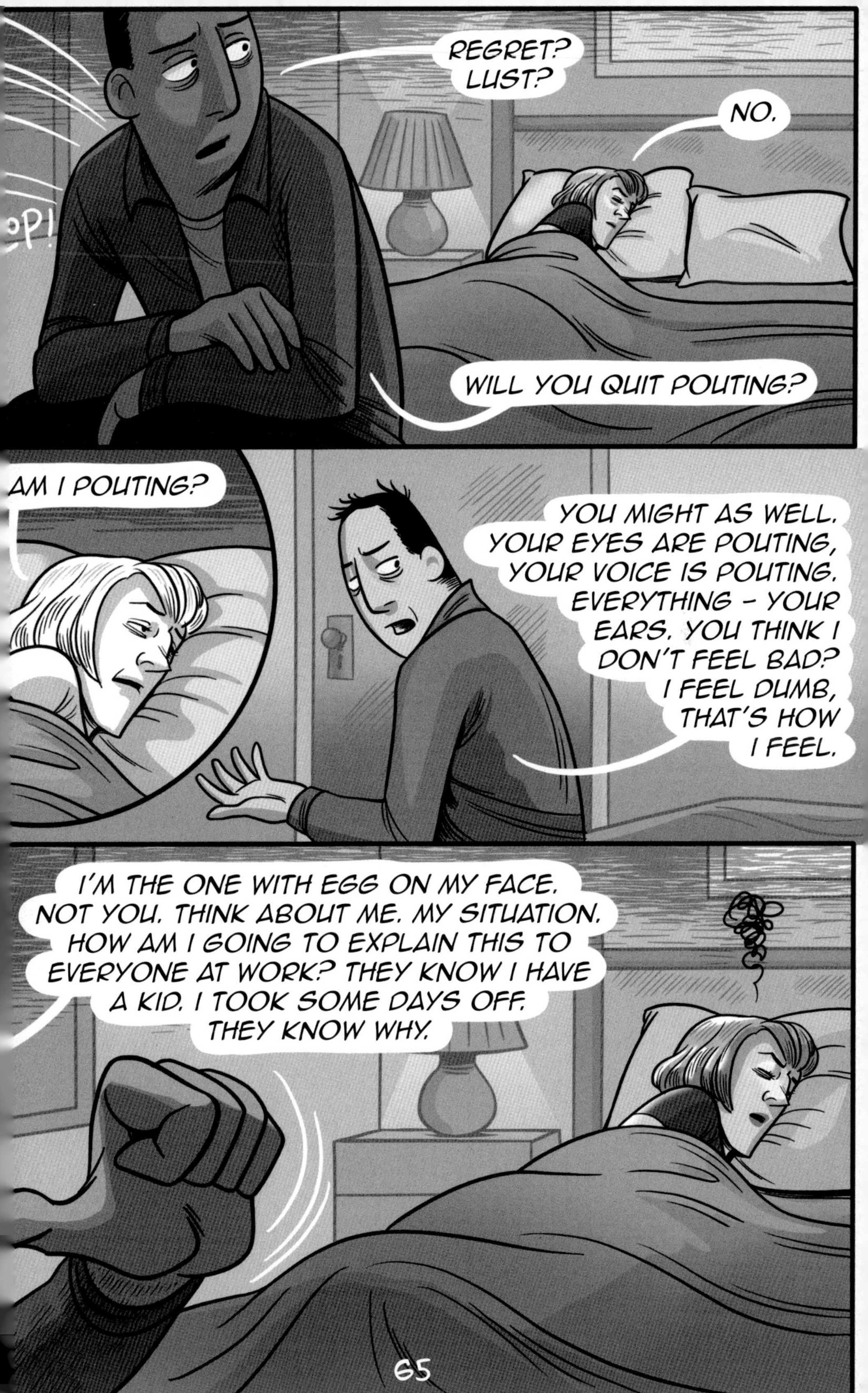

OP!
REGRET? LUST?
NO.
WILL YOU QUIT POUTING?
AM I POUTING?
YOU MIGHT AS WELL. YOUR EYES ARE POUTING, YOUR VOICE IS POUTING. EVERYTHING - YOUR EARS. YOU THINK I DON'T FEEL BAD? I FEEL DUMB, THAT'S HOW I FEEL.
I'M THE ONE WITH EGG ON MY FACE. NOT YOU. THINK ABOUT ME. MY SITUATION. HOW AM I GOING TO EXPLAIN THIS TO EVERYONE AT WORK? THEY KNOW I HAVE A KID. I TOOK SOME DAYS OFF. THEY KNOW WHY.

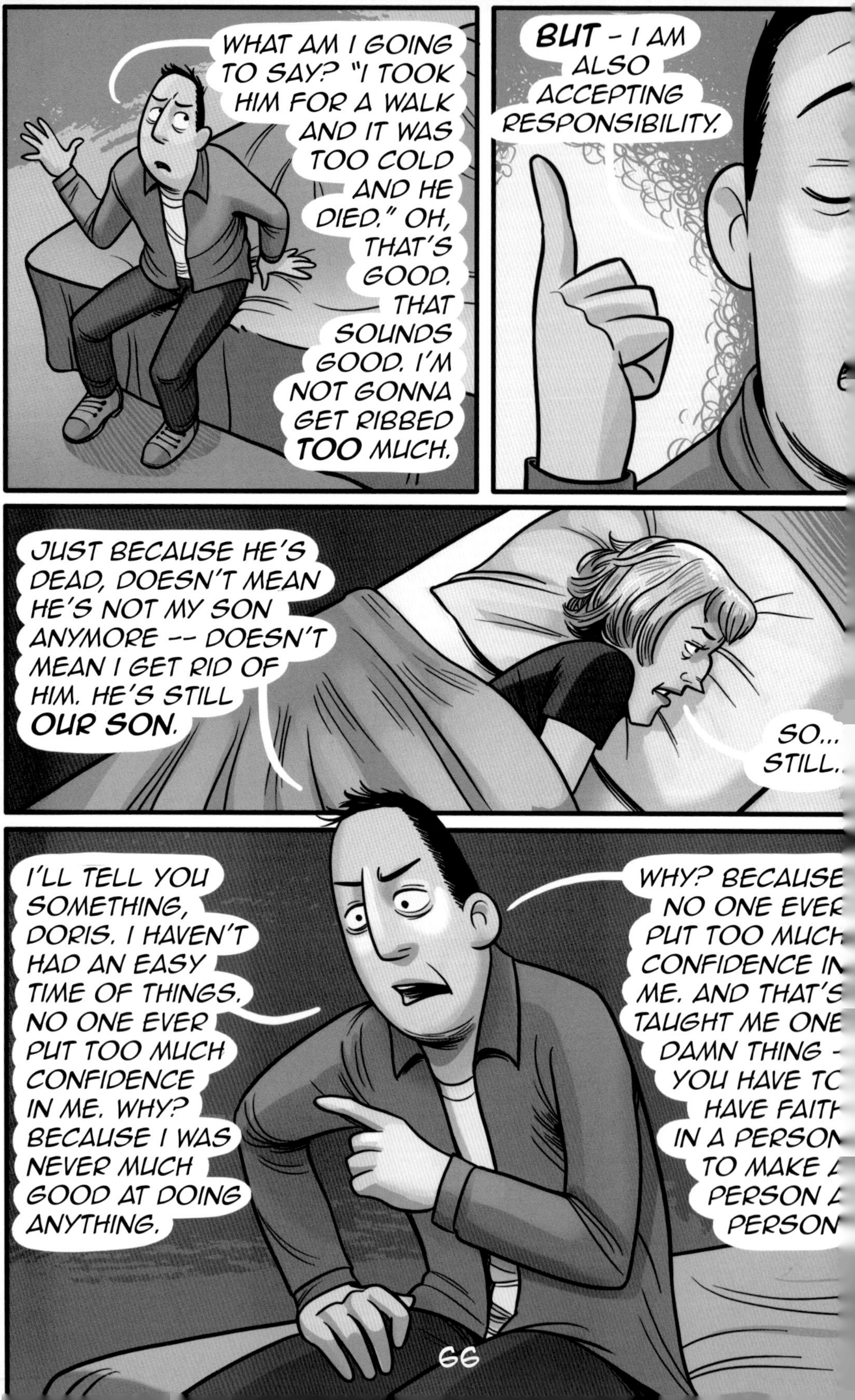
WHAT AM I GOING TO SAY? "I TOOK HIM FOR A WALK AND IT WAS TOO COLD AND HE DIED." OH, THAT'S GOOD. THAT SOUNDS GOOD. I'M NOT GONNA GET RIBBED TOO MUCH.
BUT - I AM ALSO ACCEPTING RESPONSIBILITY.
JUST BECAUSE HE'S DEAD, DOESN'T MEAN HE'S NOT MY SON ANYMORE -- DOESN'T MEAN I GET RID OF HIM. HE'S STILL OUR SON.
SO... STILL..
I'LL TELL YOU SOMETHING, DORIS. I HAVEN'T HAD AN EASY TIME OF THINGS. NO ONE EVER PUT TOO MUCH CONFIDENCE IN ME. WHY? BECAUSE I WAS NEVER MUCH GOOD AT DOING ANYTHING.
WHY? BECAUSE NO ONE EVER PUT TOO MUCH CONFIDENCE IN ME. AND THAT'S TAUGHT ME ONE DAMN THING - YOU HAVE TO HAVE FAITH IN A PERSON TO MAKE A PERSON A PERSON

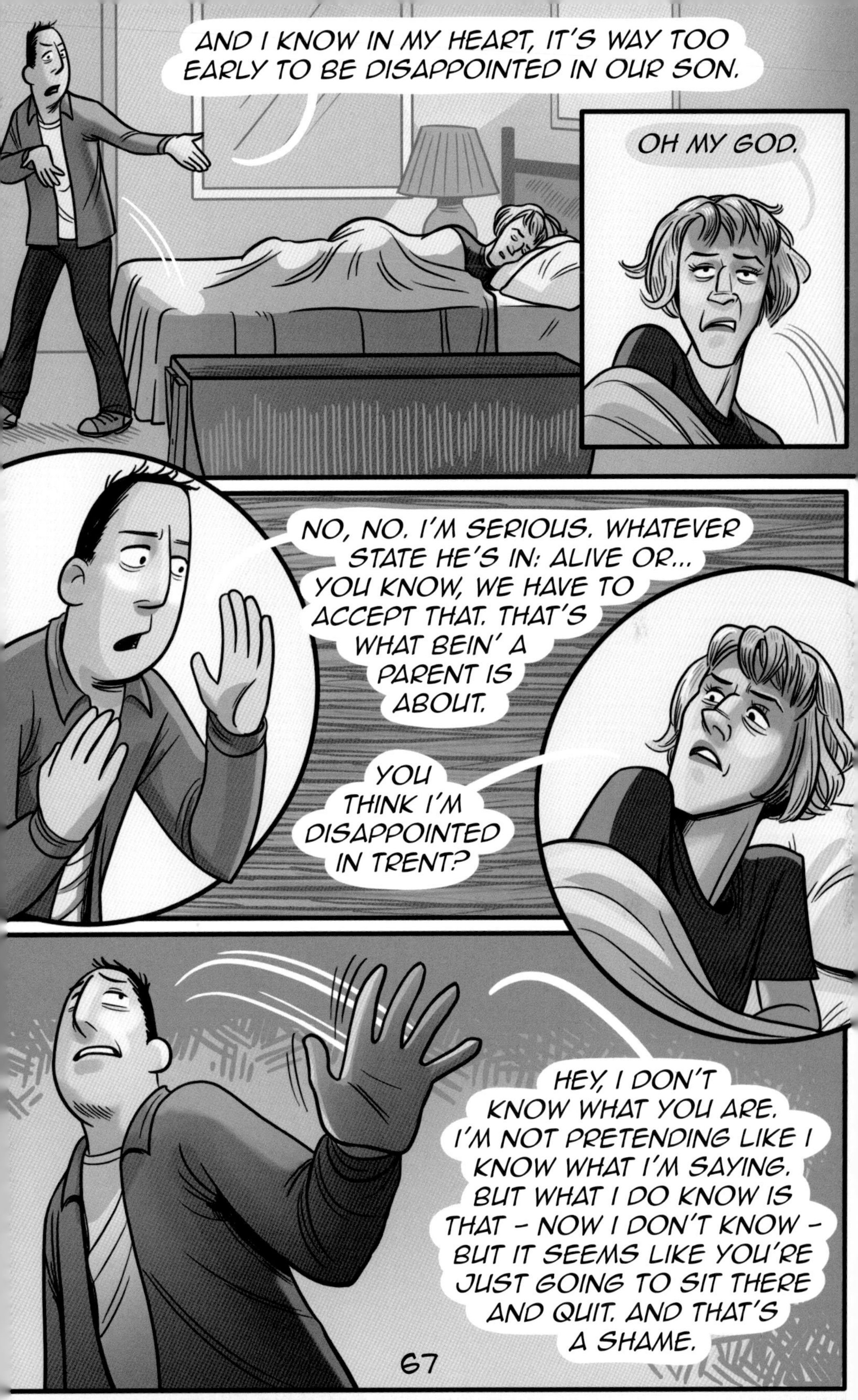
AND I KNOW IN MY HEART, IT'S WAY TOO EARLY TO BE DISAPPOINTED IN OUR SON.
OH MY GOD.
NO, NO. I'M SERIOUS. WHATEVER STATE HE'S IN: ALIVE OR... YOU KNOW, WE HAVE TO ACCEPT THAT. THAT'S WHAT BEIN' A PARENT IS ABOUT.
YOU THINK I'M DISAPPOINTED IN TRENT?
HEY, I DON'T KNOW WHAT YOU ARE. I'M NOT PRETENDING LIKE I KNOW WHAT I'M SAYING. BUT WHAT I DO KNOW IS THAT - NOW I DON'T KNOW - BUT IT SEEMS LIKE YOU'RE JUST GOING TO SIT THERE AND QUIT. AND THAT'S A SHAME.

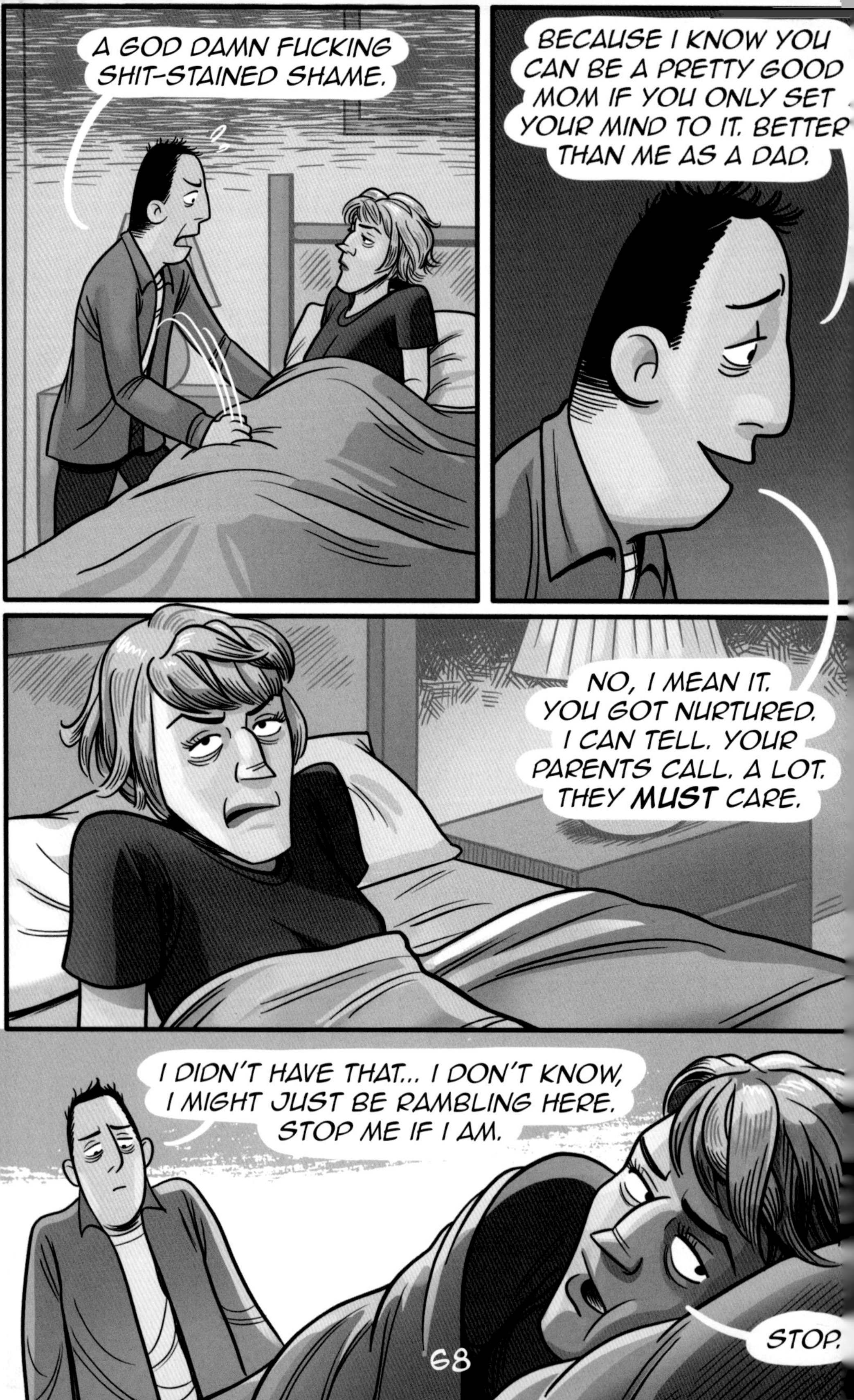
A GOD DAMN FUCKING SHIT-STAINED SHAME.
BECAUSE I KNOW YOU CAN BE A PRETTY GOOD MOM IF YOU ONLY SET YOUR MIND TO IT. BETTER THAN ME AS A DAD.
NO, I MEAN IT. YOU GOT NURTURED. I CAN TELL. YOUR PARENTS CALL. A LOT. THEY **MUST** CARE.
I DIDN'T HAVE THAT... I DON'T KNOW, I MIGHT JUST BE RAMBLING HERE. STOP ME IF I AM.
STOP.

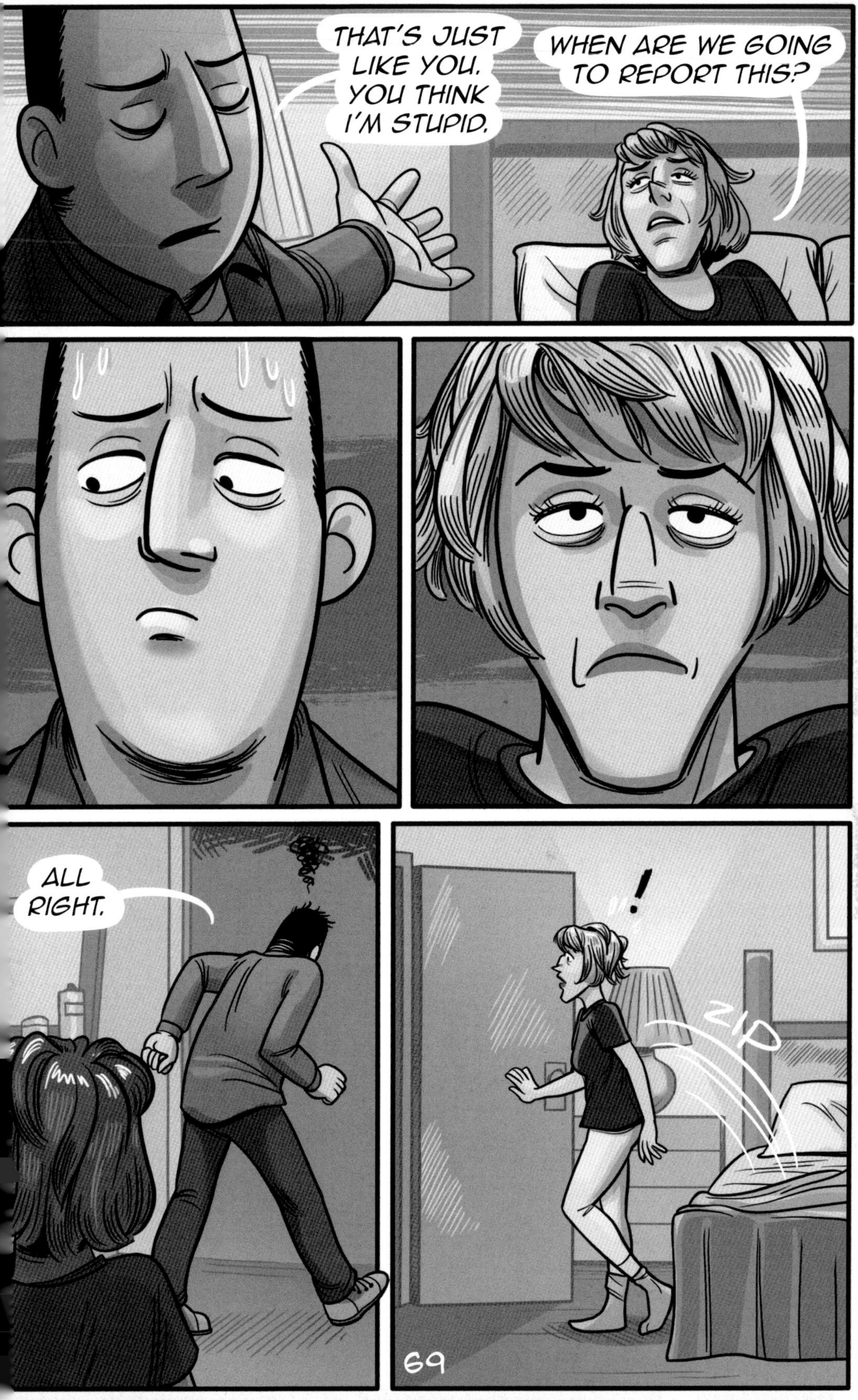
THAT'S JUST LIKE YOU. YOU THINK I'M STUPID.
WHEN ARE WE GOING TO REPORT THIS?
ALL RIGHT.
!
ZIP

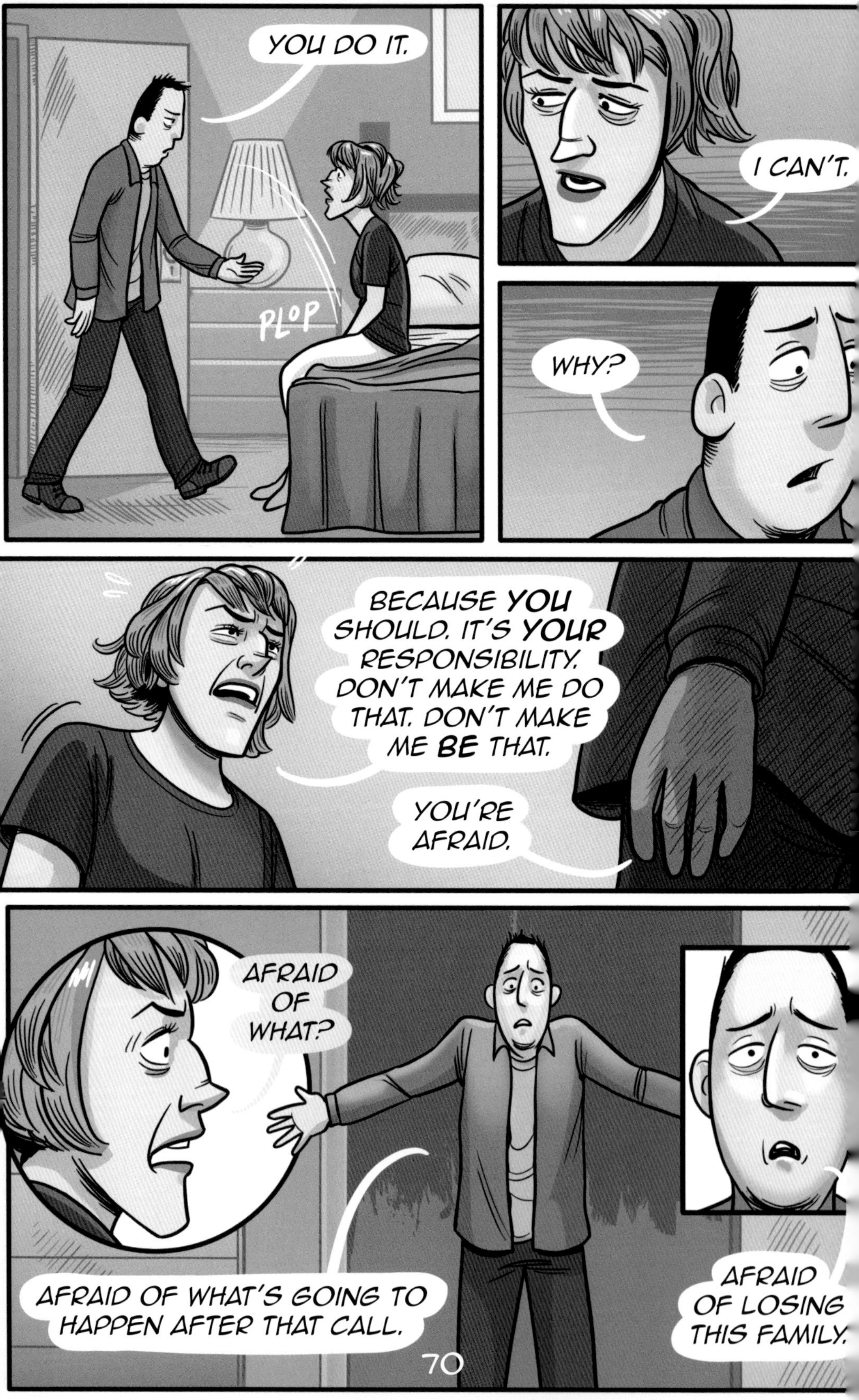
YOU DO IT.
PLOP
I CAN'T.
WHY?
BECAUSE YOU SHOULD. IT'S YOUR RESPONSIBILITY. DON'T MAKE ME DO THAT. DON'T MAKE ME BE THAT.
YOU'RE AFRAID.
AFRAID OF WHAT?
AFRAID OF WHAT'S GOING TO HAPPEN AFTER THAT CALL.
AFRAID OF LOSING THIS FAMILY.

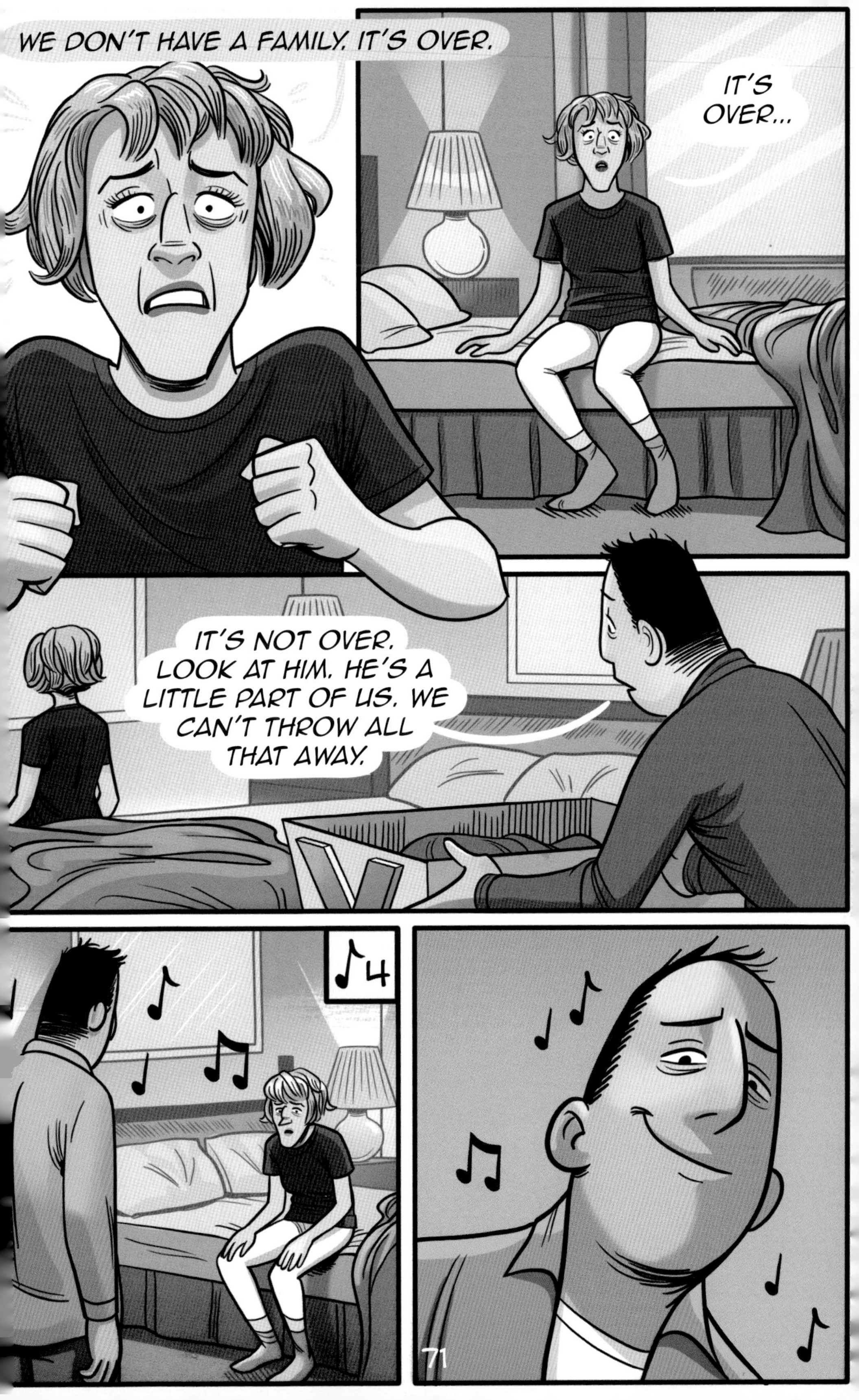
WE DON'T HAVE A FAMILY. IT'S OVER.
IT'S OVER...
IT'S NOT OVER. LOOK AT HIM. HE'S A LITTLE PART OF US. WE CAN'T THROW ALL THAT AWAY.
♪4

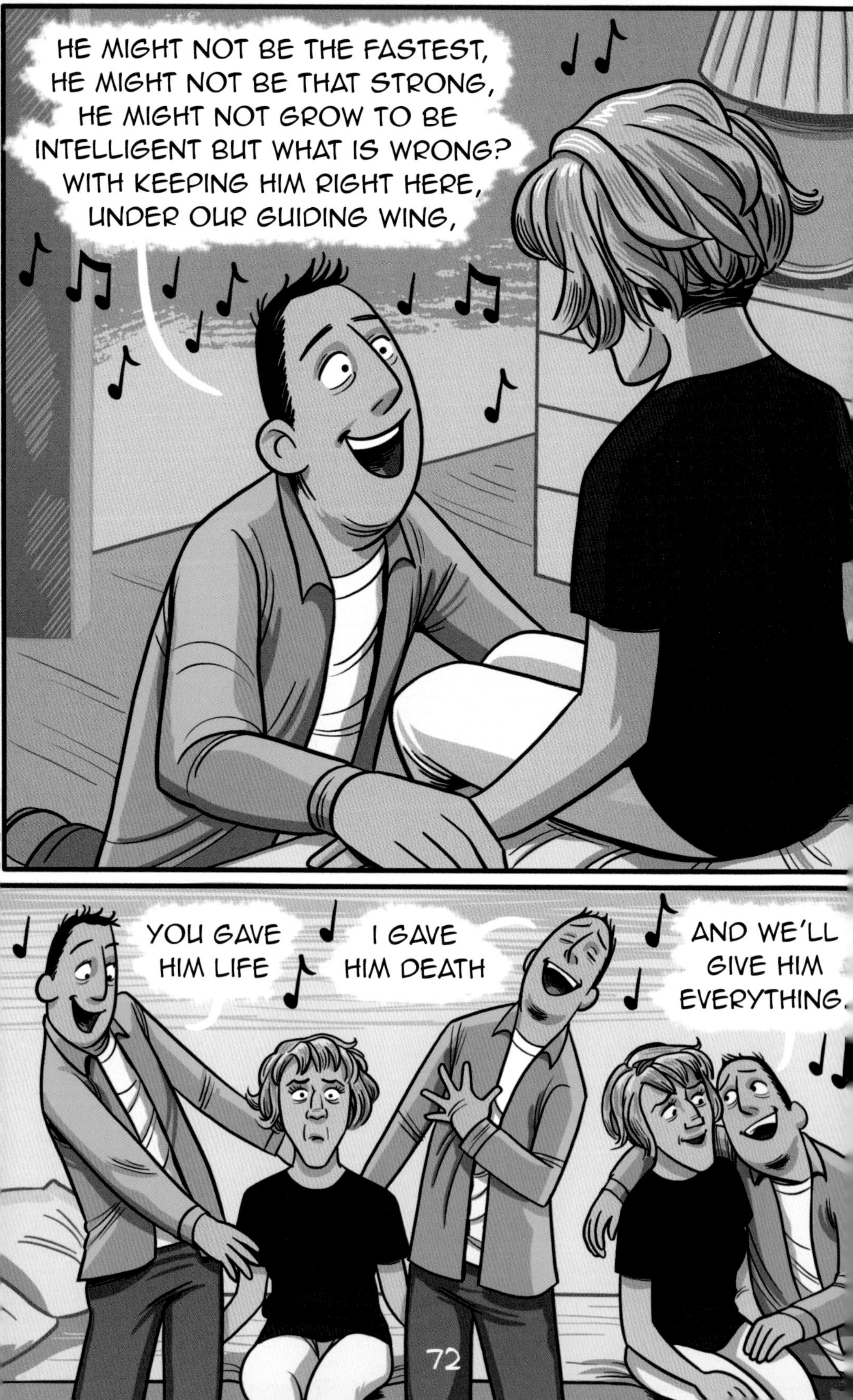
HE MIGHT NOT BE THE FASTEST, HE MIGHT NOT BE THAT STRONG, HE MIGHT NOT GROW TO BE INTELLIGENT BUT WHAT IS WRONG? WITH KEEPING HIM RIGHT HERE, UNDER OUR GUIDING WING,
YOU GAVE HIM LIFE
I GAVE HIM DEATH
AND WE'LL GIVE HIM EVERYTHING.

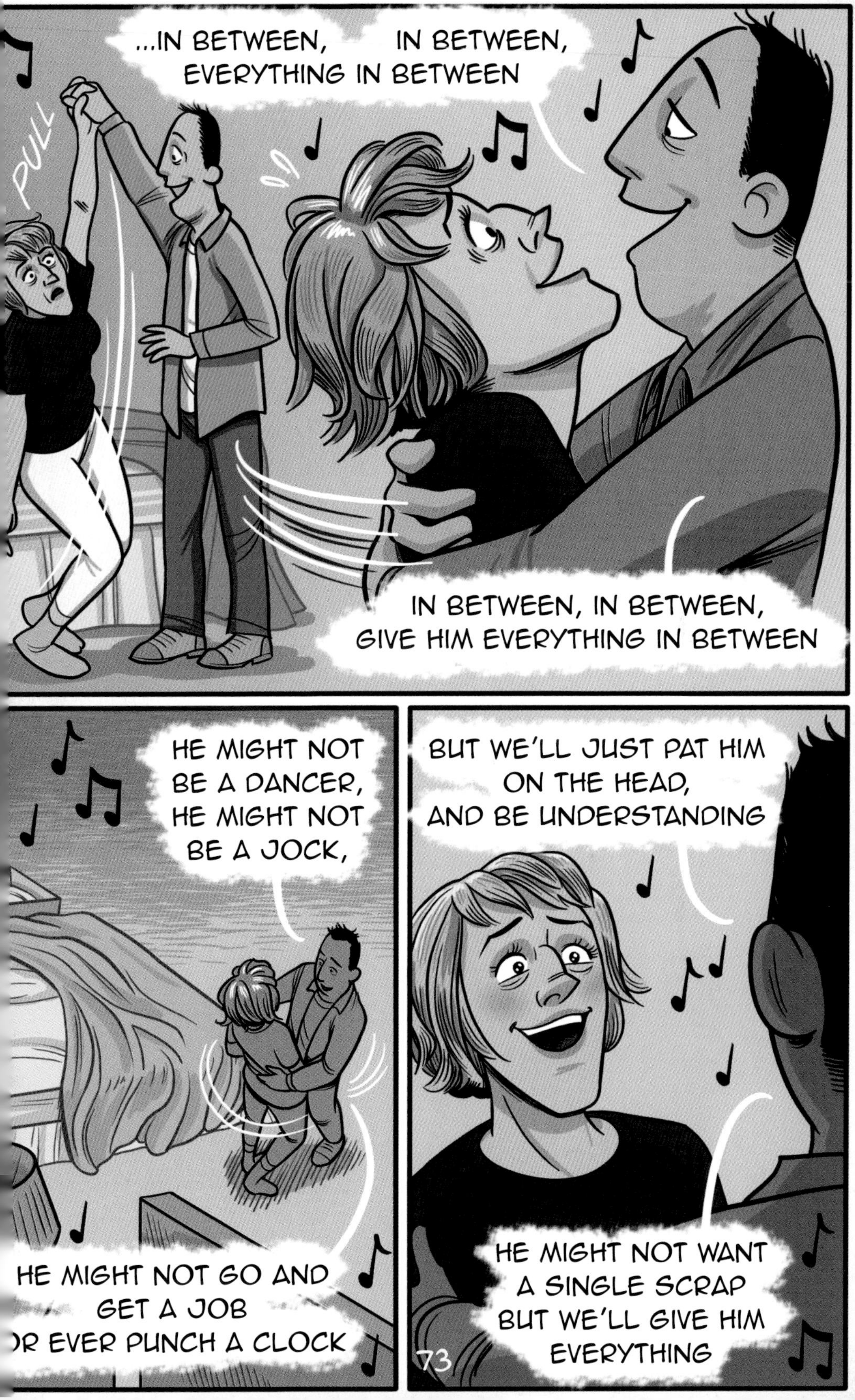
...IN BETWEEN, IN BETWEEN, EVERYTHING IN BETWEEN
PULL
IN BETWEEN, IN BETWEEN, GIVE HIM EVERYTHING IN BETWEEN
HE MIGHT NOT BE A DANCER, HE MIGHT NOT BE A JOCK,
HE MIGHT NOT GO AND GET A JOB
OR EVER PUNCH A CLOCK
BUT WE'LL JUST PAT HIM ON THE HEAD, AND BE UNDERSTANDING
HE MIGHT NOT WANT A SINGLE SCRAP BUT WE'LL GIVE HIM EVERYTHING

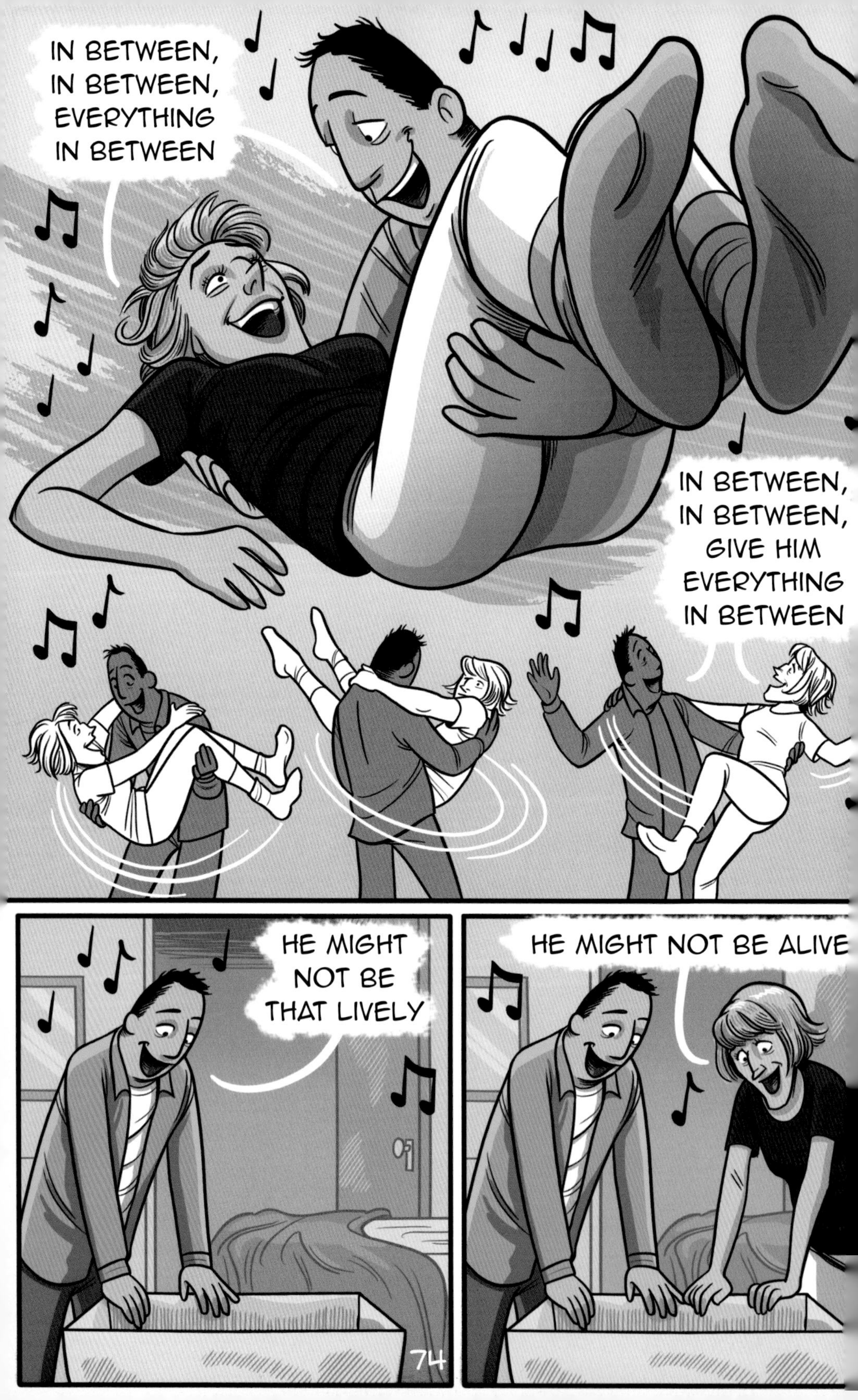

IN BETWEEN, IN BETWEEN, EVERYTHING IN BETWEEN
IN BETWEEN, IN BETWEEN, GIVE HIM EVERYTHING IN BETWEEN
HE MIGHT NOT BE THAT LIVELY
HE MIGHT NOT BE ALIVE

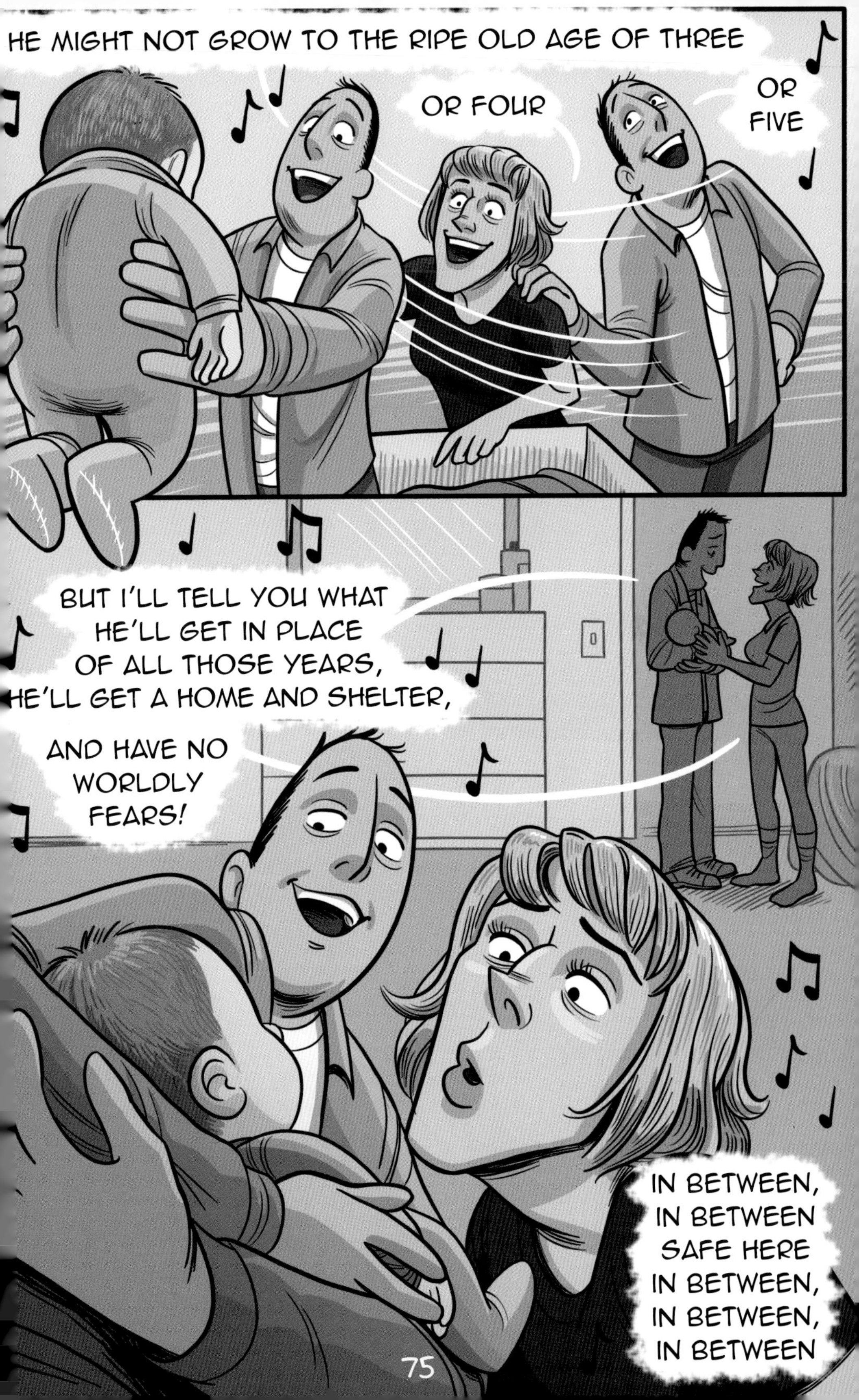
HE MIGHT NOT GROW TO THE RIPE OLD AGE OF THREE
OR FOUR
OR FIVE
BUT I'LL TELL YOU WHAT HE'LL GET IN PLACE OF ALL THOSE YEARS, HE'LL GET A HOME AND SHELTER,
AND HAVE NO WORLDLY FEARS!
IN BETWEEN, IN BETWEEN SAFE HERE IN BETWEEN, IN BETWEEN, IN BETWEEN

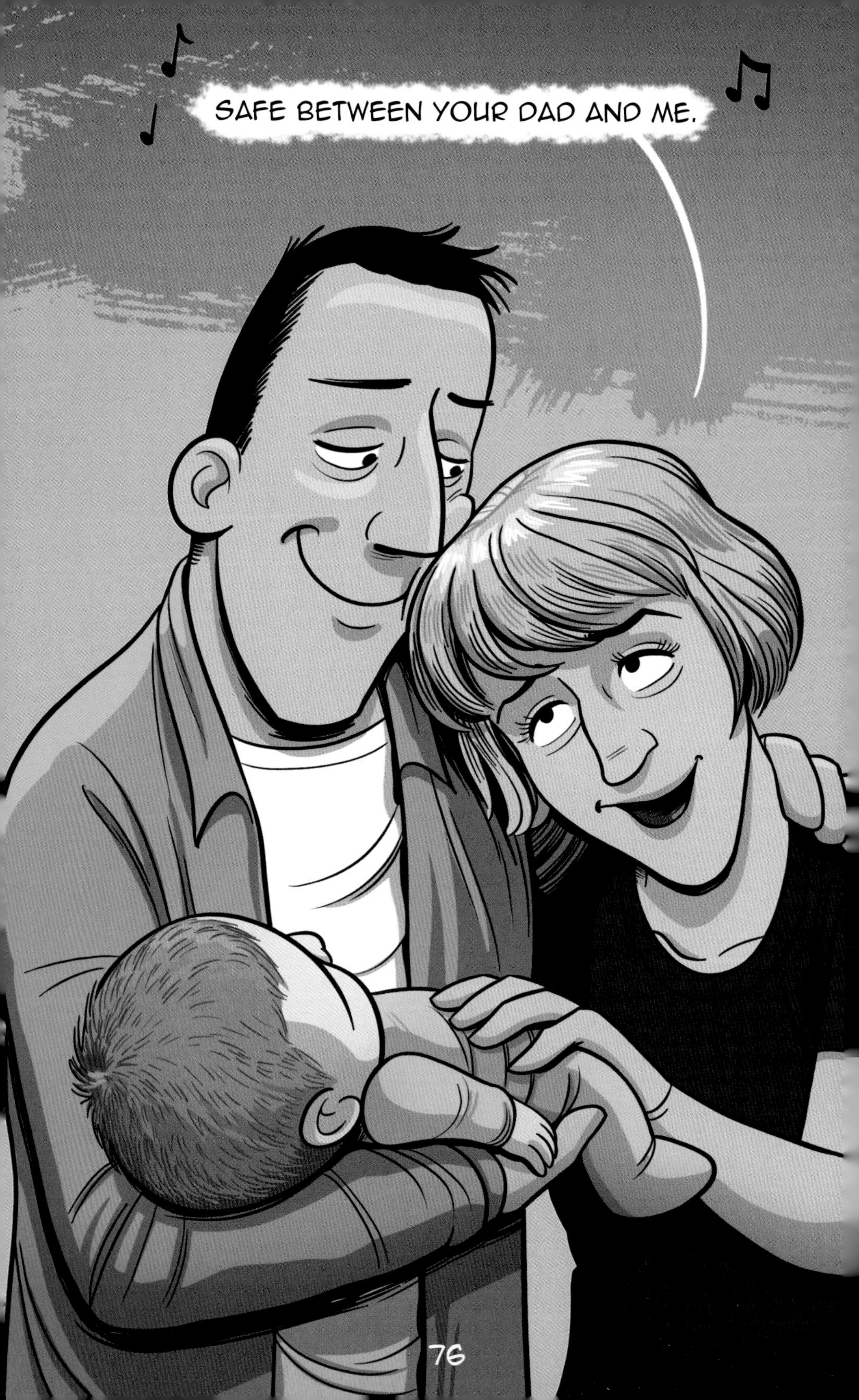
SAFE BETWEEN YOUR DAD AND ME.

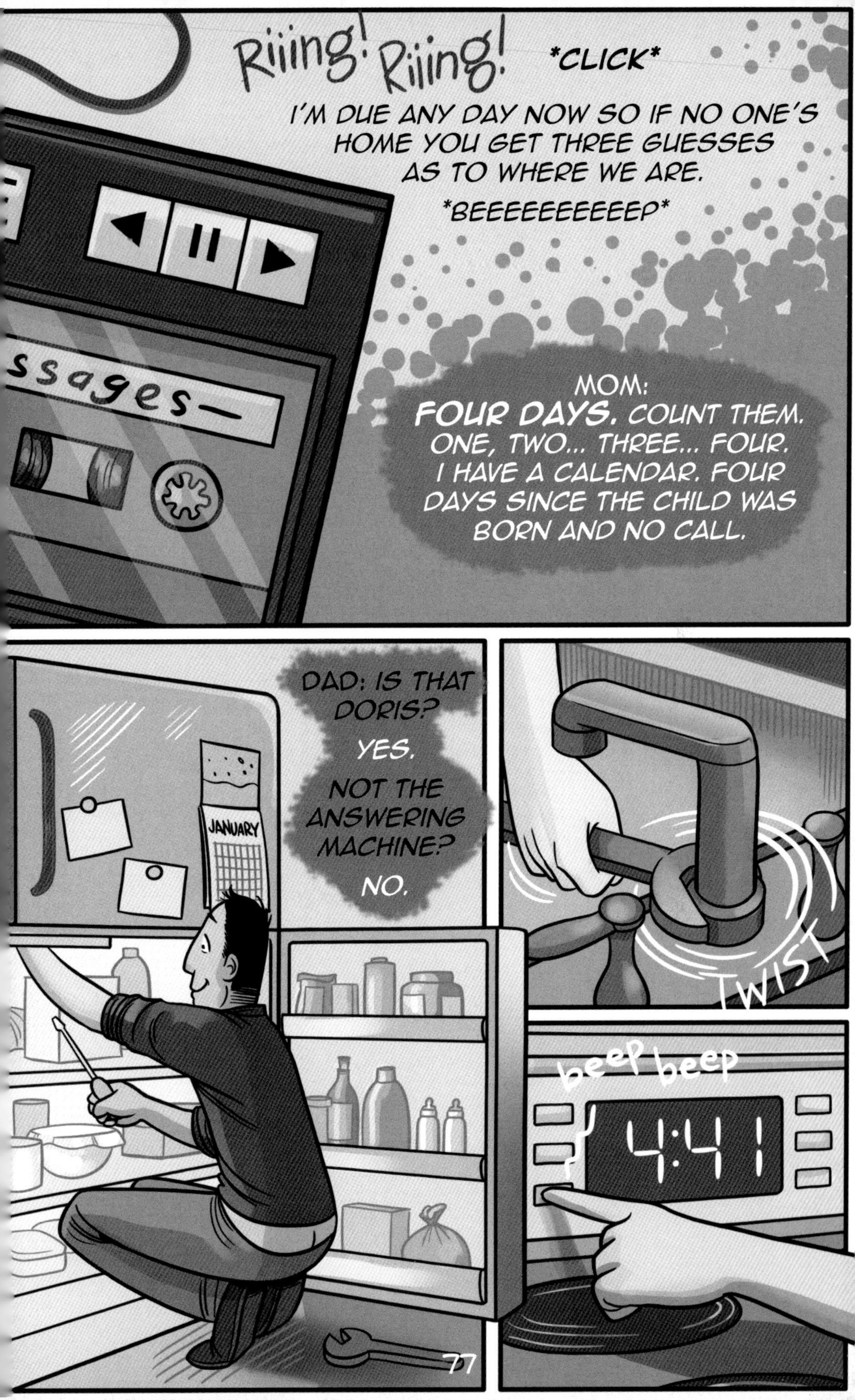
Riiing! Riiing!
CLICK
I'M DUE ANY DAY NOW SO IF NO ONE'S HOME YOU GET THREE GUESSES AS TO WHERE WE ARE.
BEEEEEEEEEEEP
ssages—
MOM: FOUR DAYS. COUNT THEM. ONE, TWO... THREE... FOUR. I HAVE A CALENDAR. FOUR DAYS SINCE THE CHILD WAS BORN AND NO CALL.
JANUARY
DAD: IS THAT DORIS?
YES.
NOT THE ANSWERING MACHINE?
NO.
TWIST
beep beep
4:41

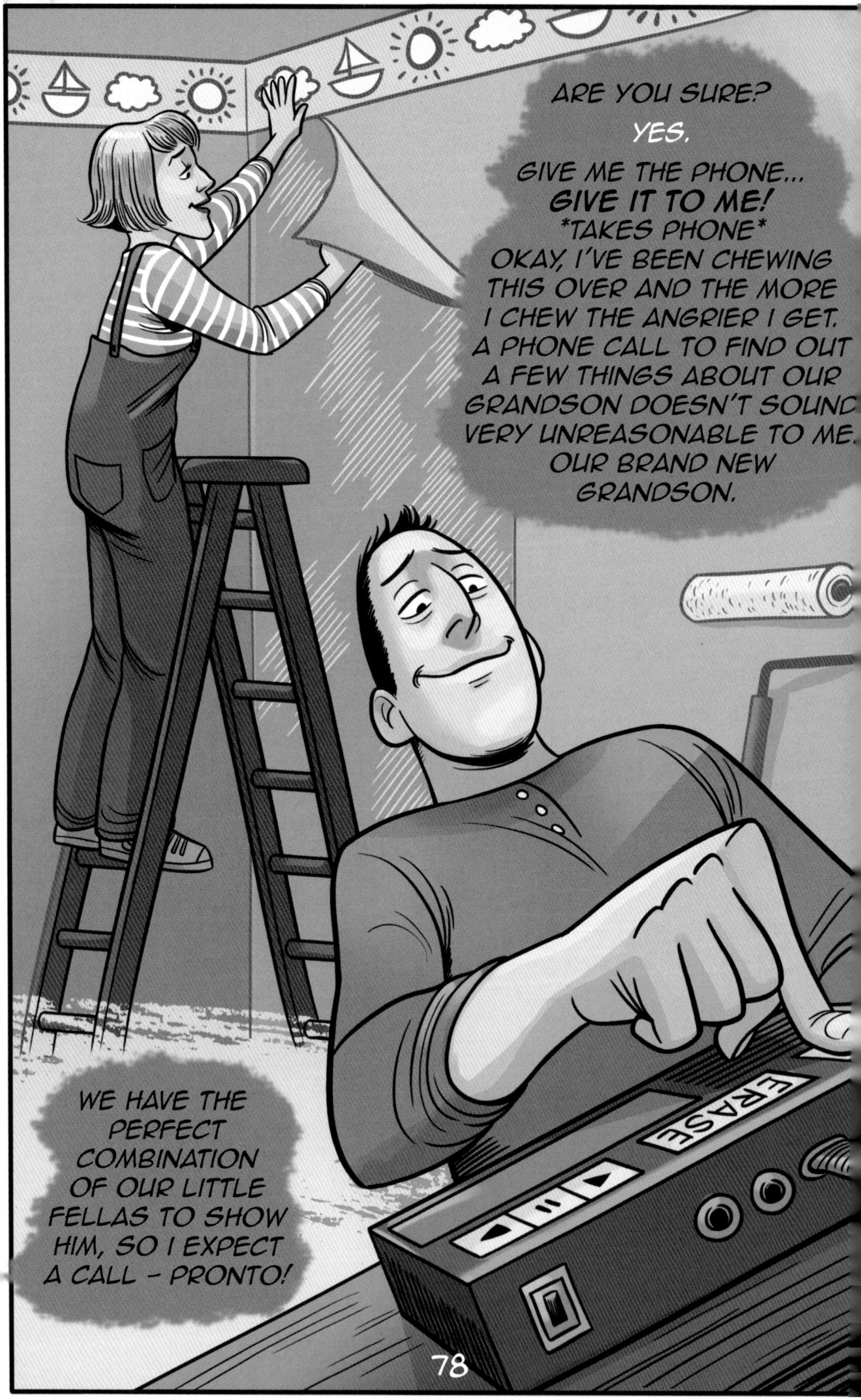
ARE YOU SURE?
YES.
GIVE ME THE PHONE... **GIVE IT TO ME!** *TAKES PHONE* OKAY, I'VE BEEN CHEWING THIS OVER AND THE MORE I CHEW THE ANGRIER I GET. A PHONE CALL TO FIND OUT A FEW THINGS ABOUT OUR GRANDSON DOESN'T SOUND VERY UNREASONABLE TO ME. OUR BRAND NEW GRANDSON.
WE HAVE THE PERFECT COMBINATION OF OUR LITTLE FELLAS TO SHOW HIM, SO I EXPECT A CALL - PRONTO!
ERASE

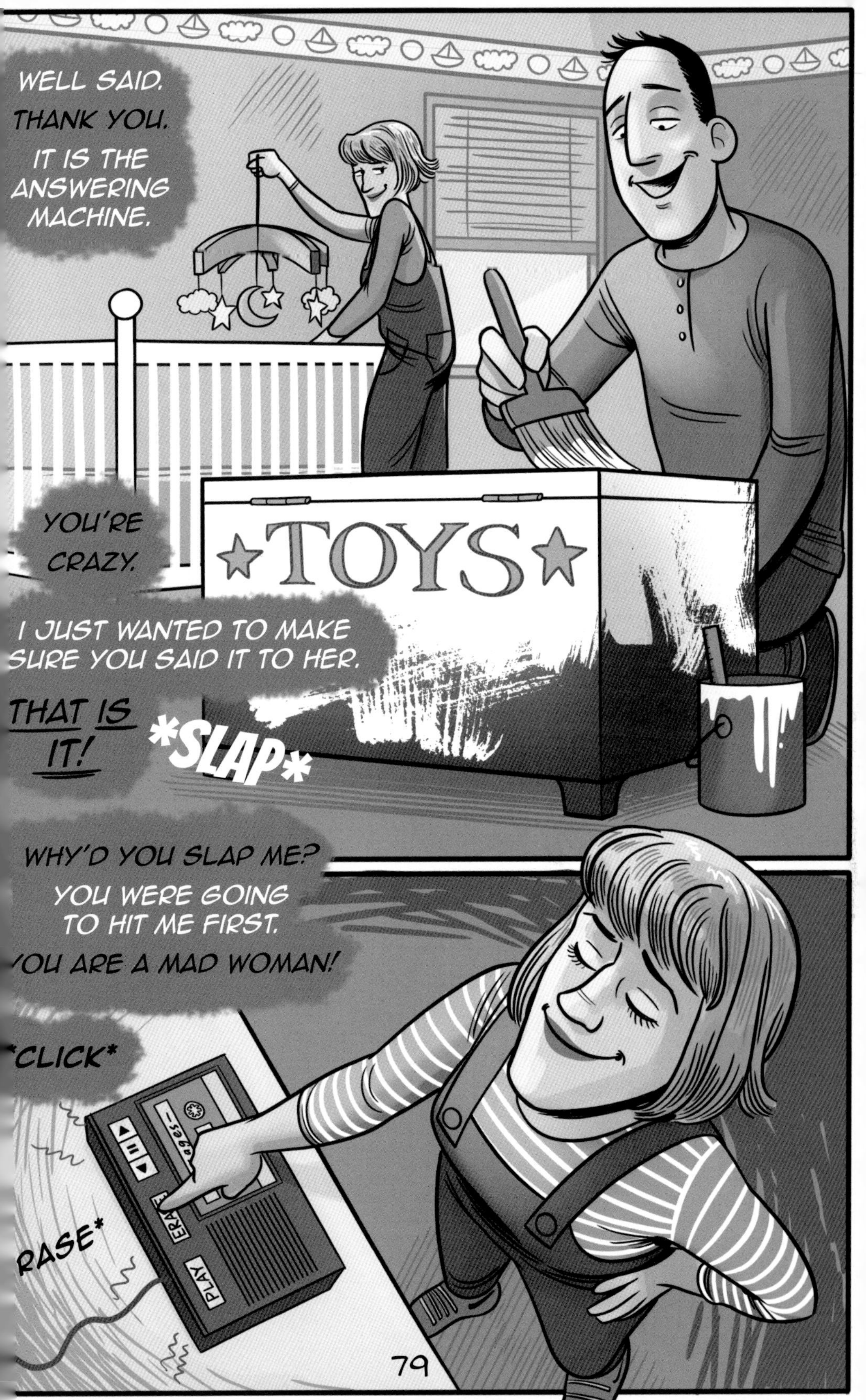

WELL SAID.
THANK YOU.
IT IS THE ANSWERING MACHINE.
TOYS
YOU'RE CRAZY.
I JUST WANTED TO MAKE SURE YOU SAID IT TO HER.
THAT IS IT!
SLAP
WHY'D YOU SLAP ME?
YOU WERE GOING TO HIT ME FIRST.
YOU ARE A MAD WOMAN!
CLICK
RASE*
ERASE
PLAY

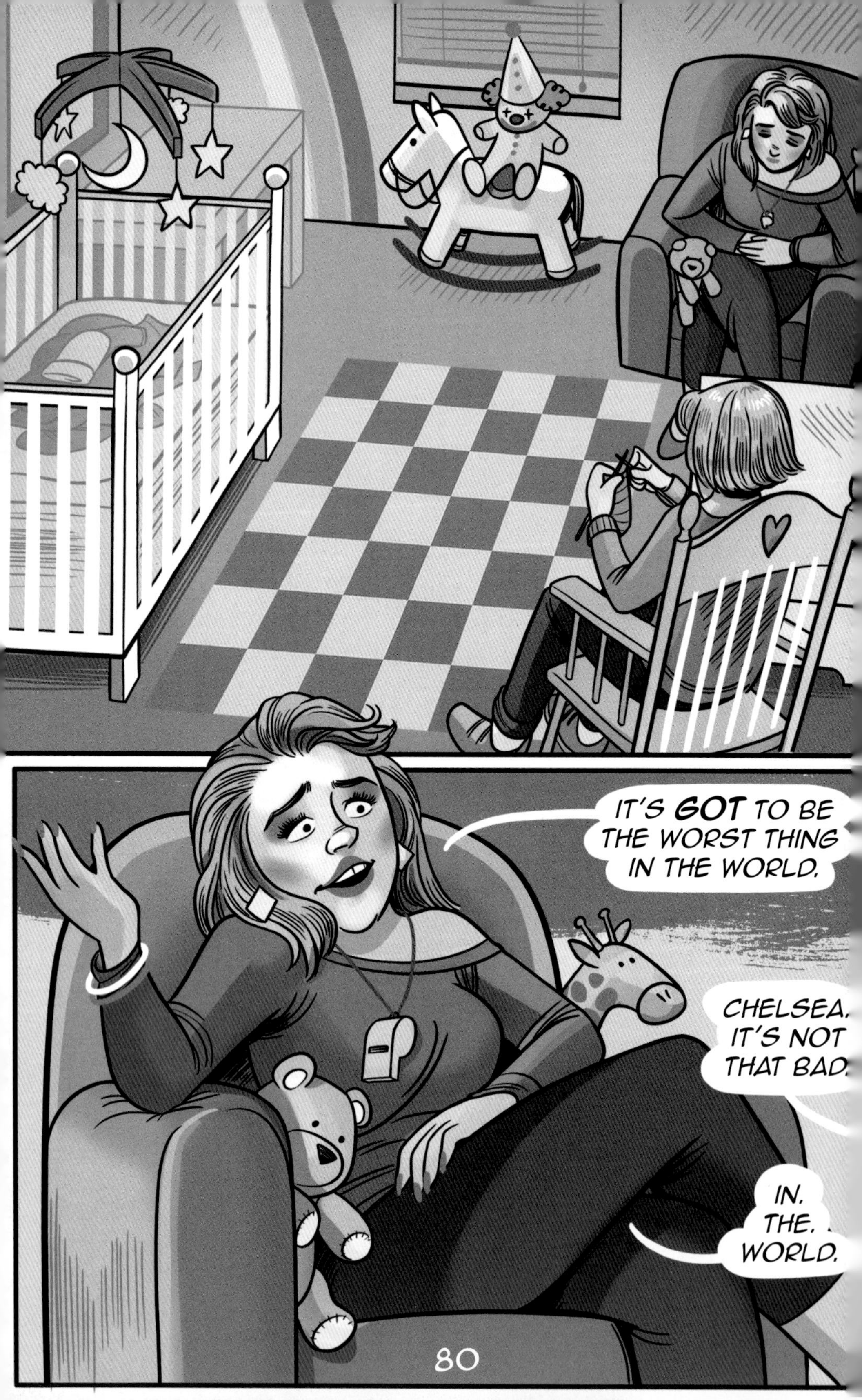
IT'S **GOT** TO BE THE WORST THING IN THE WORLD.
CHELSEA. IT'S NOT THAT BAD.
IN. THE. WORLD.

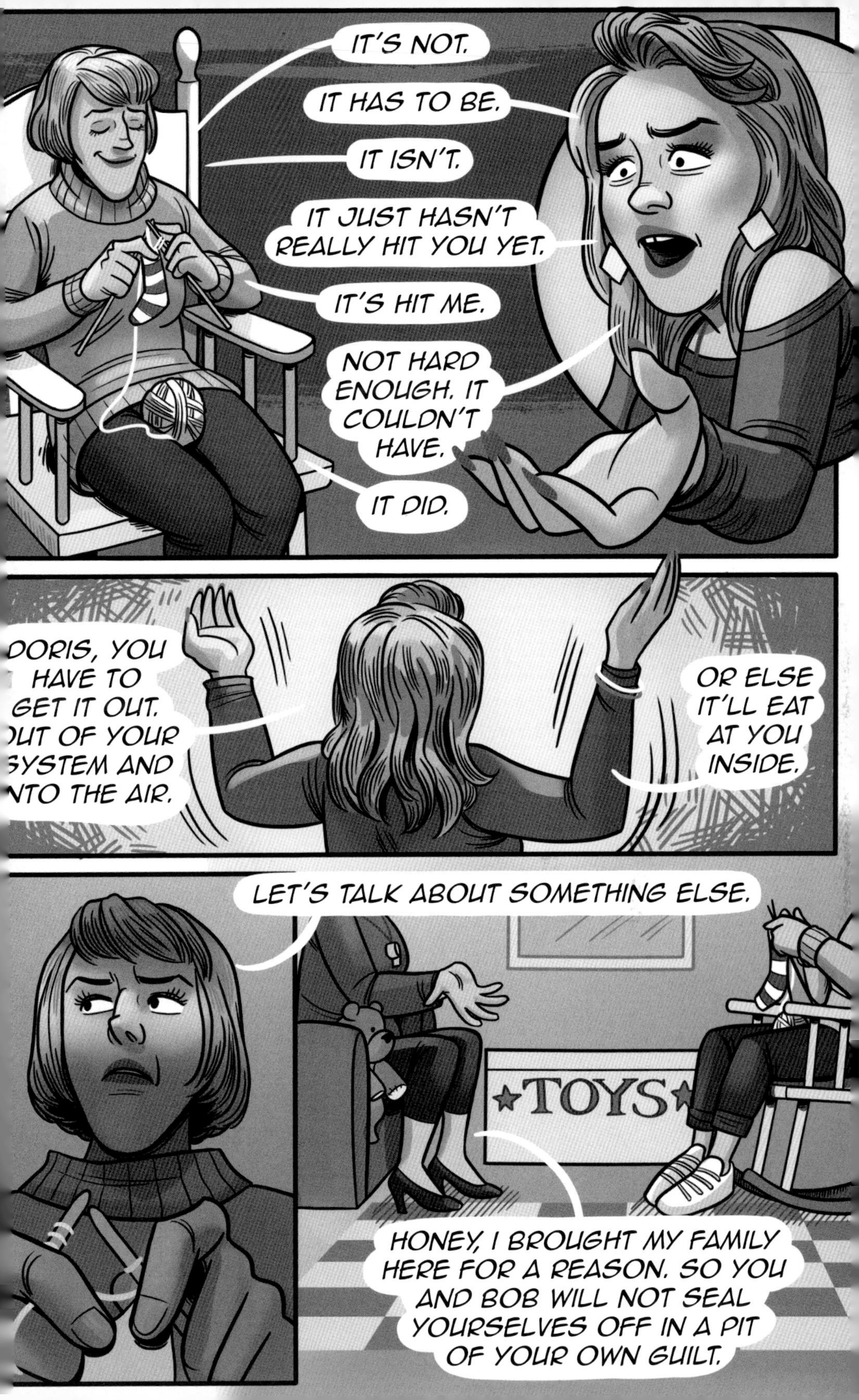
IT'S NOT.
IT HAS TO BE.
IT ISN'T.
IT JUST HASN'T REALLY HIT YOU YET.
IT'S HIT ME.
NOT HARD ENOUGH. IT COULDN'T HAVE.
IT DID.
DORIS, YOU HAVE TO GET IT OUT. UT OF YOUR YSTEM AND NTO THE AIR.
OR ELSE IT'LL EAT AT YOU INSIDE.
LET'S TALK ABOUT SOMETHING ELSE.
TOYS
HONEY, I BROUGHT MY FAMILY HERE FOR A REASON. SO YOU AND BOB WILL NOT SEAL YOURSELVES OFF IN A PIT OF YOUR OWN GUILT.

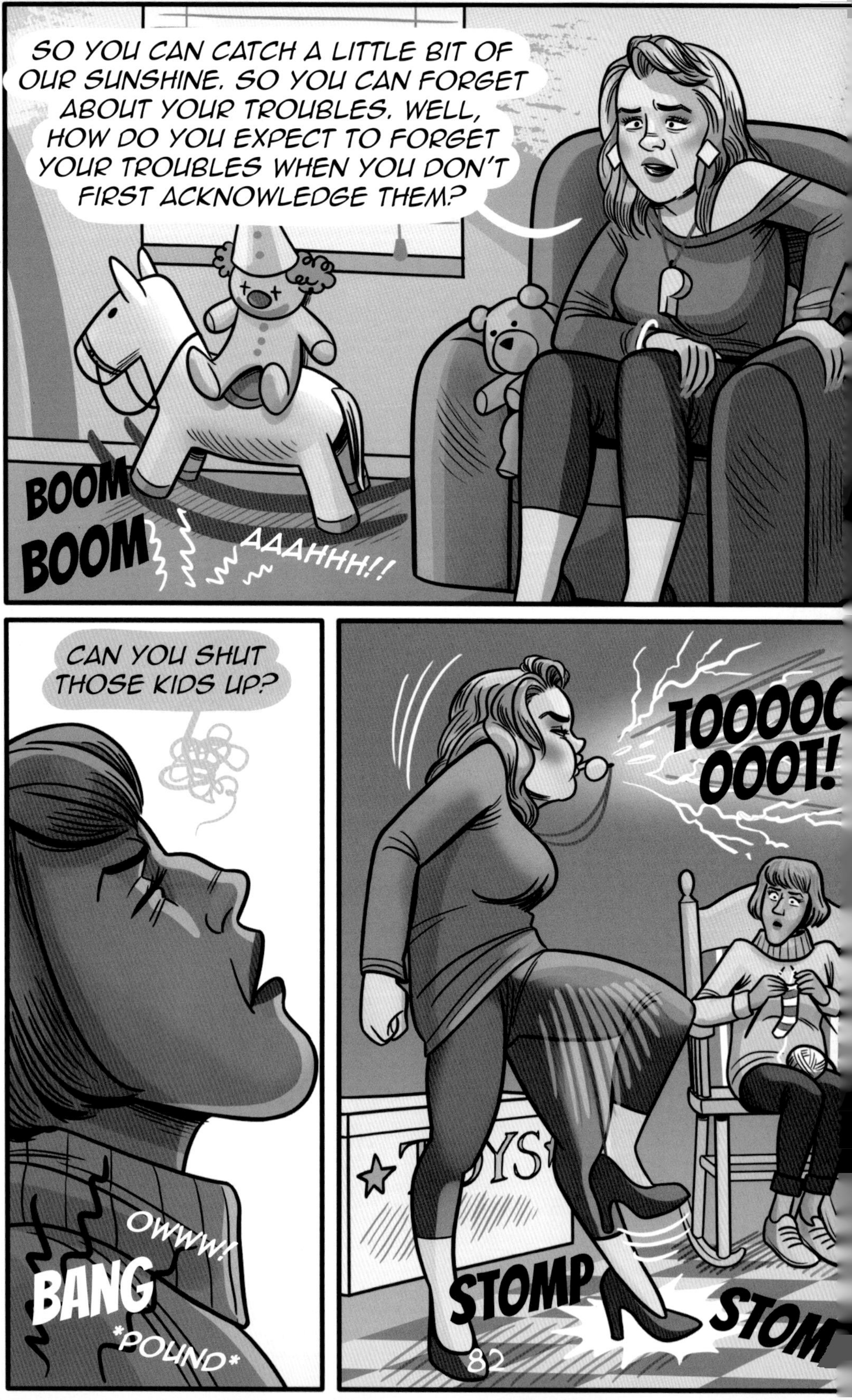

SO YOU CAN CATCH A LITTLE BIT OF OUR SUNSHINE. SO YOU CAN FORGET ABOUT YOUR TROUBLES. WELL, HOW DO YOU EXPECT TO FORGET YOUR TROUBLES WHEN YOU DON'T FIRST ACKNOWLEDGE THEM?
BOOM
BOOM
AAAHHHH!!
CAN YOU SHUT THOSE KIDS UP?
OWWW!
BANG
POUND
TOOOOO
OOOT!
TOYS
STOMP
STOM

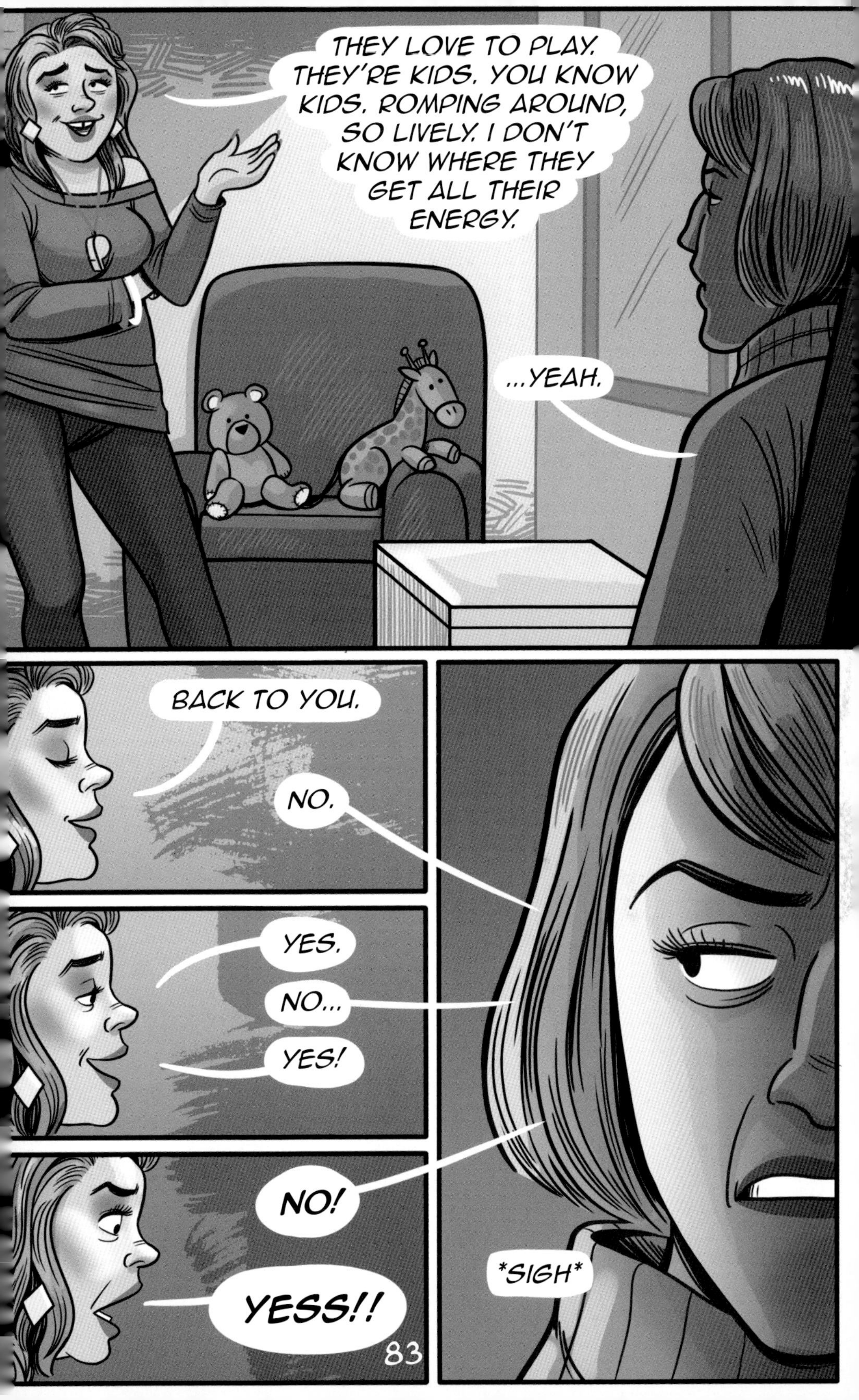
THEY LOVE TO PLAY. THEY'RE KIDS. YOU KNOW KIDS. ROMPING AROUND, SO LIVELY. I DON'T KNOW WHERE THEY GET ALL THEIR ENERGY.
...YEAH.
BACK TO YOU.
NO.
YES.
NO...
YES!
NO!
YESS!!
SIGH

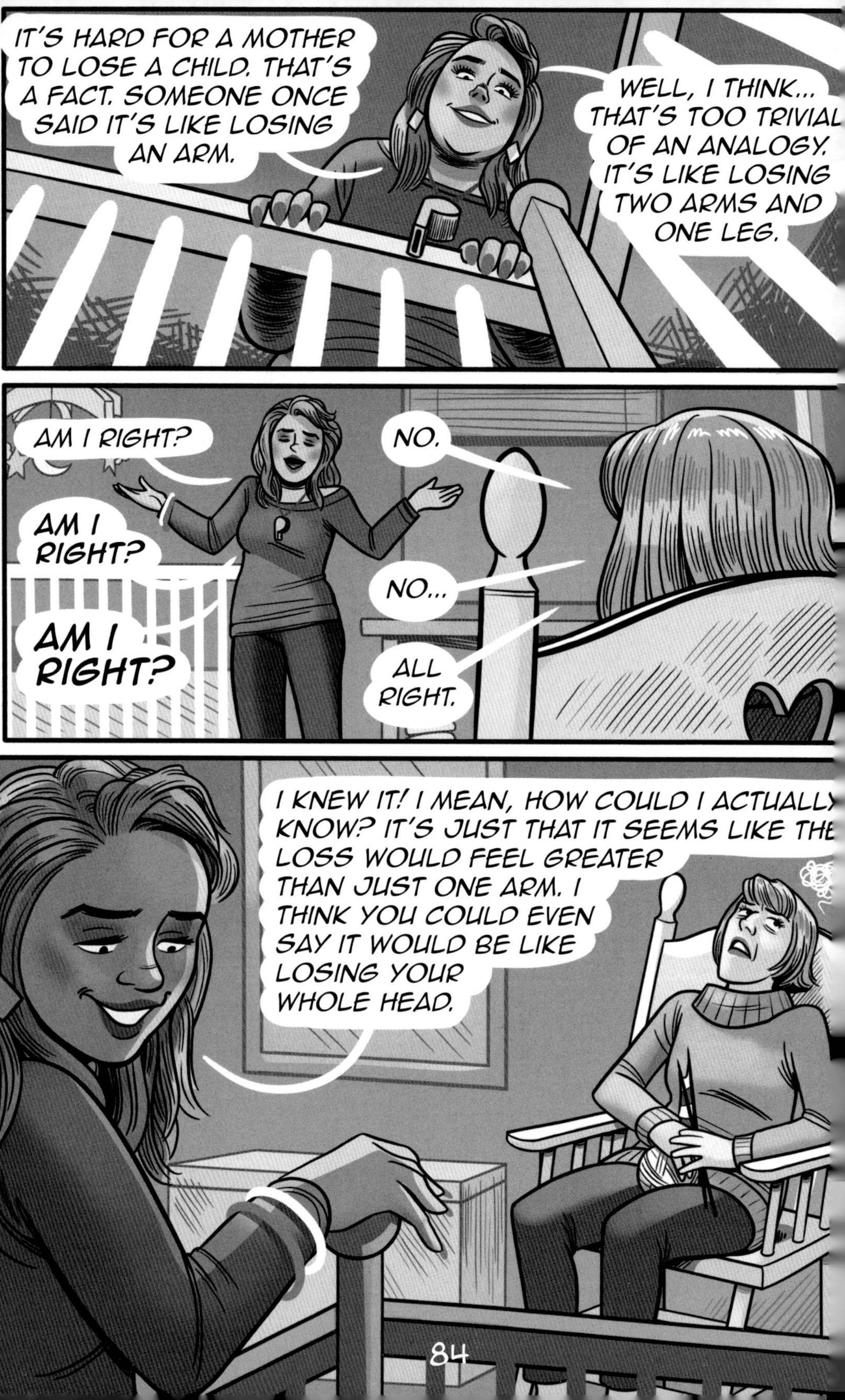
IT'S HARD FOR A MOTHER TO LOSE A CHILD. THAT'S A FACT. SOMEONE ONCE SAID IT'S LIKE LOSING AN ARM.
WELL, I THINK... THAT'S TOO TRIVIAL OF AN ANALOGY. IT'S LIKE LOSING TWO ARMS AND ONE LEG.
AM I RIGHT?
NO.
AM I RIGHT?
NO...
AM I RIGHT?
ALL RIGHT.
I KNEW IT! I MEAN, HOW COULD I ACTUALLY KNOW? IT'S JUST THAT IT SEEMS LIKE THE LOSS WOULD FEEL GREATER THAN JUST ONE ARM. I THINK YOU COULD EVEN SAY IT WOULD BE LIKE LOSING YOUR WHOLE HEAD.

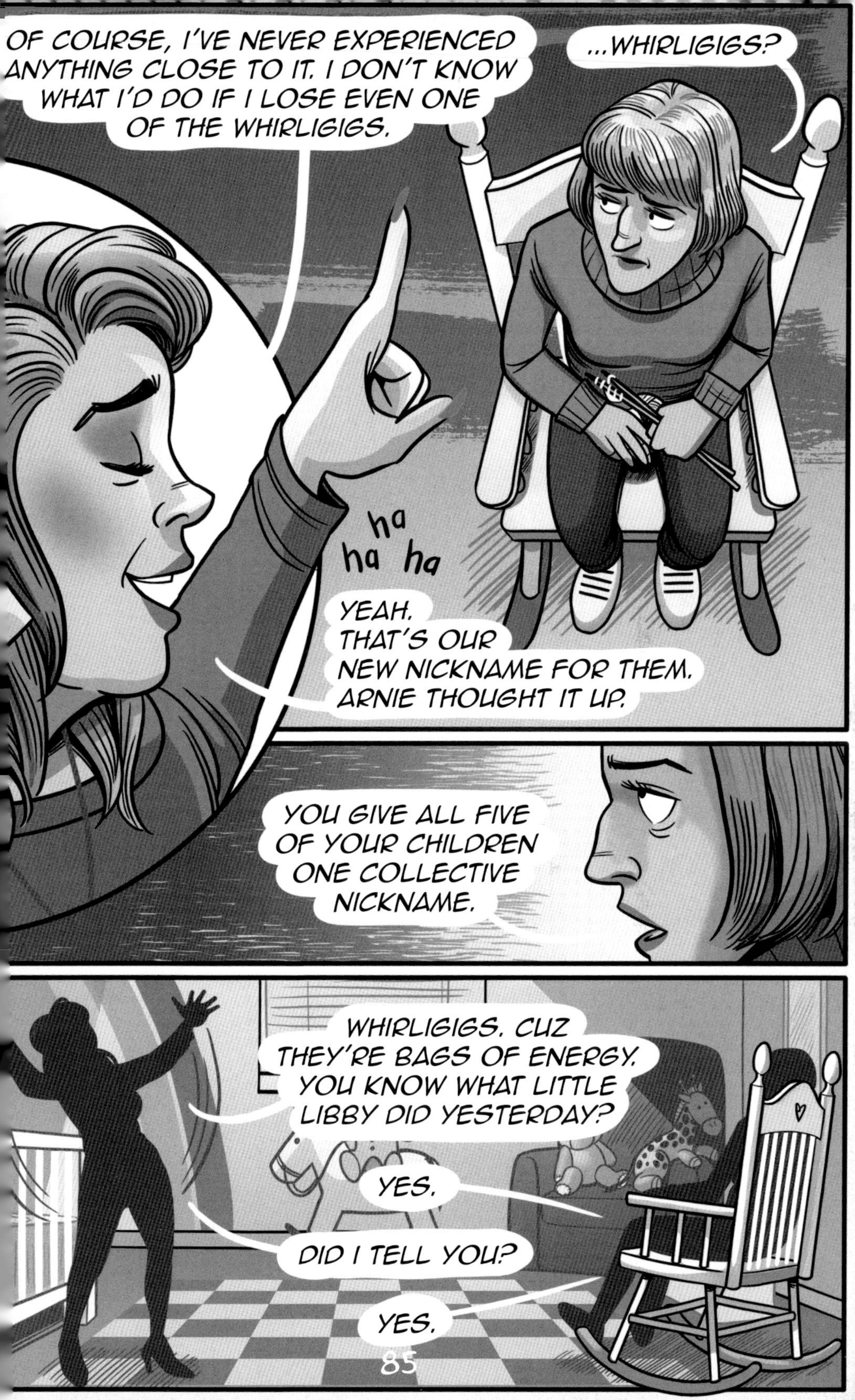
OF COURSE, I'VE NEVER EXPERIENCED ANYTHING CLOSE TO IT. I DON'T KNOW WHAT I'D DO IF I LOSE EVEN ONE OF THE WHIRLIGIGS.
...WHIRLIGIGS?
ha ha ha
YEAH. THAT'S OUR NEW NICKNAME FOR THEM. ARNIE THOUGHT IT UP.
YOU GIVE ALL FIVE OF YOUR CHILDREN ONE COLLECTIVE NICKNAME.
WHIRLIGIGS. CUZ THEY'RE BAGS OF ENERGY. YOU KNOW WHAT LITTLE LIBBY DID YESTERDAY?
YES.
DID I TELL YOU?
YES.

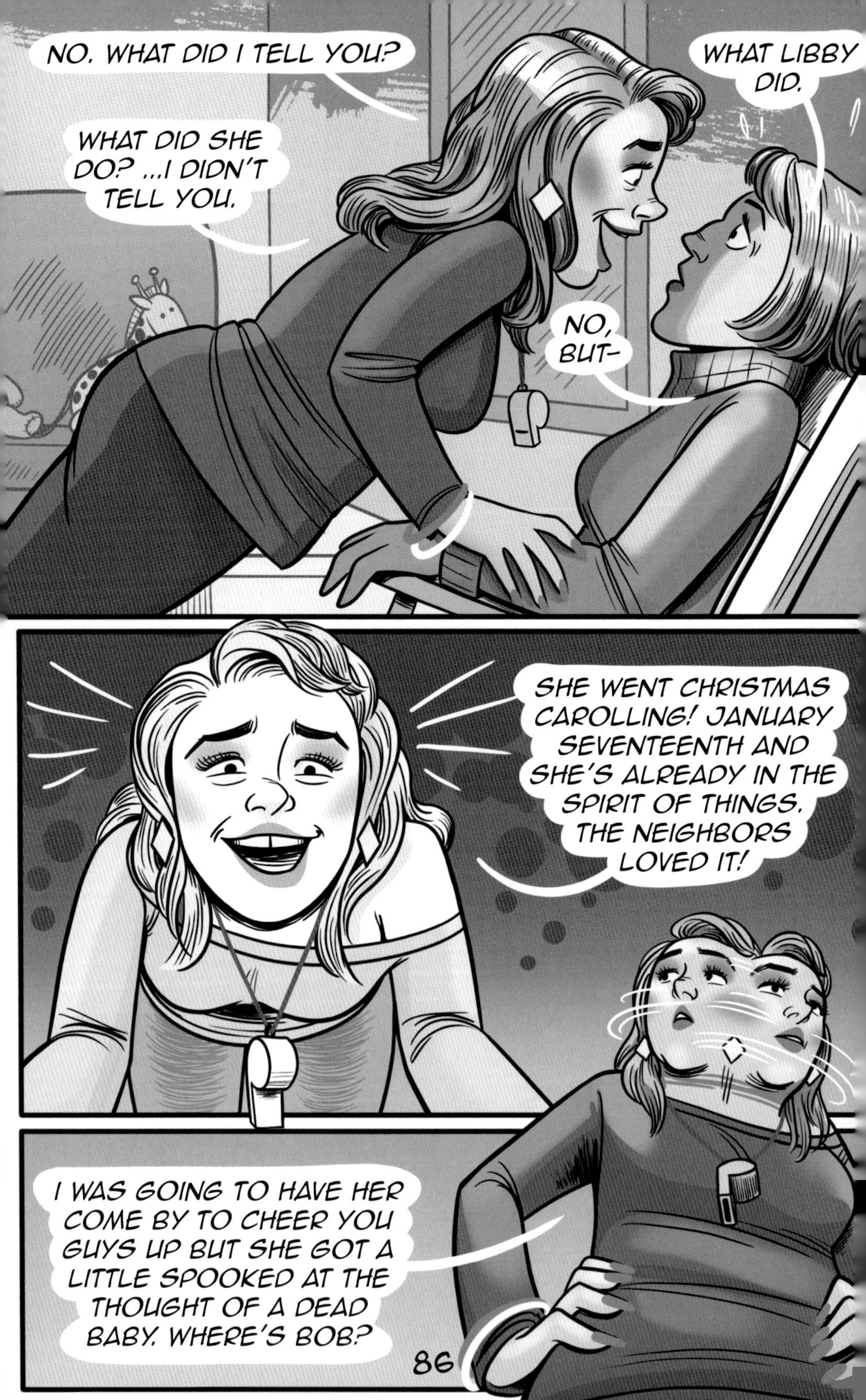

NO. WHAT DID I TELL YOU?
WHAT LIBBY DID.
WHAT DID SHE DO? ...I DIDN'T TELL YOU.
NO, BUT-
SHE WENT CHRISTMAS CAROLLING! JANUARY SEVENTEENTH AND SHE'S ALREADY IN THE SPIRIT OF THINGS. THE NEIGHBORS LOVED IT!
I WAS GOING TO HAVE HER COME BY TO CHEER YOU GUYS UP BUT SHE GOT A LITTLE SPOOKED AT THE THOUGHT OF A DEAD BABY. WHERE'S BOB?

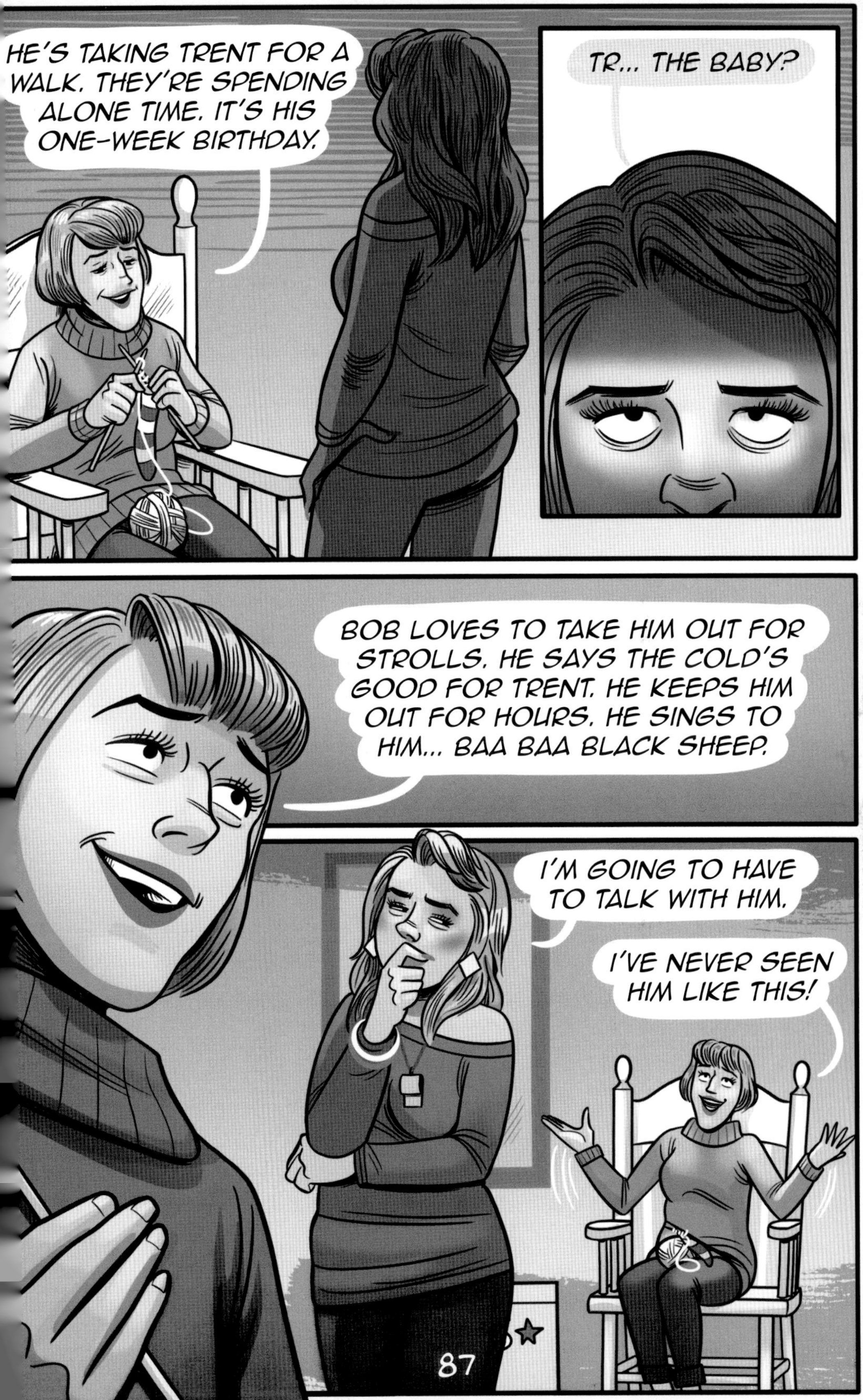

HE'S TAKING TRENT FOR A WALK. THEY'RE SPENDING ALONE TIME. IT'S HIS ONE-WEEK BIRTHDAY.
TR... THE BABY?
BOB LOVES TO TAKE HIM OUT FOR STROLLS. HE SAYS THE COLD'S GOOD FOR TRENT. HE KEEPS HIM OUT FOR HOURS. HE SINGS TO HIM... BAA BAA BLACK SHEEP.
I'M GOING TO HAVE TO TALK WITH HIM.
I'VE NEVER SEEN HIM LIKE THIS!

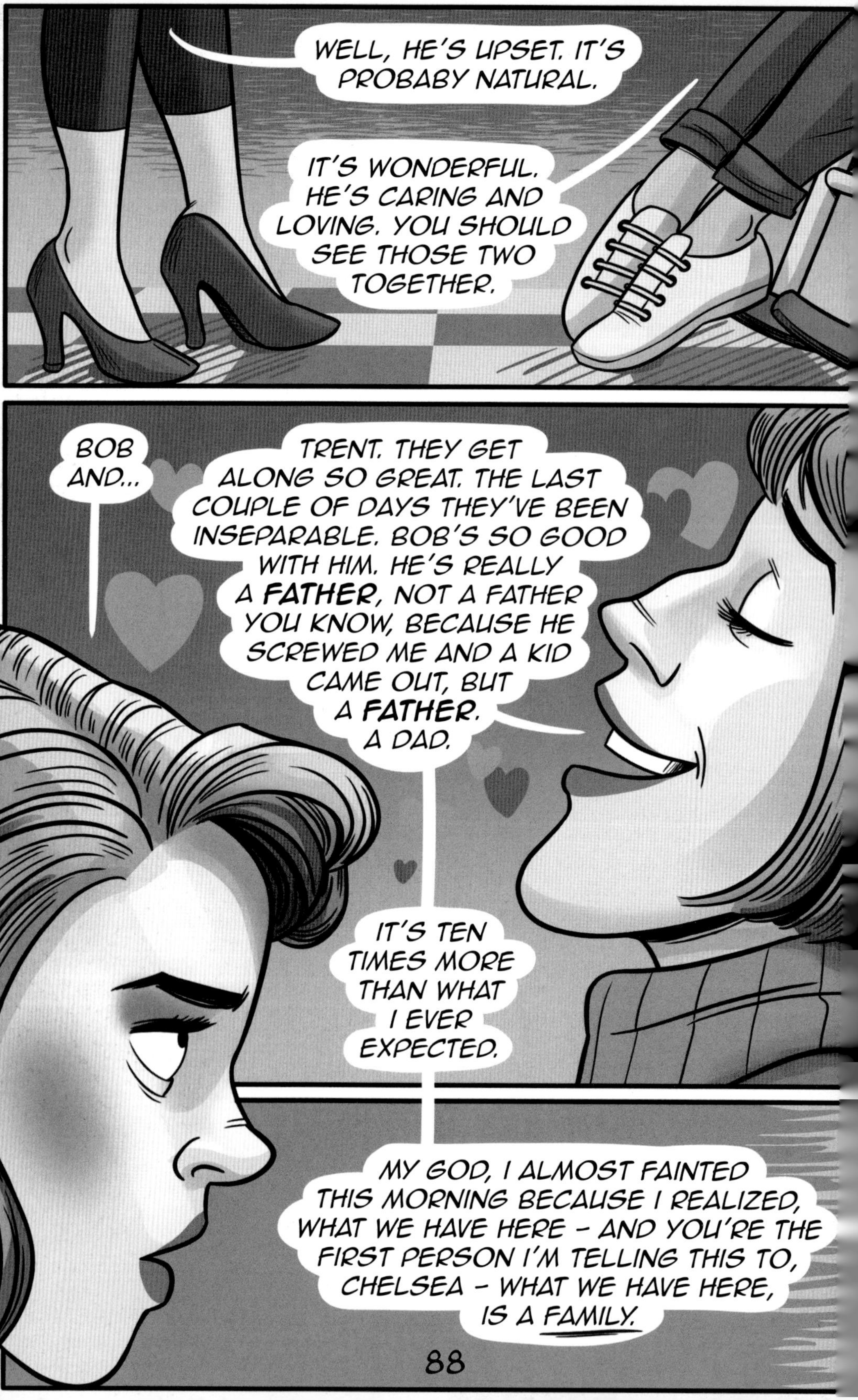
WELL, HE'S UPSET. IT'S PROBABY NATURAL.
IT'S WONDERFUL. HE'S CARING AND LOVING. YOU SHOULD SEE THOSE TWO TOGETHER.
BOB AND...
TRENT. THEY GET ALONG SO GREAT. THE LAST COUPLE OF DAYS THEY'VE BEEN INSEPARABLE. BOB'S SO GOOD WITH HIM. HE'S REALLY A **FATHER**, NOT A FATHER YOU KNOW, BECAUSE HE SCREWED ME AND A KID CAME OUT, BUT A **FATHER**. A DAD.
IT'S TEN TIMES MORE THAN WHAT I EVER EXPECTED.
MY GOD, I ALMOST FAINTED THIS MORNING BECAUSE I REALIZED, WHAT WE HAVE HERE - AND YOU'RE THE FIRST PERSON I'M TELLING THIS TO, CHELSEA - WHAT WE HAVE HERE, IS A FAMILY.

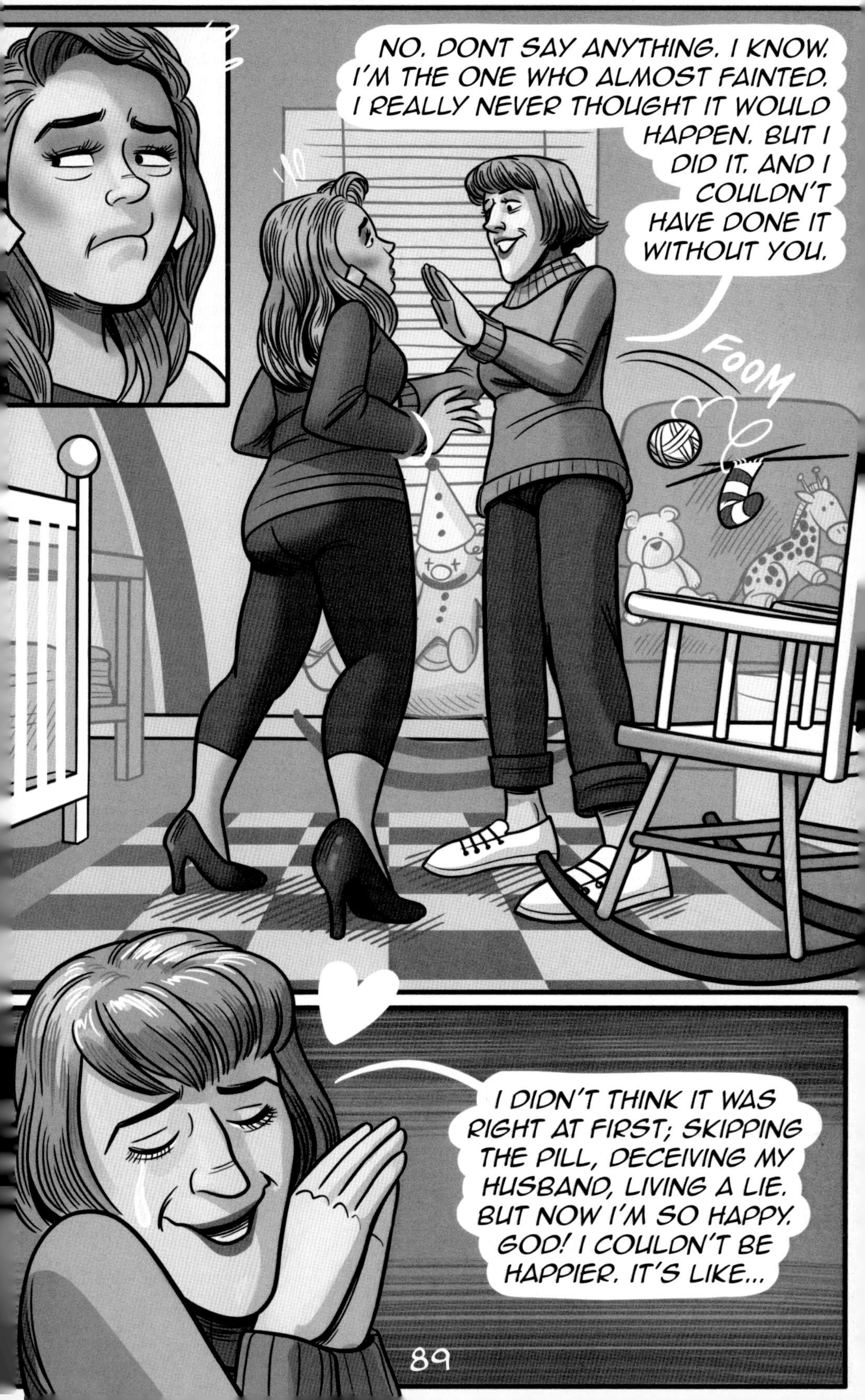
NO. DONT SAY ANYTHING. I KNOW. I'M THE ONE WHO ALMOST FAINTED. I REALLY NEVER THOUGHT IT WOULD HAPPEN. BUT I DID IT. AND I COULDN'T HAVE DONE IT WITHOUT YOU.
FOOM
I DIDN'T THINK IT WAS RIGHT AT FIRST; SKIPPING THE PILL, DECEIVING MY HUSBAND, LIVING A LIE. BUT NOW I'M SO HAPPY. GOD! I COULDN'T BE HAPPIER. IT'S LIKE...

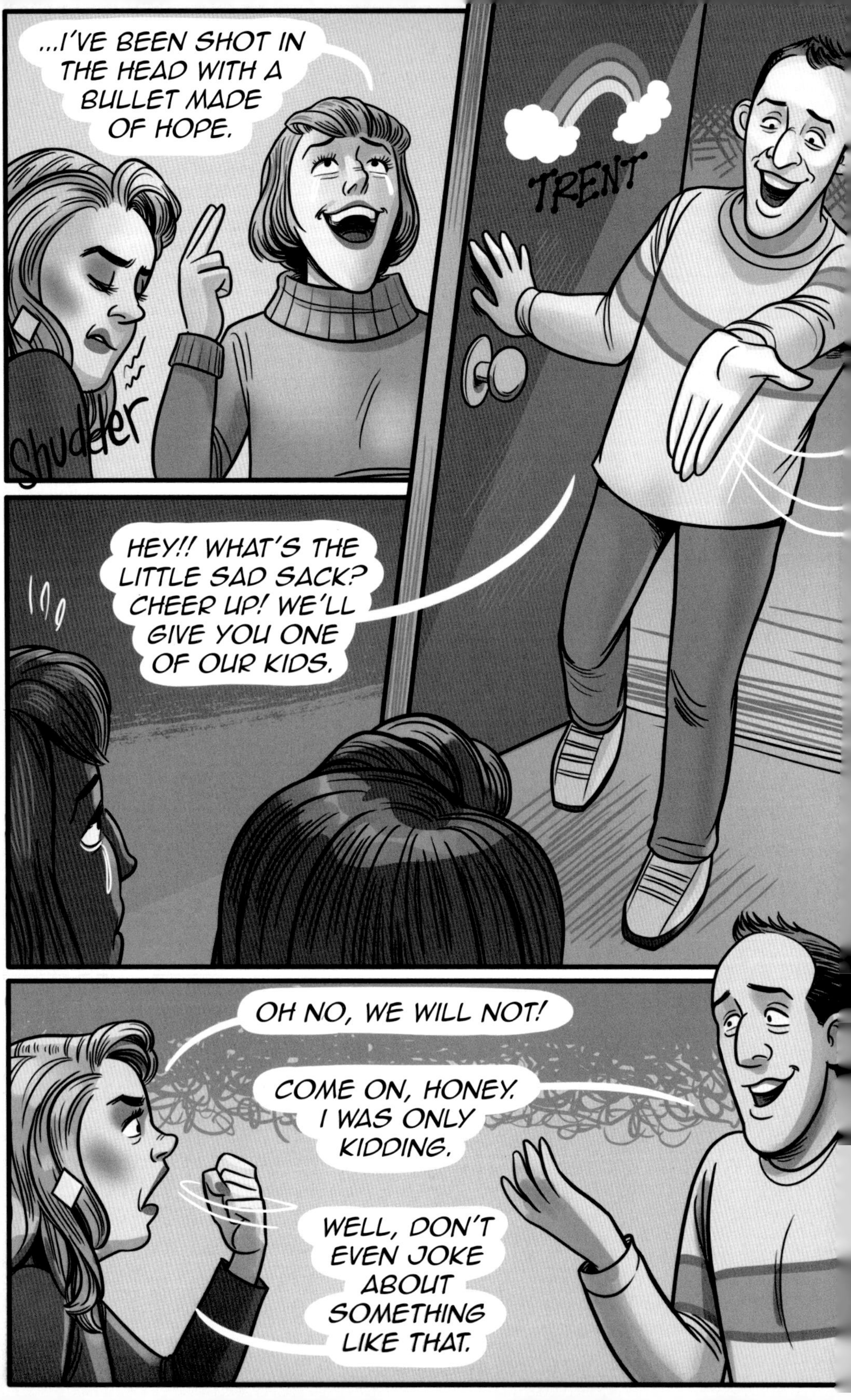

...I'VE BEEN SHOT IN THE HEAD WITH A BULLET MADE OF HOPE.
Shudder
TRENT
HEY!! WHAT'S THE LITTLE SAD SACK? CHEER UP! WE'LL GIVE YOU ONE OF OUR KIDS.
OH NO, WE WILL NOT!
COME ON, HONEY. I WAS ONLY KIDDING.
WELL, DON'T EVEN JOKE ABOUT SOMETHING LIKE THAT.

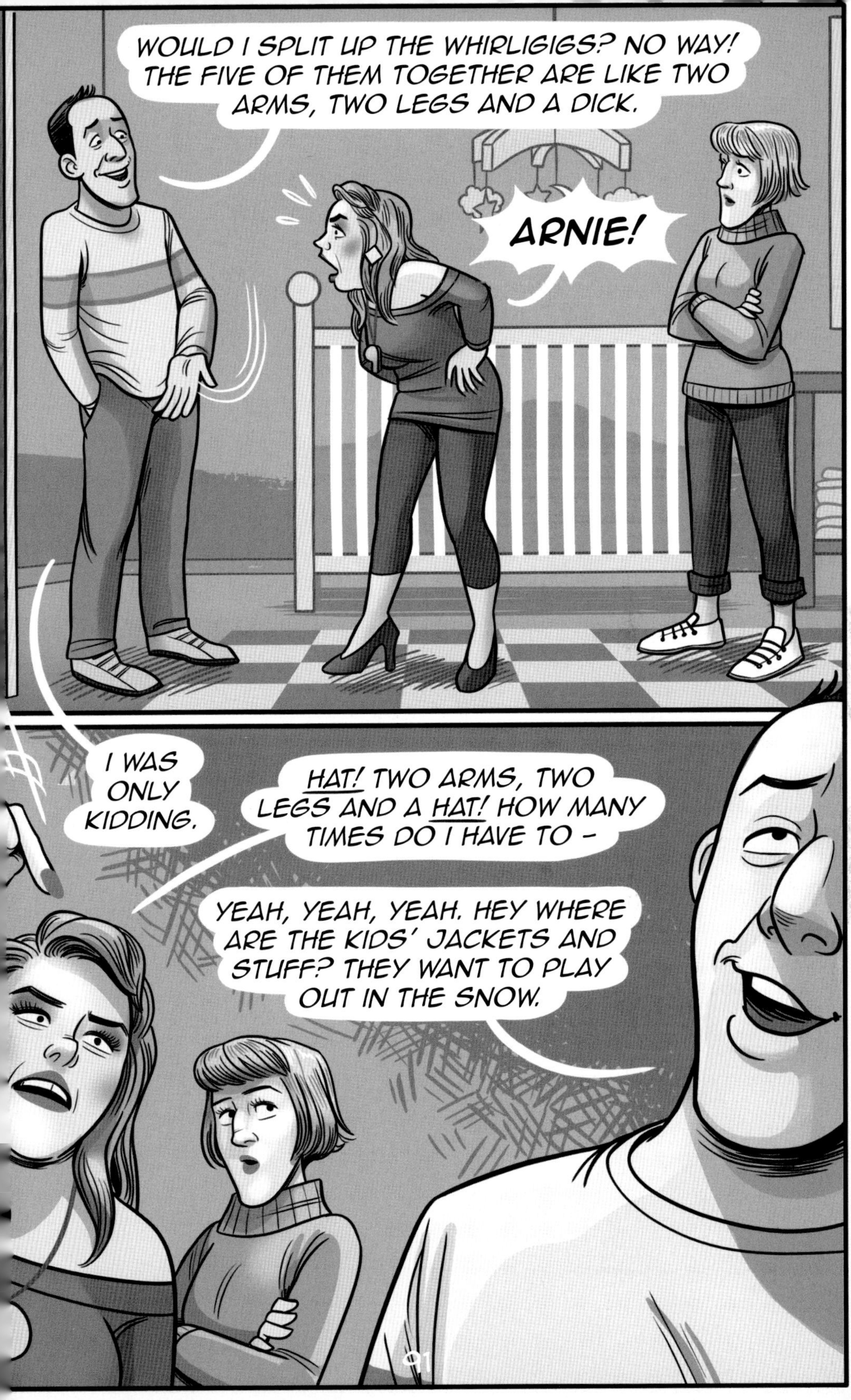
WOULD I SPLIT UP THE WHIRLIGIGS? NO WAY! THE FIVE OF THEM TOGETHER ARE LIKE TWO ARMS, TWO LEGS AND A DICK.
ARNIE!
I WAS ONLY KIDDING.
HAT! TWO ARMS, TWO LEGS AND A HAT! HOW MANY TIMES DO I HAVE TO –
YEAH, YEAH, YEAH. HEY WHERE ARE THE KIDS' JACKETS AND STUFF? THEY WANT TO PLAY OUT IN THE SNOW.

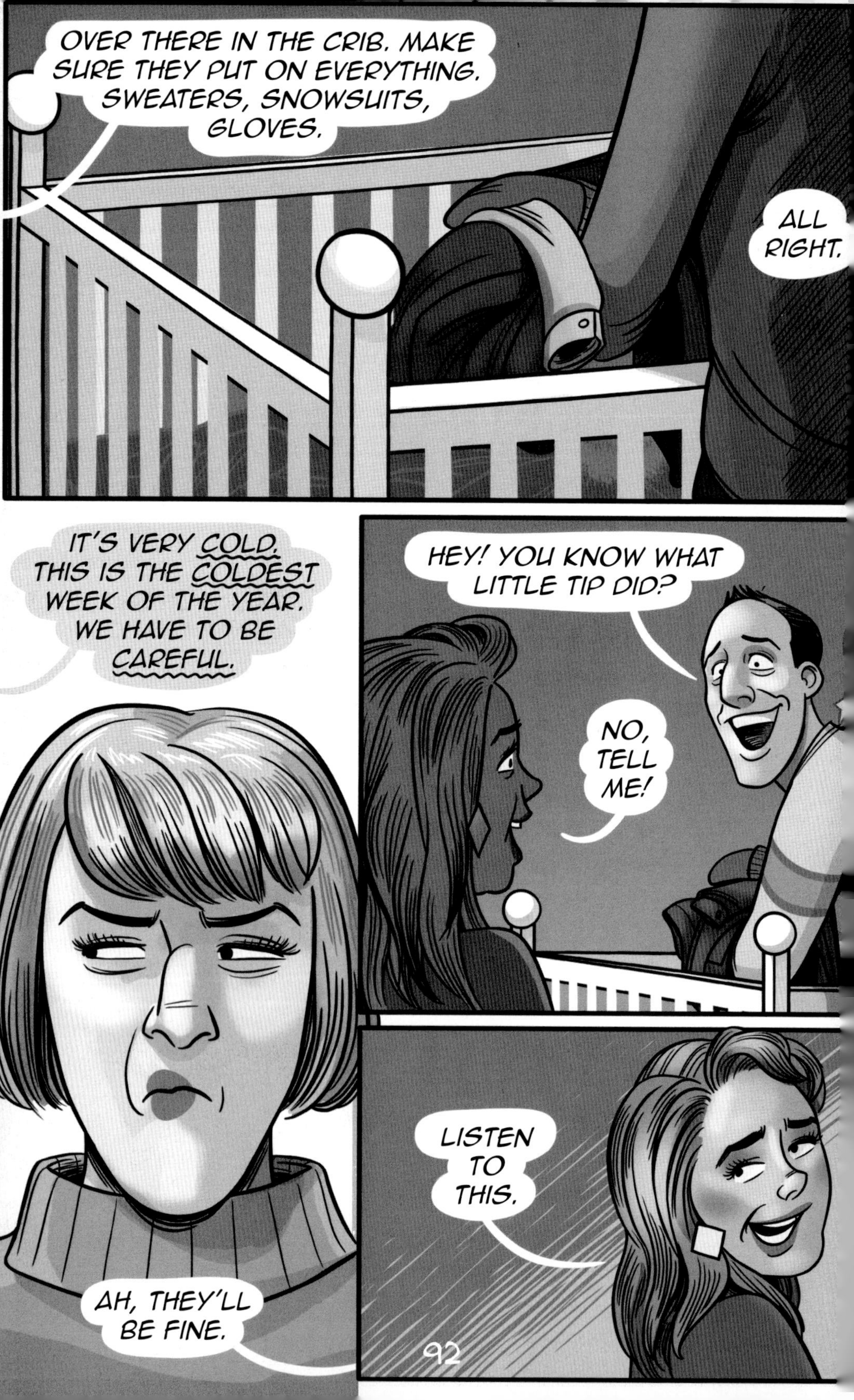
OVER THERE IN THE CRIB. MAKE SURE THEY PUT ON EVERYTHING. SWEATERS, SNOWSUITS, GLOVES.
ALL RIGHT.
IT'S VERY COLD. THIS IS THE COLDEST WEEK OF THE YEAR. WE HAVE TO BE CAREFUL.
AH, THEY'LL BE FINE.
HEY! YOU KNOW WHAT LITTLE TIP DID?
NO, TELL ME!
LISTEN TO THIS.

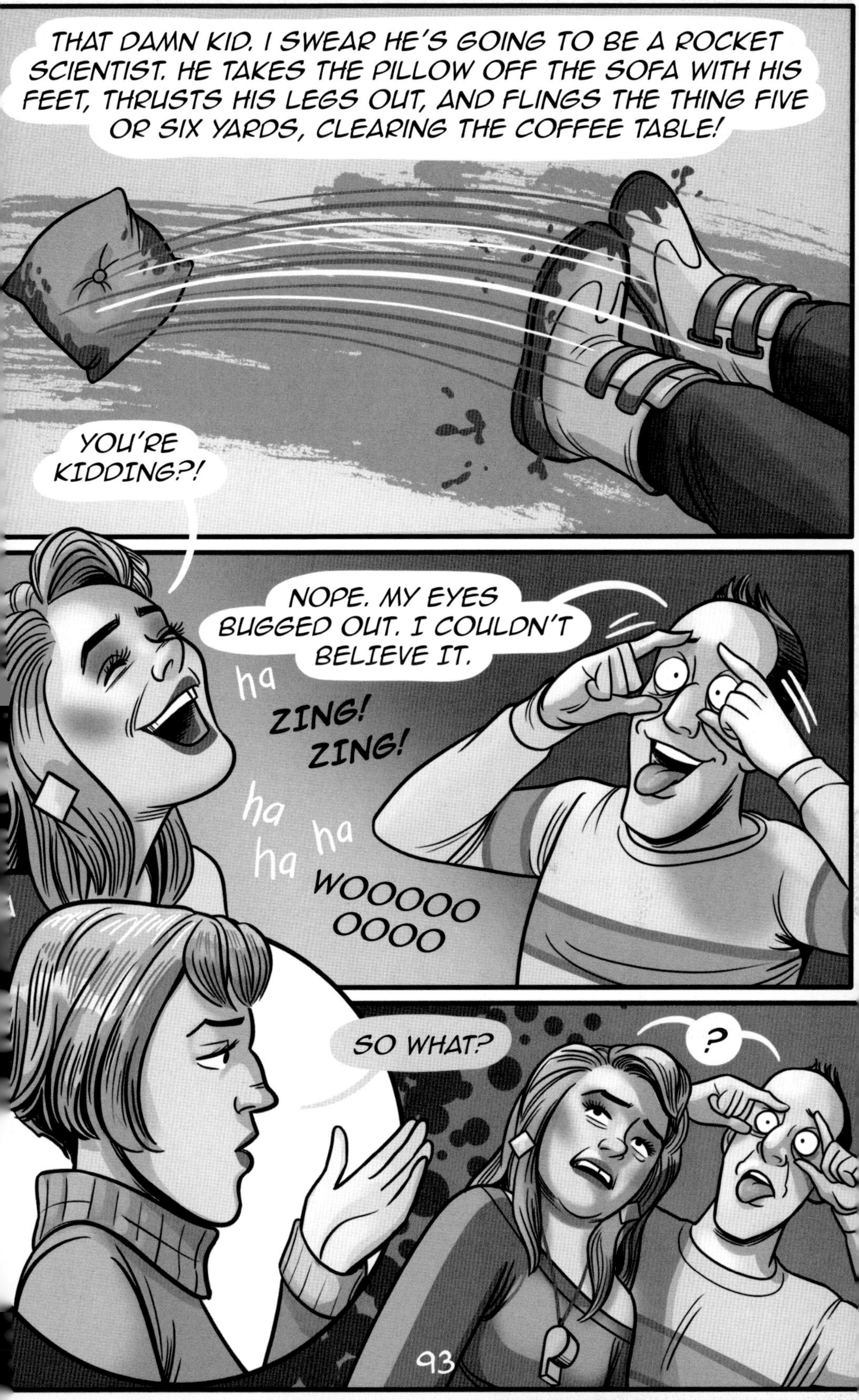
THAT DAMN KID. I SWEAR HE'S GOING TO BE A ROCKET SCIENTIST. HE TAKES THE PILLOW OFF THE SOFA WITH HIS FEET, THRUSTS HIS LEGS OUT, AND FLINGS THE THING FIVE OR SIX YARDS, CLEARING THE COFFEE TABLE!
YOU'RE KIDDING?!
NOPE. MY EYES BUGGED OUT. I COULDN'T BELIEVE IT.
ha
ZING!
ZING!
ha
ha
ha
WOOOOO OOOO
SO WHAT?
?

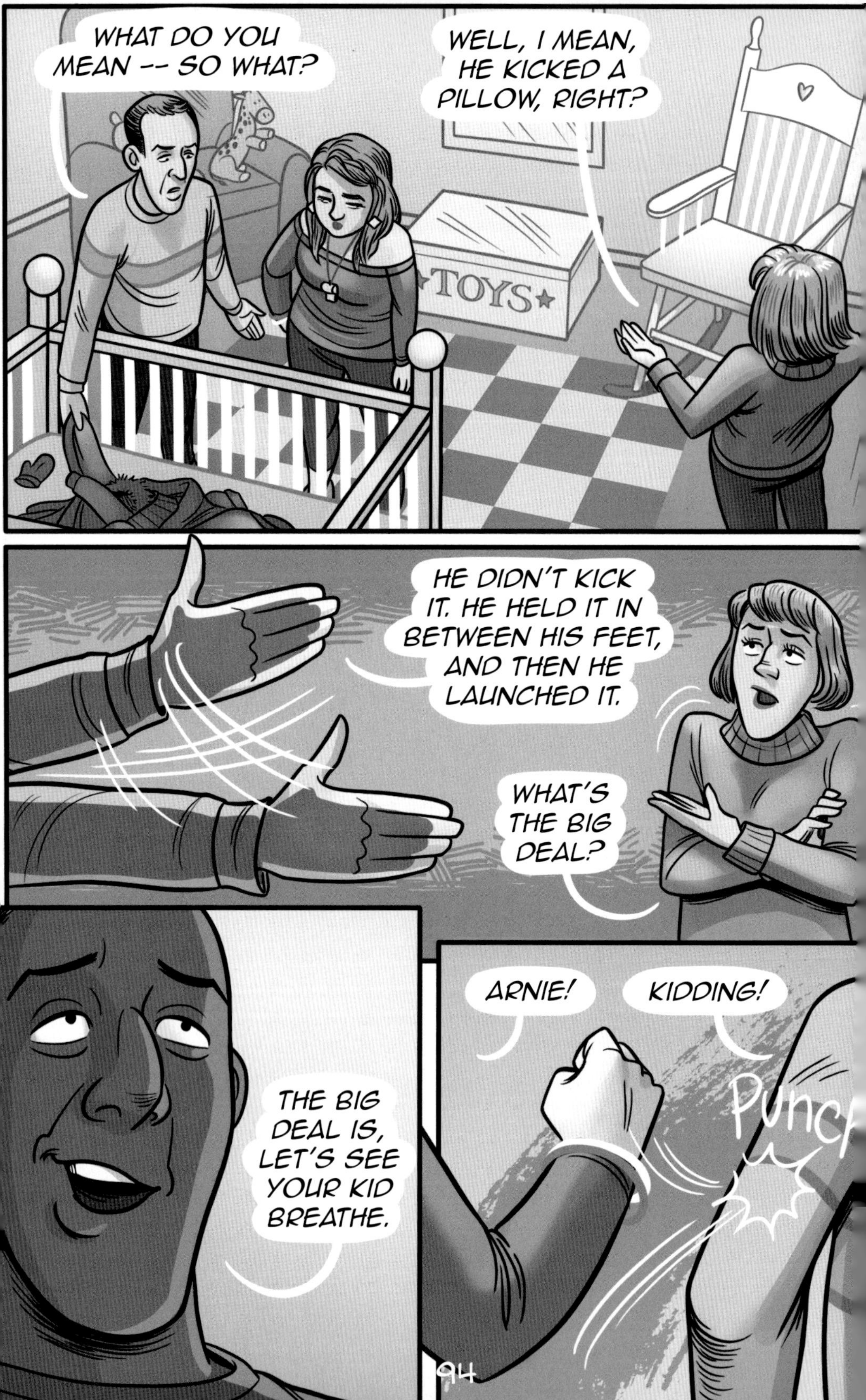
WHAT DO YOU MEAN -- SO WHAT?
WELL, I MEAN, HE KICKED A PILLOW, RIGHT?
TOYS
HE DIDN'T KICK IT. HE HELD IT IN BETWEEN HIS FEET, AND THEN HE LAUNCHED IT.
WHAT'S THE BIG DEAL?
THE BIG DEAL IS, LET'S SEE YOUR KID BREATHE.
ARNIE!
KIDDING!
Punch

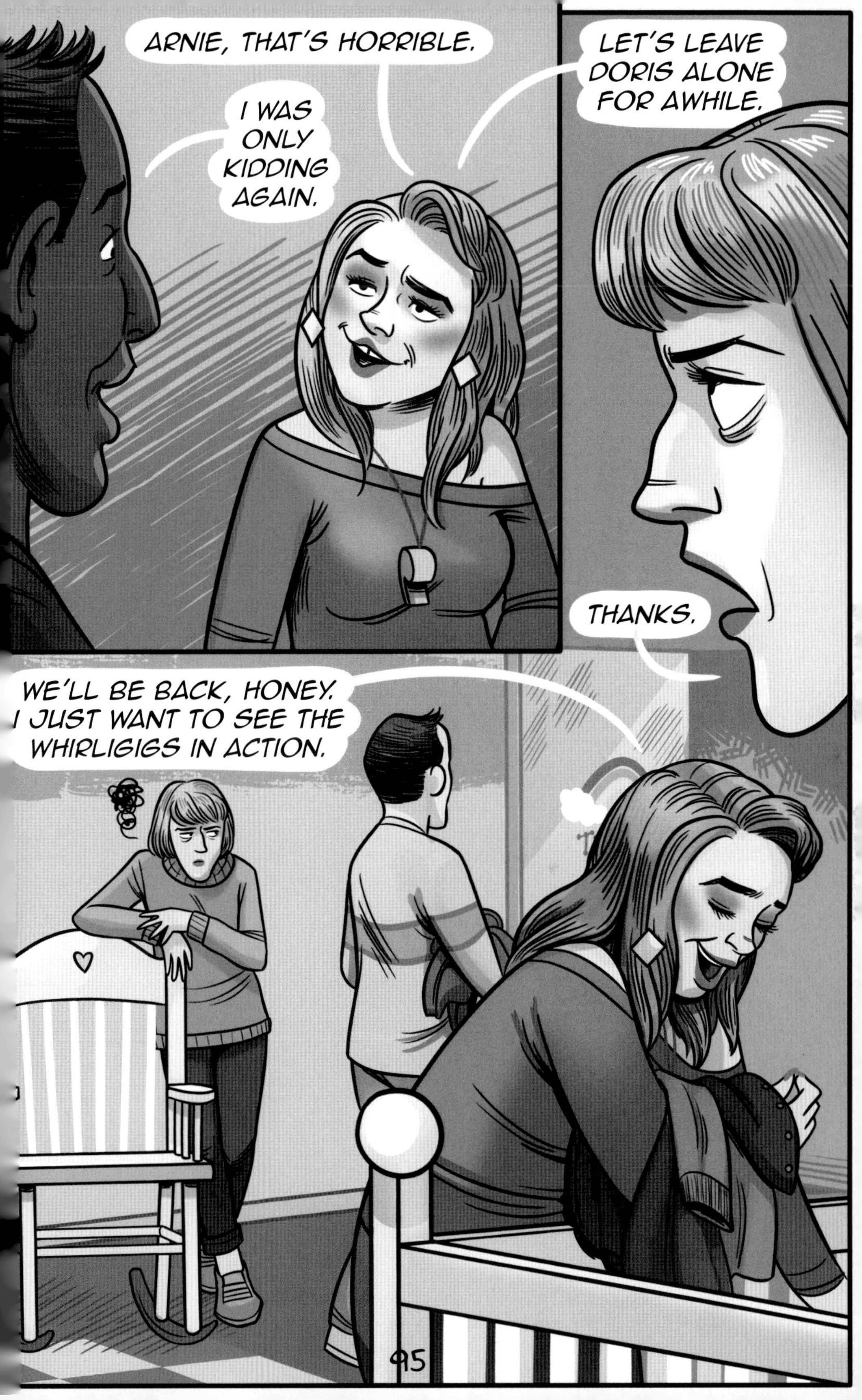
ARNIE, THAT'S HORRIBLE.
I WAS ONLY KIDDING AGAIN.
LET'S LEAVE DORIS ALONE FOR AWHILE.
THANKS.
WE'LL BE BACK, HONEY. I JUST WANT TO SEE THE WHIRLIGIGS IN ACTION.

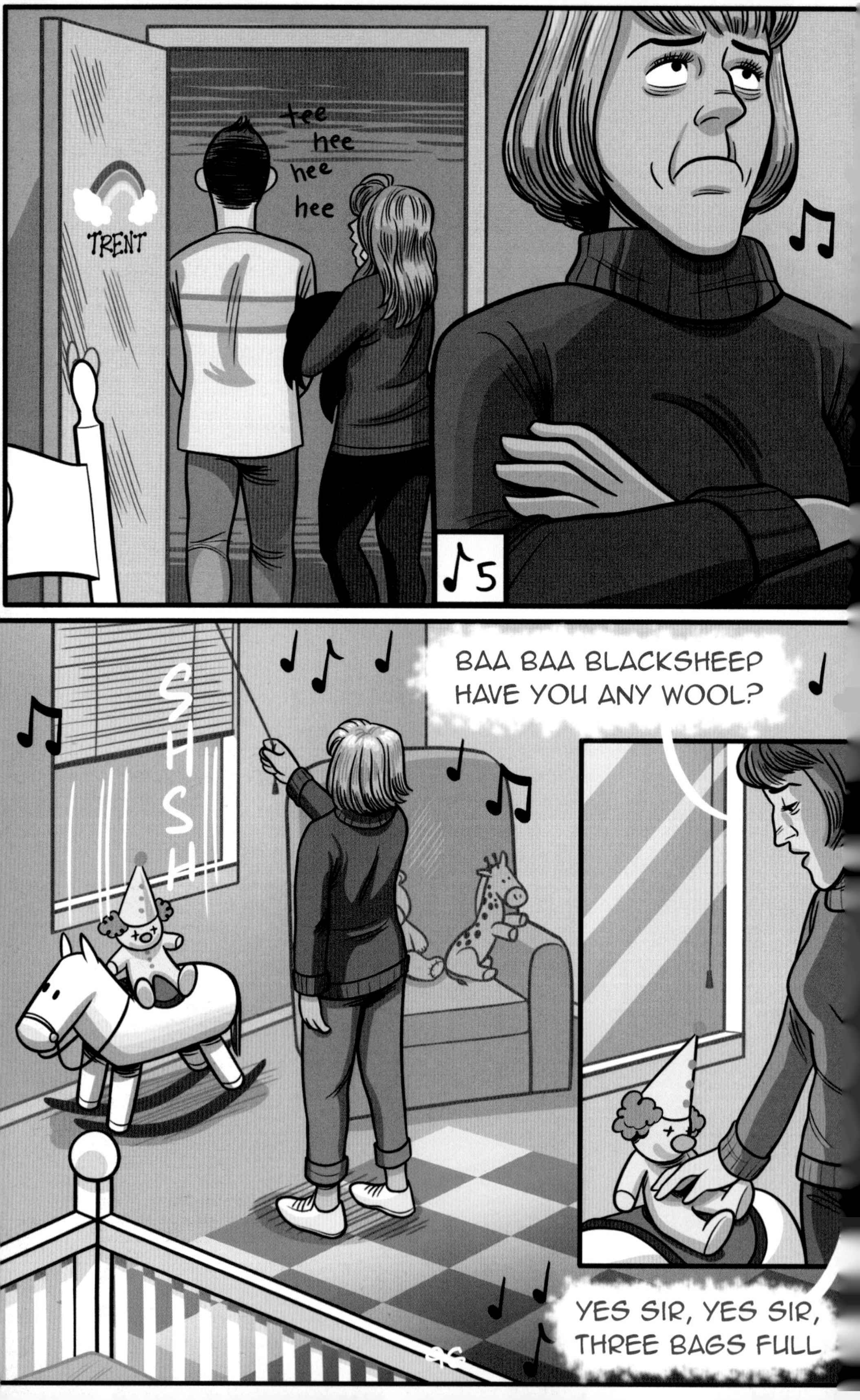

TRENT
tee hee hee hee
5
SHSH
BAA BAA BLACKSHEEP HAVE YOU ANY WOOL?
YES SIR, YES SIR, THREE BAGS FULL

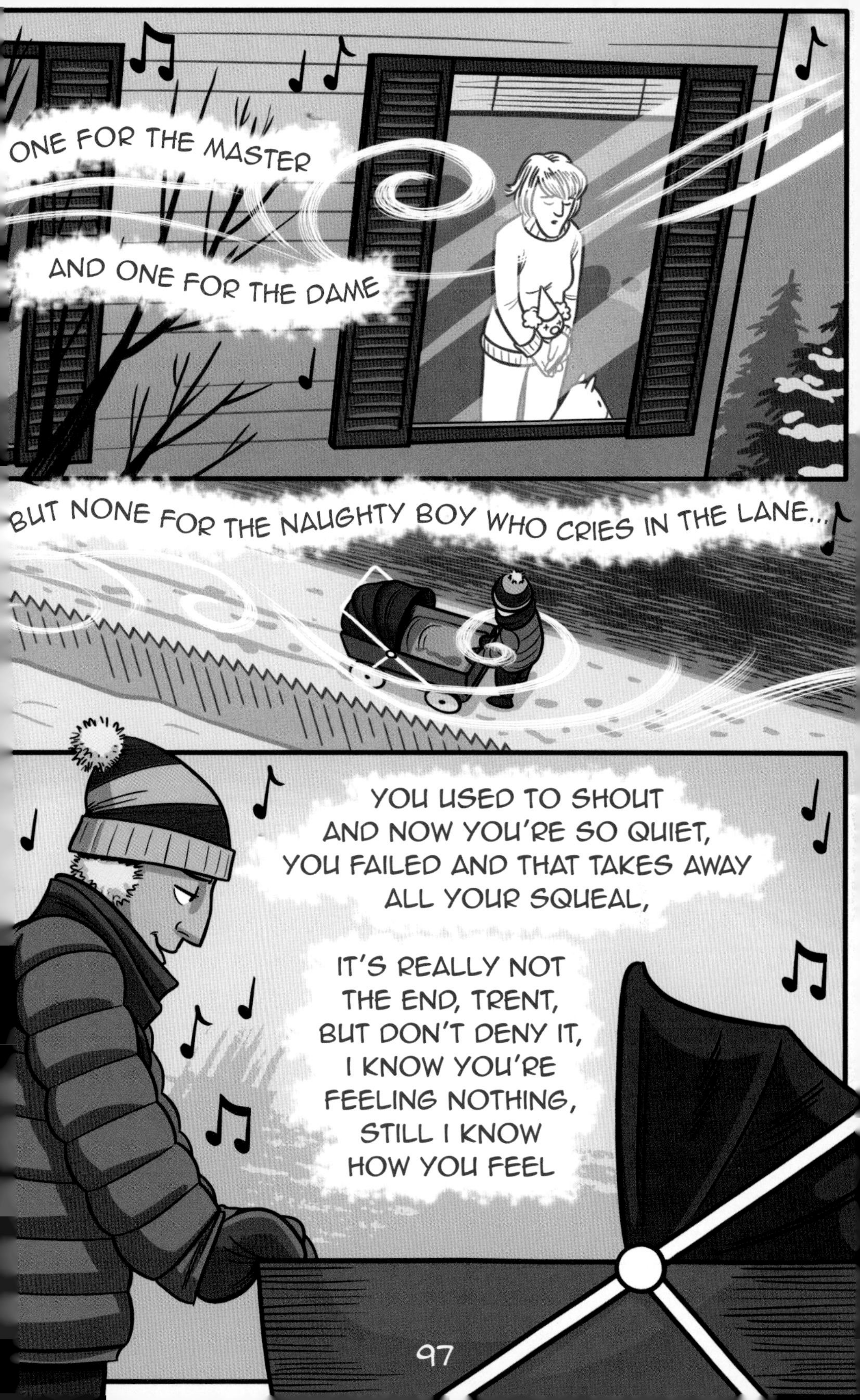
ONE FOR THE MASTER
AND ONE FOR THE DAME
BUT NONE FOR THE NAUGHTY BOY WHO CRIES IN THE LANE...
YOU USED TO SHOUT AND NOW YOU'RE SO QUIET, YOU FAILED AND THAT TAKES AWAY ALL YOUR SQUEAL,
IT'S REALLY NOT THE END, TRENT, BUT DON'T DENY IT, I KNOW YOU'RE FEELING NOTHING, STILL I KNOW HOW YOU FEEL

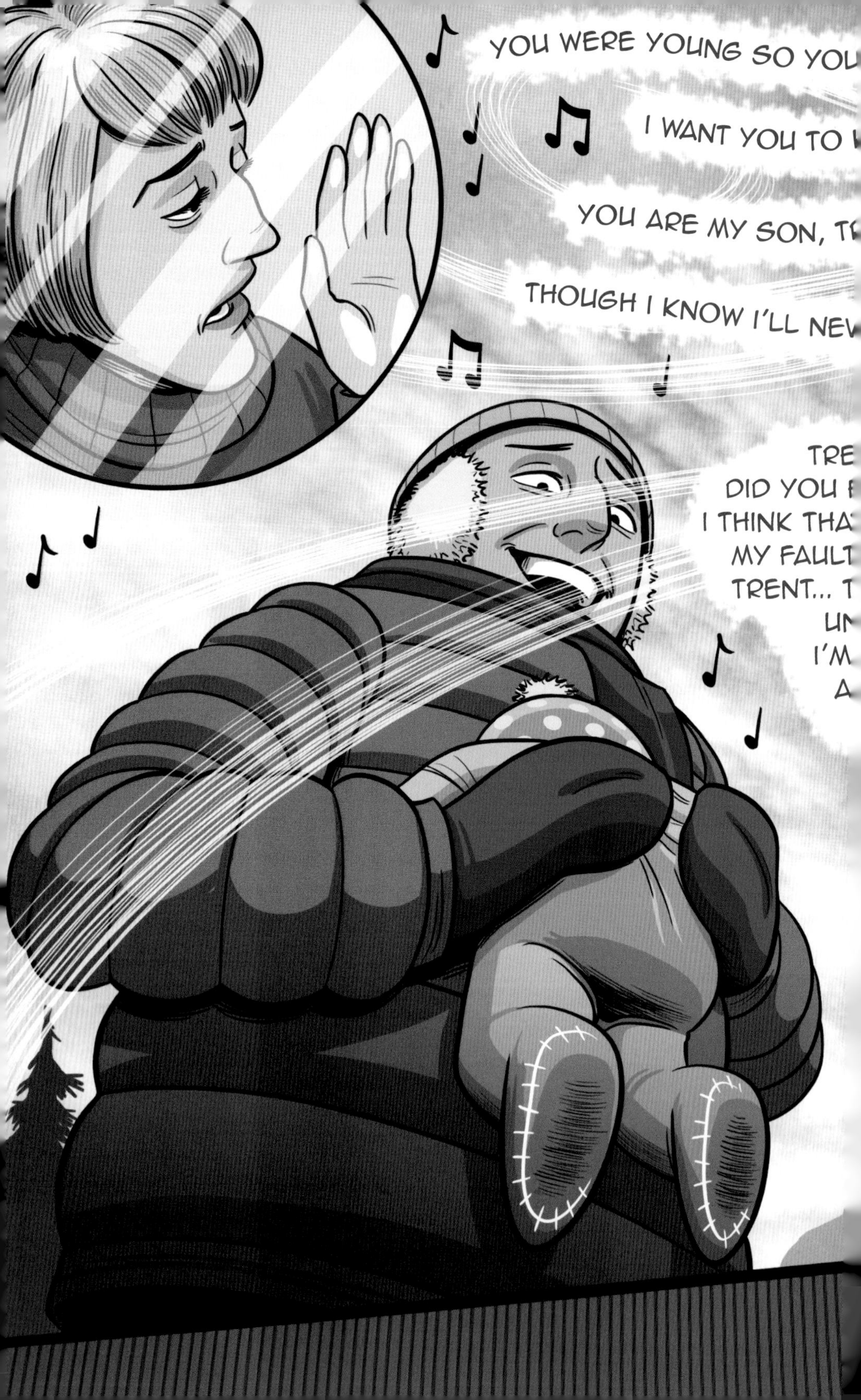
YOU WERE YOUNG SO YOU
I WANT YOU TO
YOU ARE MY SON,
THOUGH I KNOW I'LL NE
TRE
DID YOU
I THINK THA
MY FAULT
TRENT...
UN
I'M
A

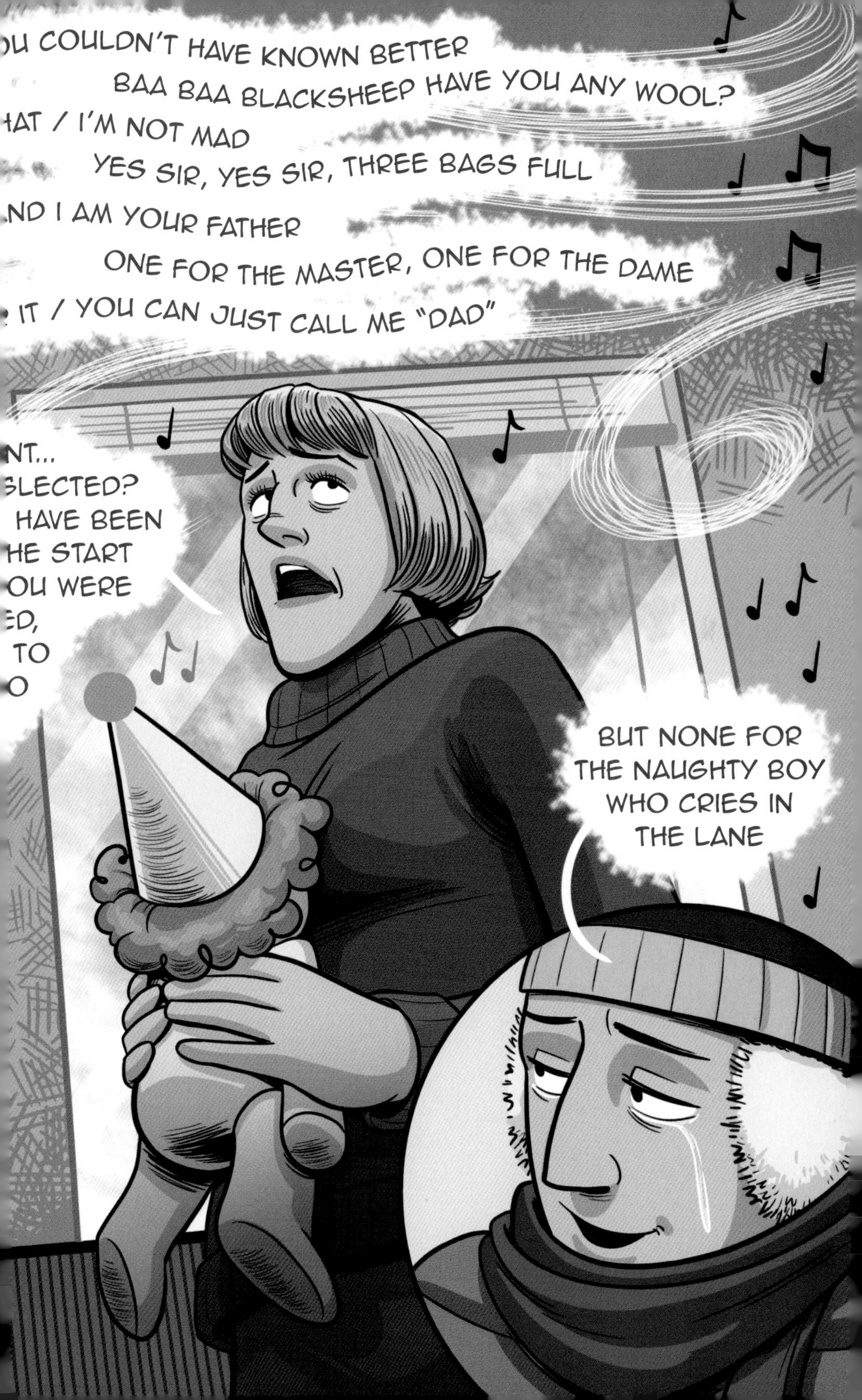

OU COULDN'T HAVE KNOWN BETTER
BAA BAA BLACKSHEEP HAVE YOU ANY WOOL?
HAT / I'M NOT MAD
YES SIR, YES SIR, THREE BAGS FULL
ND I AM YOUR FATHER
ONE FOR THE MASTER, ONE FOR THE DAME
IT / YOU CAN JUST CALL ME "DAD"
NT... GLECTED? HAVE BEEN HE START OU WERE ED, TO O
BUT NONE FOR THE NAUGHTY BOY WHO CRIES IN THE LANE

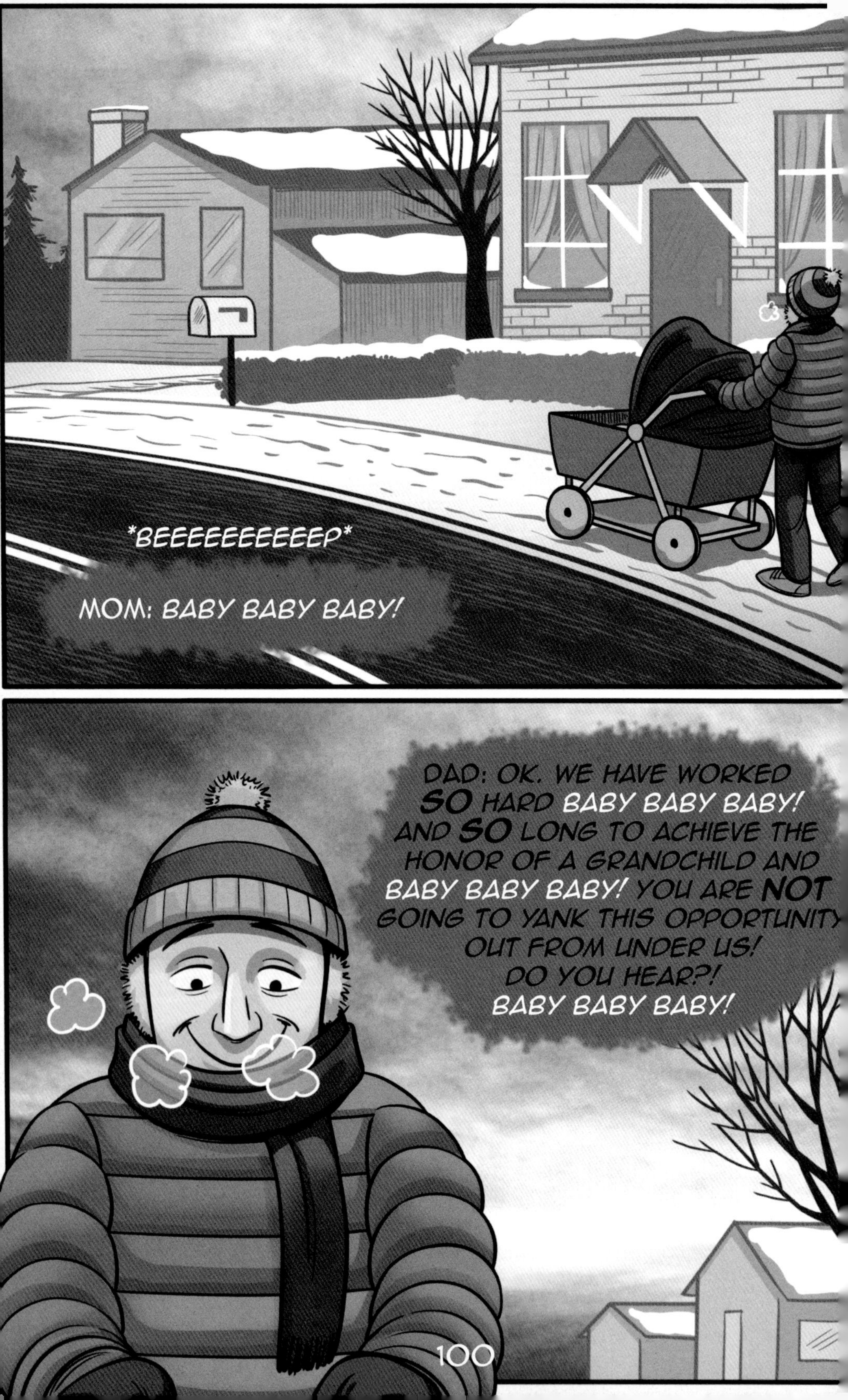
BEEEEEEEEEEP
MOM: BABY BABY BABY!
DAD: OK. WE HAVE WORKED SO HARD BABY BABY BABY! AND SO LONG TO ACHIEVE THE HONOR OF A GRANDCHILD AND BABY BABY BABY! YOU ARE NOT GOING TO YANK THIS OPPORTUNITY OUT FROM UNDER US! DO YOU HEAR?! BABY BABY BABY!

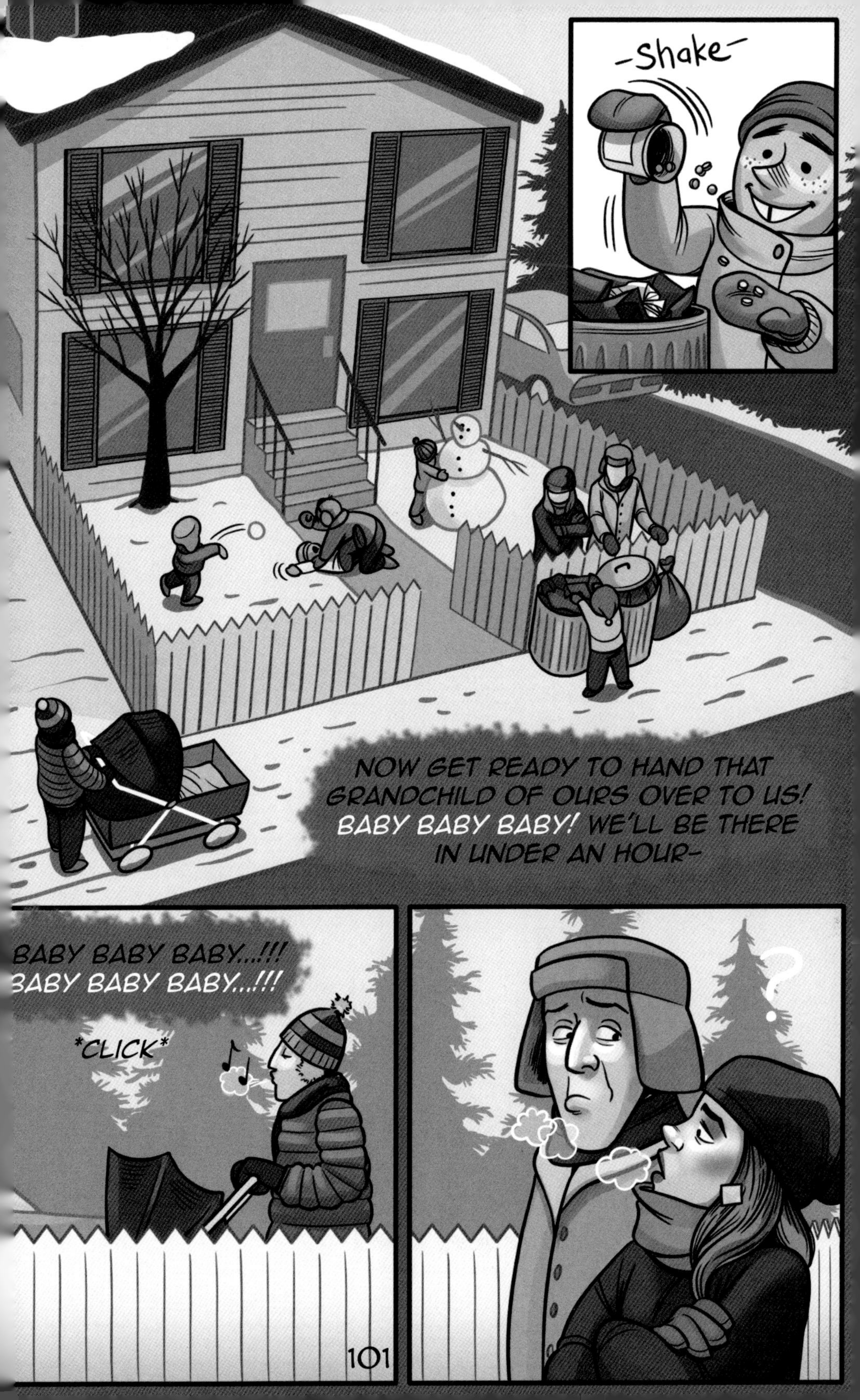

-Shake-
NOW GET READY TO HAND THAT GRANDCHILD OF OURS OVER TO US! BABY BABY BABY! WE'LL BE THERE IN UNDER AN HOUR-
BABY BABY BABY...!!!
BABY BABY BABY...!!!
CLICK
?

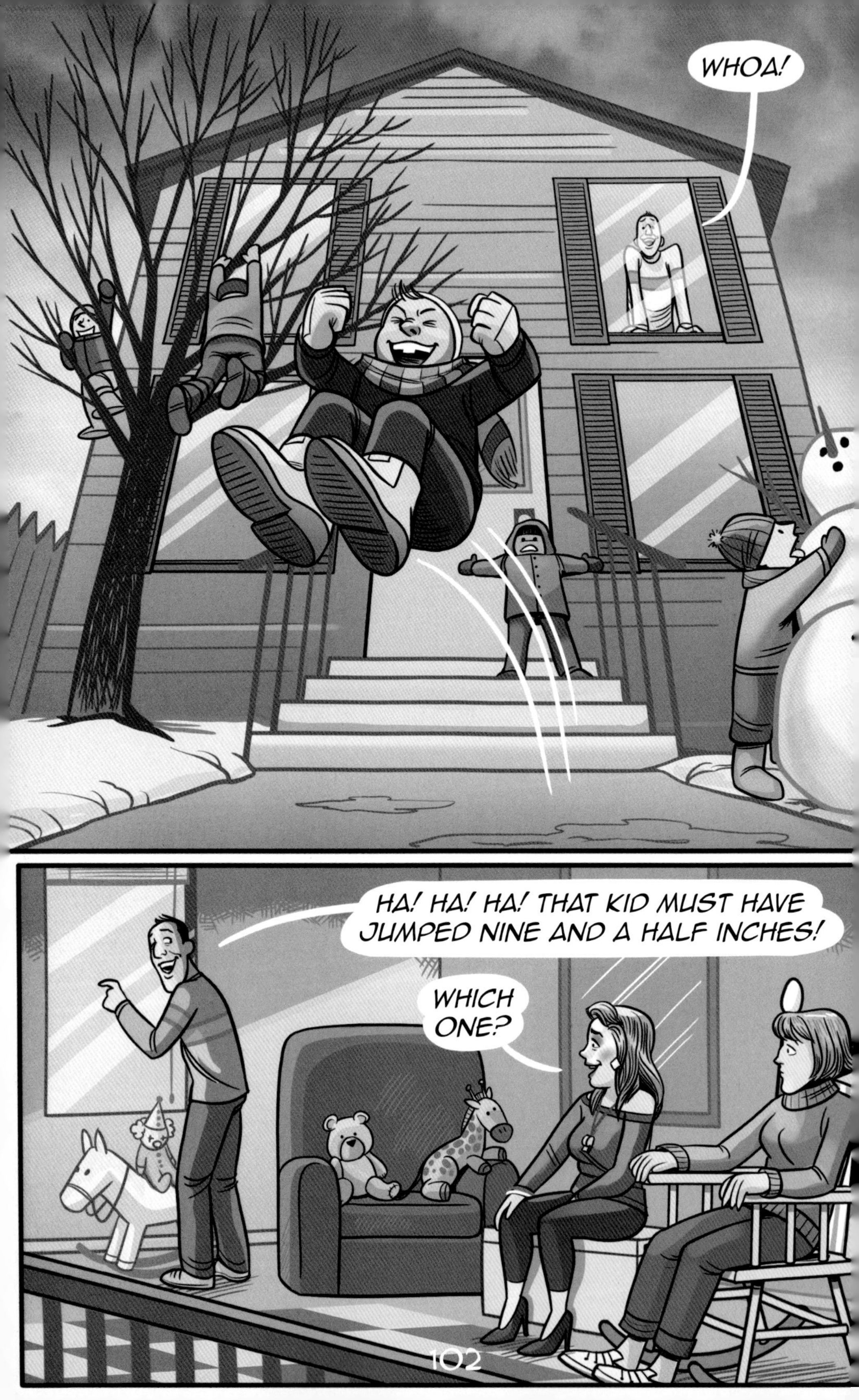
WHOA!
HA! HA! HA! THAT KID MUST HAVE JUMPED NINE AND A HALF INCHES!
WHICH ONE?

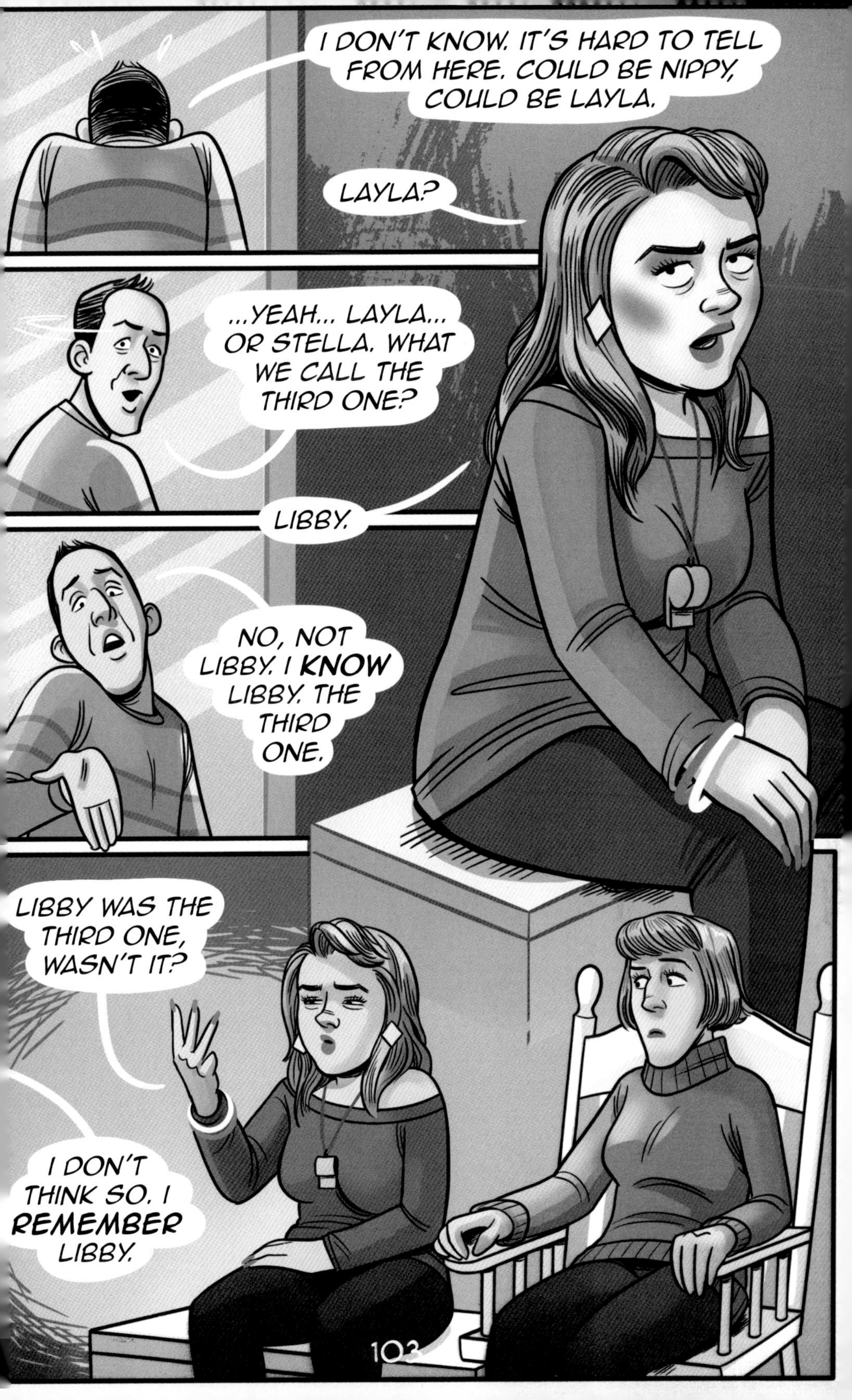
I DON'T KNOW. IT'S HARD TO TELL FROM HERE. COULD BE NIPPY, COULD BE LAYLA.
LAYLA?
...YEAH... LAYLA... OR STELLA. WHAT WE CALL THE THIRD ONE?
LIBBY.
NO, NOT LIBBY. I **KNOW** LIBBY. THE THIRD ONE.
LIBBY WAS THE THIRD ONE, WASN'T IT?
I DON'T THINK SO. I **REMEMBER** LIBBY.

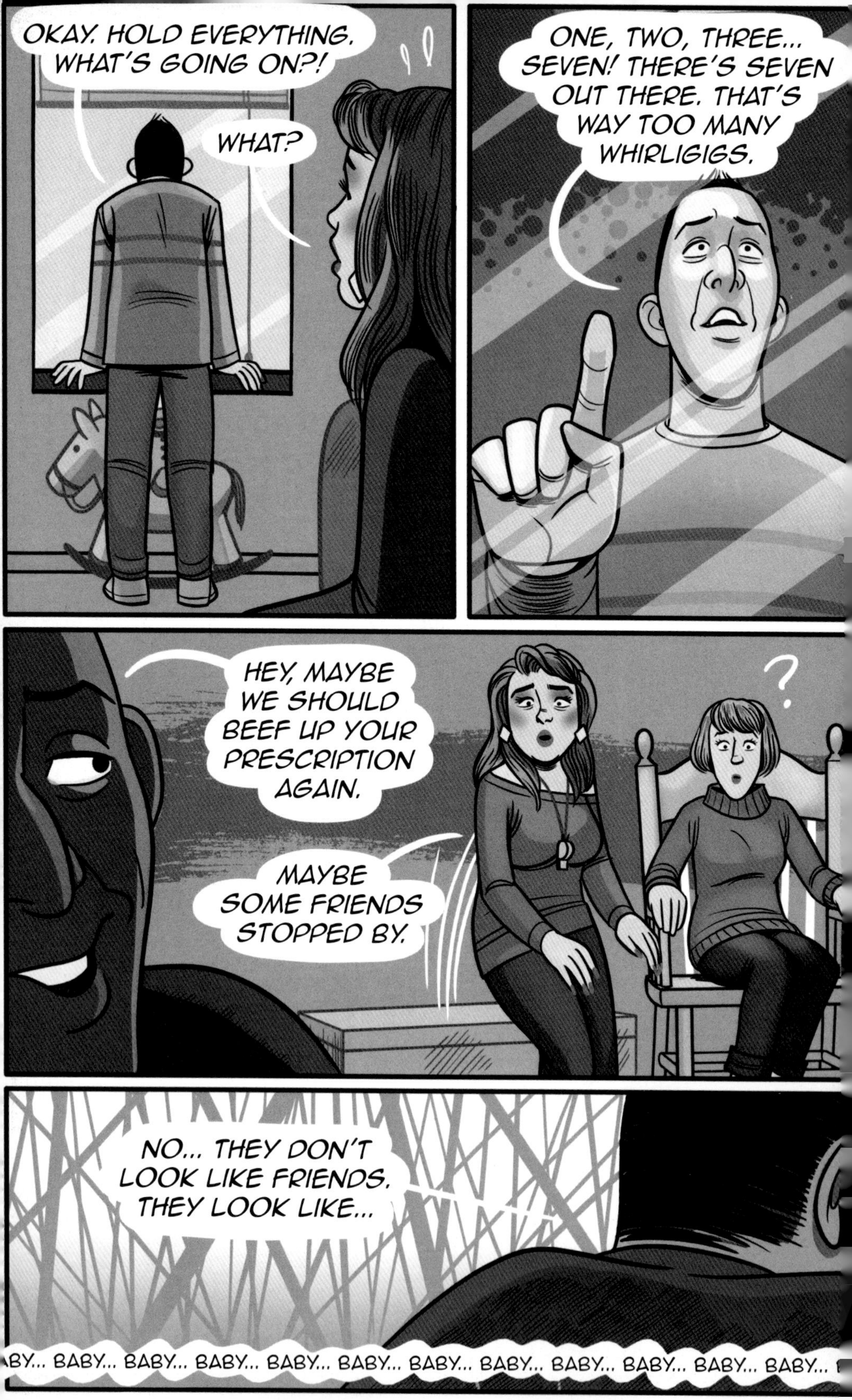
OKAY. HOLD EVERYTHING. WHAT'S GOING ON?!
WHAT?
ONE, TWO, THREE... SEVEN! THERE'S SEVEN OUT THERE. THAT'S WAY TOO MANY WHIRLIGIGS.
HEY, MAYBE WE SHOULD BEEF UP YOUR PRESCRIPTION AGAIN.
MAYBE SOME FRIENDS STOPPED BY.
NO... THEY DON'T LOOK LIKE FRIENDS. THEY LOOK LIKE...
BABY... BABY... BABY... BABY... BABY... BABY... BABY... BABY... BABY... BABY... BABY... BABY...

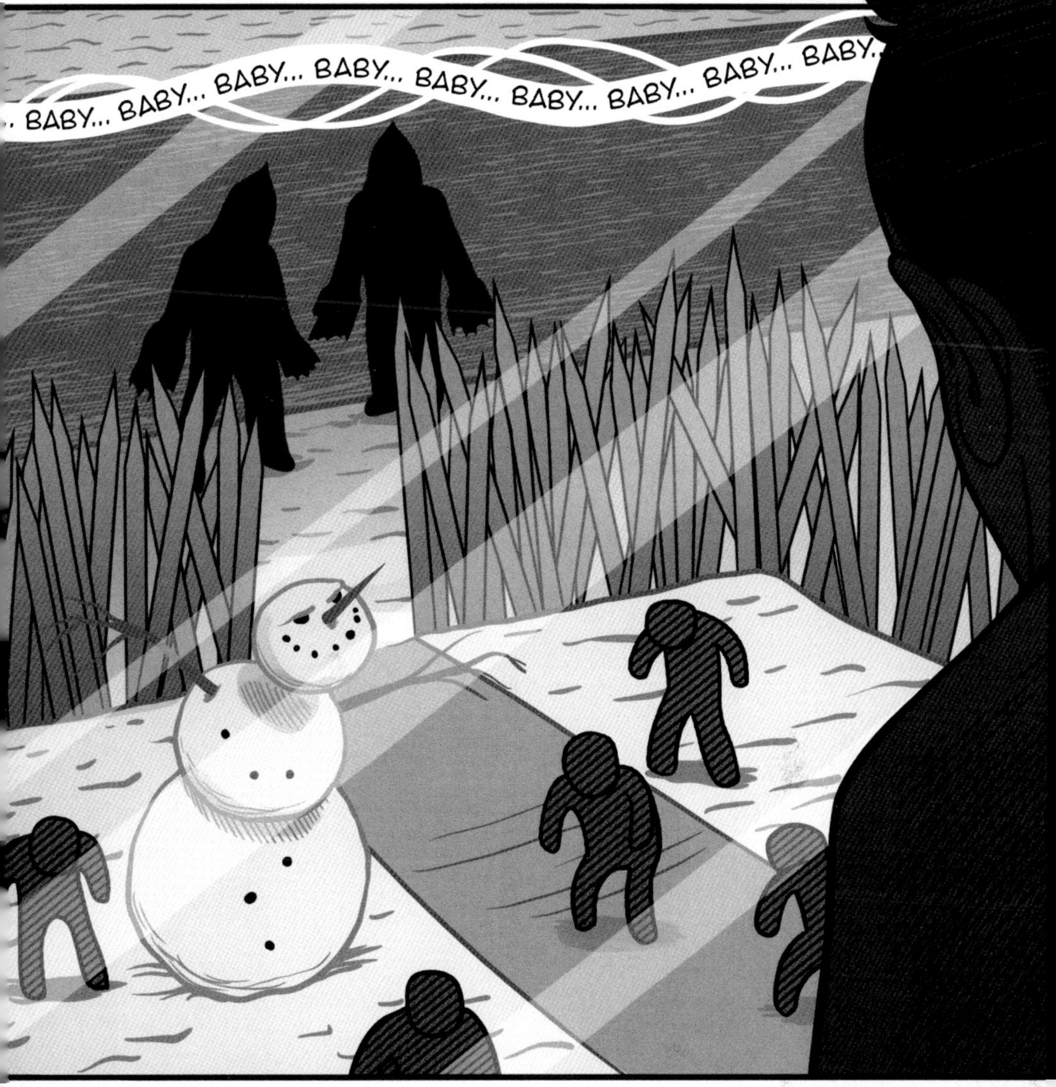
BABY... BABY... BABY... BABY... BABY... BABY... BABY... BABY... BABY...

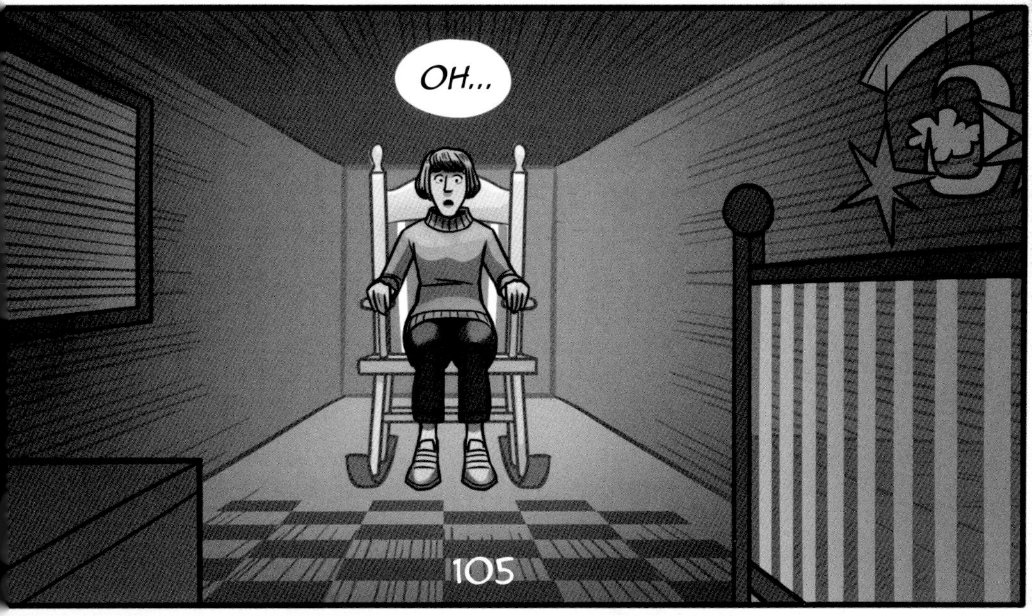
OH...

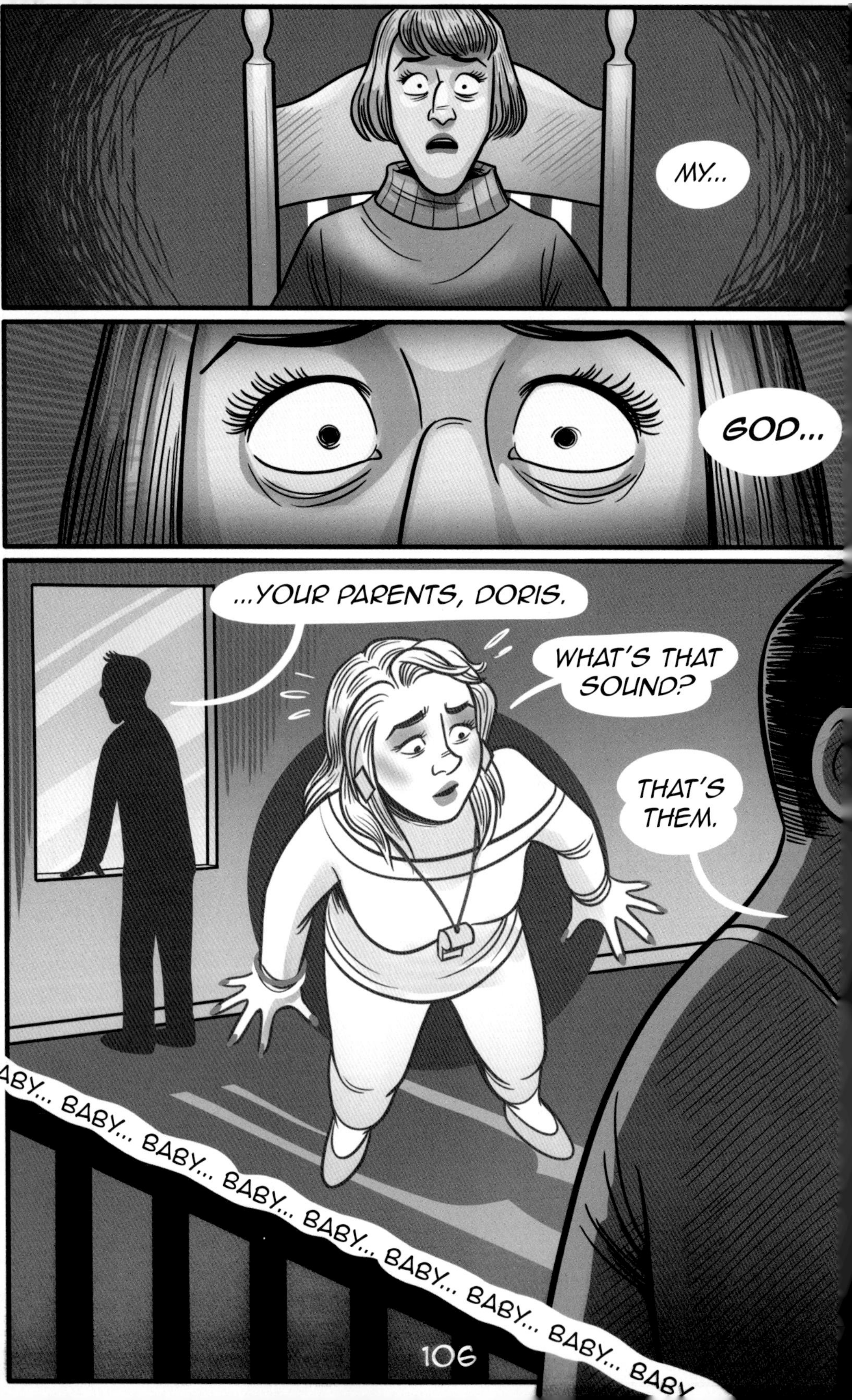
MY...
GOD...
...YOUR PARENTS, DORIS.
WHAT'S THAT SOUND?
THAT'S THEM.
ABY... BABY... BABY... BABY... BABY... BABY... BABY... BABY... BABY

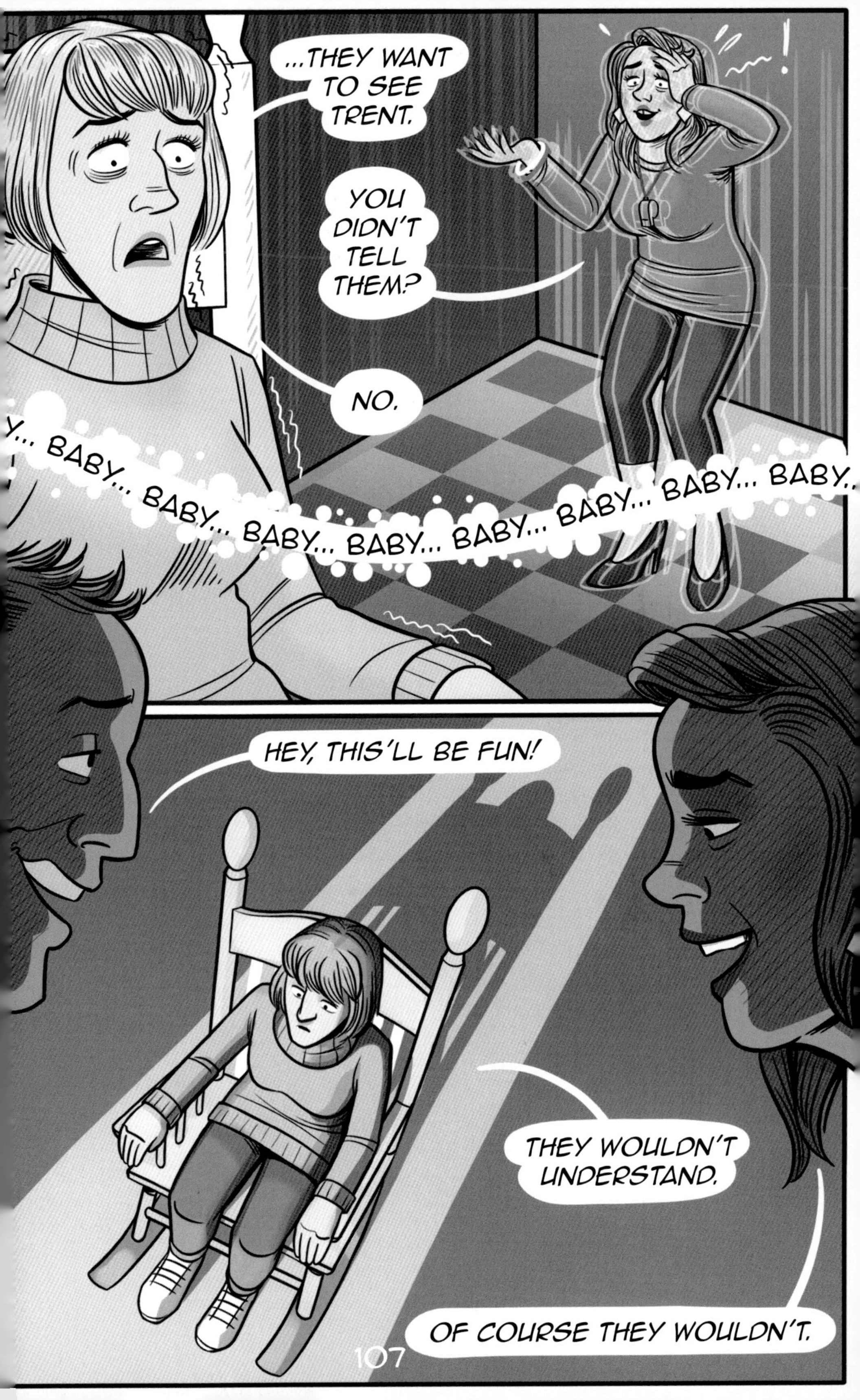
...THEY WANT TO SEE TRENT.
YOU DIDN'T TELL THEM?
NO.
Y... BABY... BABY... BABY... BABY... BABY... BABY... BABY... BABY...
HEY, THIS'LL BE FUN!
THEY WOULDN'T UNDERSTAND.
OF COURSE THEY WOULDN'T.

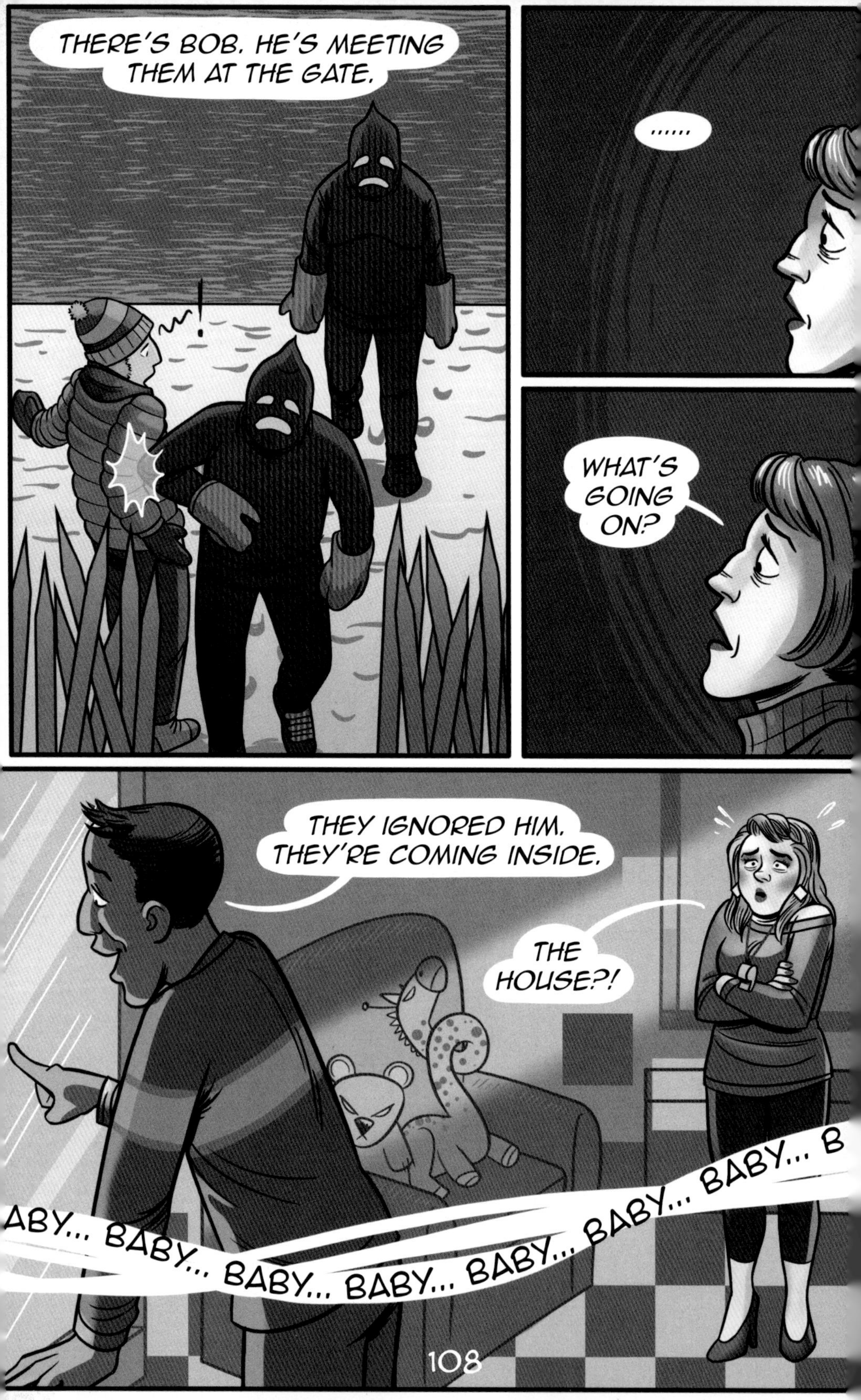
THERE'S BOB. HE'S MEETING THEM AT THE GATE.
!
......
WHAT'S GOING ON?
THEY IGNORED HIM. THEY'RE COMING INSIDE.
THE HOUSE?!
ABY... BABY... BABY... BABY... BABY... BABY... BABY... B

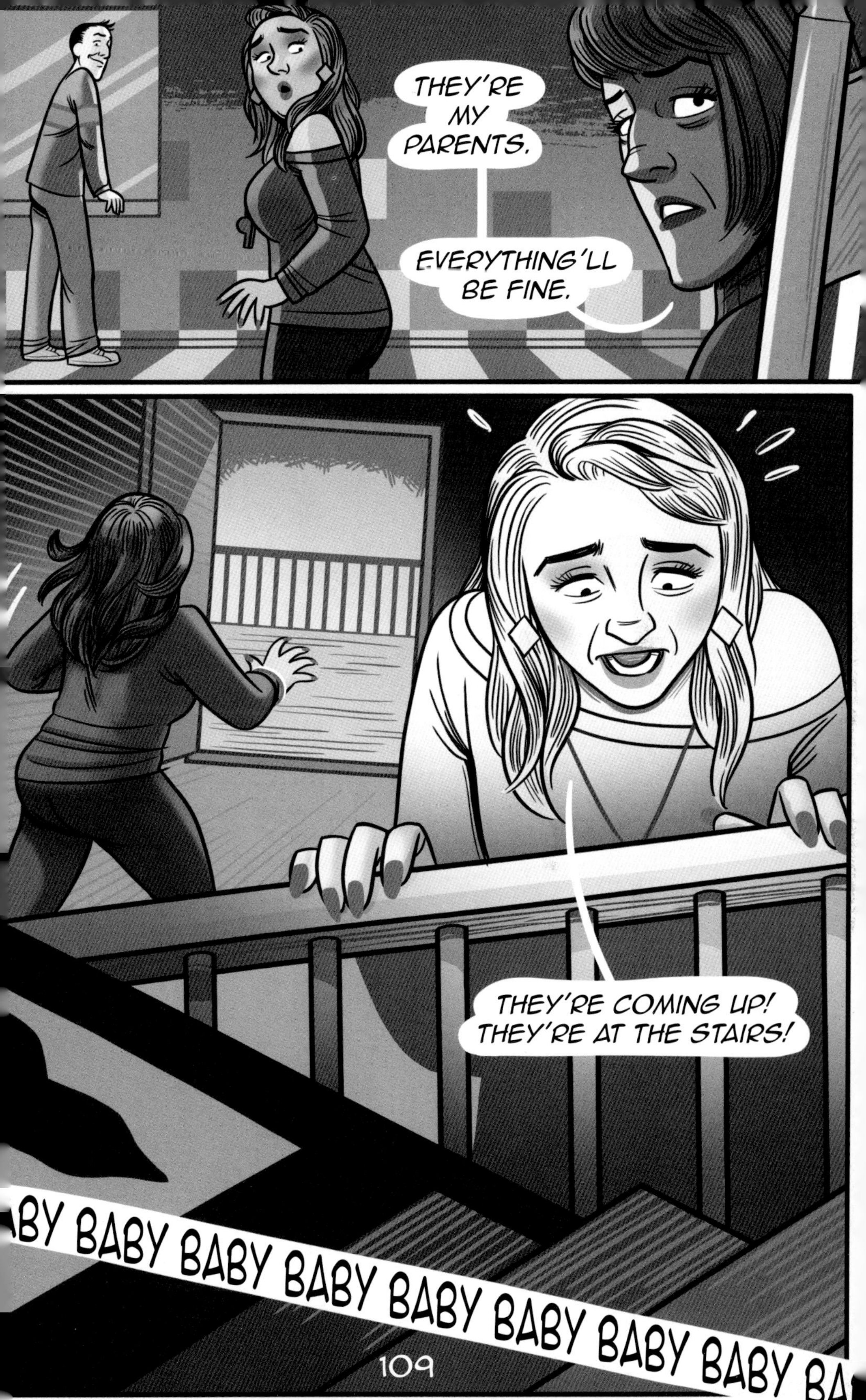
THEY'RE MY PARENTS.
EVERYTHING'LL BE FINE.
THEY'RE COMING UP! THEY'RE AT THE STAIRS!
BABY BABY BABY BABY BABY BABY BABY BABY

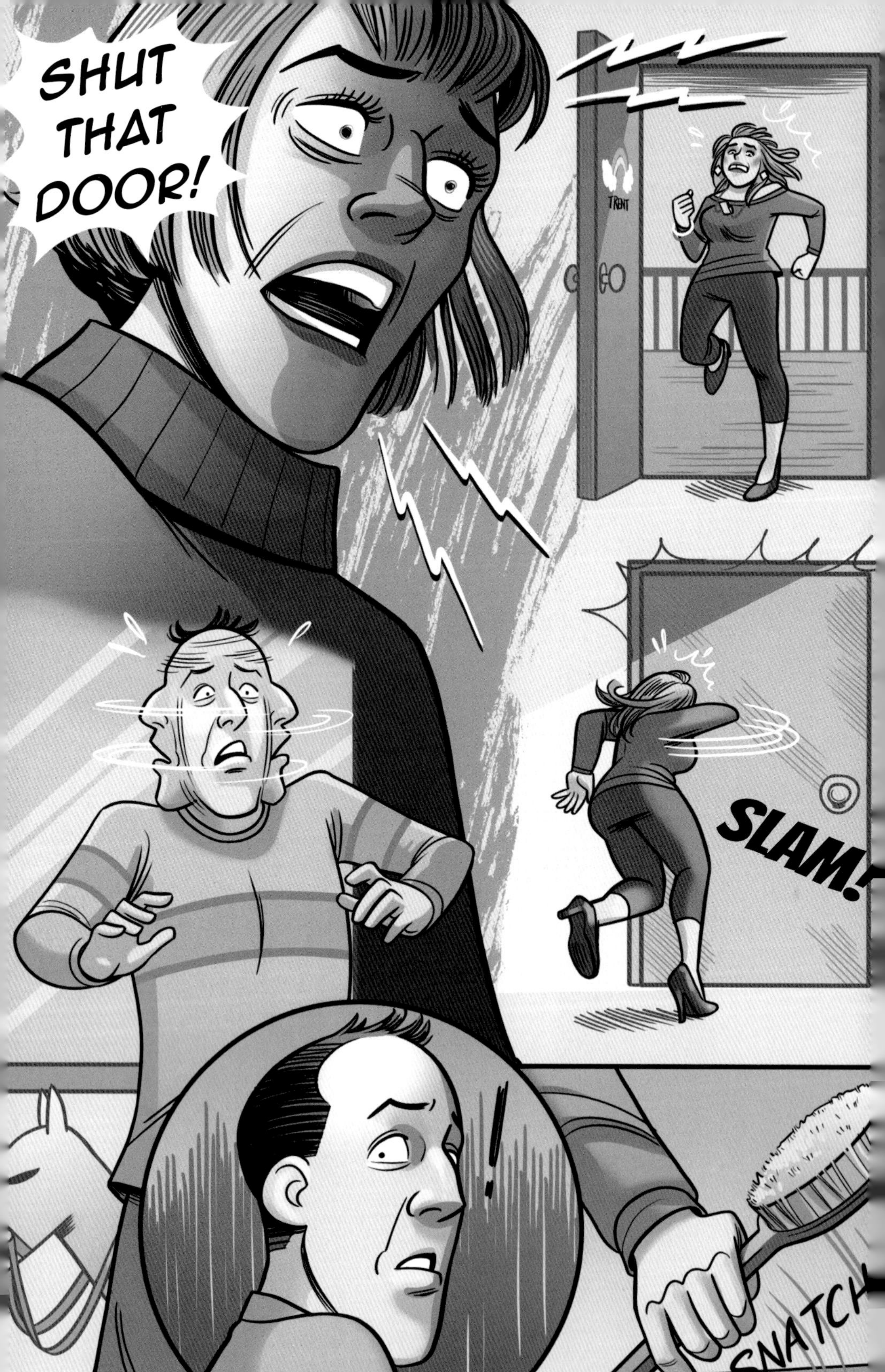
SHUT THAT DOOR!
TRENT
SLAM!
SNATCH

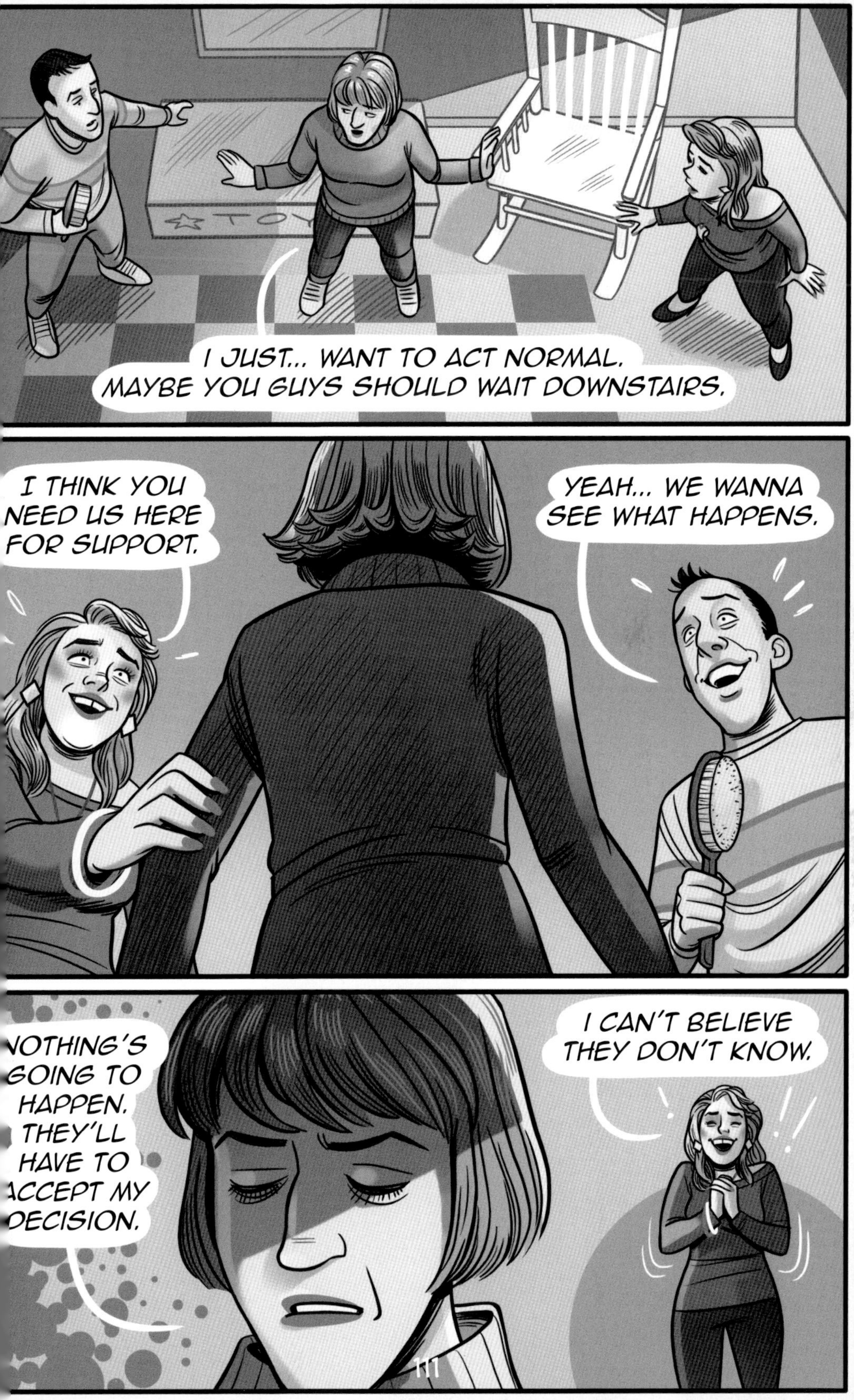

I JUST... WANT TO ACT NORMAL. MAYBE YOU GUYS SHOULD WAIT DOWNSTAIRS.
I THINK YOU NEED US HERE FOR SUPPORT.
YEAH... WE WANNA SEE WHAT HAPPENS.
NOTHING'S GOING TO HAPPEN. THEY'LL HAVE TO ACCEPT MY DECISION.
I CAN'T BELIEVE THEY DON'T KNOW.

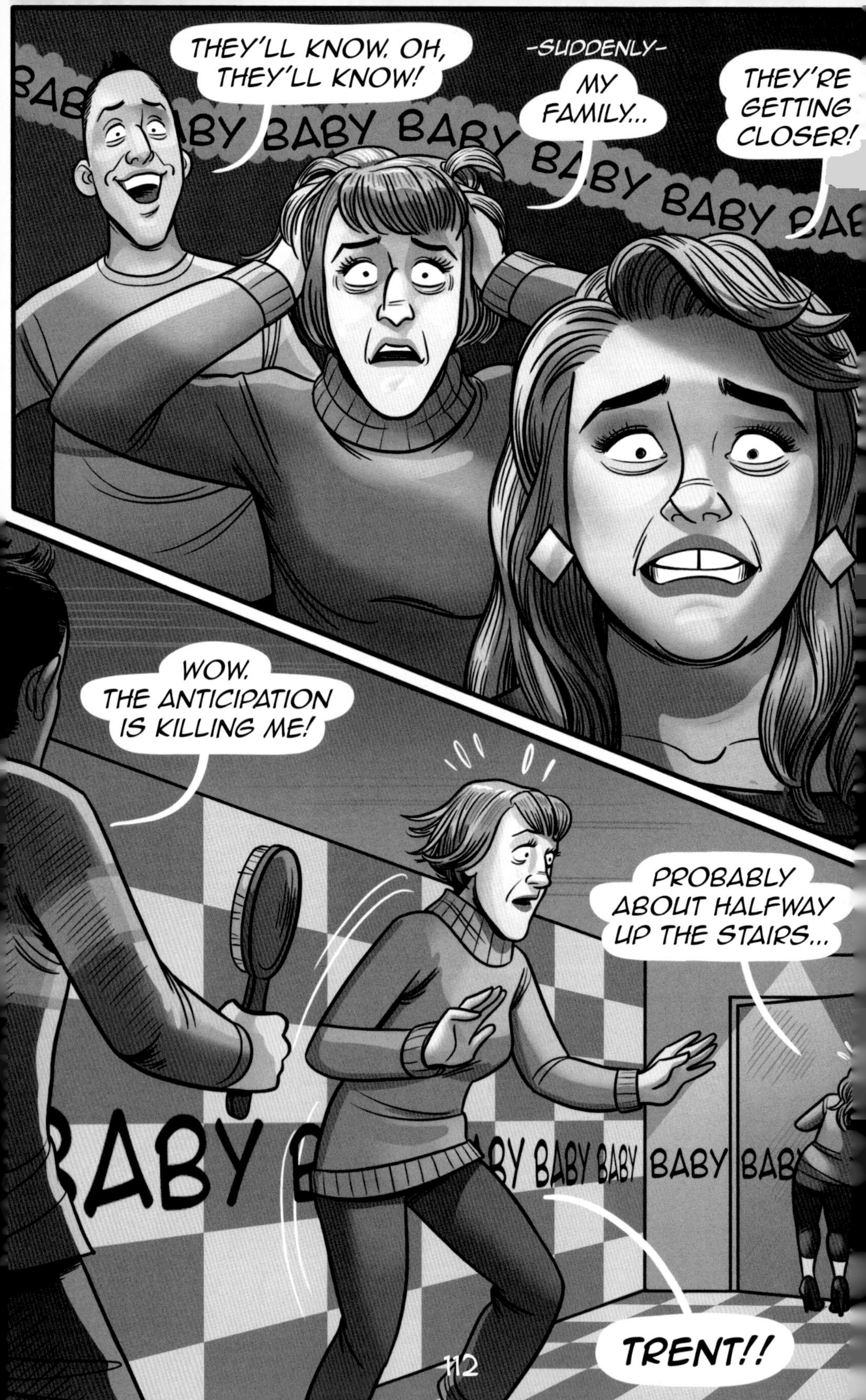
THEY'LL KNOW. OH, THEY'LL KNOW!
BABY BABY BABY BABY BABY BABY BABY BABY
-SUDDENLY-
MY FAMILY...
THEY'RE GETTING CLOSER!
WOW. THE ANTICIPATION IS KILLING ME!
PROBABLY ABOUT HALFWAY UP THE STAIRS...
BABY BABY BABY BABY BABY BABY
TRENT!!

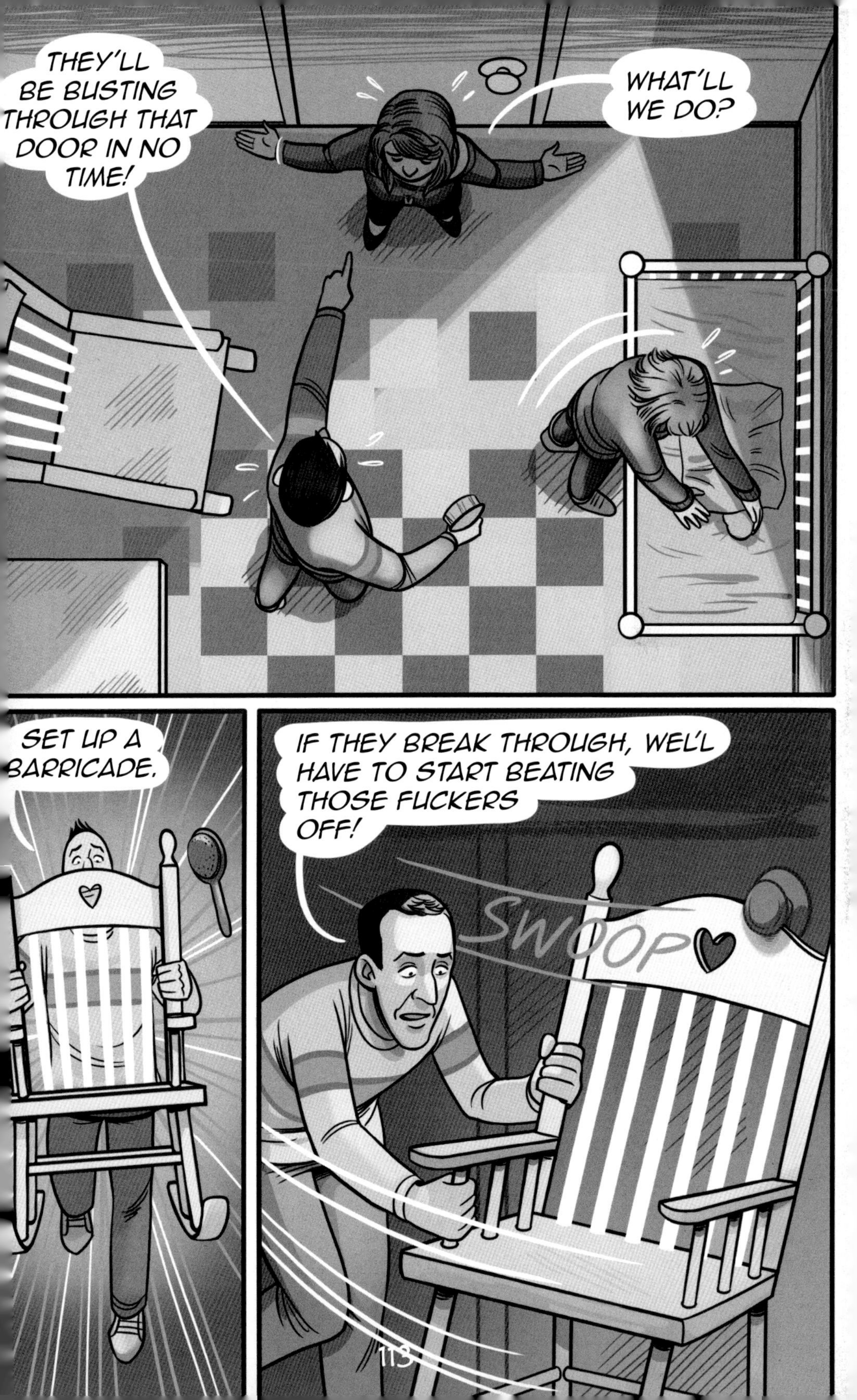
THEY'LL BE BUSTING THROUGH THAT DOOR IN NO TIME!
WHAT'LL WE DO?
SET UP A BARRICADE.
IF THEY BREAK THROUGH, WE'LL HAVE TO START BEATING THOSE FUCKERS OFF!
SWOOP

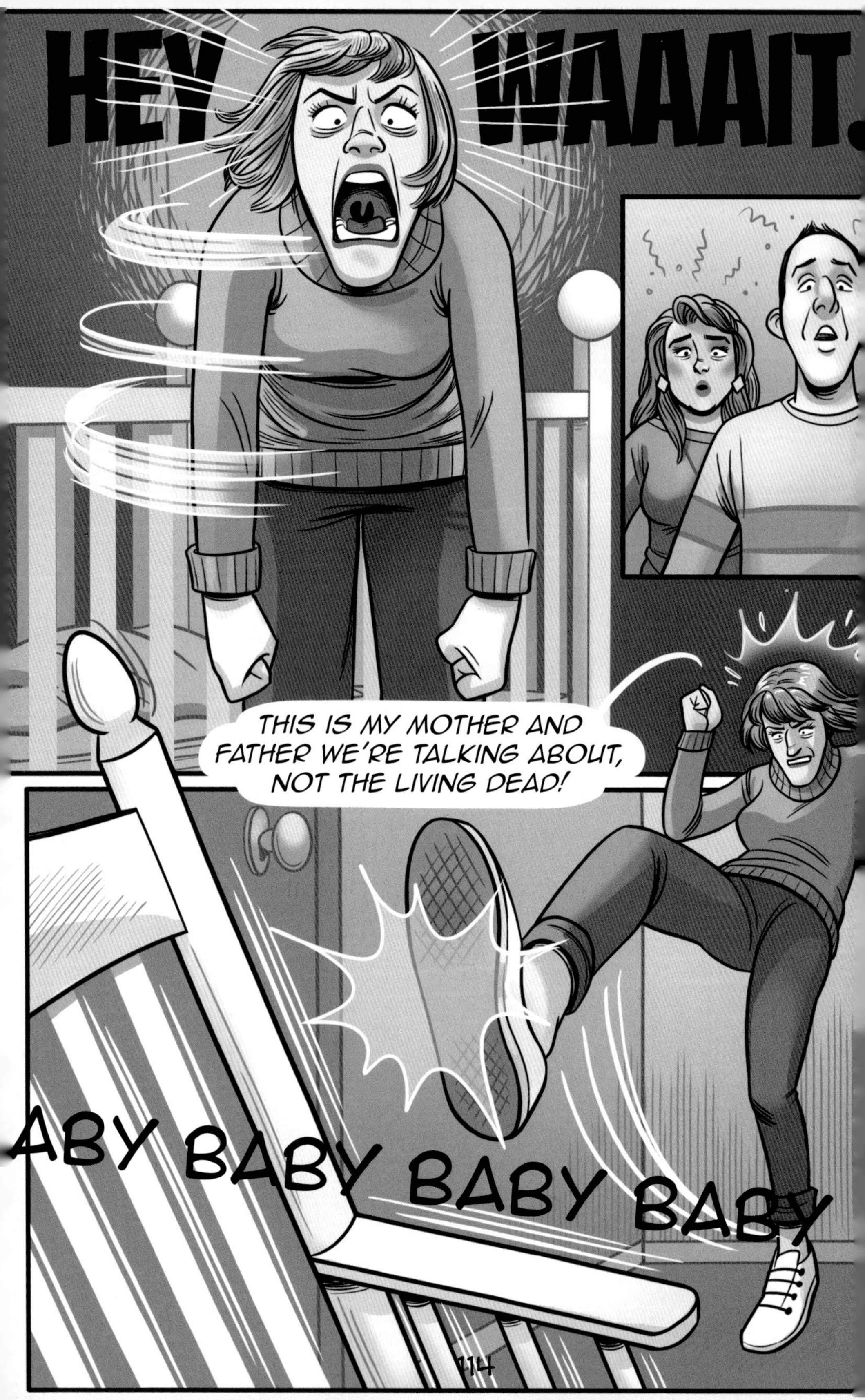
HEY WAAAIT.
THIS IS MY MOTHER AND FATHER WE'RE TALKING ABOUT, NOT THE LIVING DEAD!
ABY BABY BABY BABY BABY

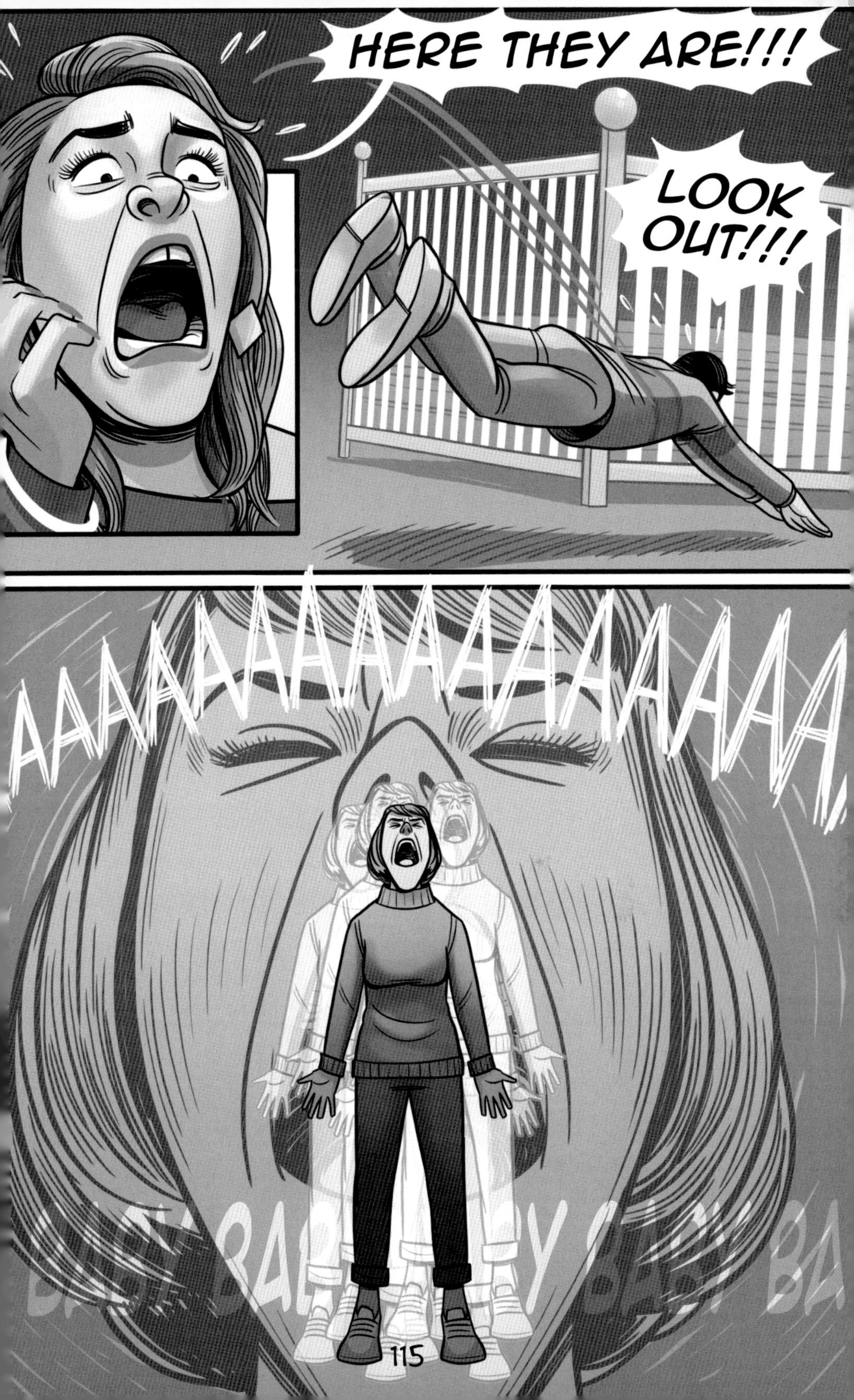
HERE THEY ARE!!!
LOOK OUT!!!
AAAAAAAAAAAAAAA

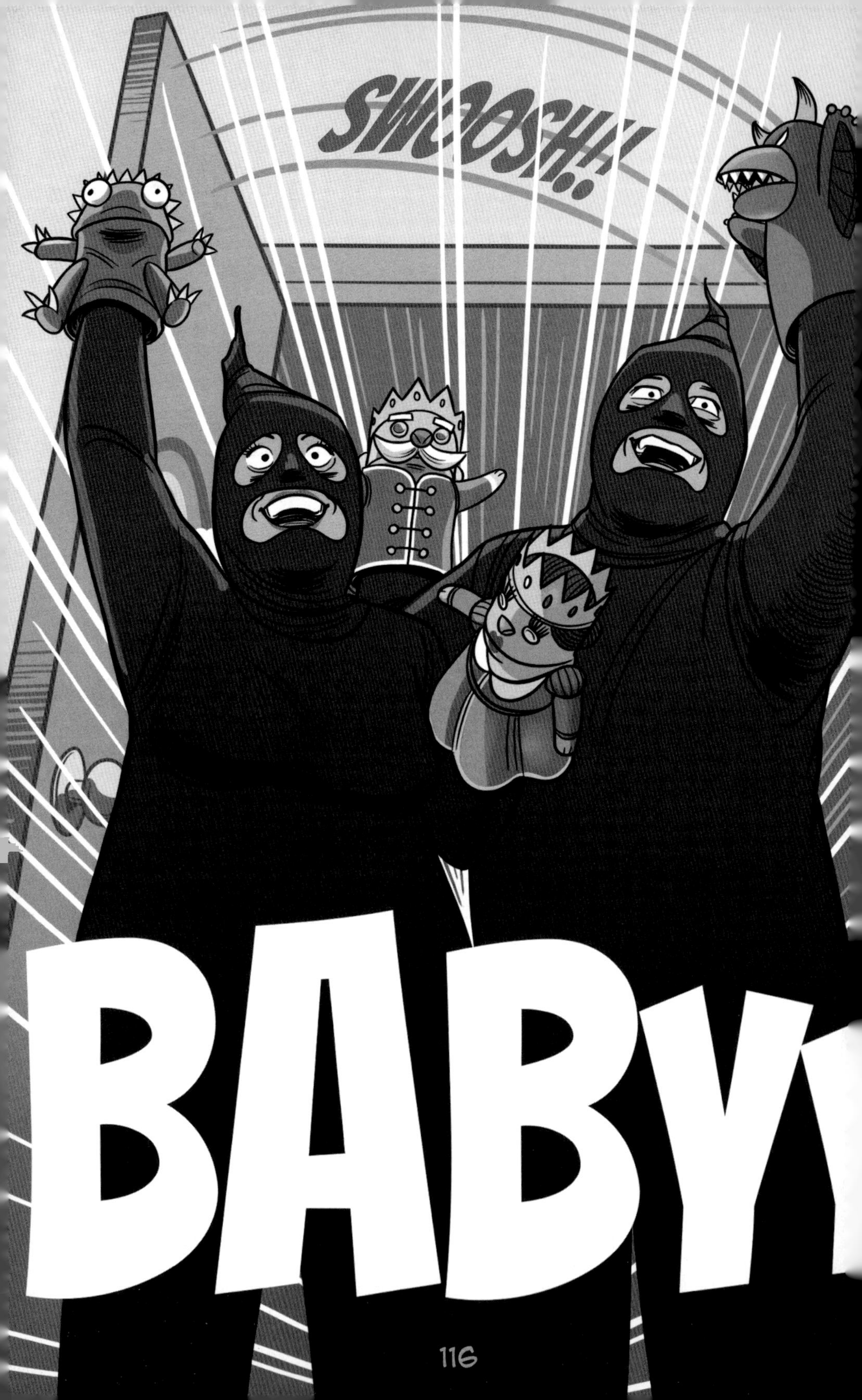
SWOOSH!!
BABY!

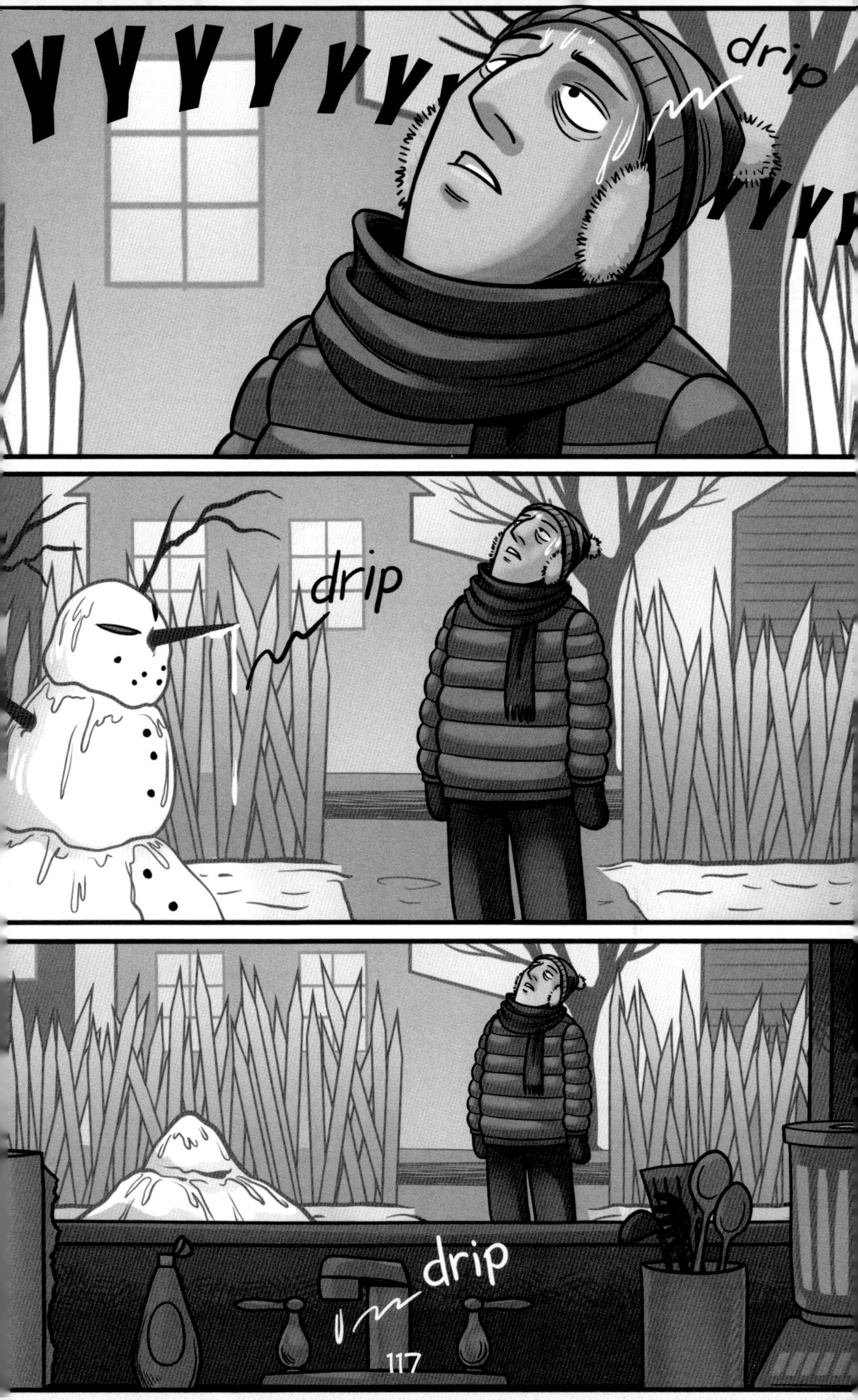
YYYYYYYY
drip
YYYY
drip
drip

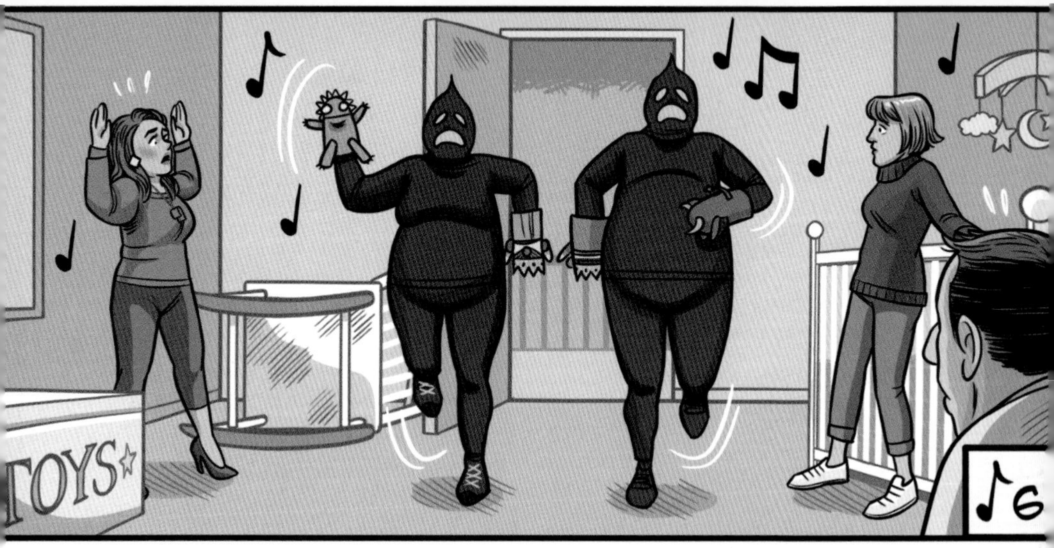
TOYS
6

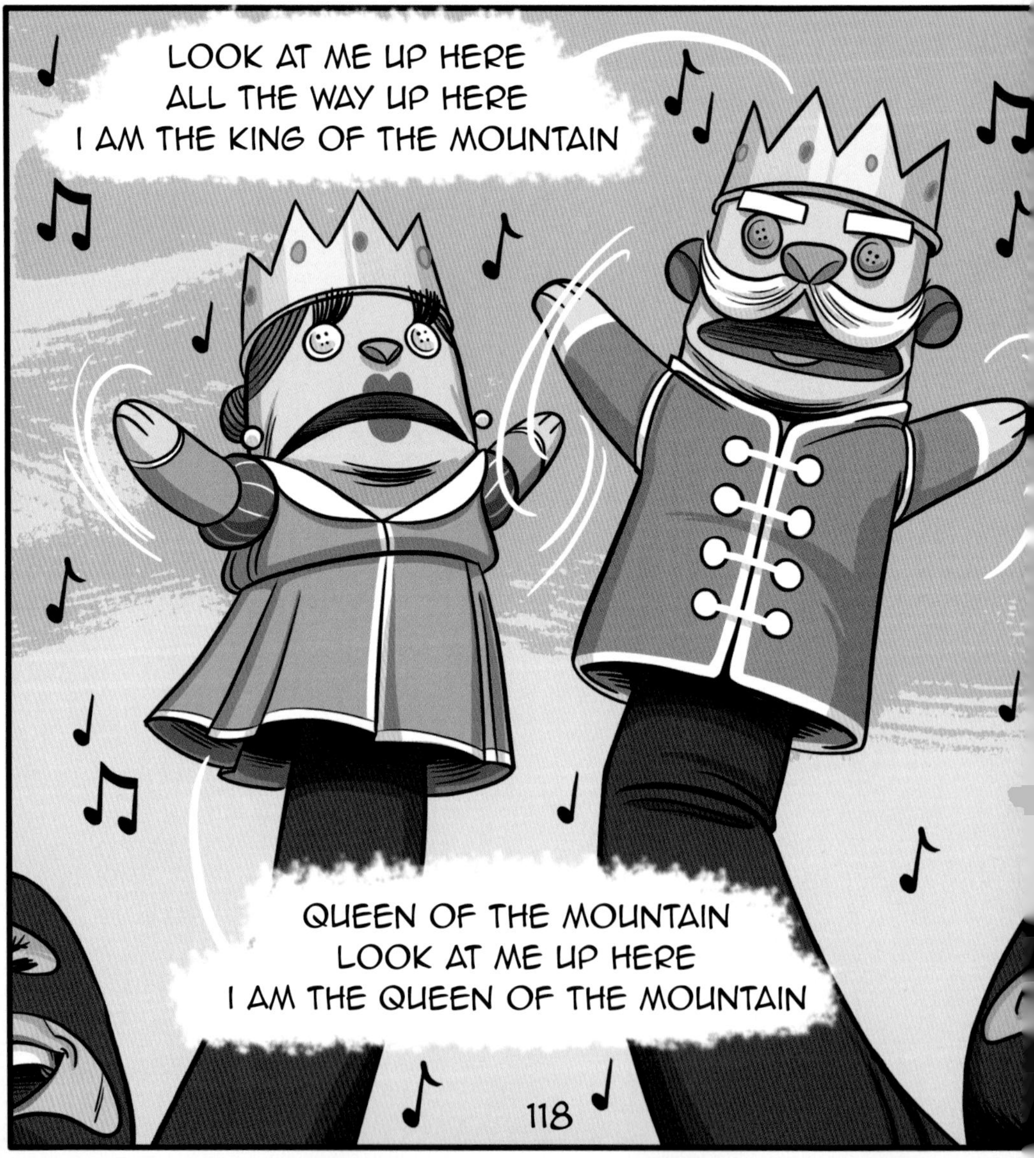
LOOK AT ME UP HERE
ALL THE WAY UP HERE
I AM THE KING OF THE MOUNTAIN
QUEEN OF THE MOUNTAIN
LOOK AT ME UP HERE
I AM THE QUEEN OF THE MOUNTAIN

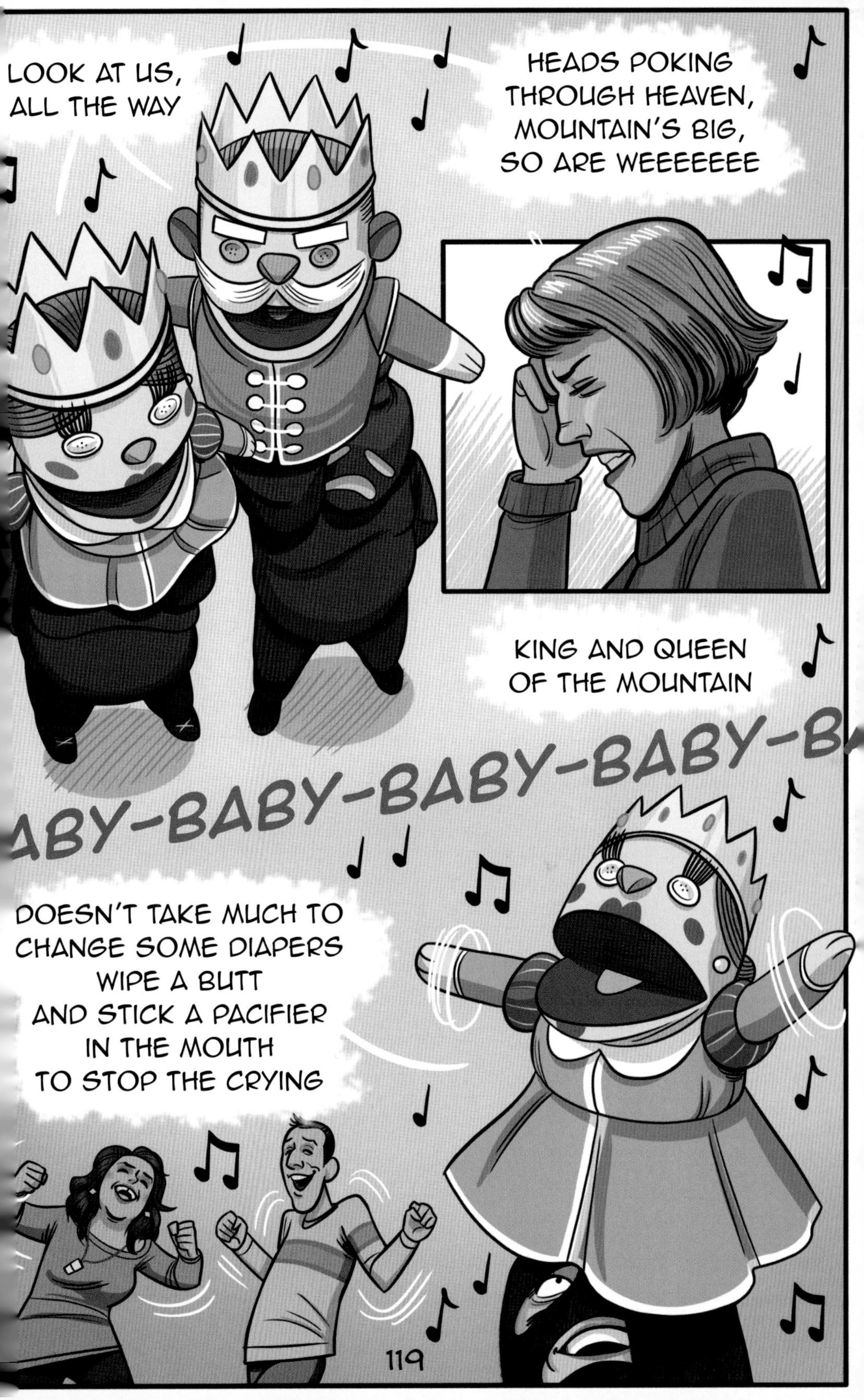
LOOK AT US,
ALL THE WAY
HEADS POKING
THROUGH HEAVEN,
MOUNTAIN'S BIG,
SO ARE WEEEEEEE
KING AND QUEEN
OF THE MOUNTAIN
ABY-BABY-BABY-BABY-B
DOESN'T TAKE MUCH TO
CHANGE SOME DIAPERS
WIPE A BUTT
AND STICK A PACIFIER
IN THE MOUTH
TO STOP THE CRYING

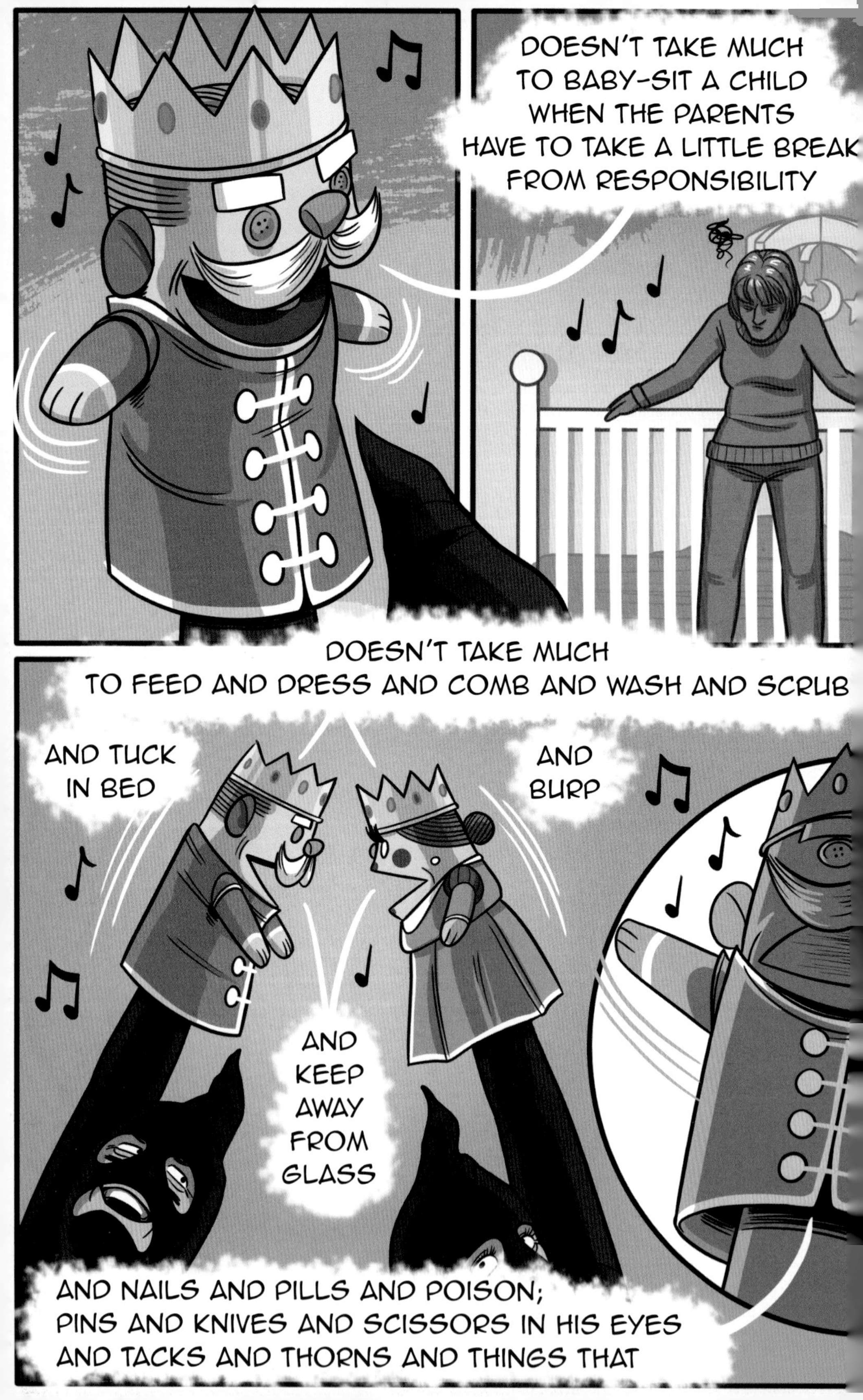
DOESN'T TAKE MUCH
TO BABY-SIT A CHILD
WHEN THE PARENTS
HAVE TO TAKE A LITTLE BREAK
FROM RESPONSIBILITY
DOESN'T TAKE MUCH
TO FEED AND DRESS AND COMB AND WASH AND SCRUB
AND TUCK IN BED
AND BURP
AND KEEP AWAY FROM GLASS
AND NAILS AND PILLS AND POISON;
PINS AND KNIVES AND SCISSORS IN HIS EYES
AND TACKS AND THORNS AND THINGS THAT

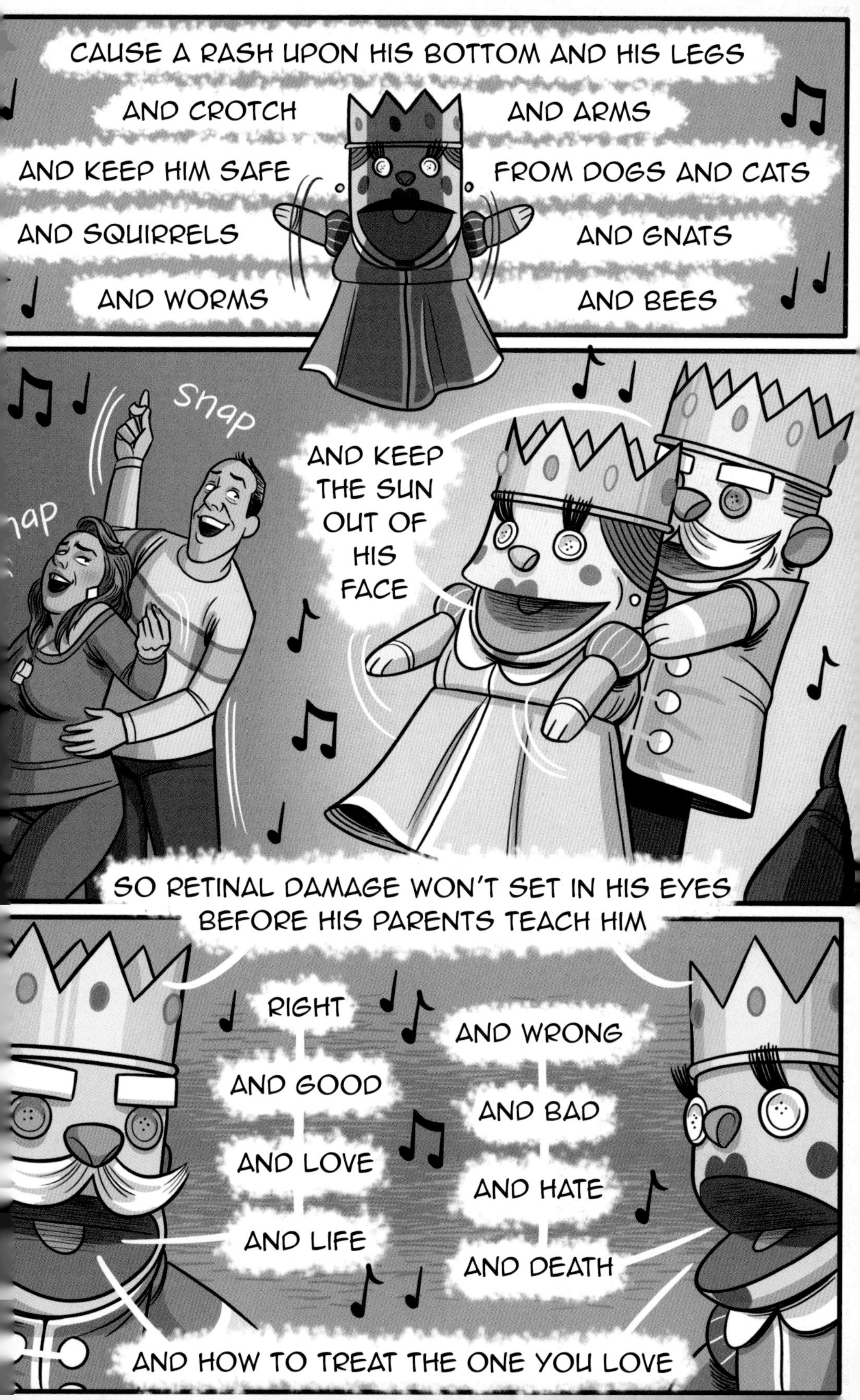
CAUSE A RASH UPON HIS BOTTOM AND HIS LEGS
AND CROTCH
AND ARMS
AND KEEP HIM SAFE
FROM DOGS AND CATS
AND SQUIRRELS
AND GNATS
AND WORMS
AND BEES
SNAP
SNAP
AND KEEP THE SUN OUT OF HIS FACE
SO RETINAL DAMAGE WON'T SET IN HIS EYES BEFORE HIS PARENTS TEACH HIM
RIGHT
AND WRONG
AND GOOD
AND BAD
AND LOVE
AND HATE
AND LIFE
AND DEATH
AND HOW TO TREAT THE ONE YOU LOVE

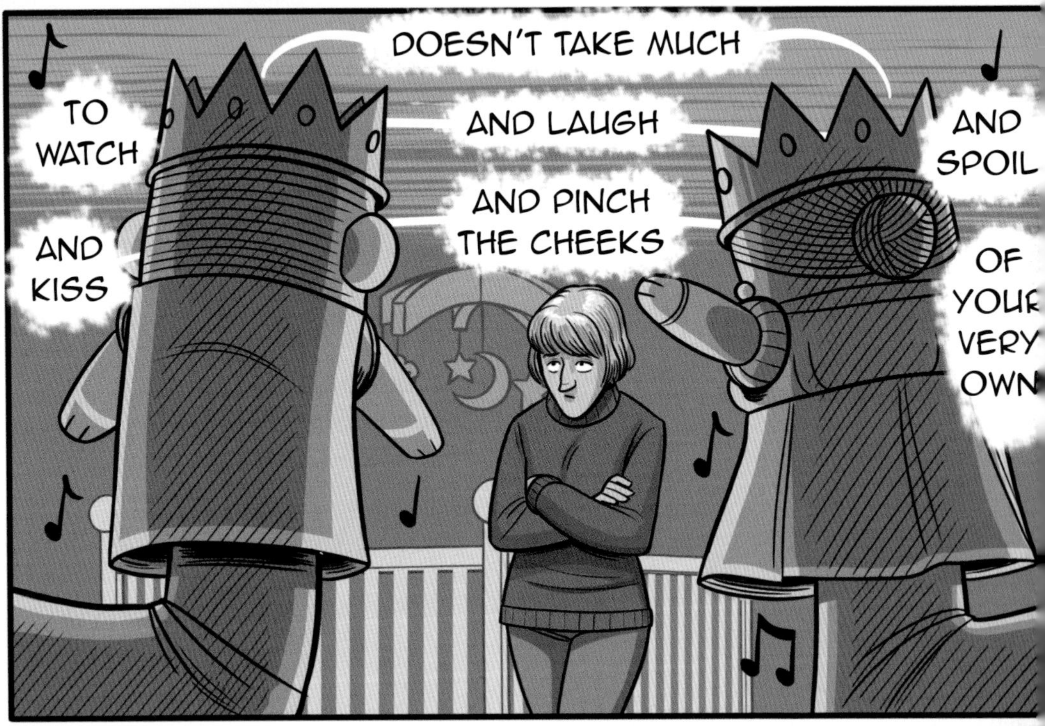
DOESN'T TAKE MUCH
TO WATCH
AND LAUGH
AND SPOIL
AND KISS
AND PINCH THE CHEEKS
OF YOUR VERY OWN

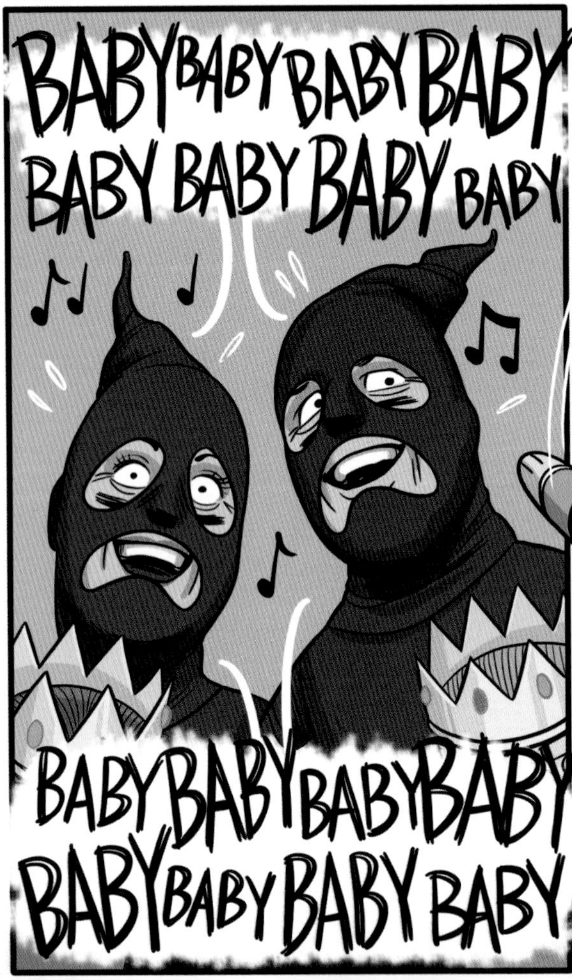
BABY BABY BABY BABY BABY BABY BABY BABY

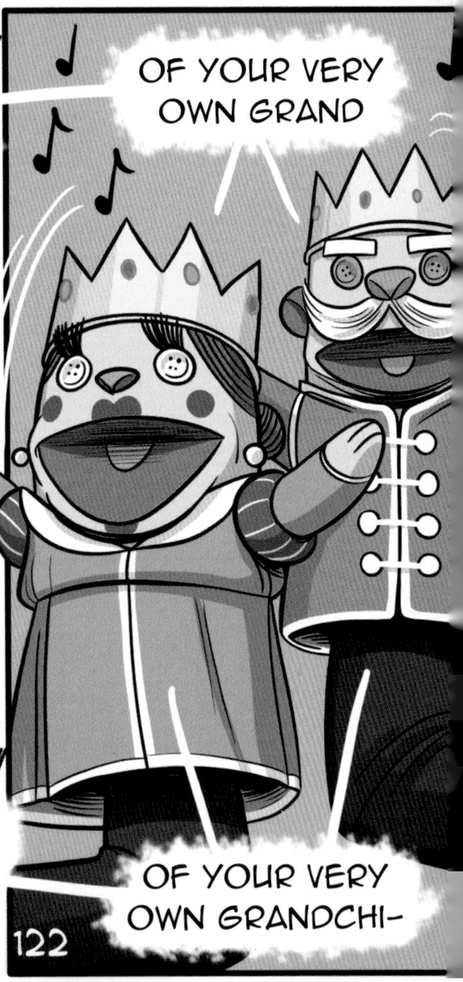
OF YOUR VERY OWN GRAND

BABY BABY BABY BABY BABY BABY BABY BABY

OF YOUR VERY OWN GRANDCHI-

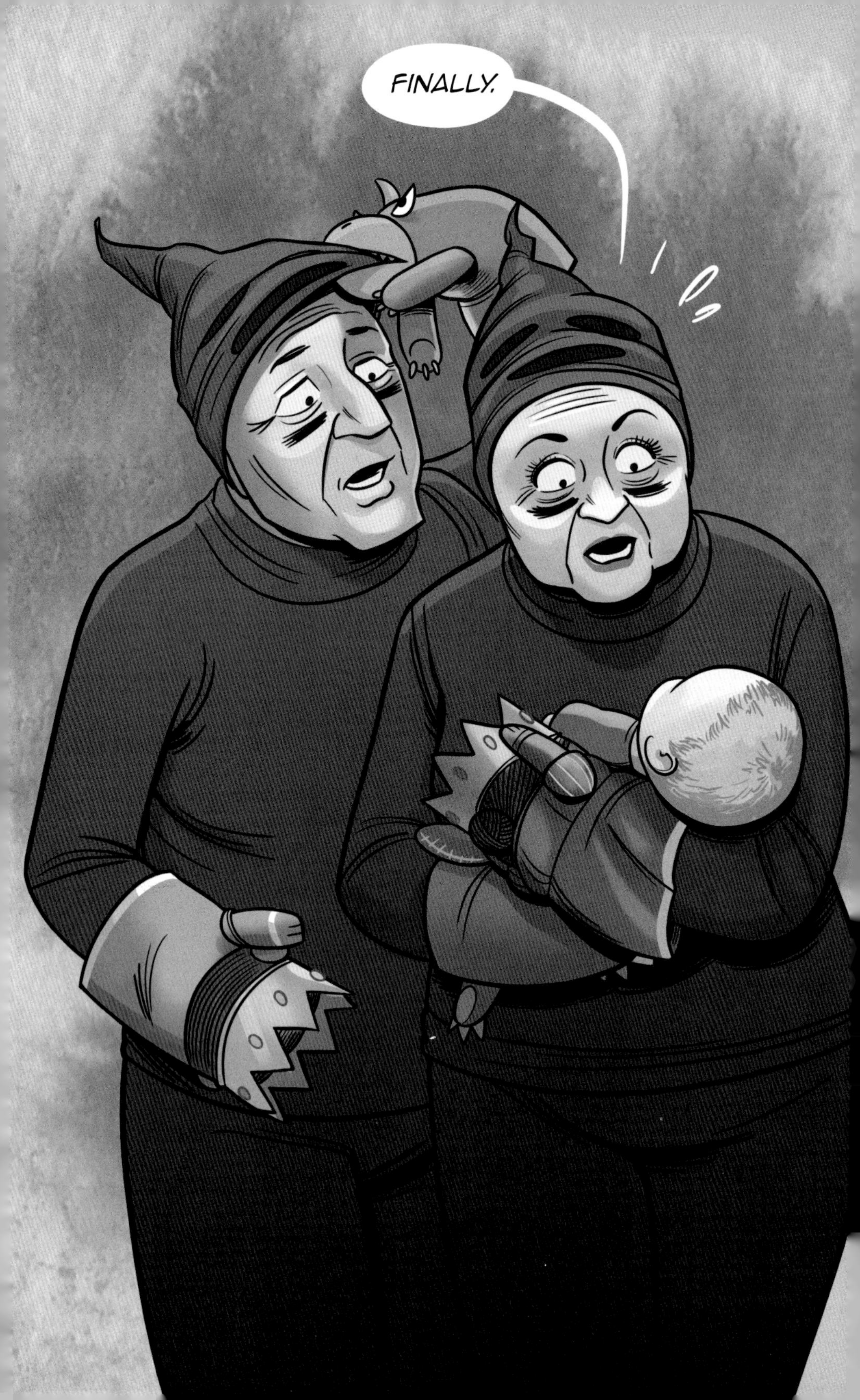
FINALLY.

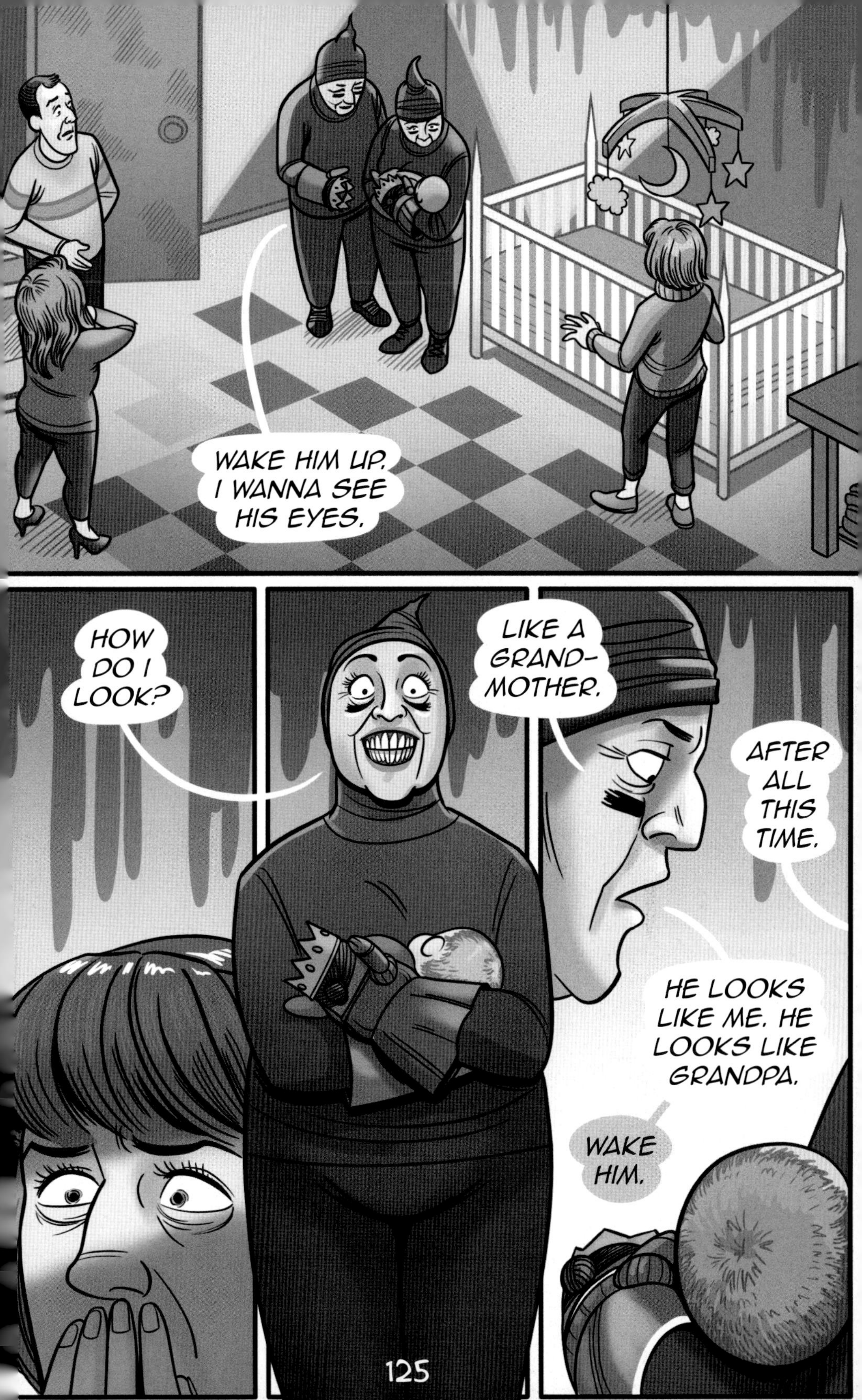
WAKE HIM UP. I WANNA SEE HIS EYES.
HOW DO I LOOK?
LIKE A GRAND-MOTHER.
AFTER ALL THIS TIME.
HE LOOKS LIKE ME. HE LOOKS LIKE GRANDPA.
WAKE HIM.

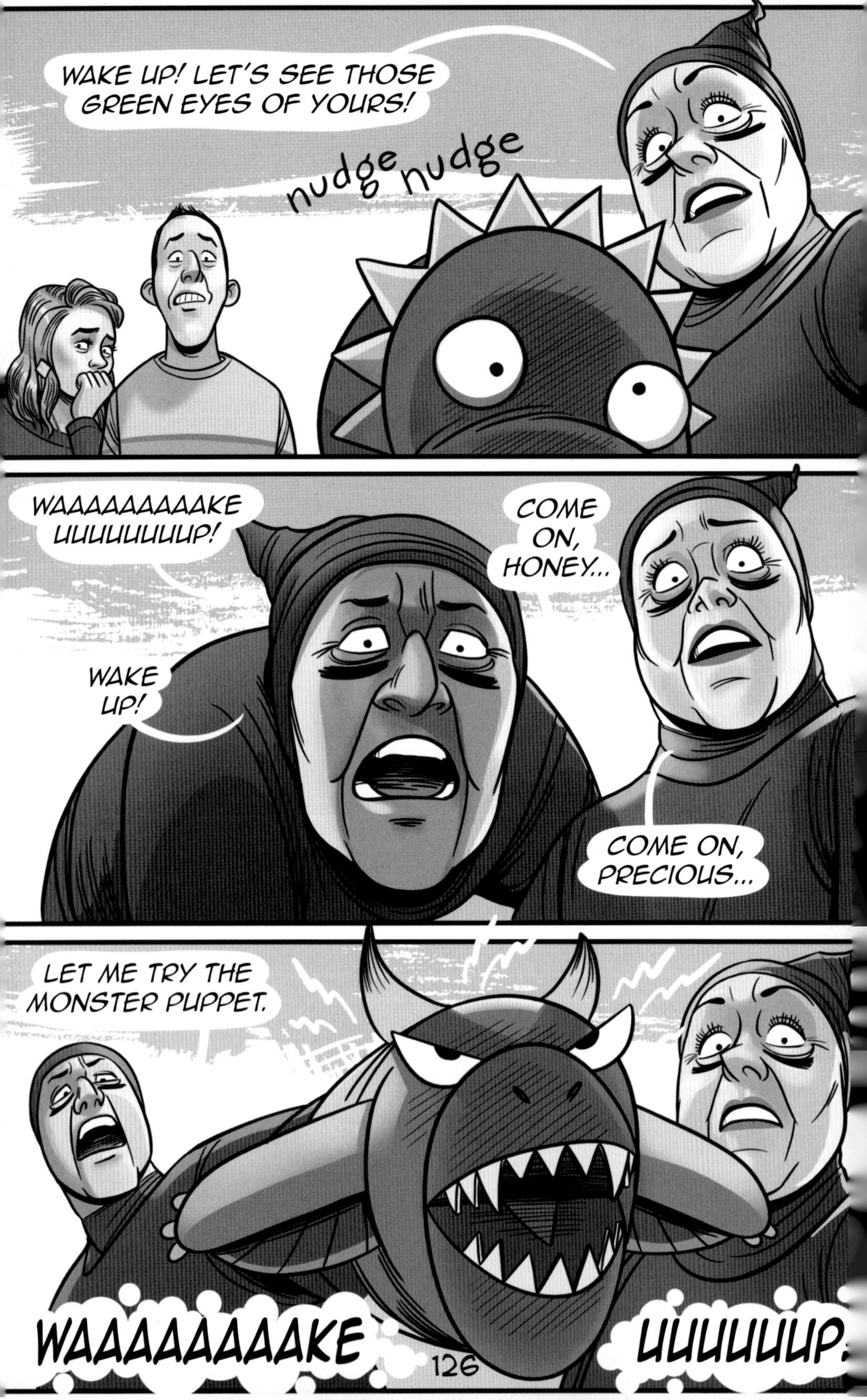

WAKE UP! LET'S SEE THOSE GREEN EYES OF YOURS!
nudge nudge
WAAAAAAAAAAKE UUUUUUUUP!
COME ON, HONEY...
WAKE UP!
COME ON, PRECIOUS...
LET ME TRY THE MONSTER PUPPET.
WAAAAAAAAAKE
UUUUUUP

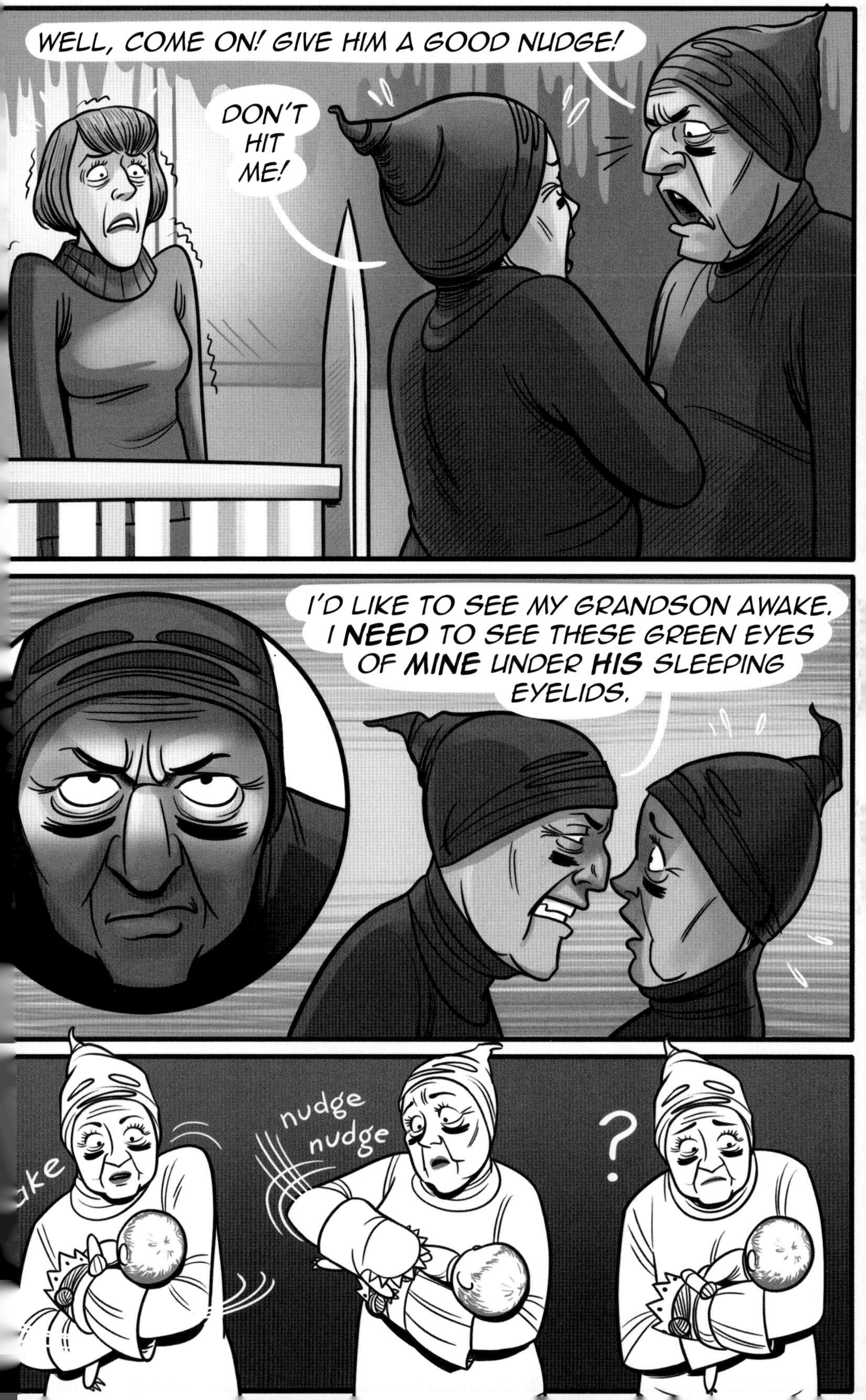
WELL, COME ON! GIVE HIM A GOOD NUDGE!
DON'T HIT ME!
I'D LIKE TO SEE MY GRANDSON AWAKE. I NEED TO SEE THESE GREEN EYES OF MINE UNDER HIS SLEEPING EYELIDS.
nudge nudge
?

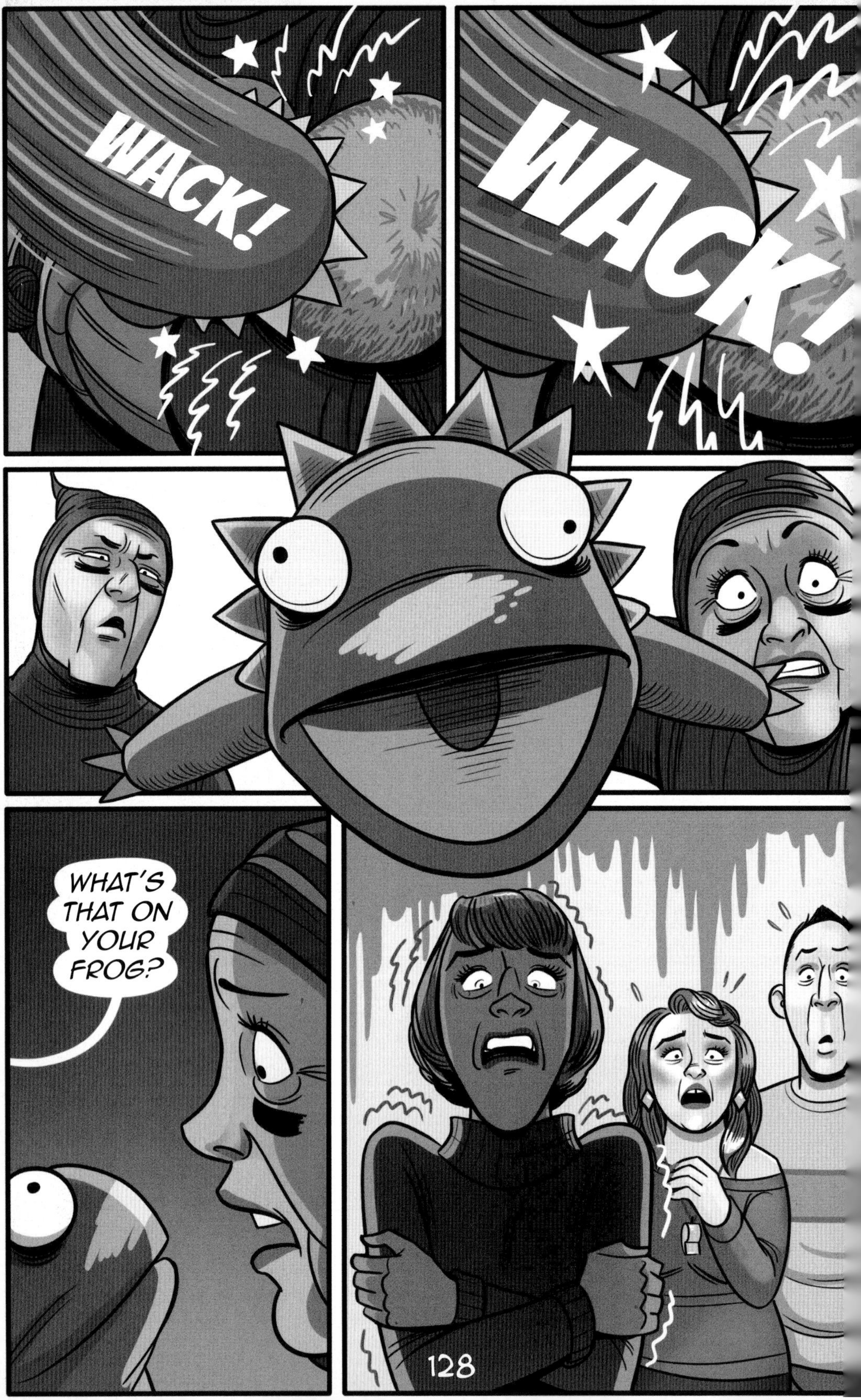
WACK!
WACK!
WHAT'S THAT ON YOUR FROG?

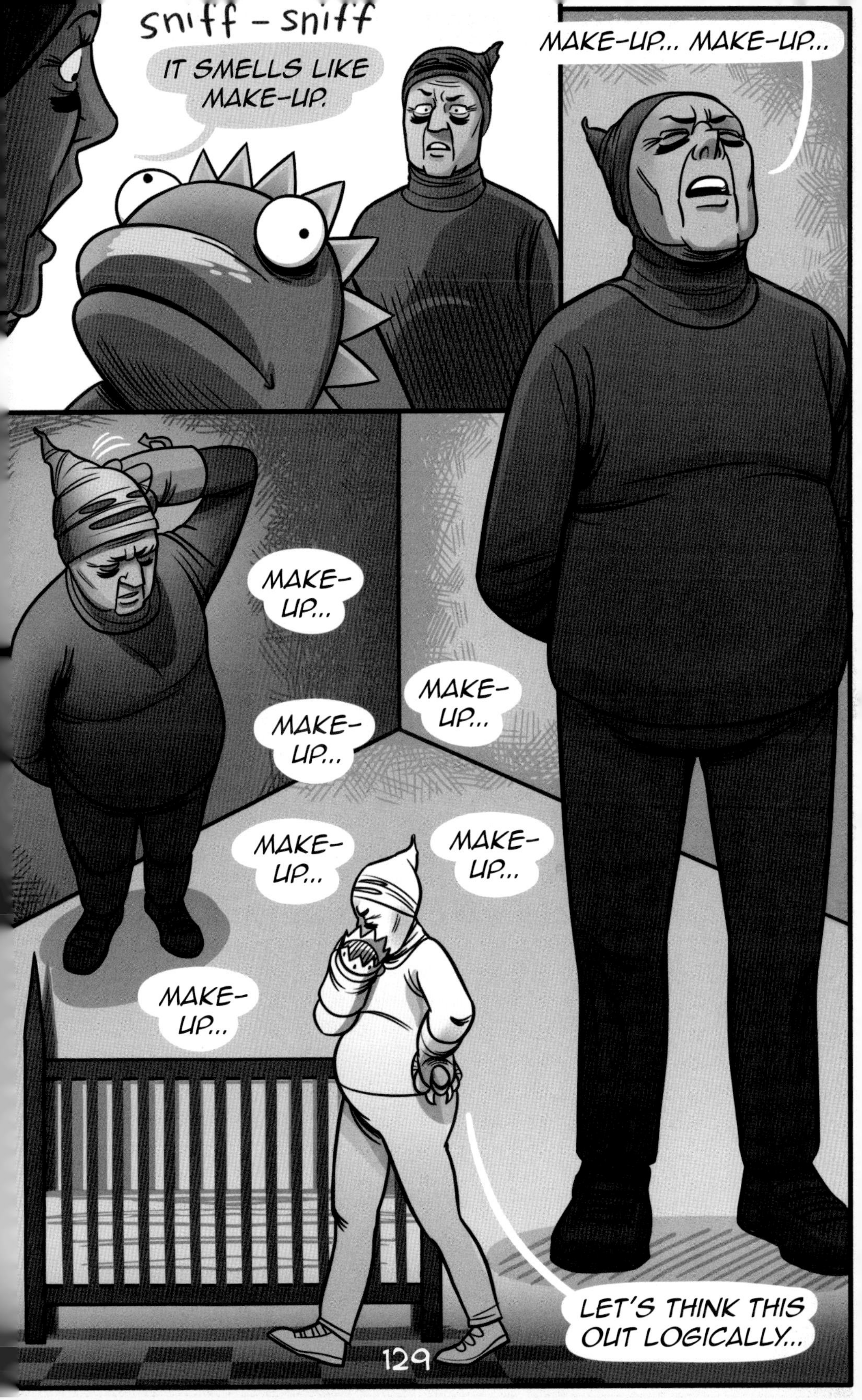
sniff - sniff
IT SMELLS LIKE MAKE-UP.
MAKE-UP... MAKE-UP...
MAKE-UP...
MAKE-UP...
MAKE-UP...
MAKE-UP...
MAKE-UP...
MAKE-UP...
LET'S THINK THIS OUT LOGICALLY...

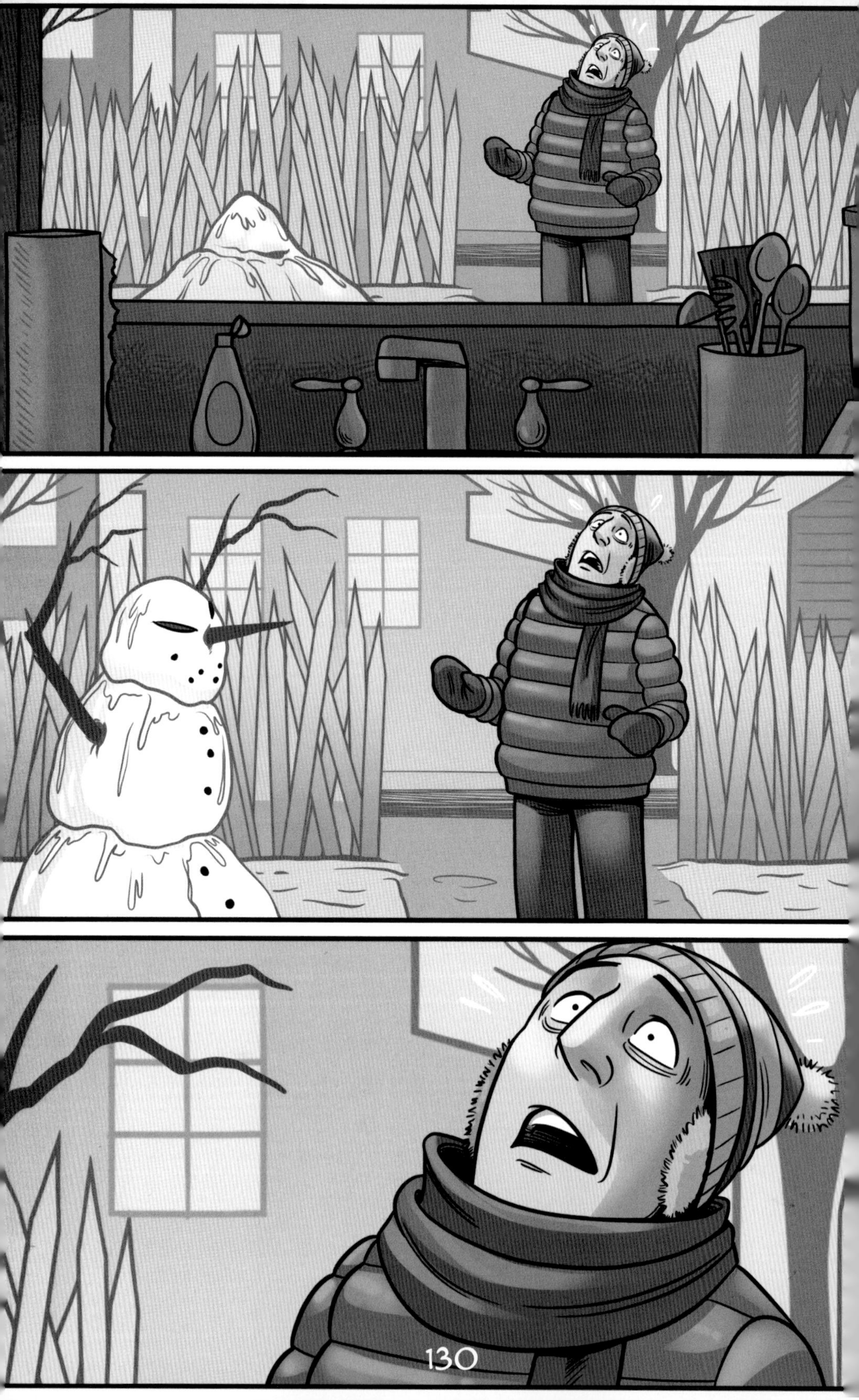

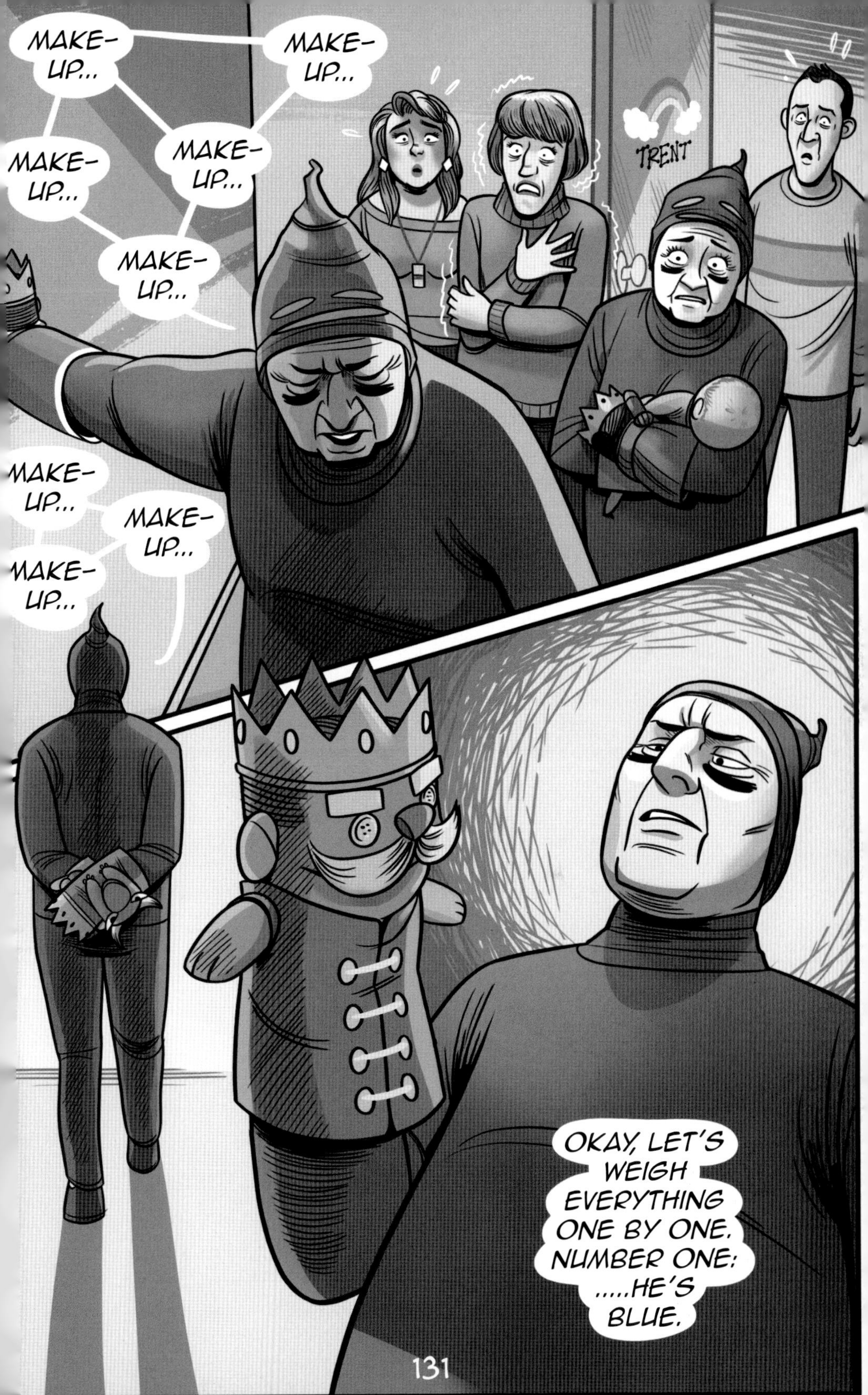
MAKE-UP...
MAKE-UP...
MAKE-UP...
MAKE-UP...
MAKE-UP...
TRENT
MAKE-UP...
MAKE-UP...
MAKE-UP...
OKAY, LET'S WEIGH EVERYTHING ONE BY ONE. NUMBER ONE: .....HE'S BLUE.

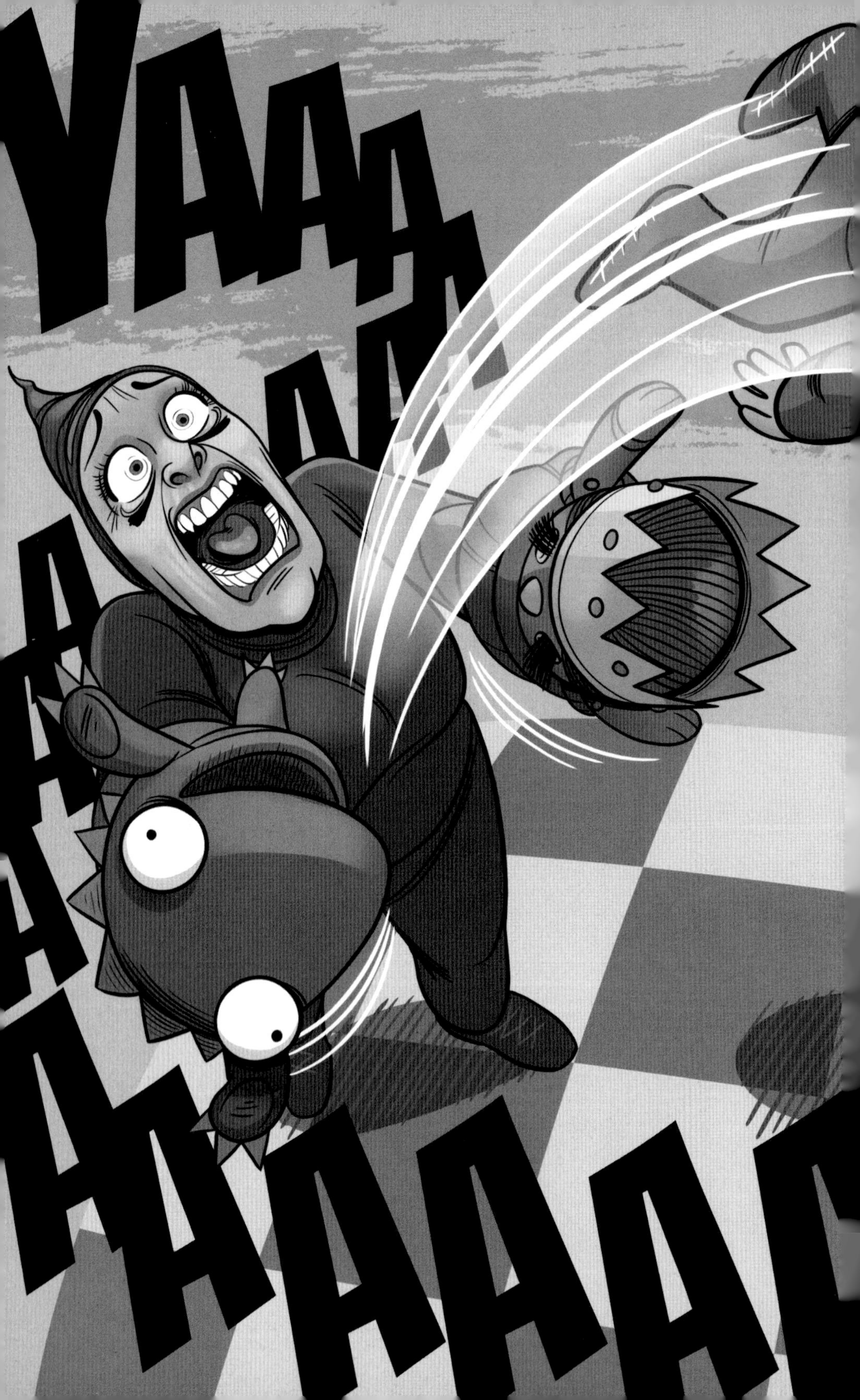
YAAAAAAAAAAAAAAA

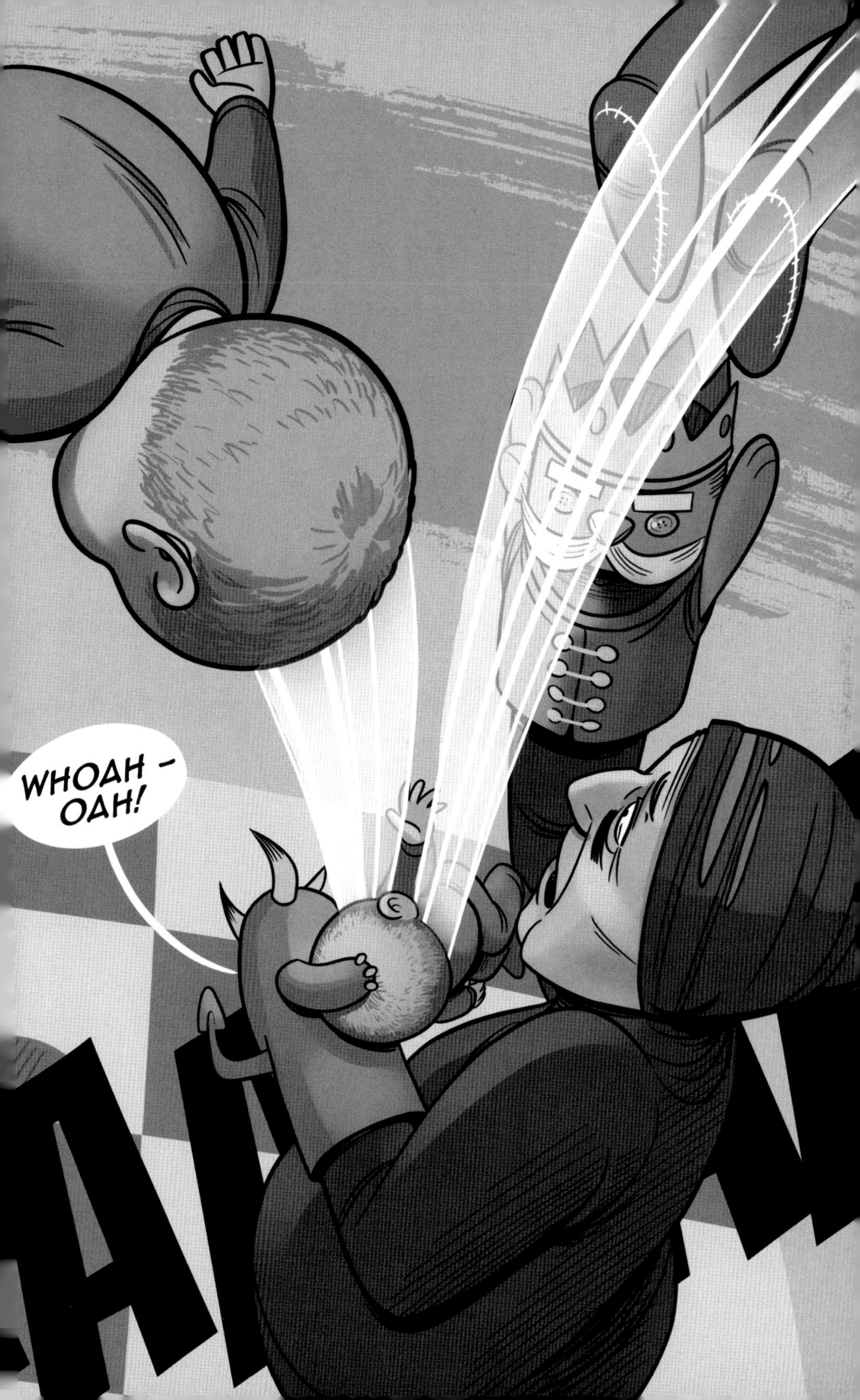
WHOAH - OAH!

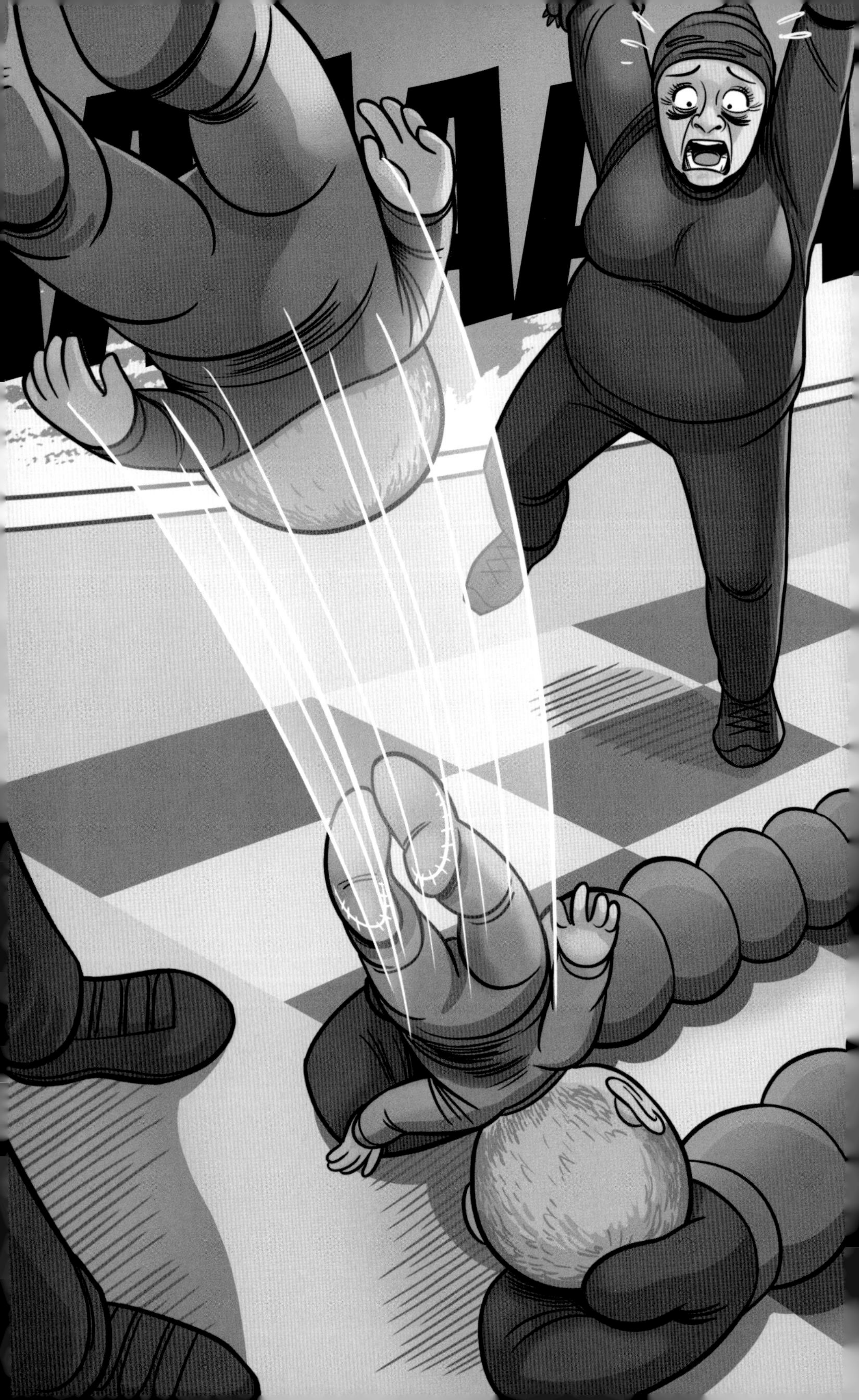

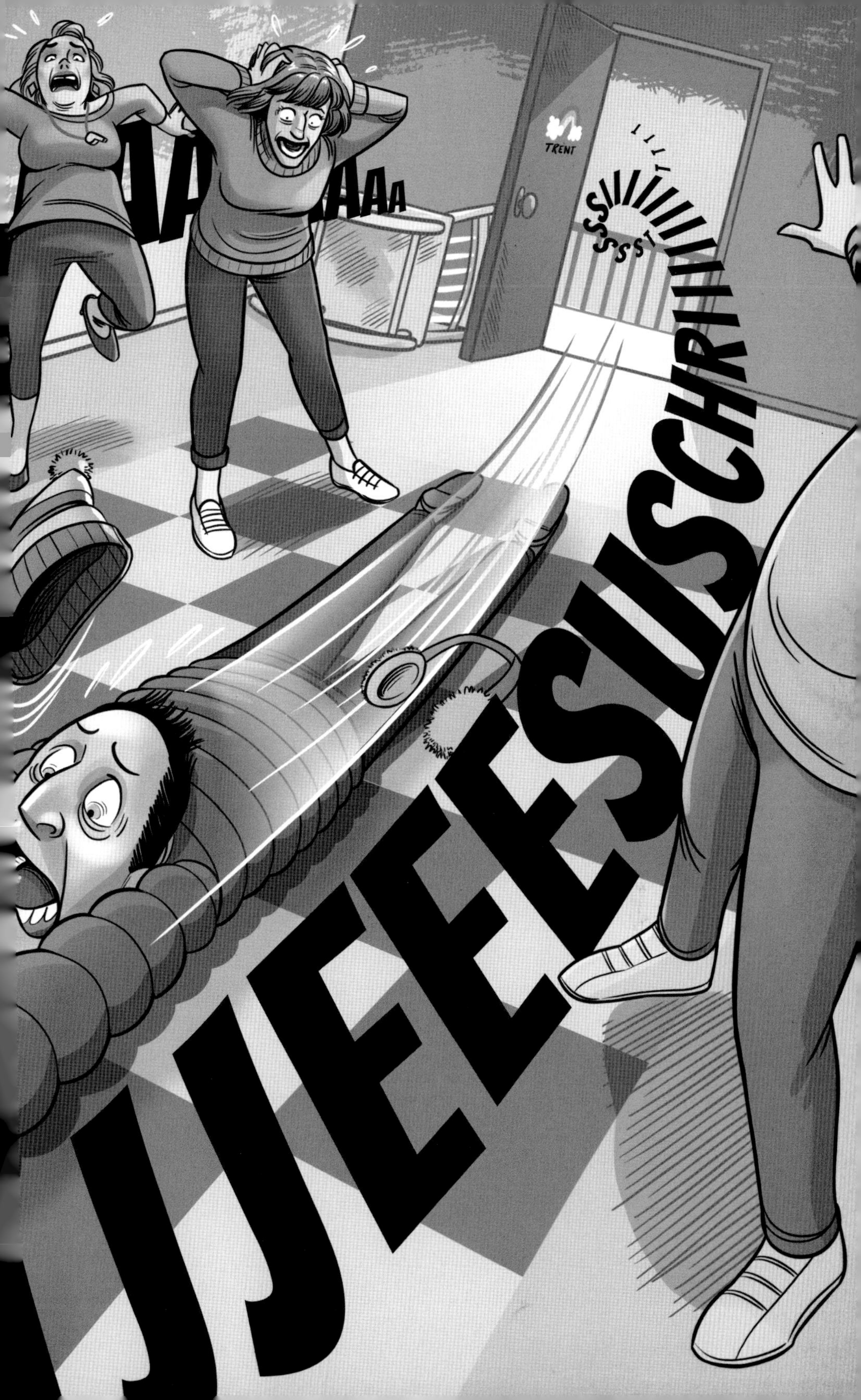
AA
AAAa
TRENT
SSSSSST
JJEEESUSCHRIIIIIIIIIII

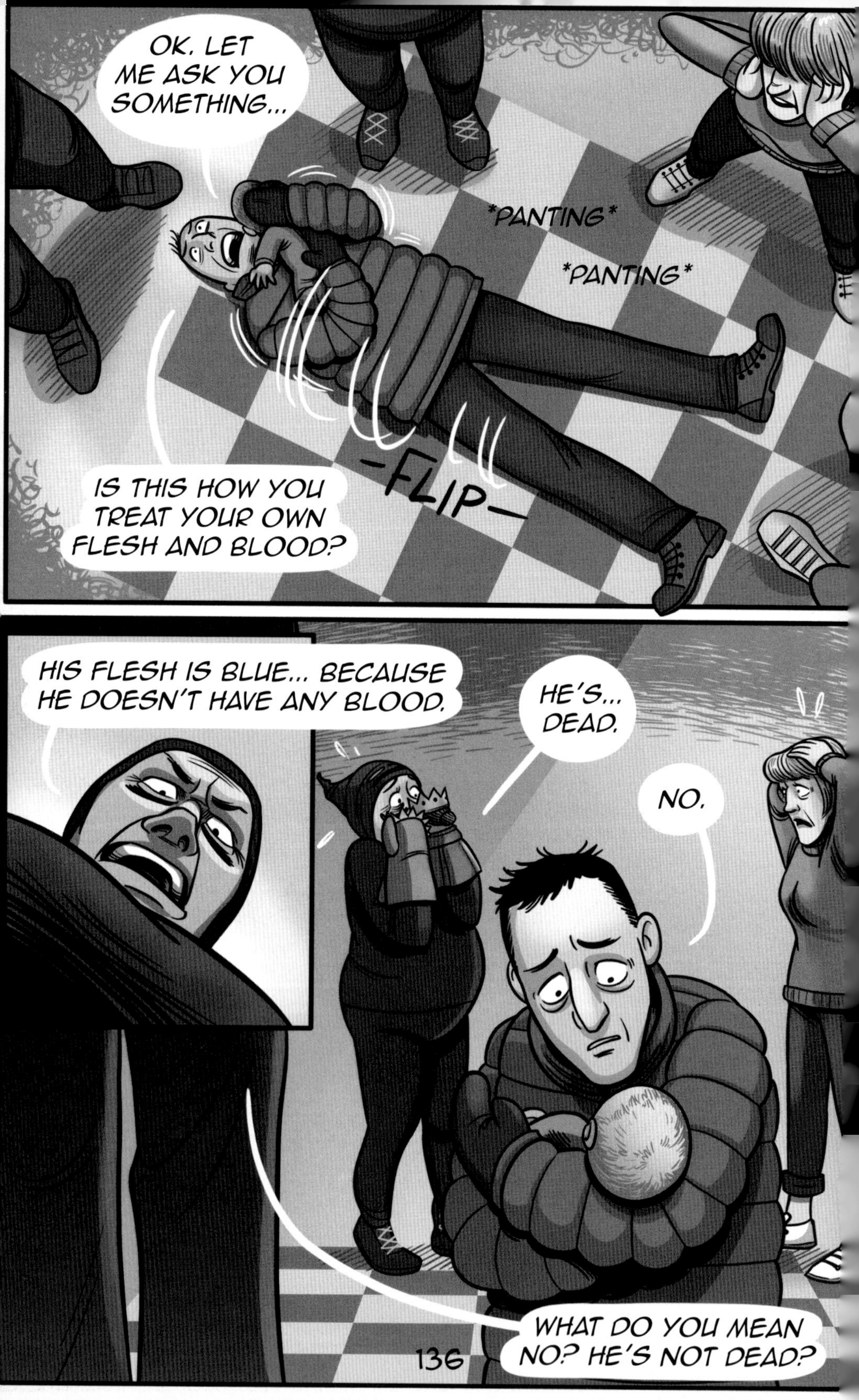
OK, LET ME ASK YOU SOMETHING...
PANTING
PANTING
-FLIP-
IS THIS HOW YOU TREAT YOUR OWN FLESH AND BLOOD?
HIS FLESH IS BLUE... BECAUSE HE DOESN'T HAVE ANY BLOOD.
HE'S... DEAD.
NO.
WHAT DO YOU MEAN NO? HE'S NOT DEAD?

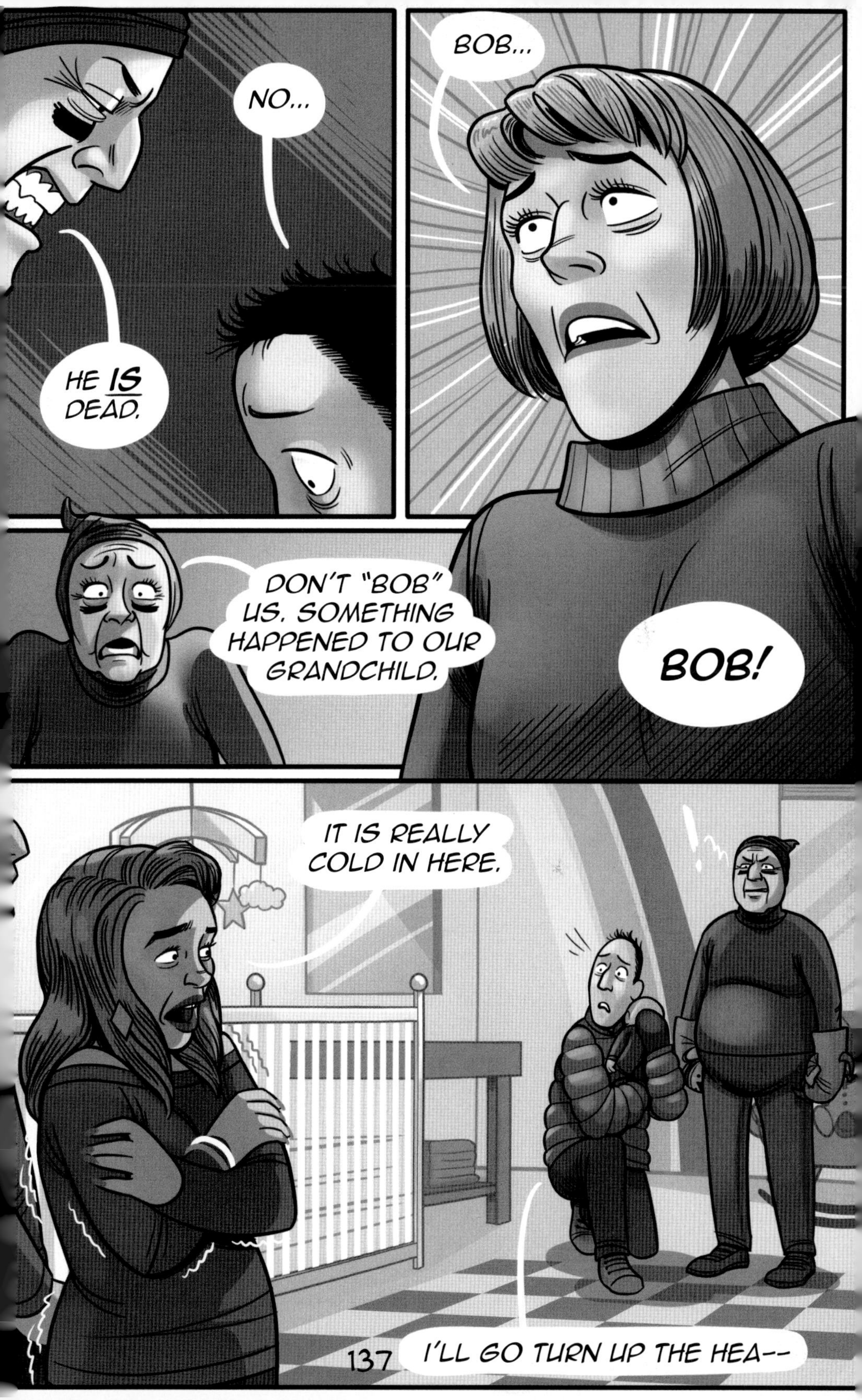
NO...
HE **IS** DEAD.
BOB...
DON'T "BOB" US. SOMETHING HAPPENED TO OUR GRANDCHILD.
BOB!
IT IS REALLY COLD IN HERE.
I'LL GO TURN UP THE HEA--

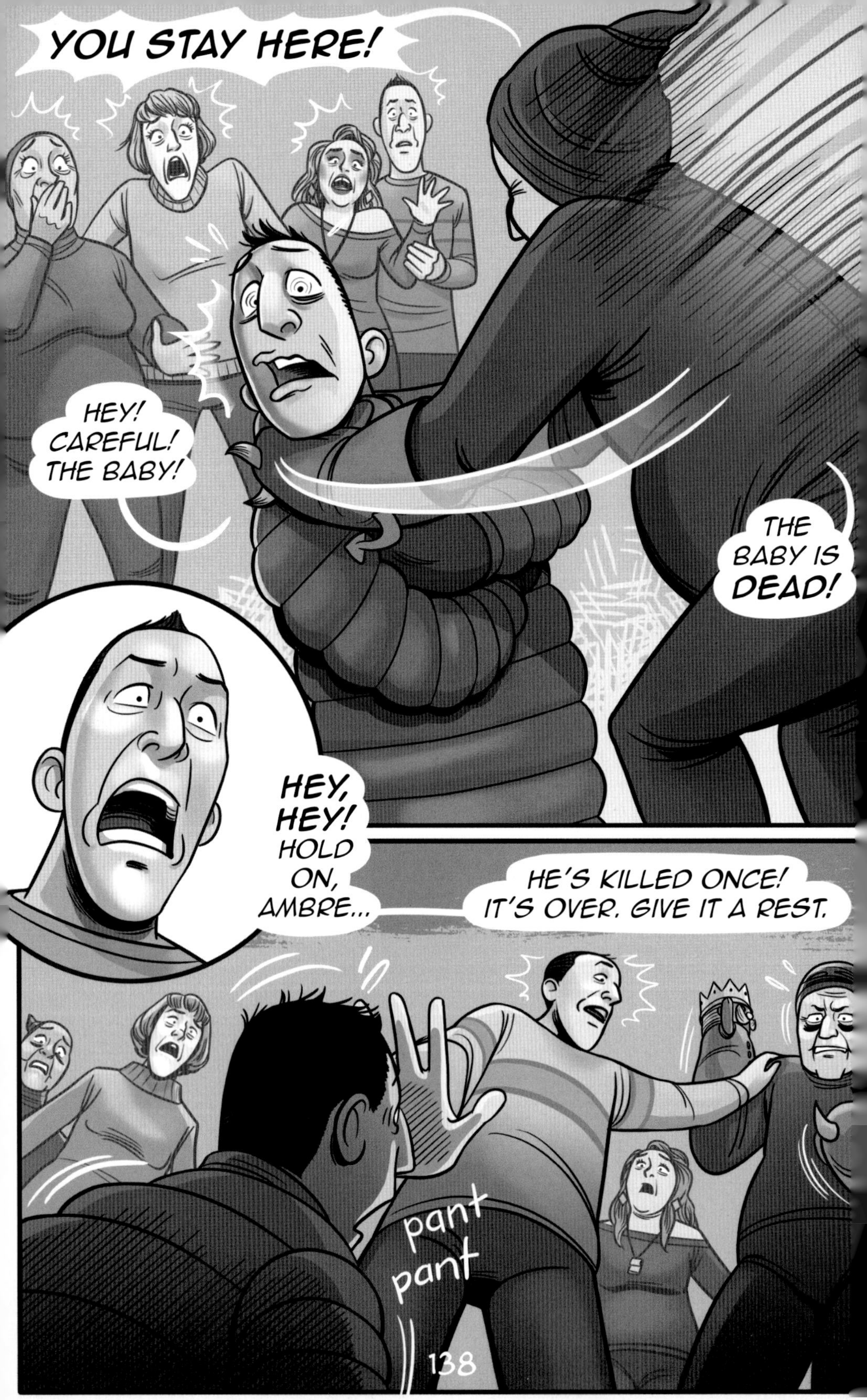

YOU STAY HERE!
HEY! CAREFUL! THE BABY!
THE BABY IS DEAD!
HEY, HEY! HOLD ON, AMBRE...
HE'S KILLED ONCE! IT'S OVER. GIVE IT A REST.
pant pant

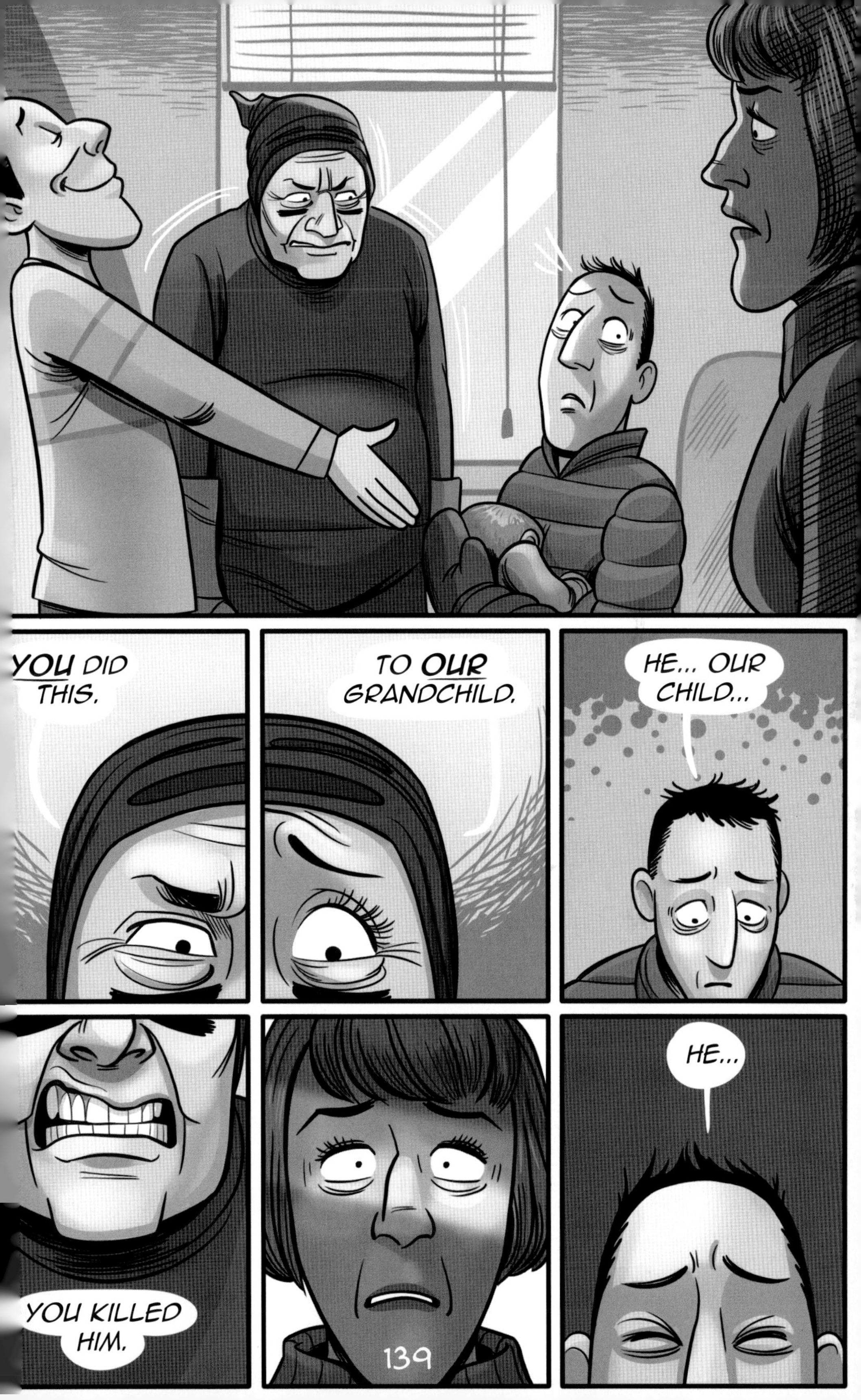
YOU DID THIS.
TO OUR GRANDCHILD.
HE... OUR CHILD...
YOU KILLED HIM.
HE...

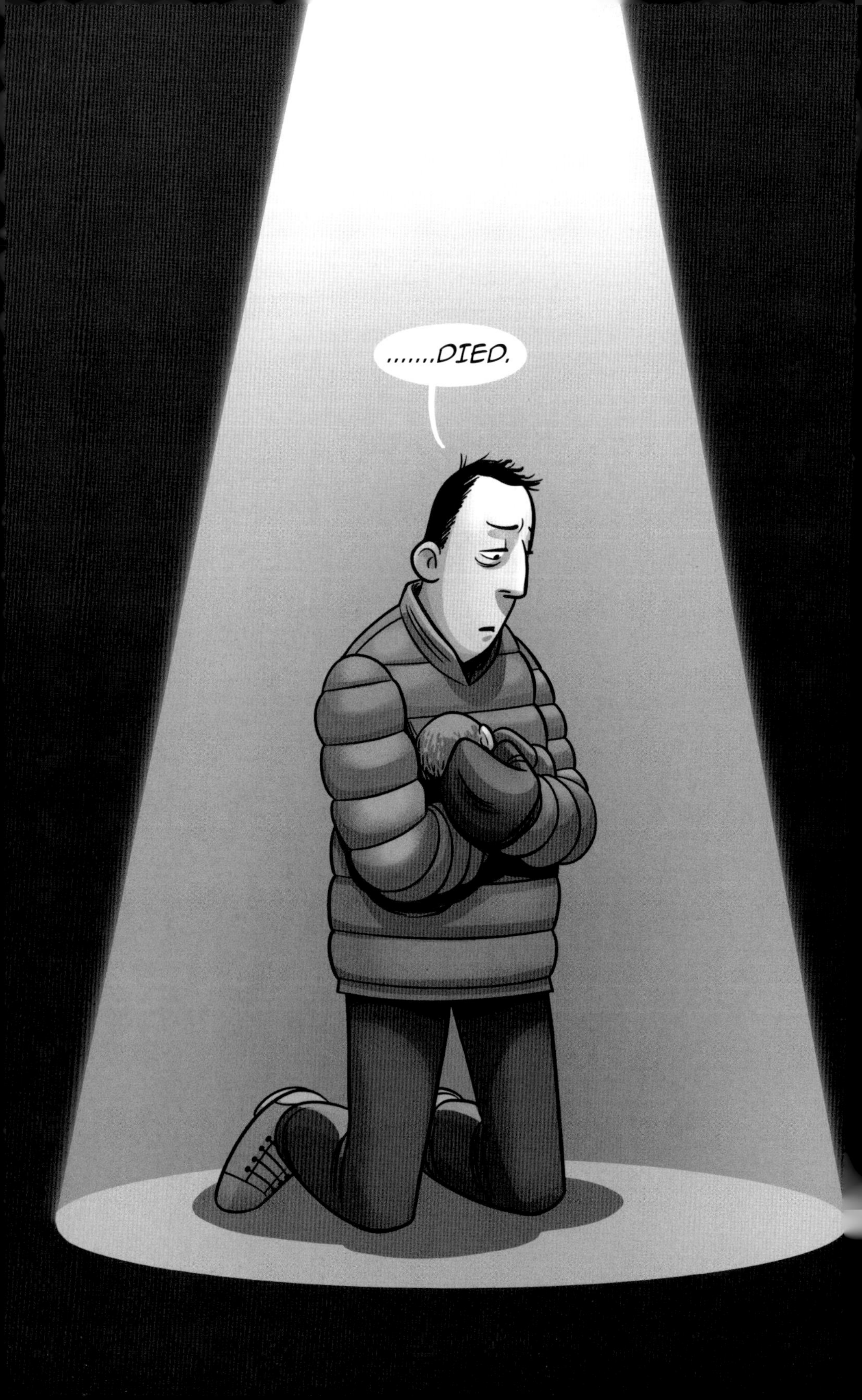
.......DIED.

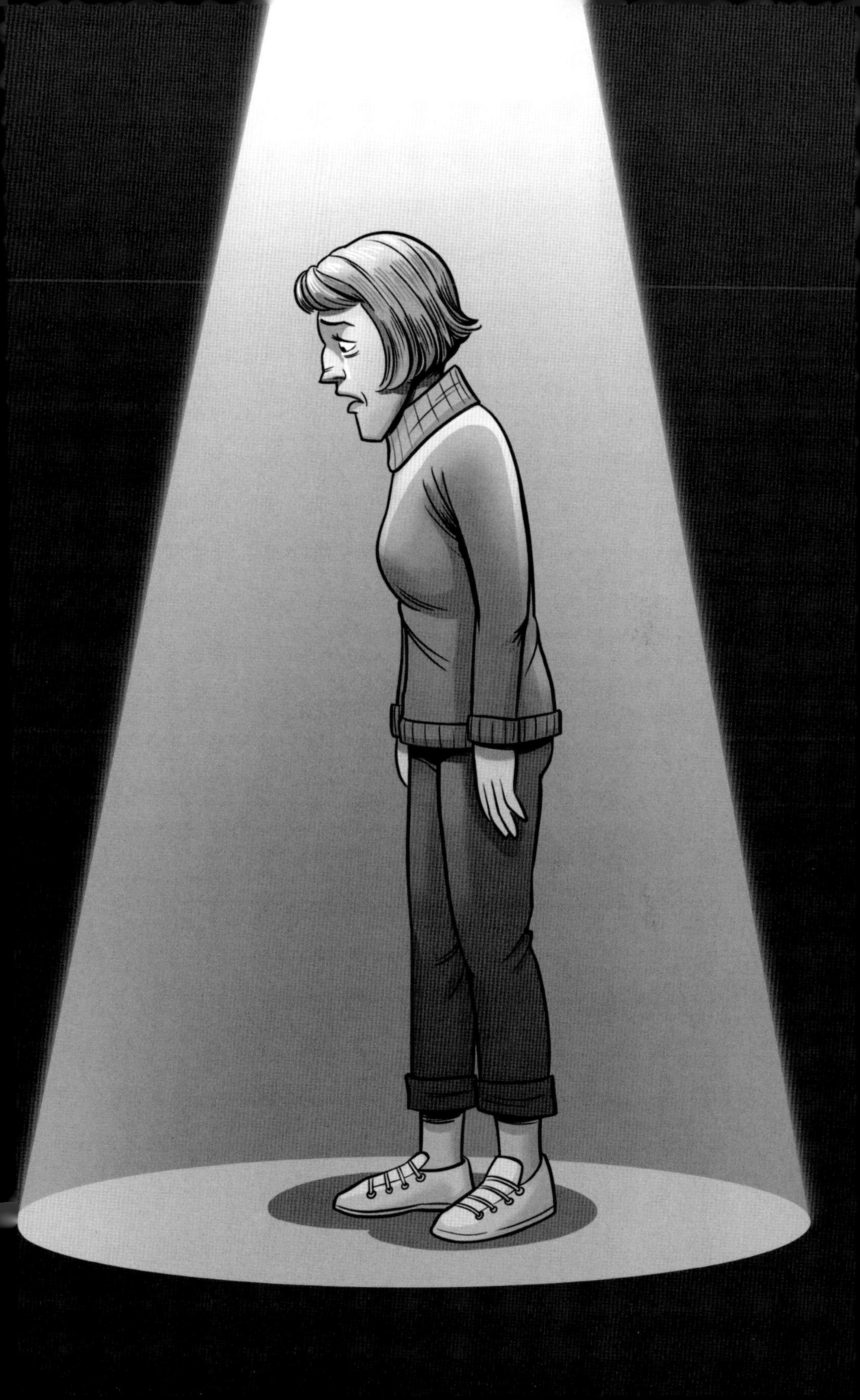

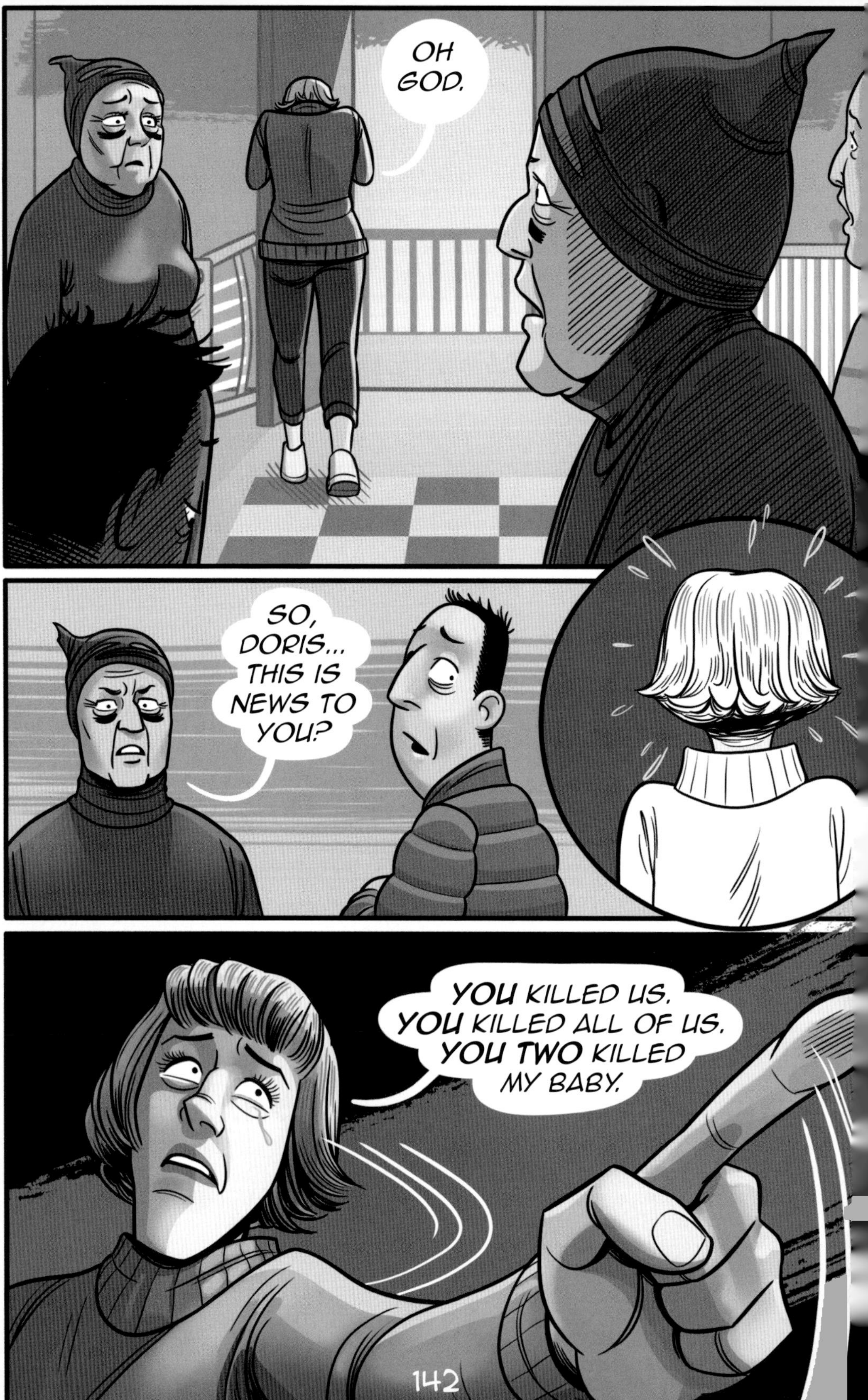
OH GOD.
SO, DORIS... THIS IS NEWS TO YOU?
YOU KILLED US. YOU KILLED ALL OF US. YOU TWO KILLED MY BABY.

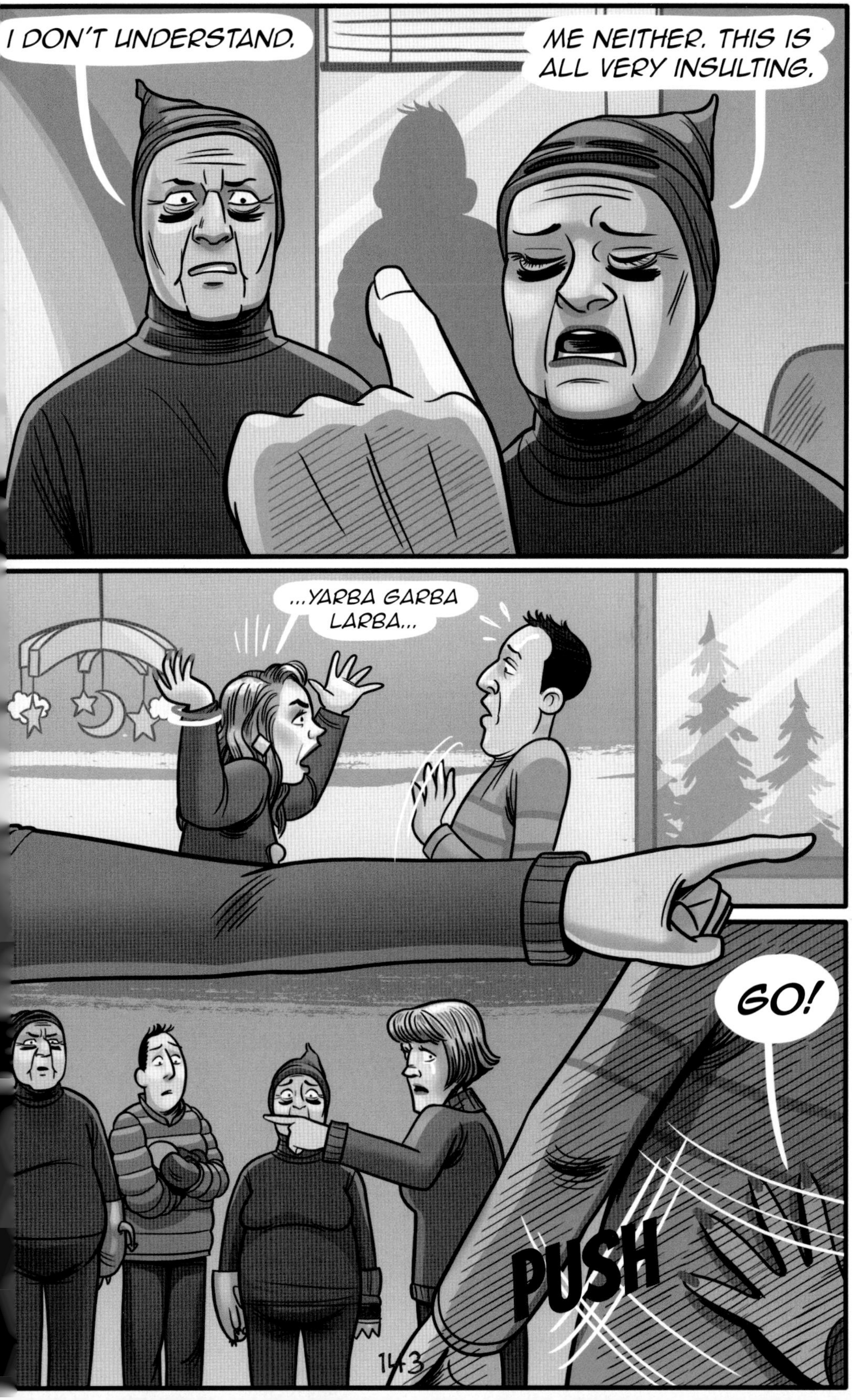
I DON'T UNDERSTAND.
ME NEITHER. THIS IS ALL VERY INSULTING.
...YARBA GARBA LARBA...
GO!
PUSH

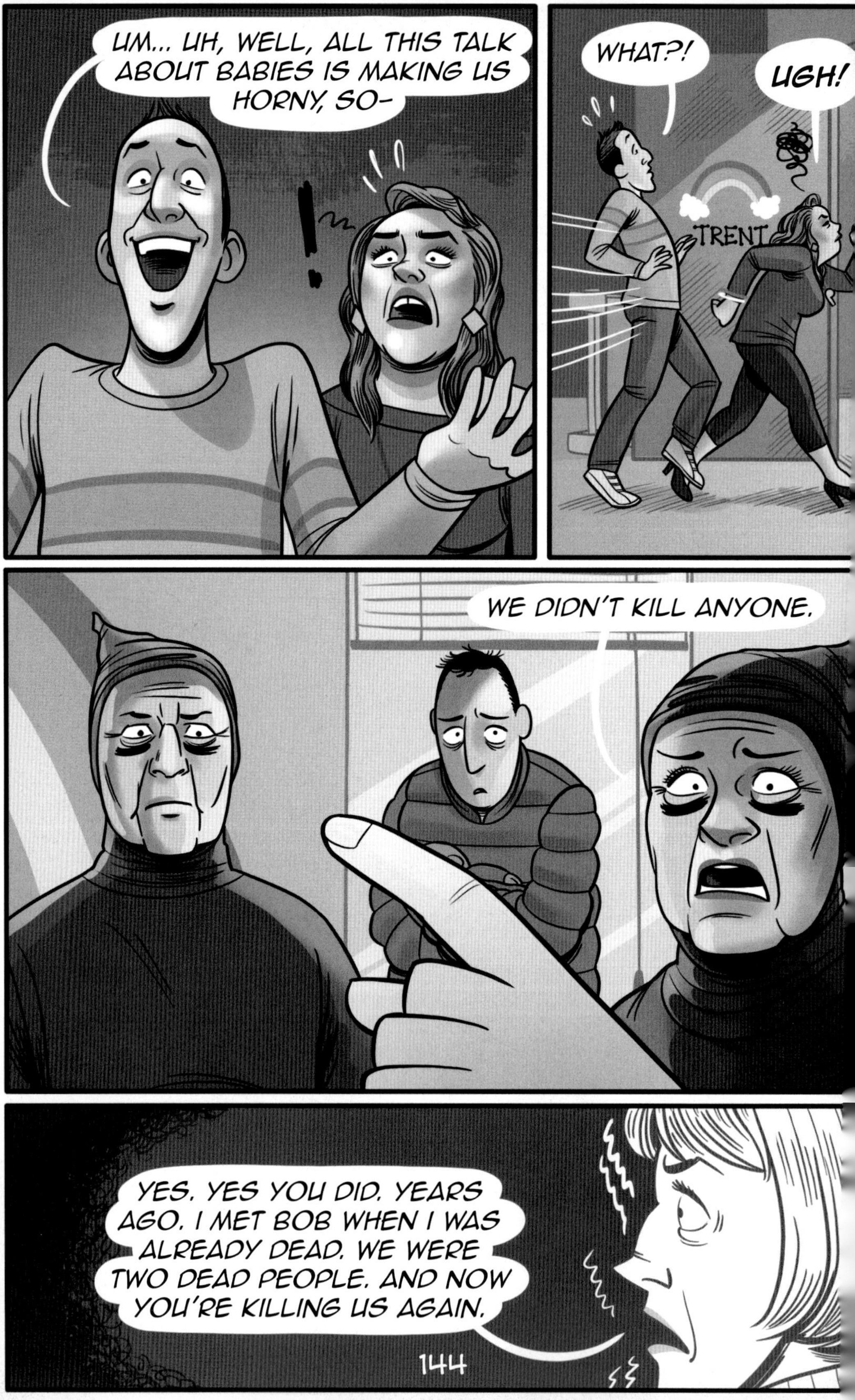
UM... UH, WELL, ALL THIS TALK ABOUT BABIES IS MAKING US HORNY, SO-
WHAT?!
UGH!
TRENT
WE DIDN'T KILL ANYONE.
YES. YES YOU DID. YEARS AGO. I MET BOB WHEN I WAS ALREADY DEAD. WE WERE TWO DEAD PEOPLE. AND NOW YOU'RE KILLING US AGAIN.

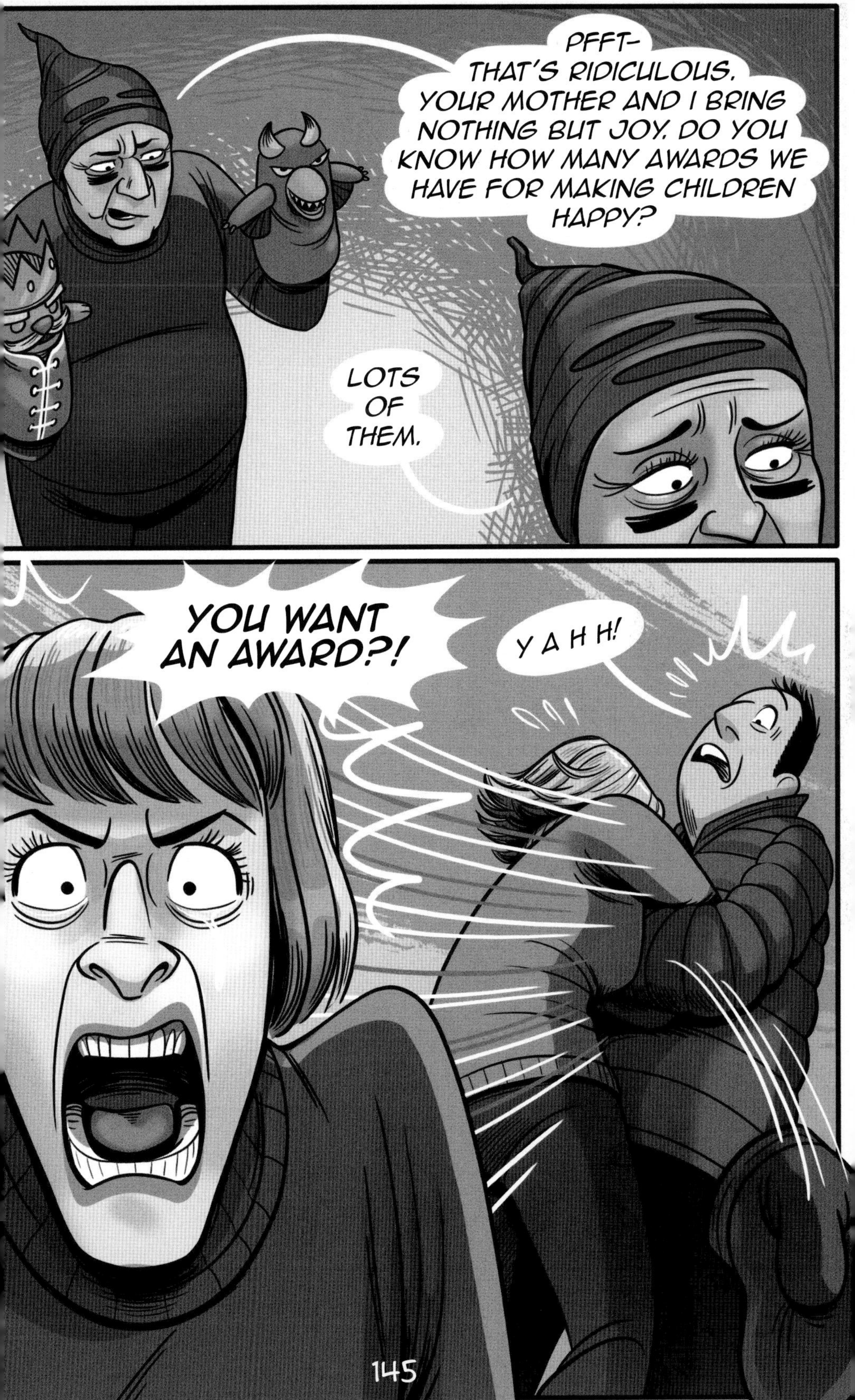
PFFT- THAT'S RIDICULOUS. YOUR MOTHER AND I BRING NOTHING BUT JOY. DO YOU KNOW HOW MANY AWARDS WE HAVE FOR MAKING CHILDREN HAPPY?
LOTS OF THEM.
YOU WANT AN AWARD?!
YAHH!

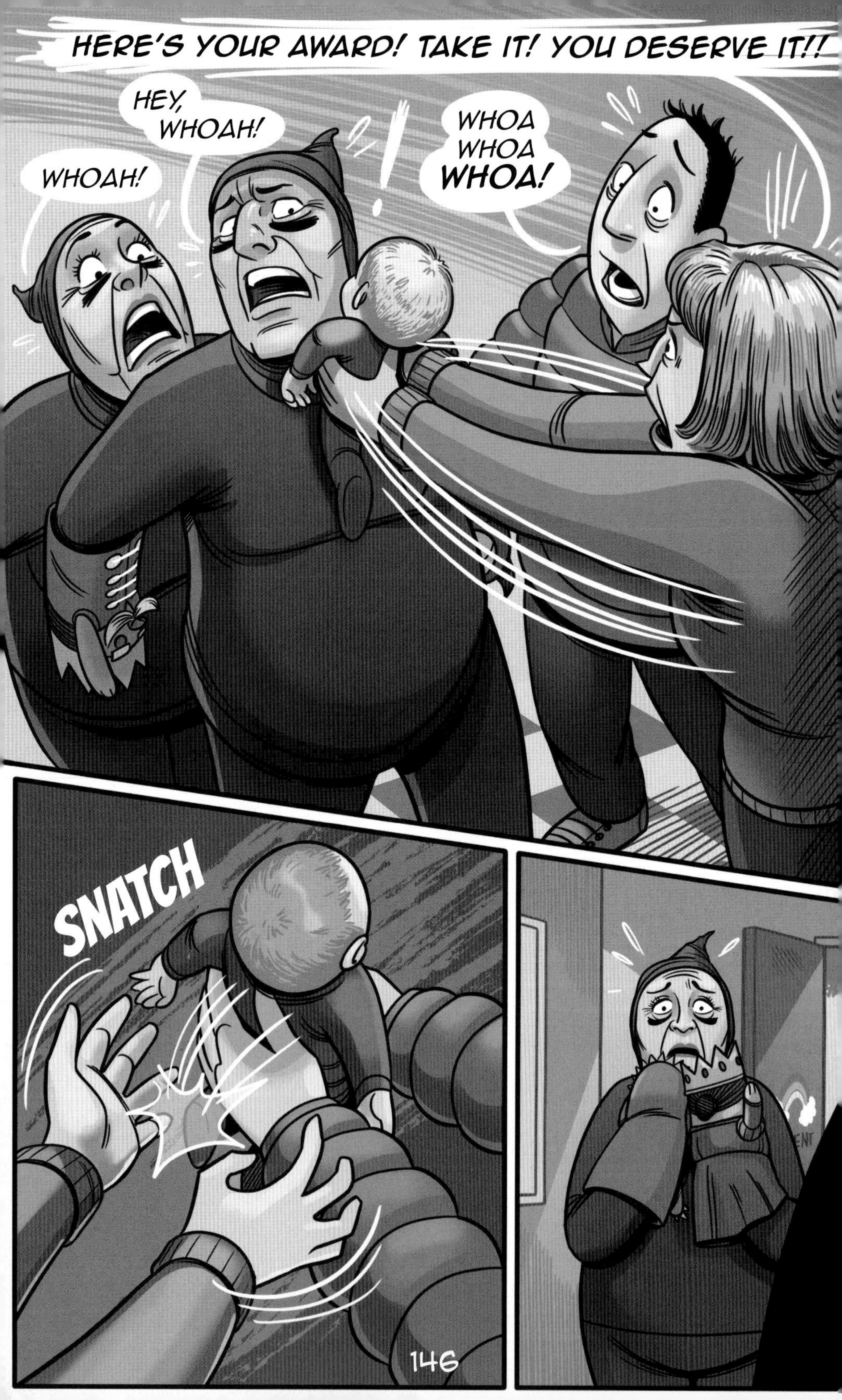
HERE'S YOUR AWARD! TAKE IT! YOU DESERVE IT!!
WHOAH!
HEY, WHOAH!
WHOA WHOA WHOA!
SNATCH

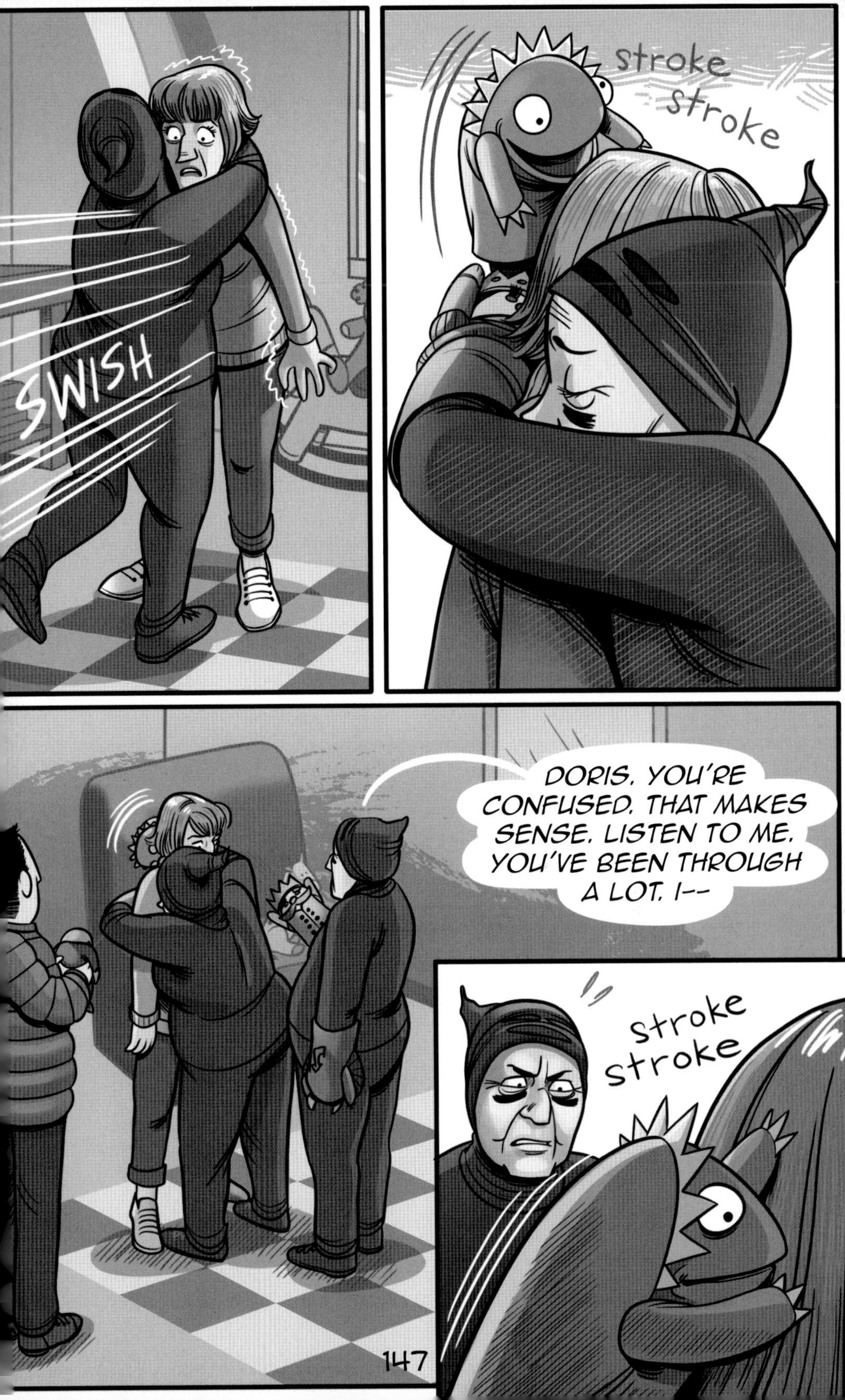
SWISH
stroke
stroke
DORIS. YOU'RE CONFUSED. THAT MAKES SENSE. LISTEN TO ME. YOU'VE BEEN THROUGH A LOT. I--
stroke
stroke

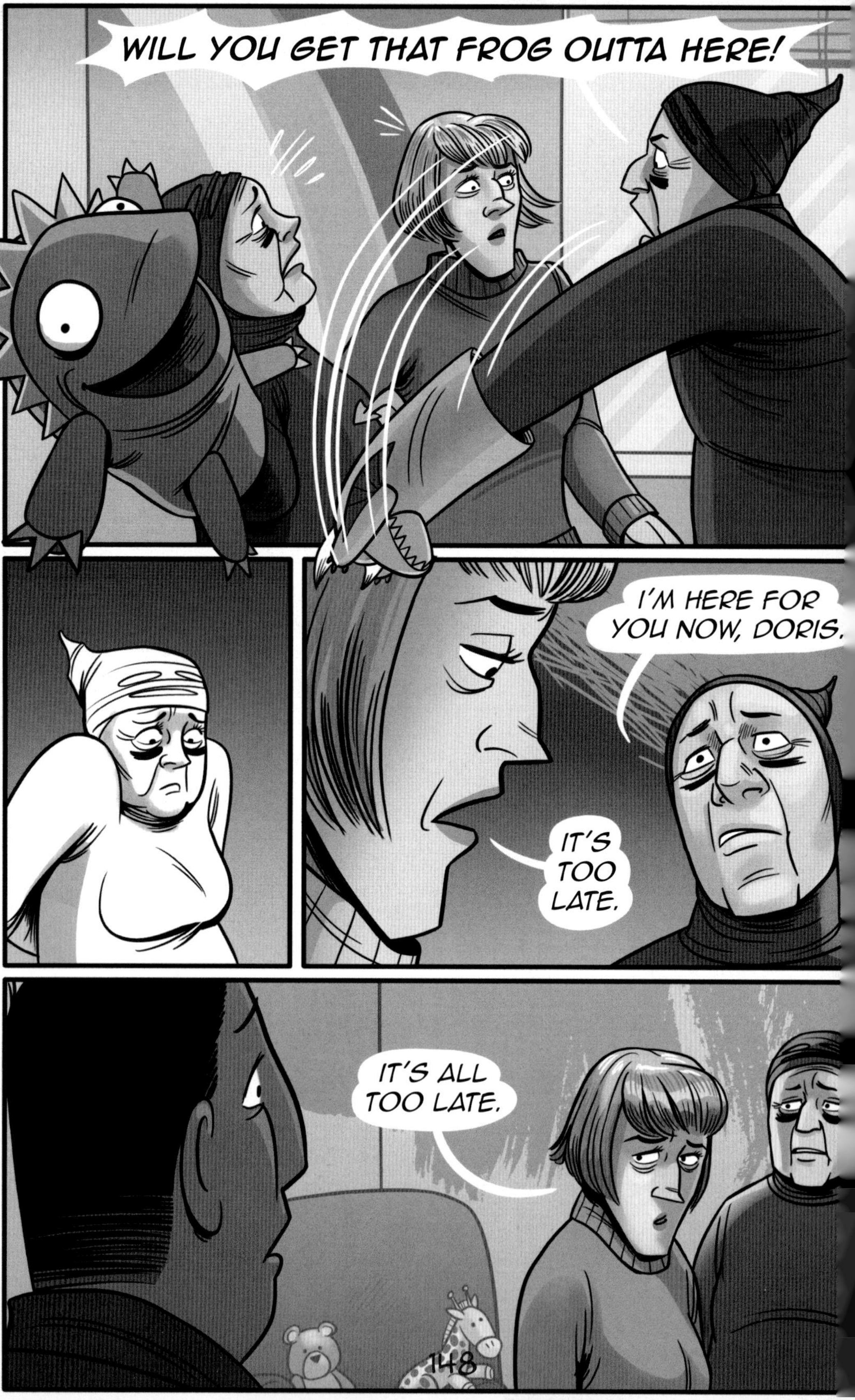

WILL YOU GET THAT FROG OUTTA HERE!
I'M HERE FOR YOU NOW, DORIS.
IT'S TOO LATE.
IT'S ALL TOO LATE.

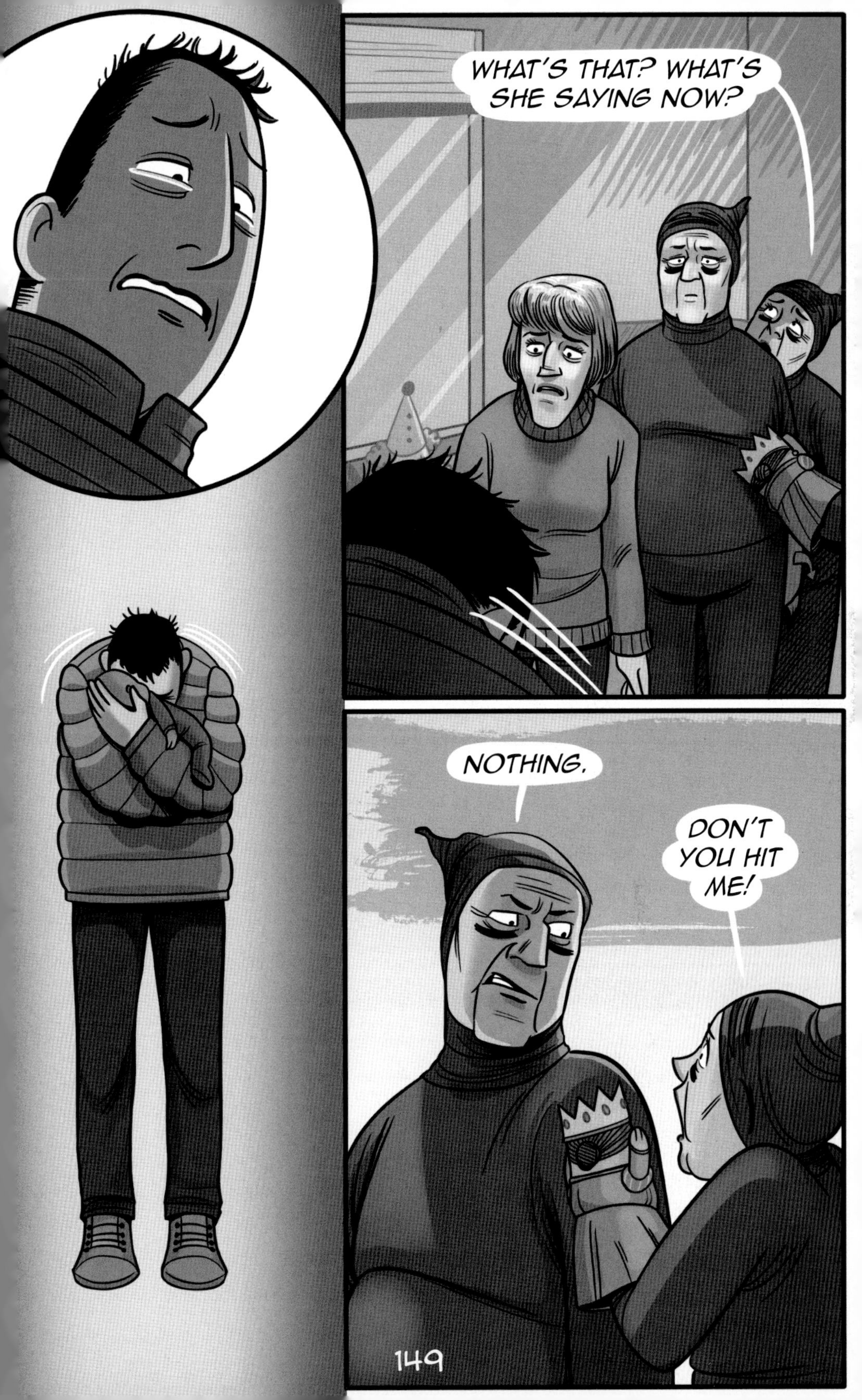
WHAT'S THAT? WHAT'S SHE SAYING NOW?
NOTHING.
DON'T YOU HIT ME!
149

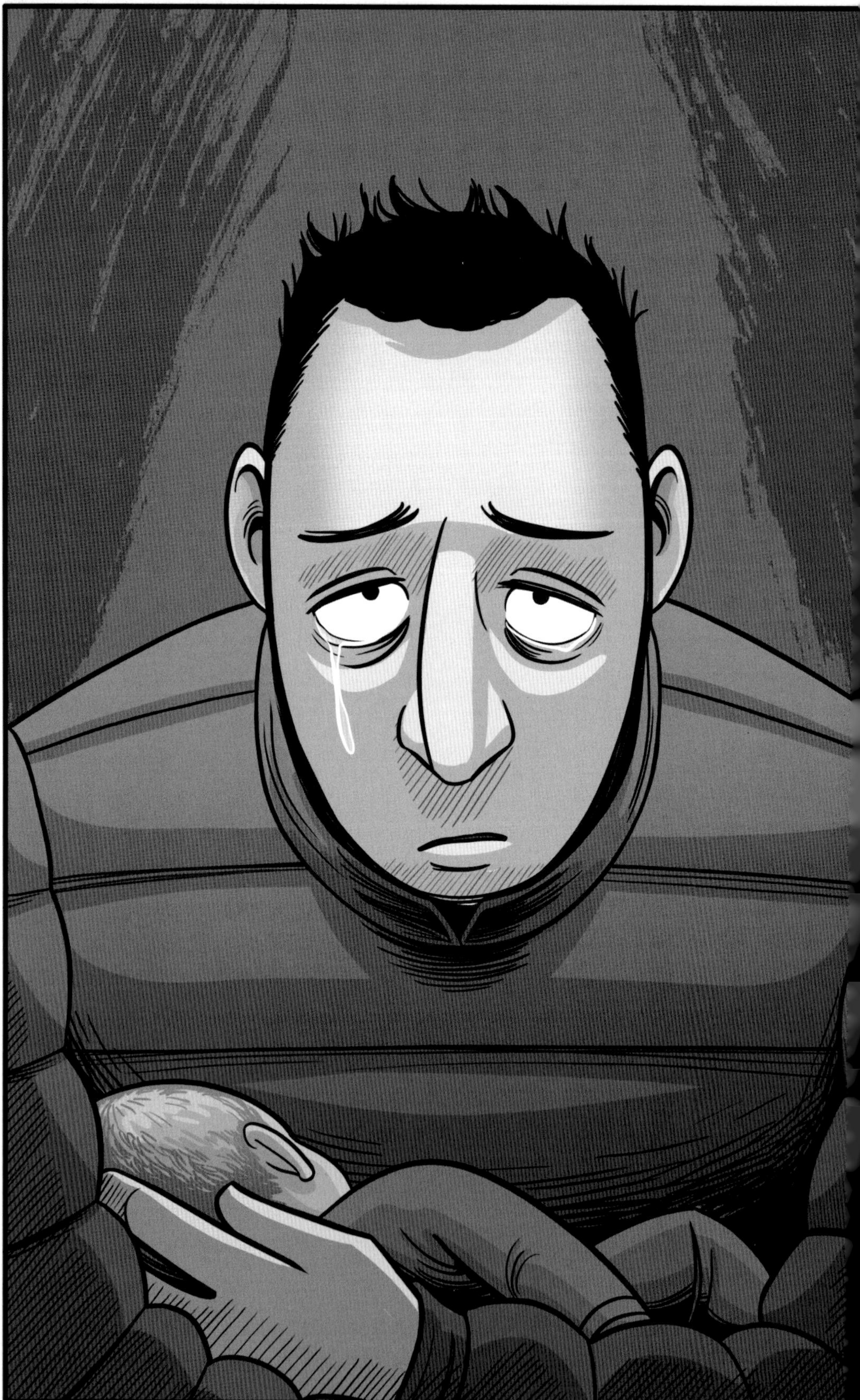

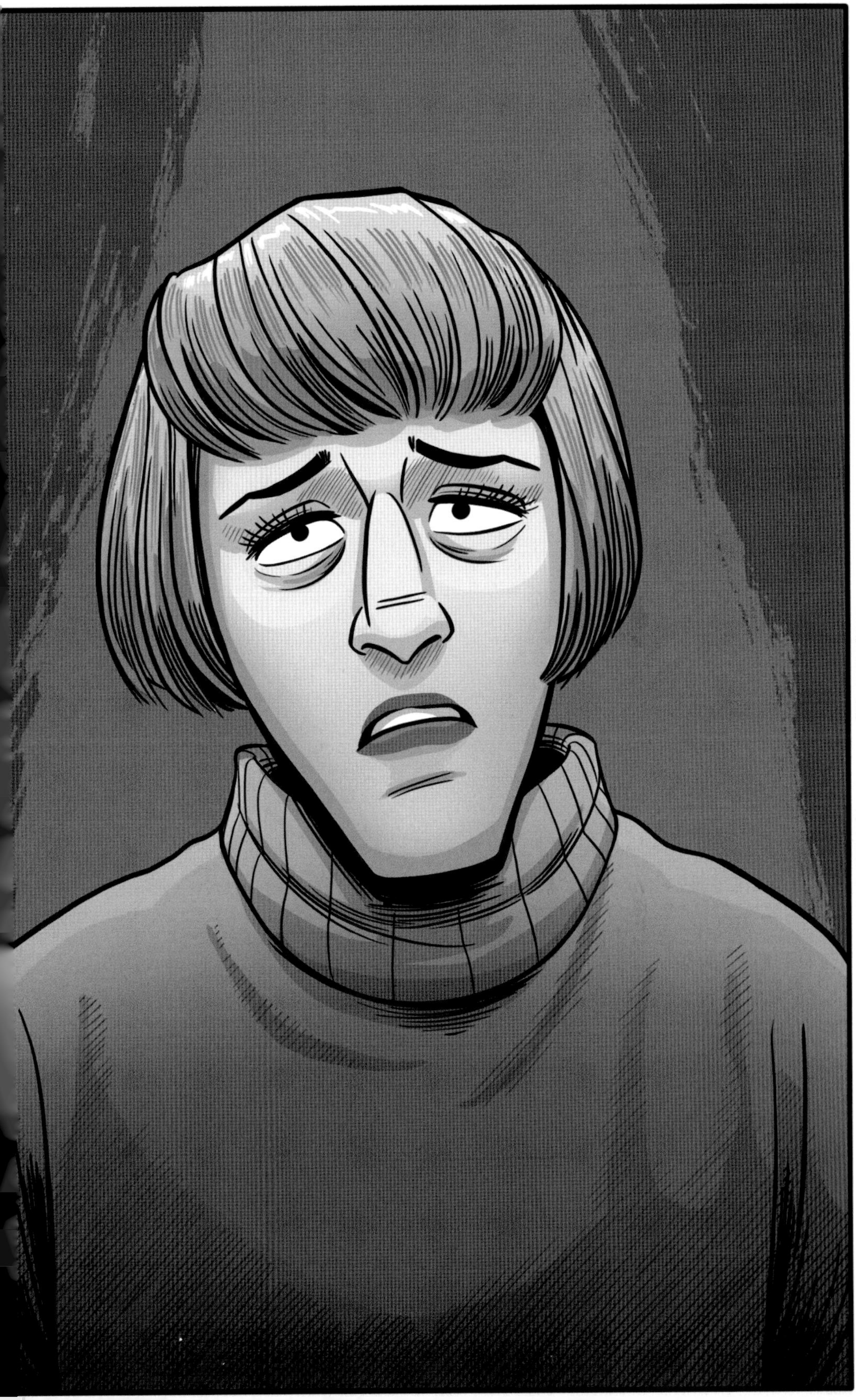

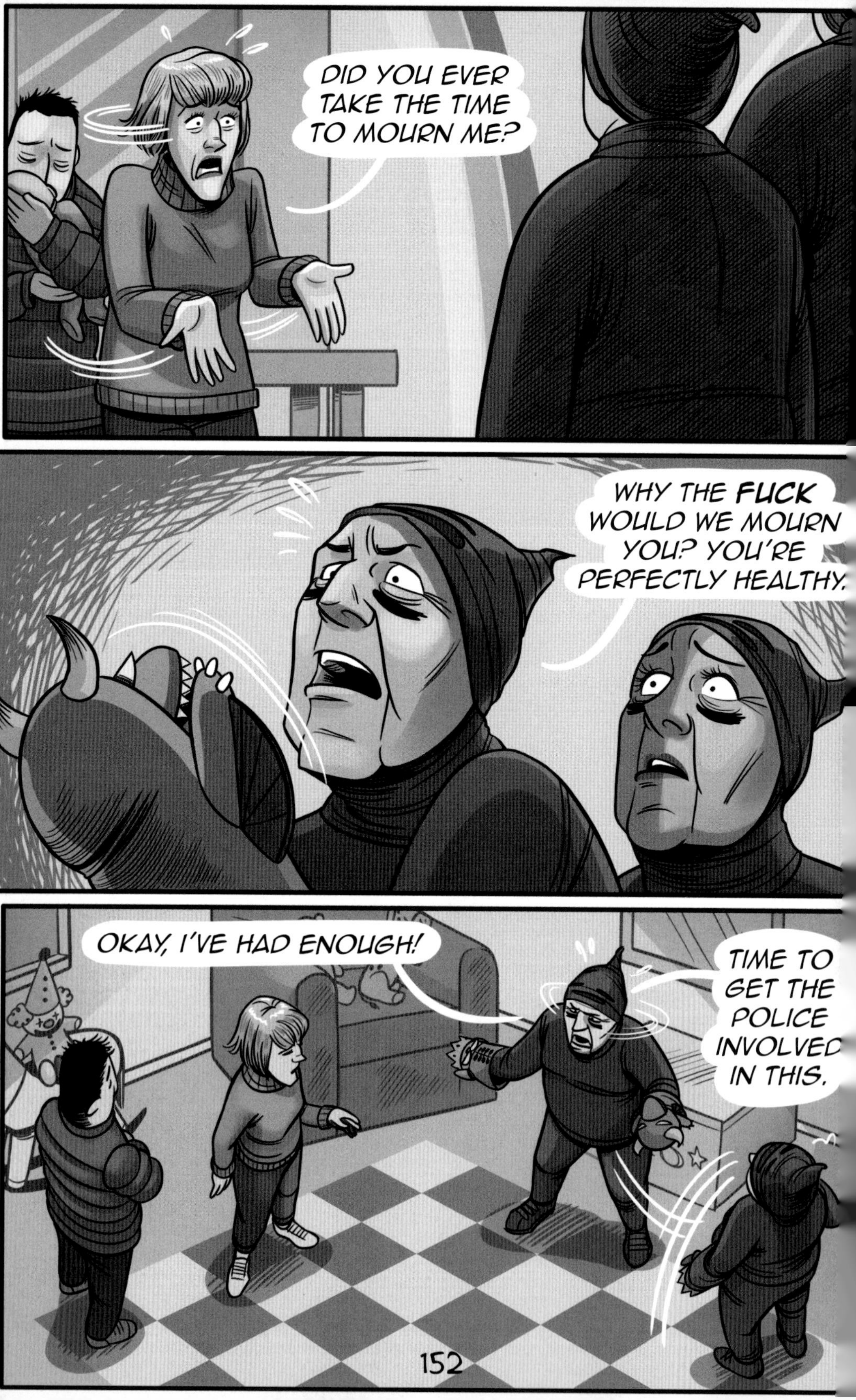
DID YOU EVER TAKE THE TIME TO MOURN ME?
WHY THE **FUCK** WOULD WE MOURN YOU? YOU'RE PERFECTLY HEALTHY.
OKAY, I'VE HAD ENOUGH!
TIME TO GET THE POLICE INVOLVED IN THIS.

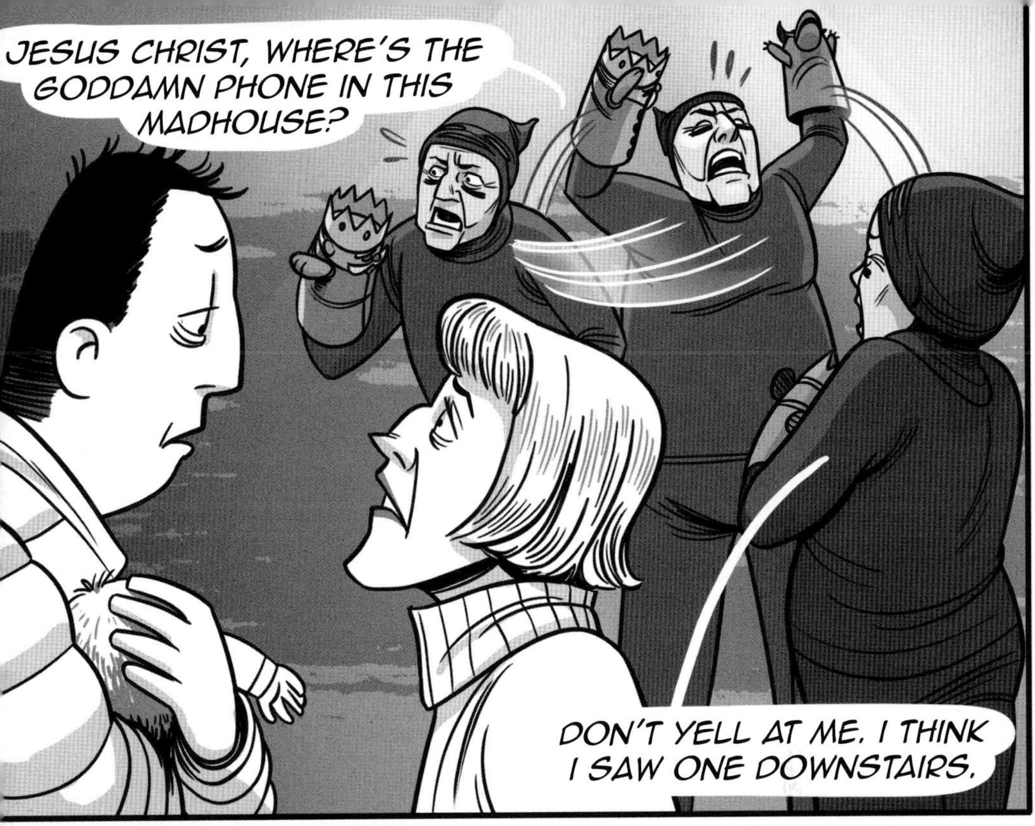
JESUS CHRIST, WHERE'S THE GODDAMN PHONE IN THIS MADHOUSE?
DON'T YELL AT ME. I THINK I SAW ONE DOWNSTAIRS.

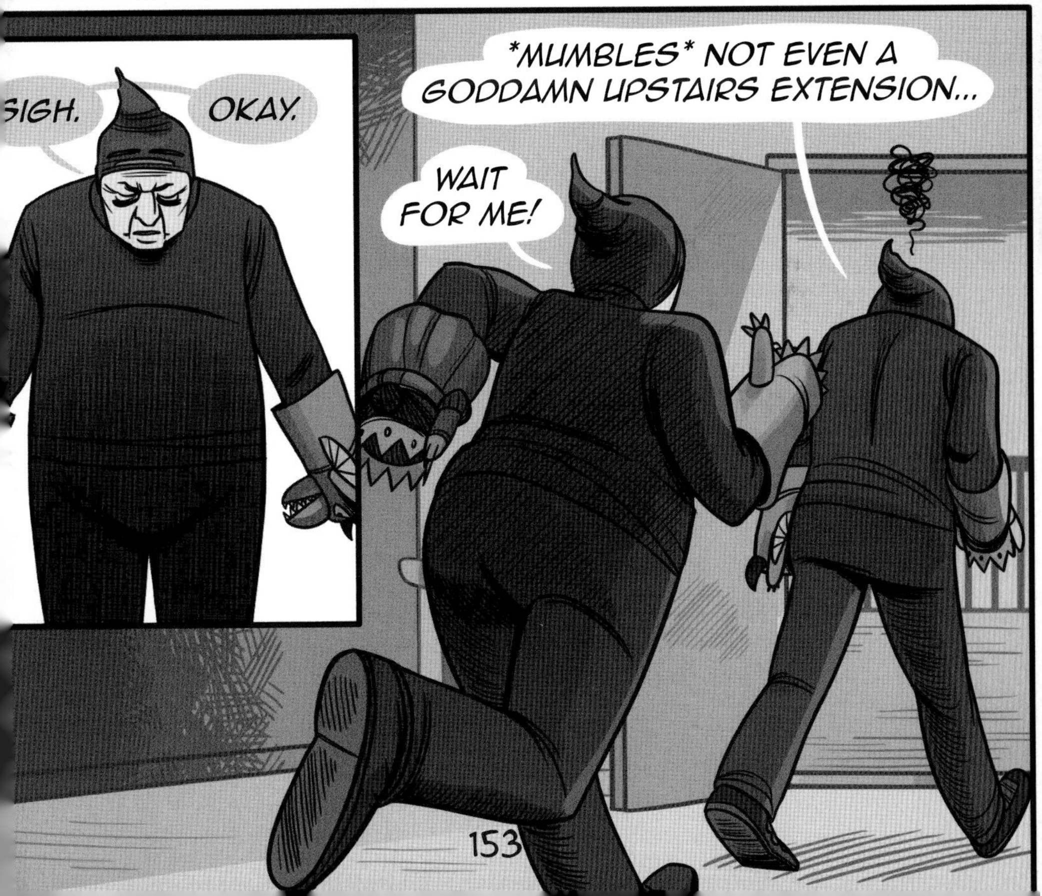
SIGH.
OKAY.
MUMBLES NOT EVEN A GODDAMN UPSTAIRS EXTENSION...
WAIT FOR ME!

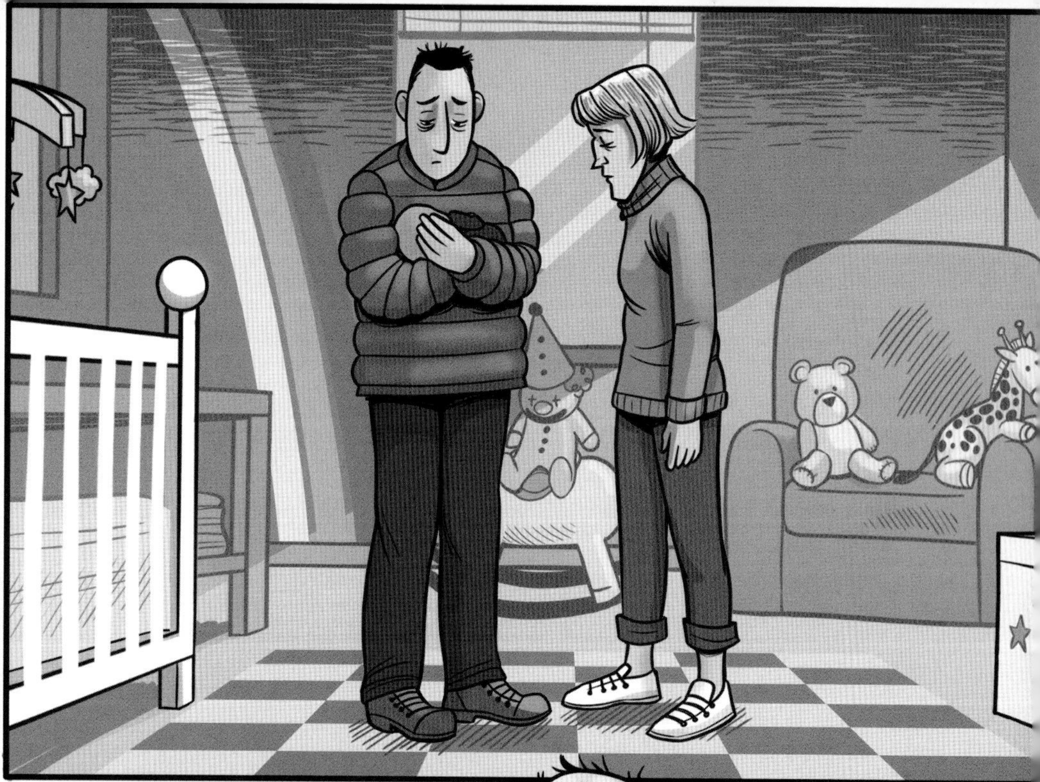

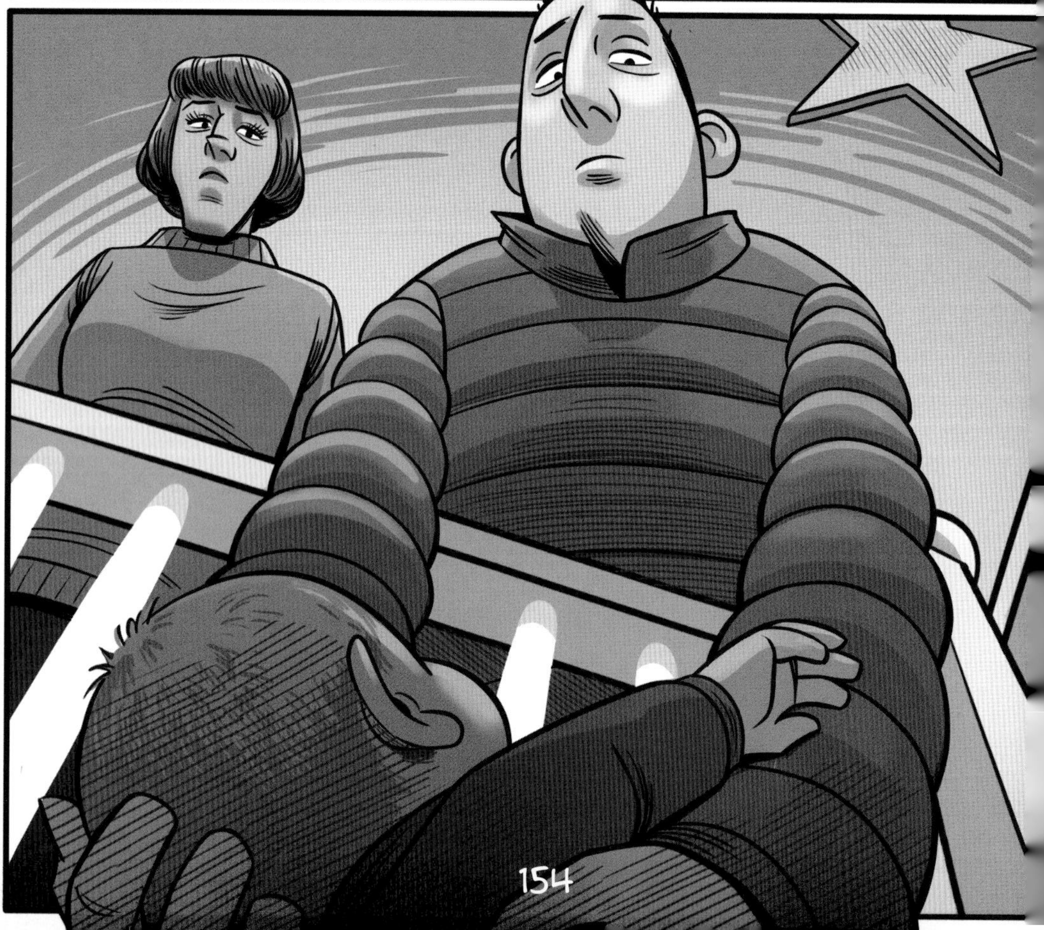

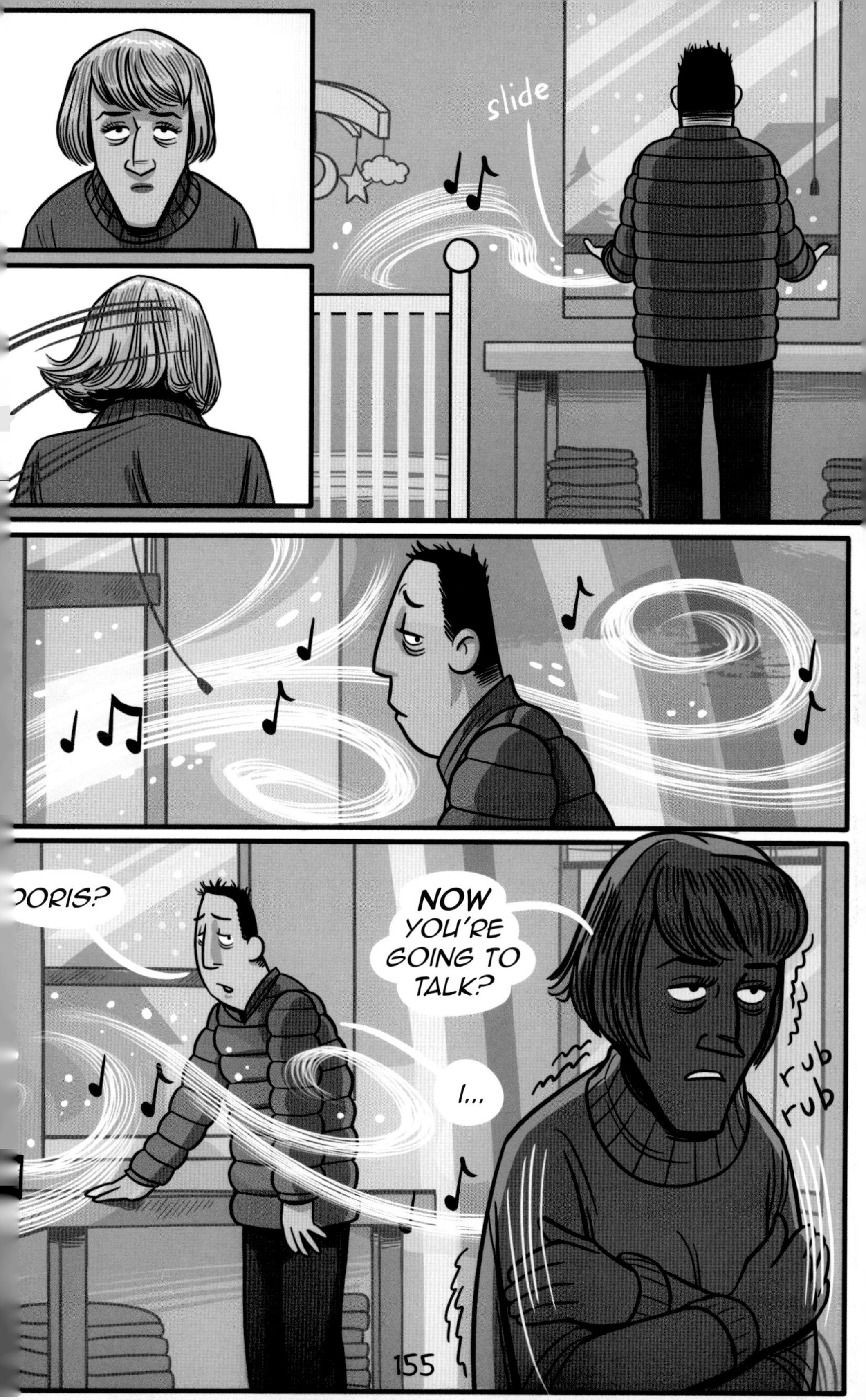
slide
DORIS?
NOW YOU'RE GOING TO TALK?
I...
rub rub

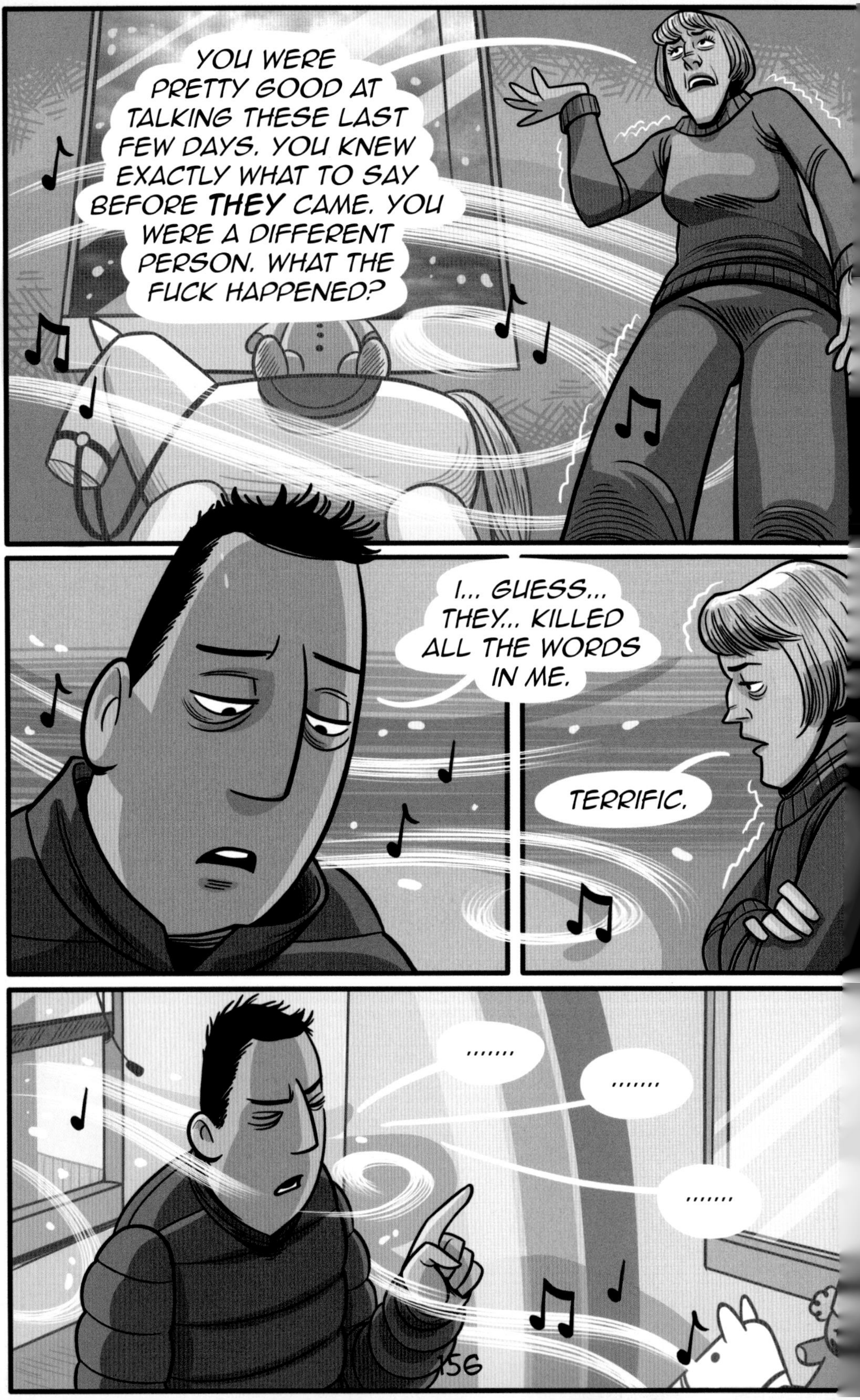
YOU WERE PRETTY GOOD AT TALKING THESE LAST FEW DAYS. YOU KNEW EXACTLY WHAT TO SAY BEFORE THEY CAME. YOU WERE A DIFFERENT PERSON. WHAT THE FUCK HAPPENED?
I... GUESS... THEY... KILLED ALL THE WORDS IN ME.
TERRIFIC.
....
....
....

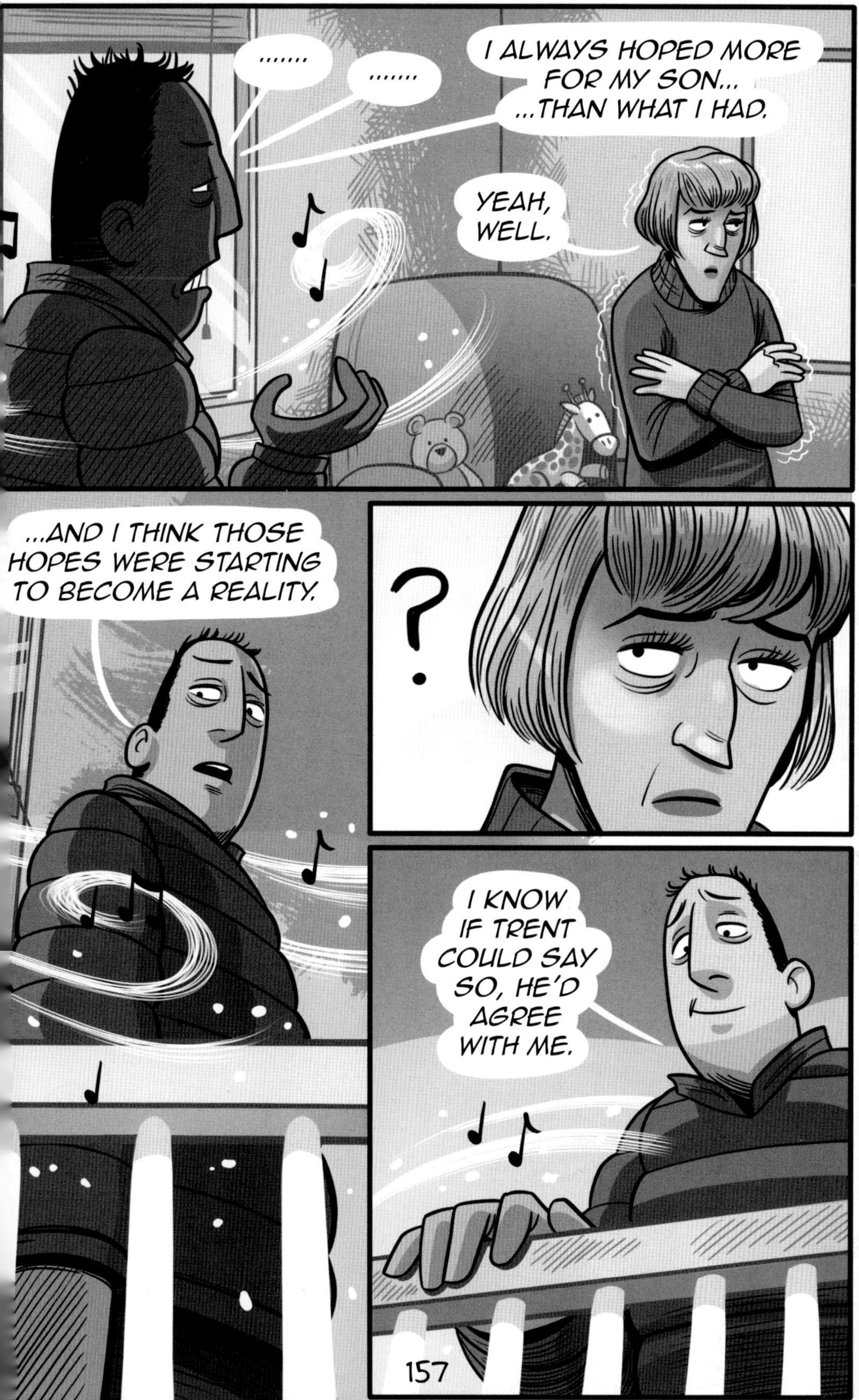
....
....
I ALWAYS HOPED MORE FOR MY SON... ...THAN WHAT I HAD.
YEAH, WELL.
...AND I THINK THOSE HOPES WERE STARTING TO BECOME A REALITY.
?
I KNOW IF TRENT COULD SAY SO, HE'D AGREE WITH ME.

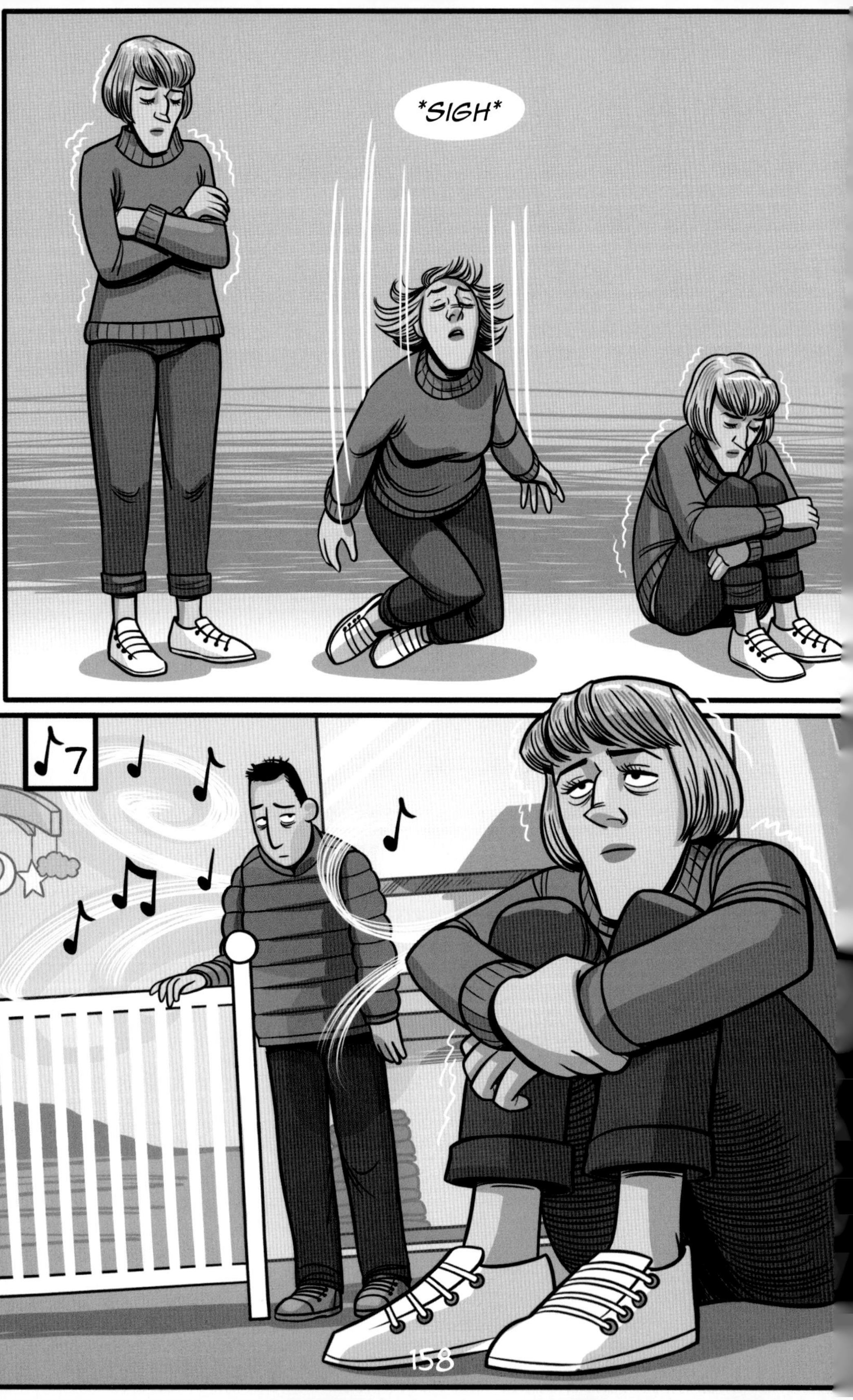
SIGH
7

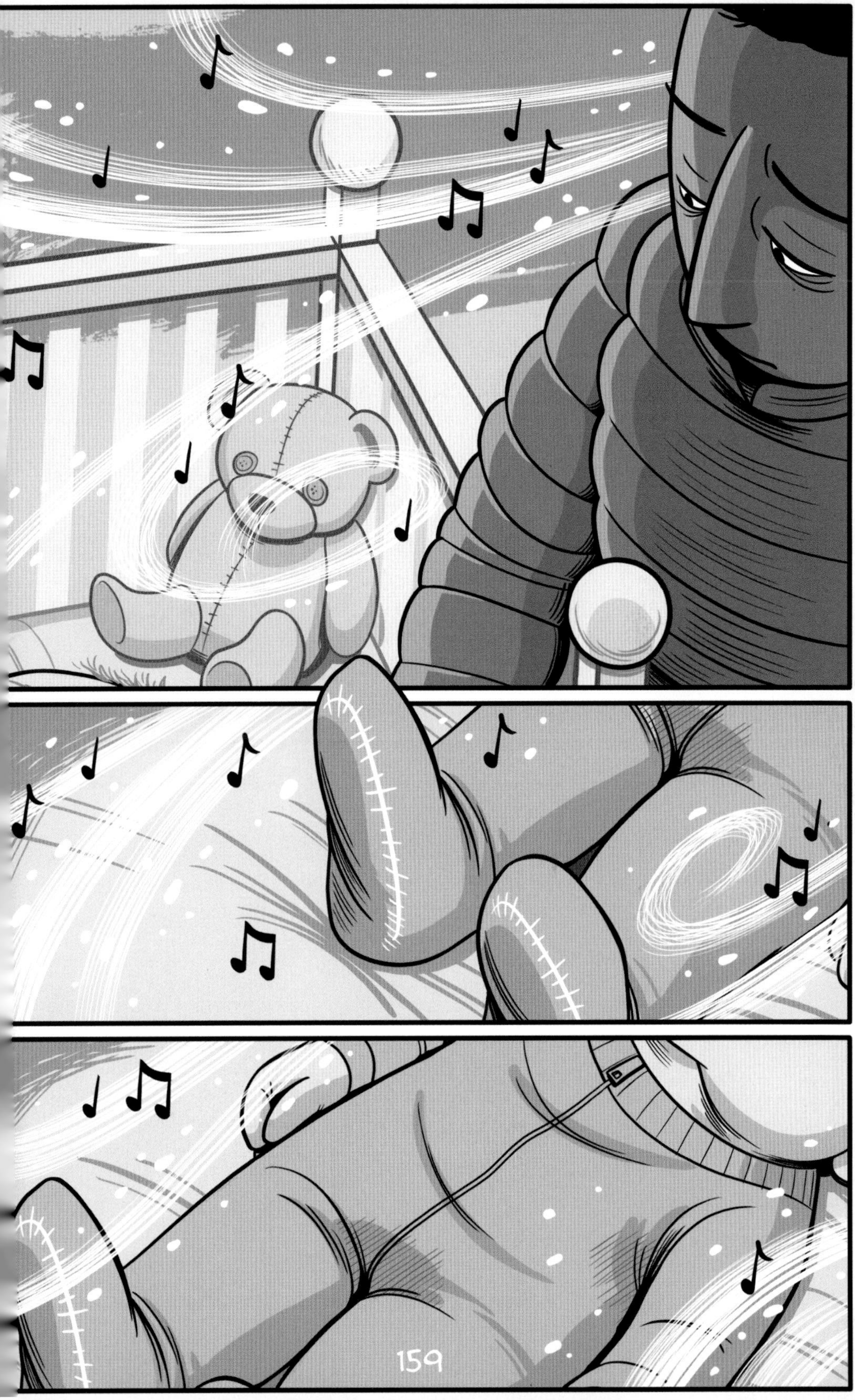

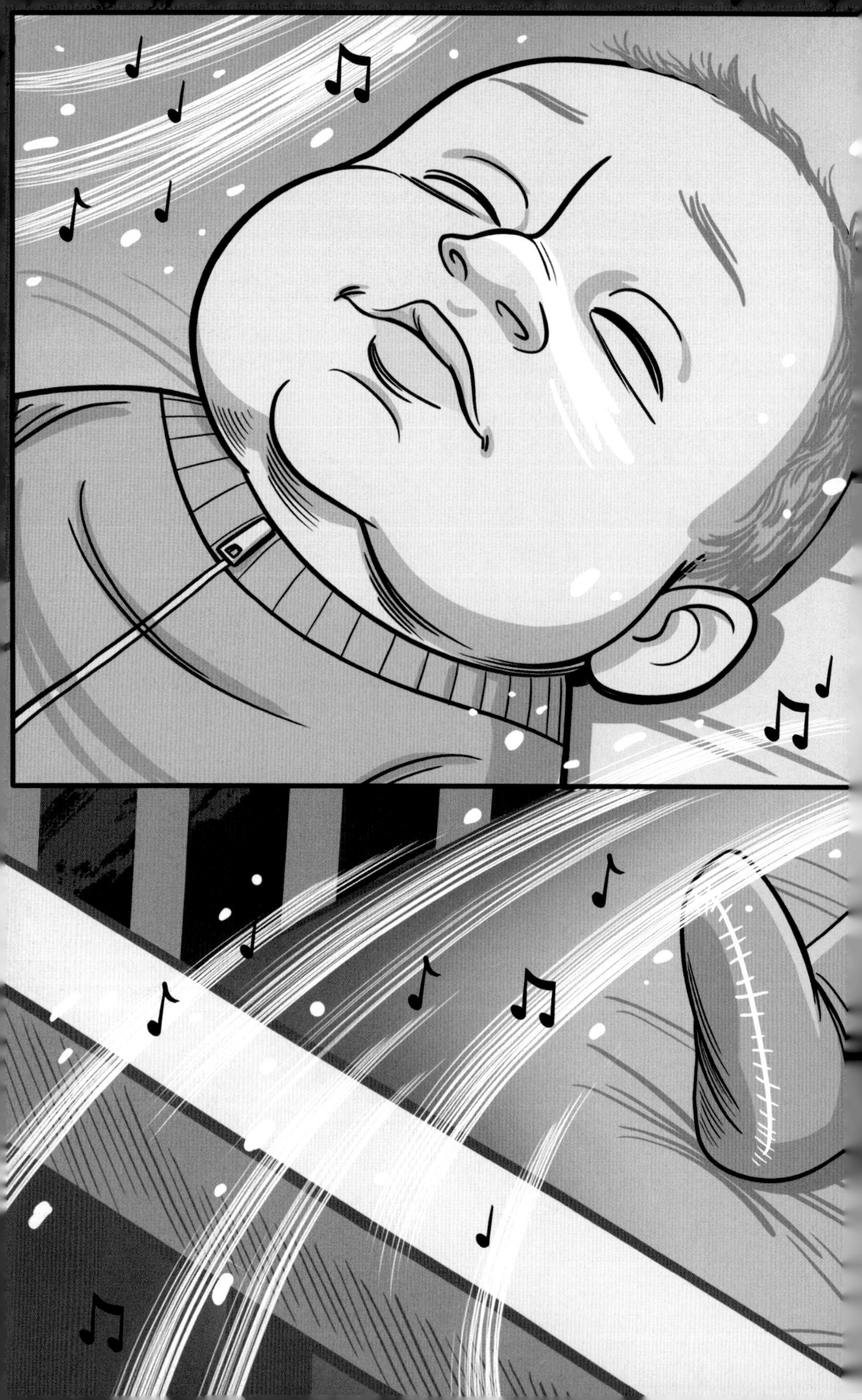

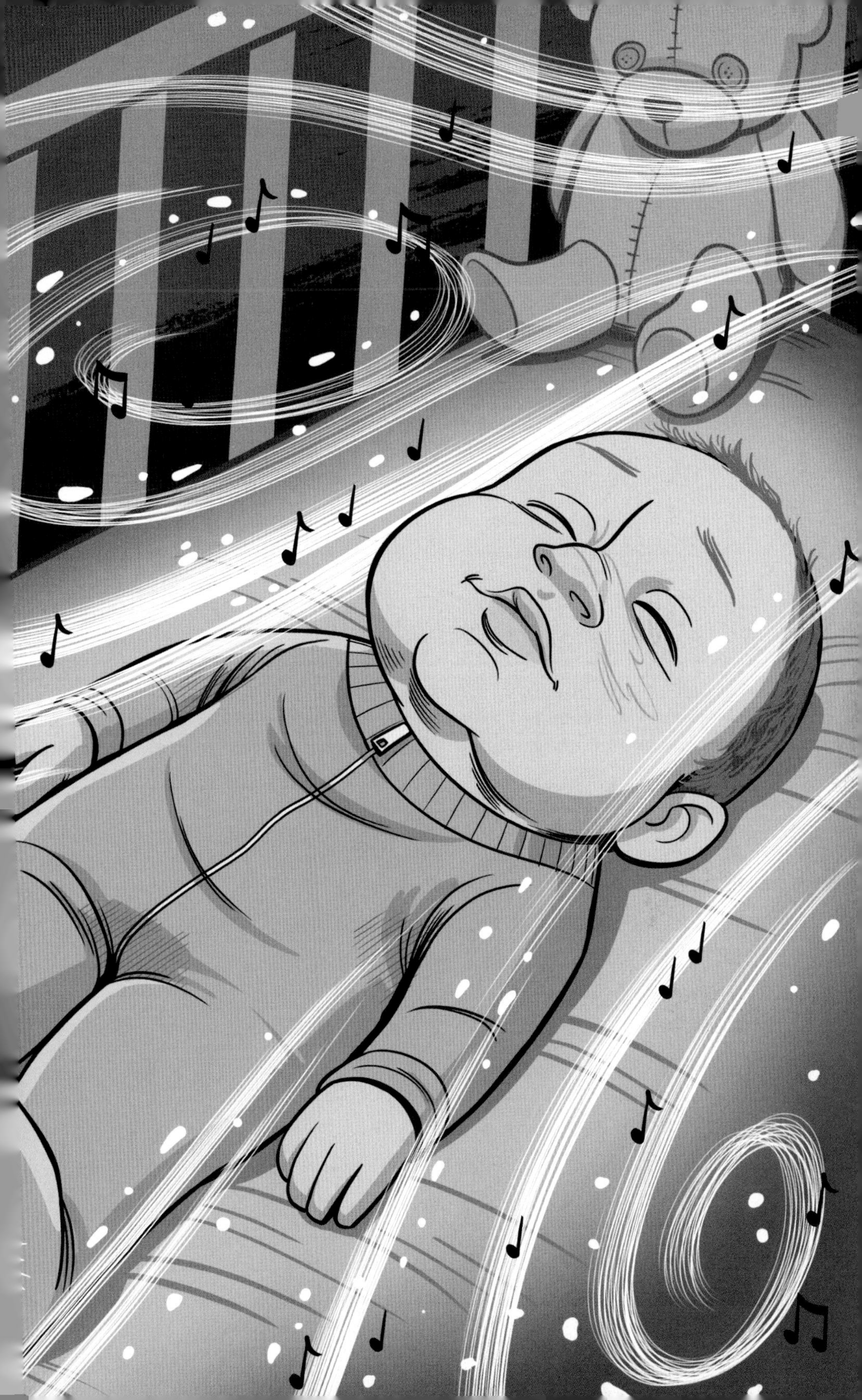

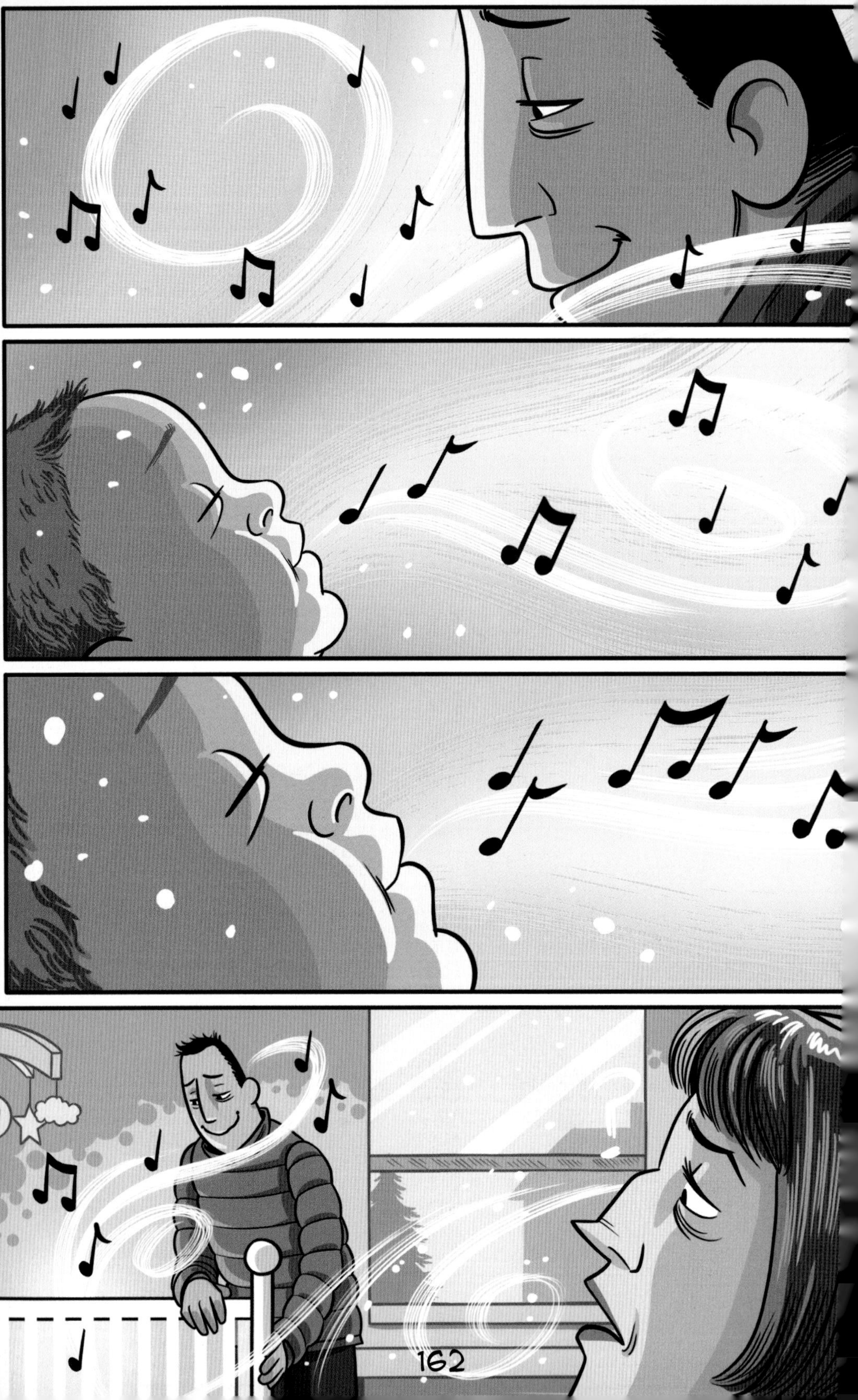

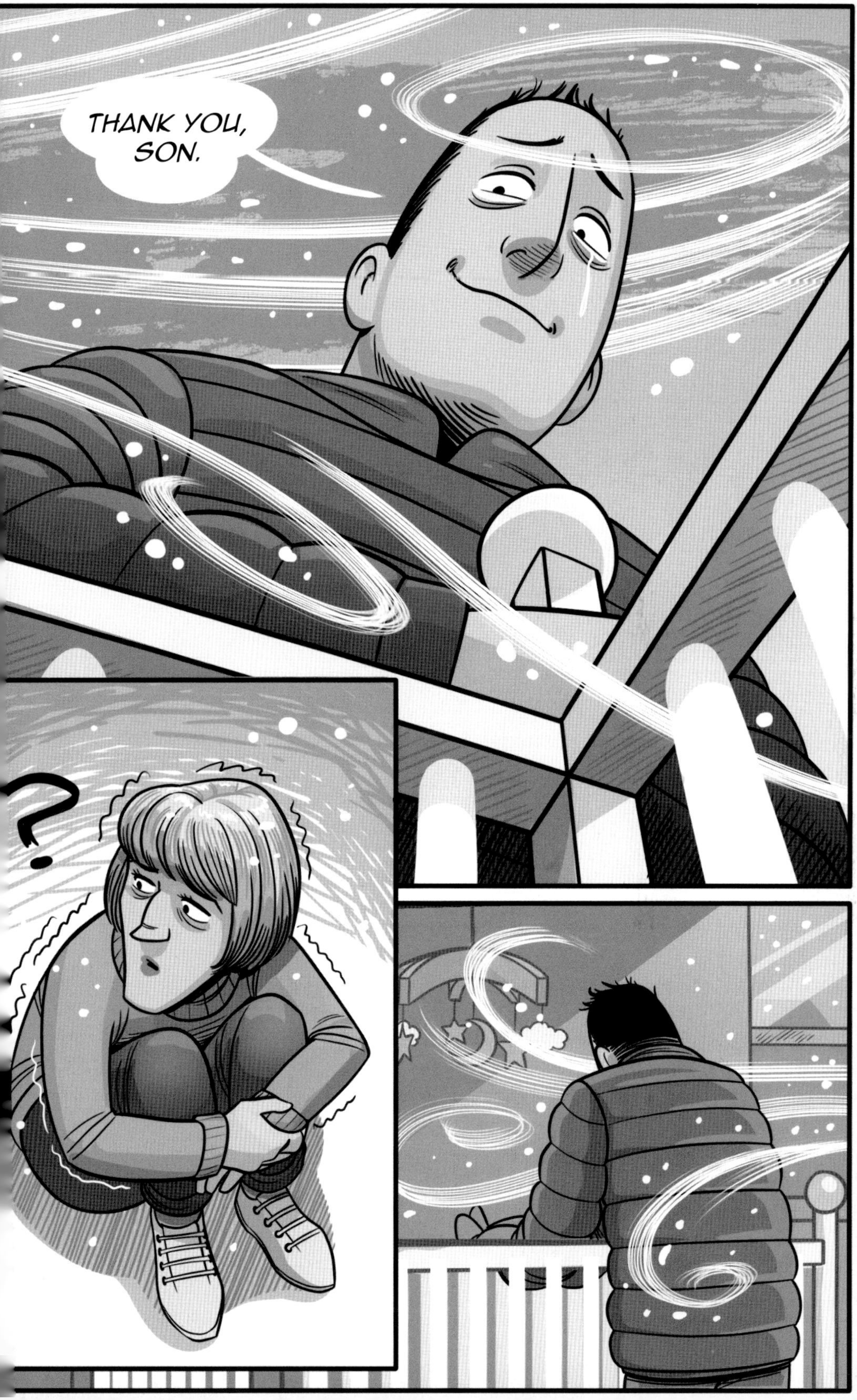
THANK YOU, SON.
?

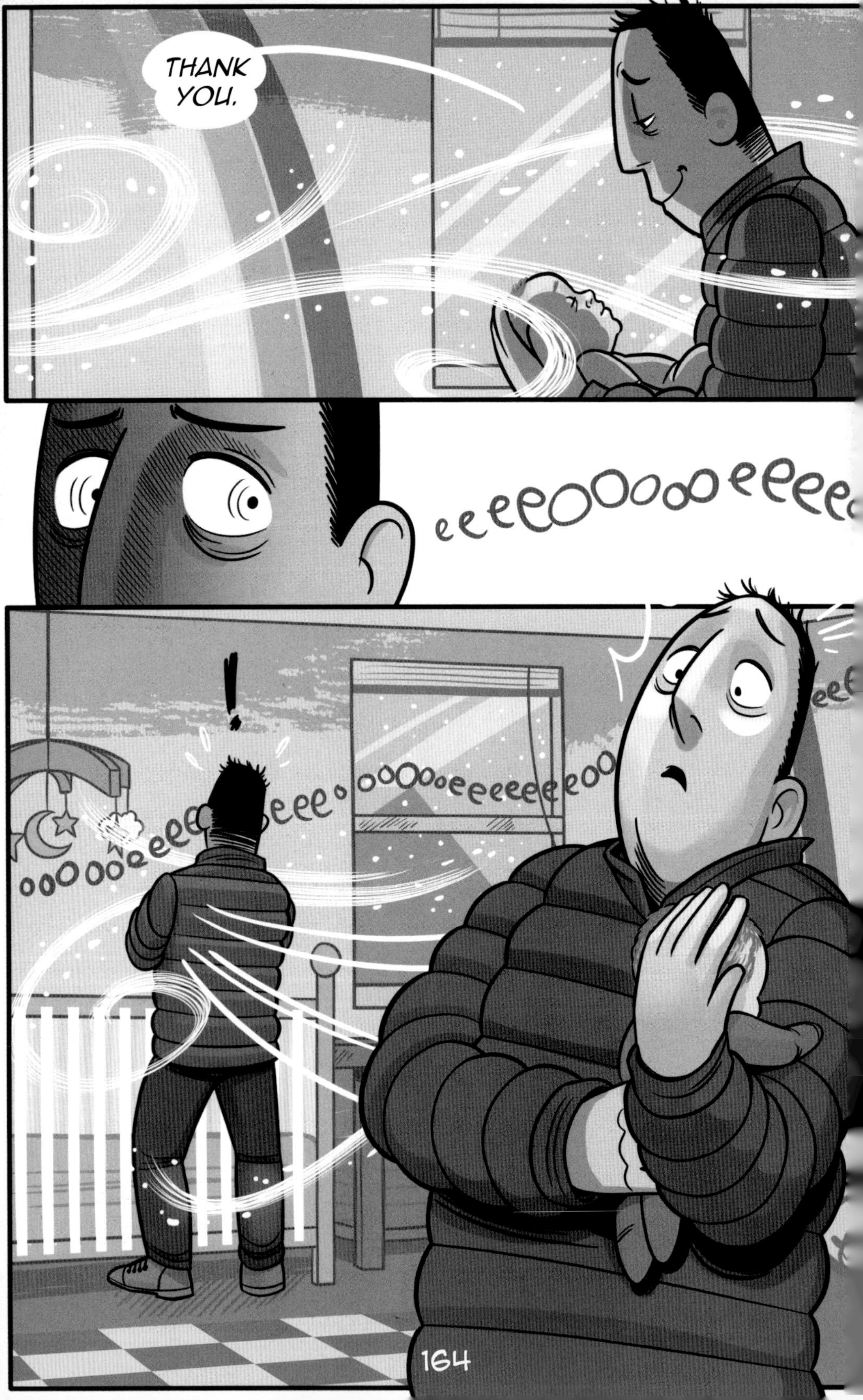
THANK YOU.
eeeeOOOooo eeee
!
oooOOoo eeeee eeeeoooOOooeeeeeeeeOO
eee

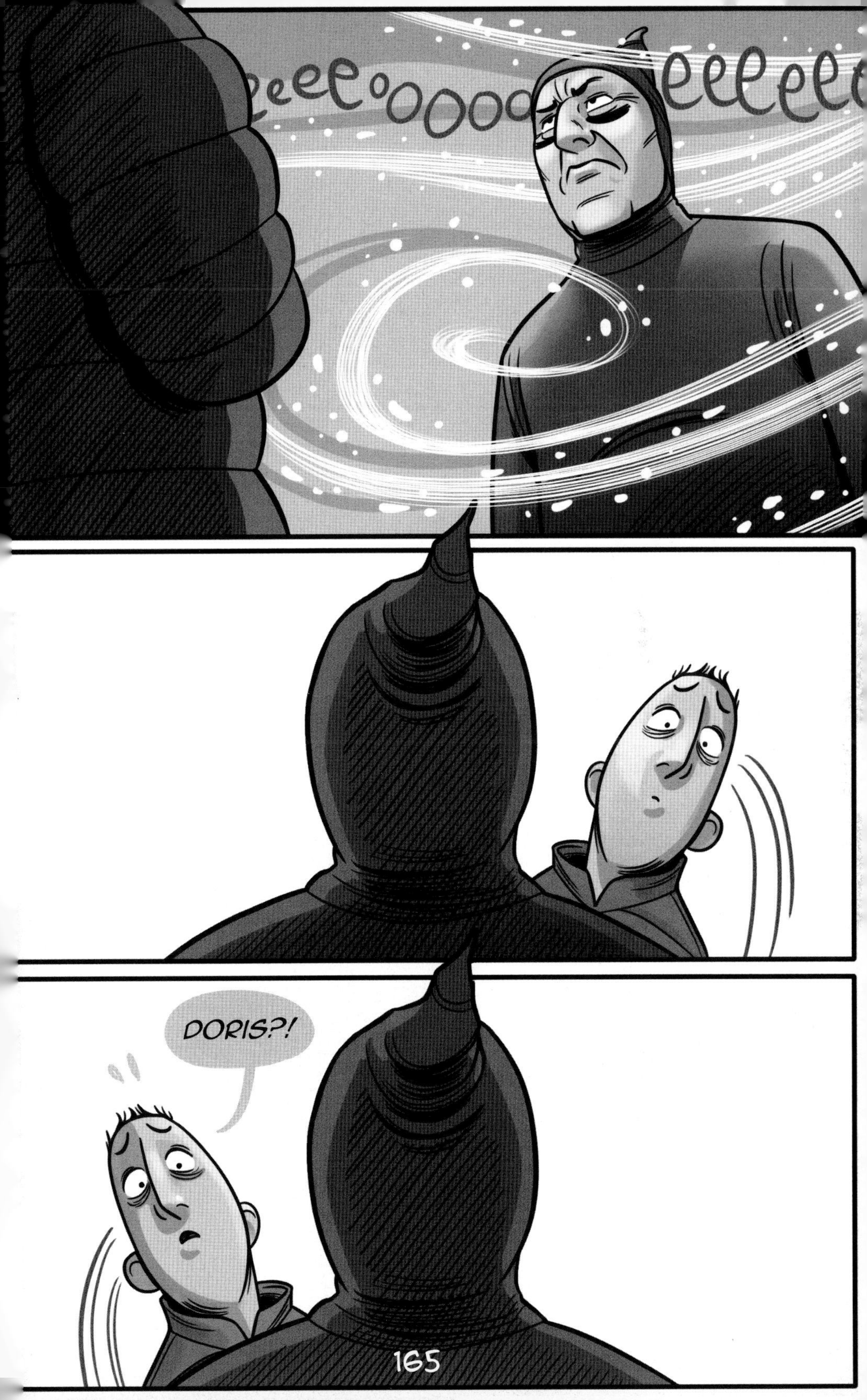
eeeeoooooeeeeee
DORIS?!

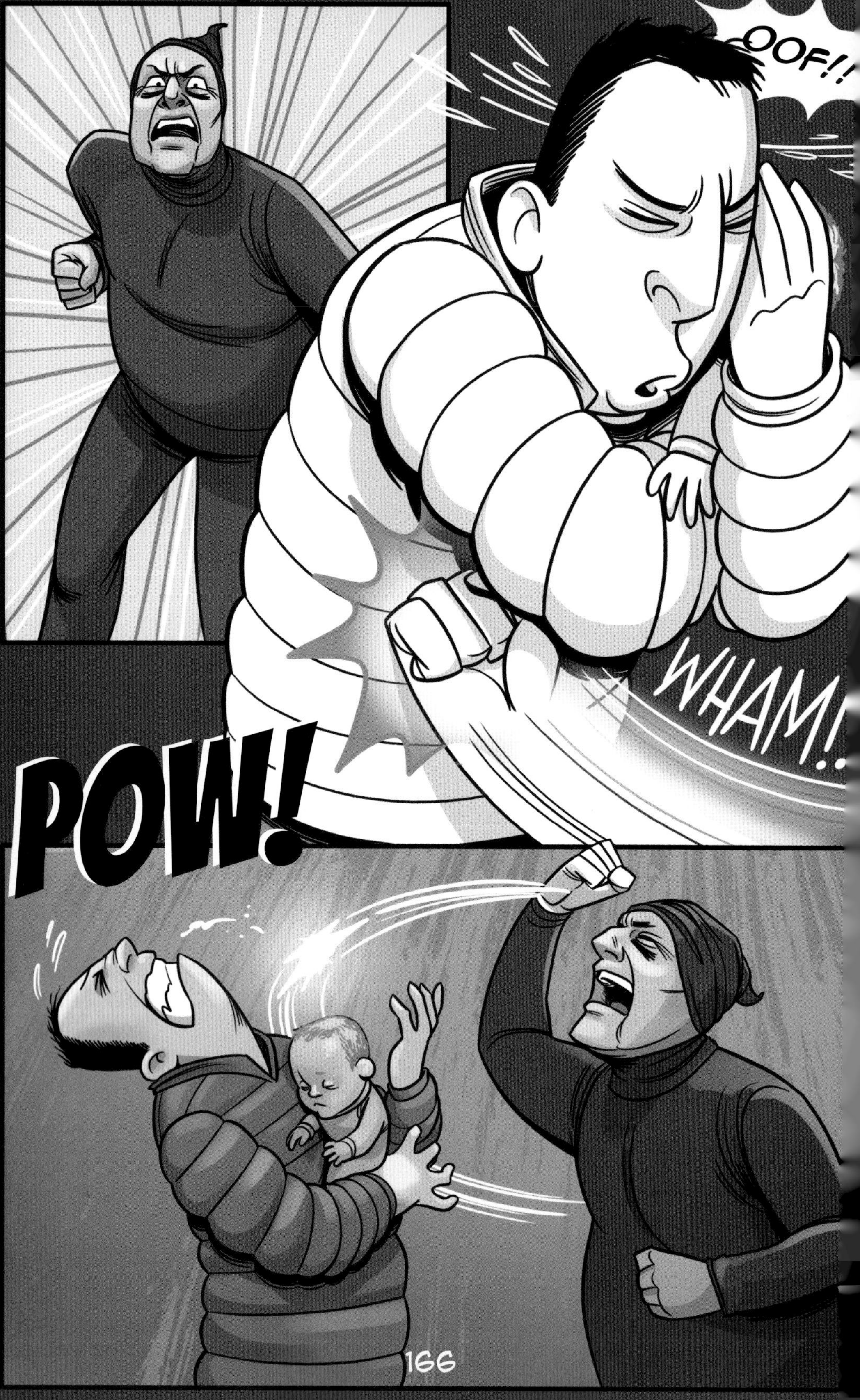
OOF!!
WHAM!!
POW!

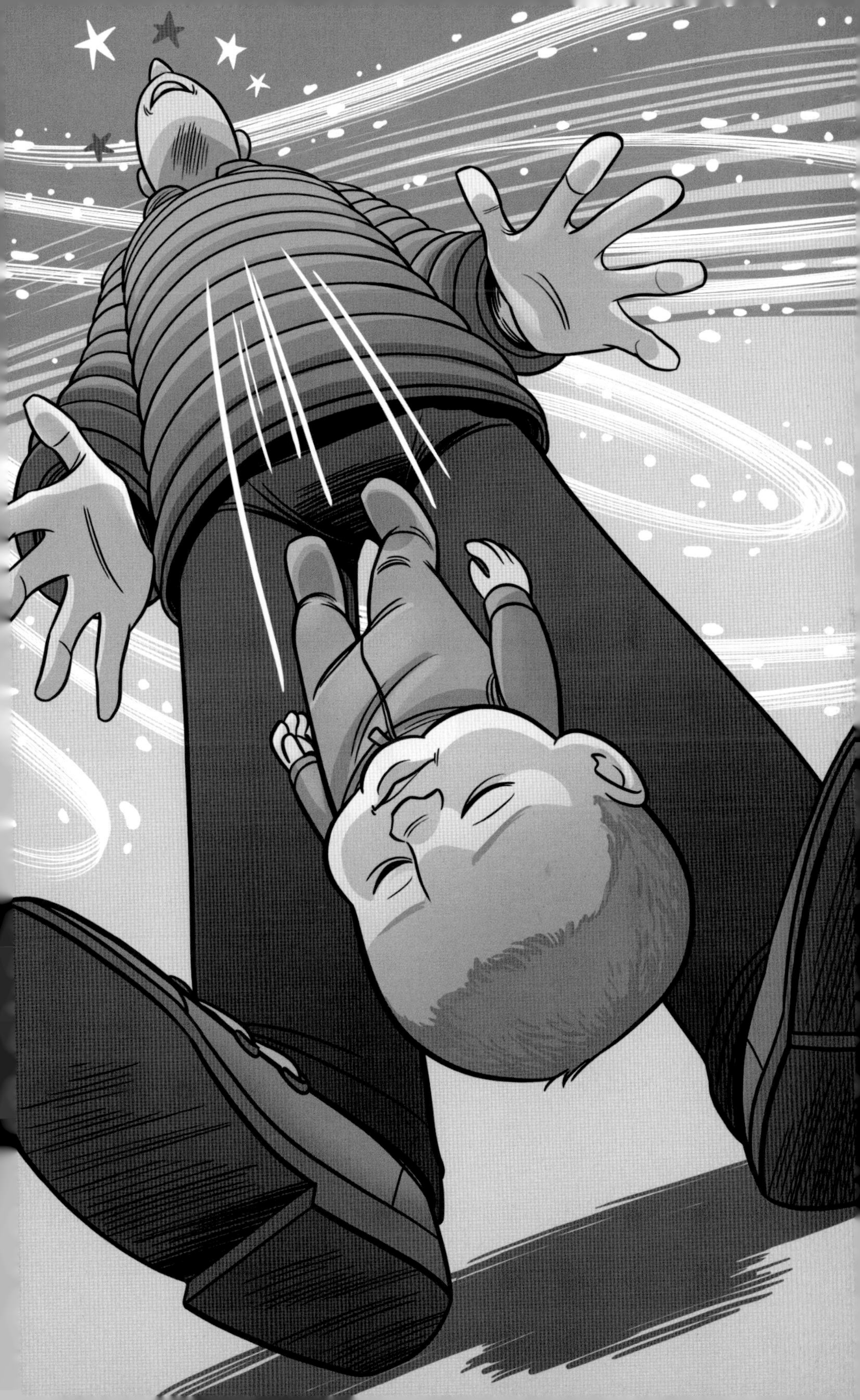

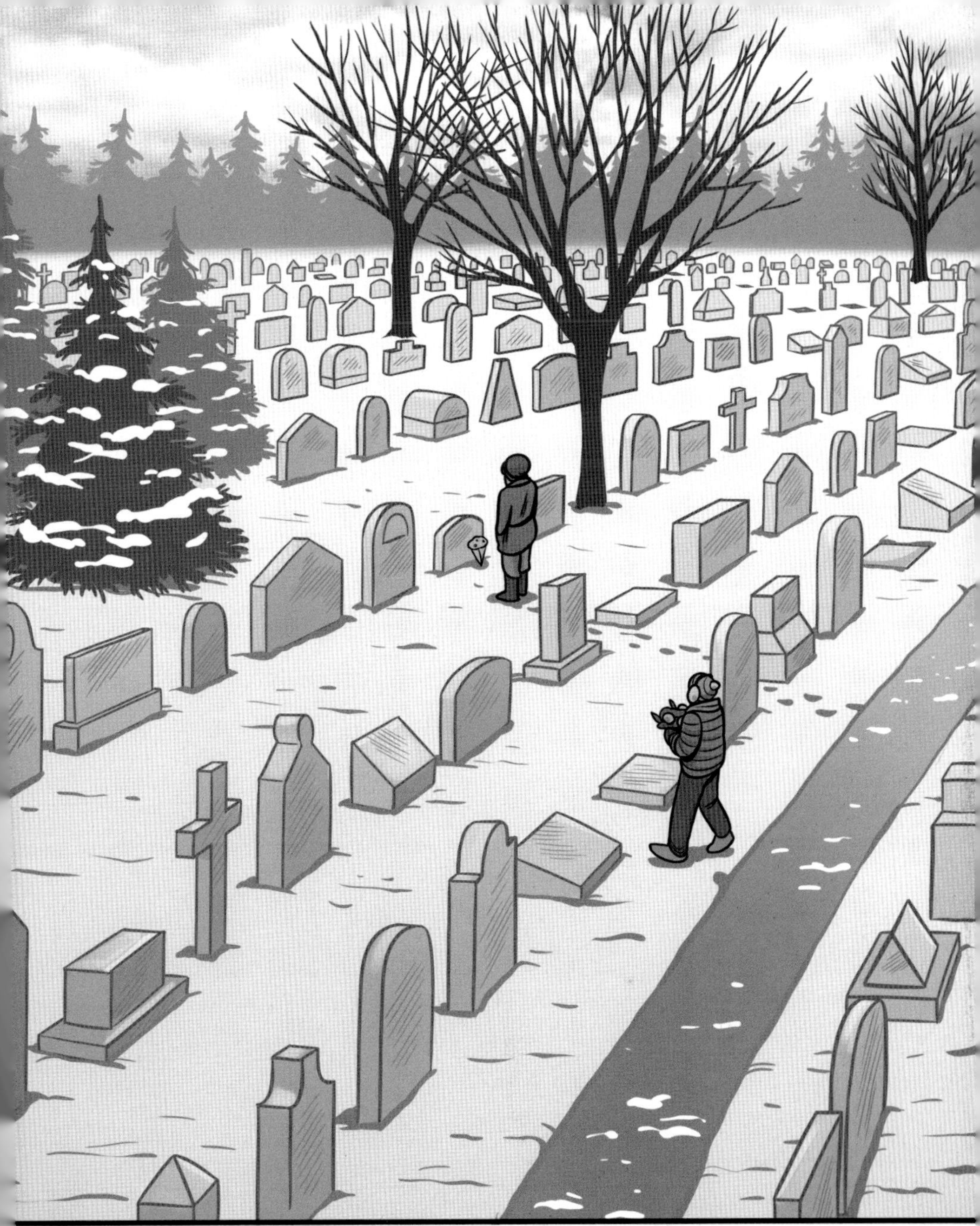

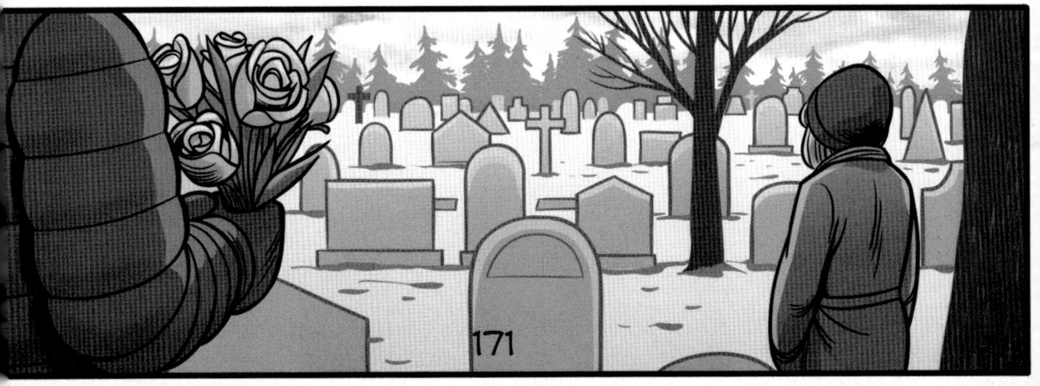

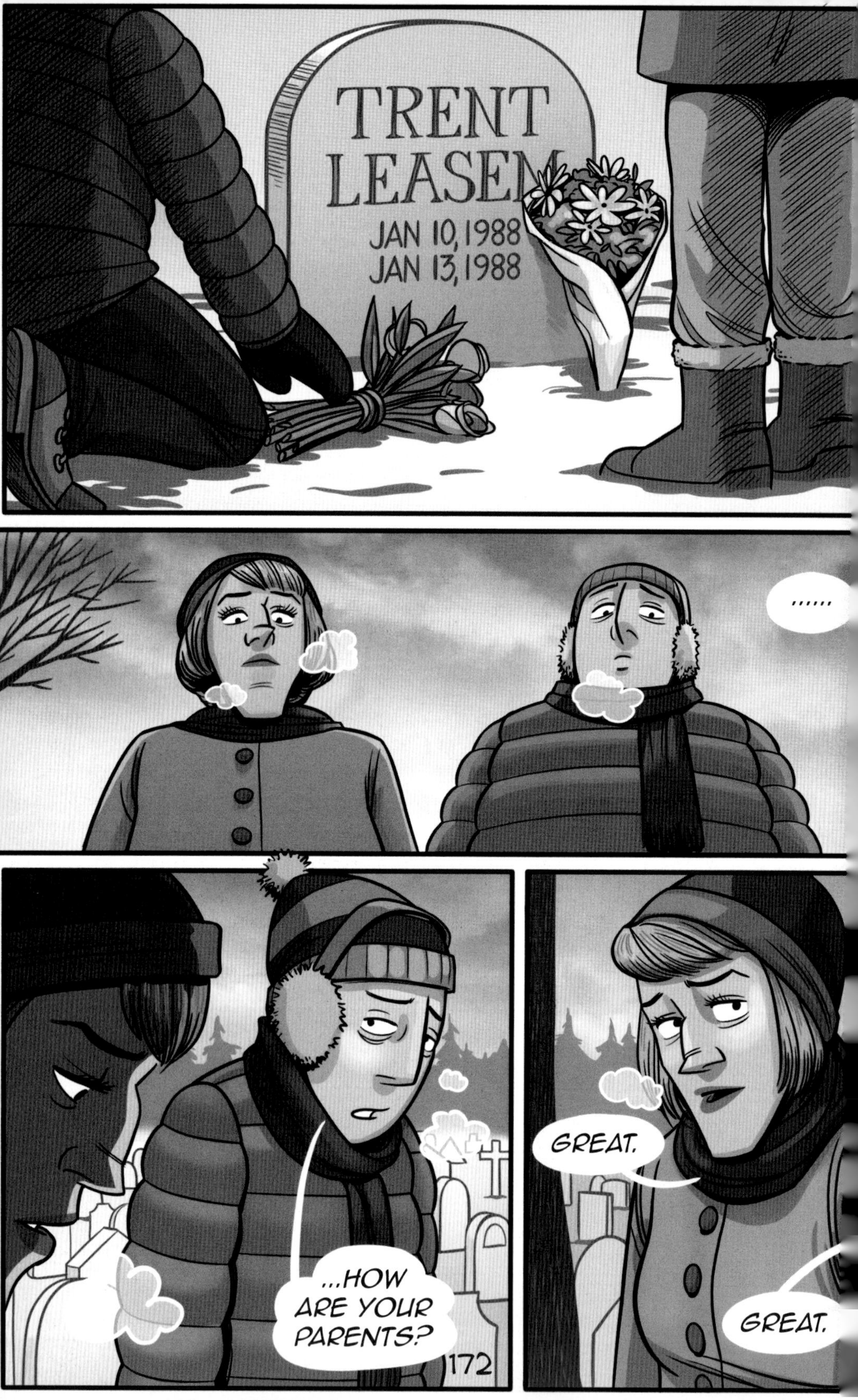
TRENT
LEASEM
JAN 10, 1988
JAN 13, 1988
......
...HOW ARE YOUR PARENTS?
GREAT.
GREAT.

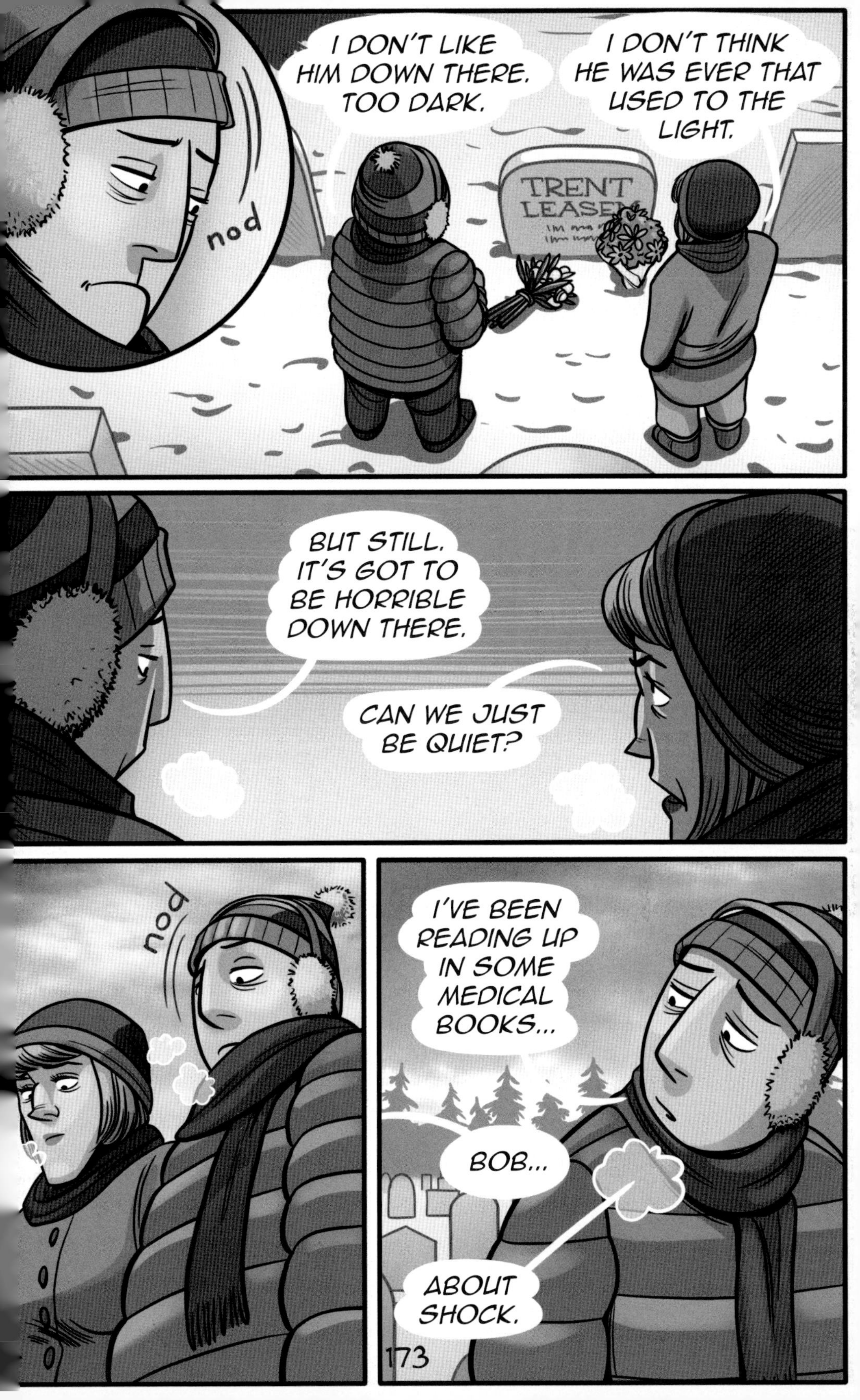
nod
I DON'T LIKE HIM DOWN THERE. TOO DARK.
I DON'T THINK HE WAS EVER THAT USED TO THE LIGHT.
TRENT LEASE
BUT STILL. IT'S GOT TO BE HORRIBLE DOWN THERE.
CAN WE JUST BE QUIET?
nod
I'VE BEEN READING UP IN SOME MEDICAL BOOKS...
BOB...
ABOUT SHOCK.

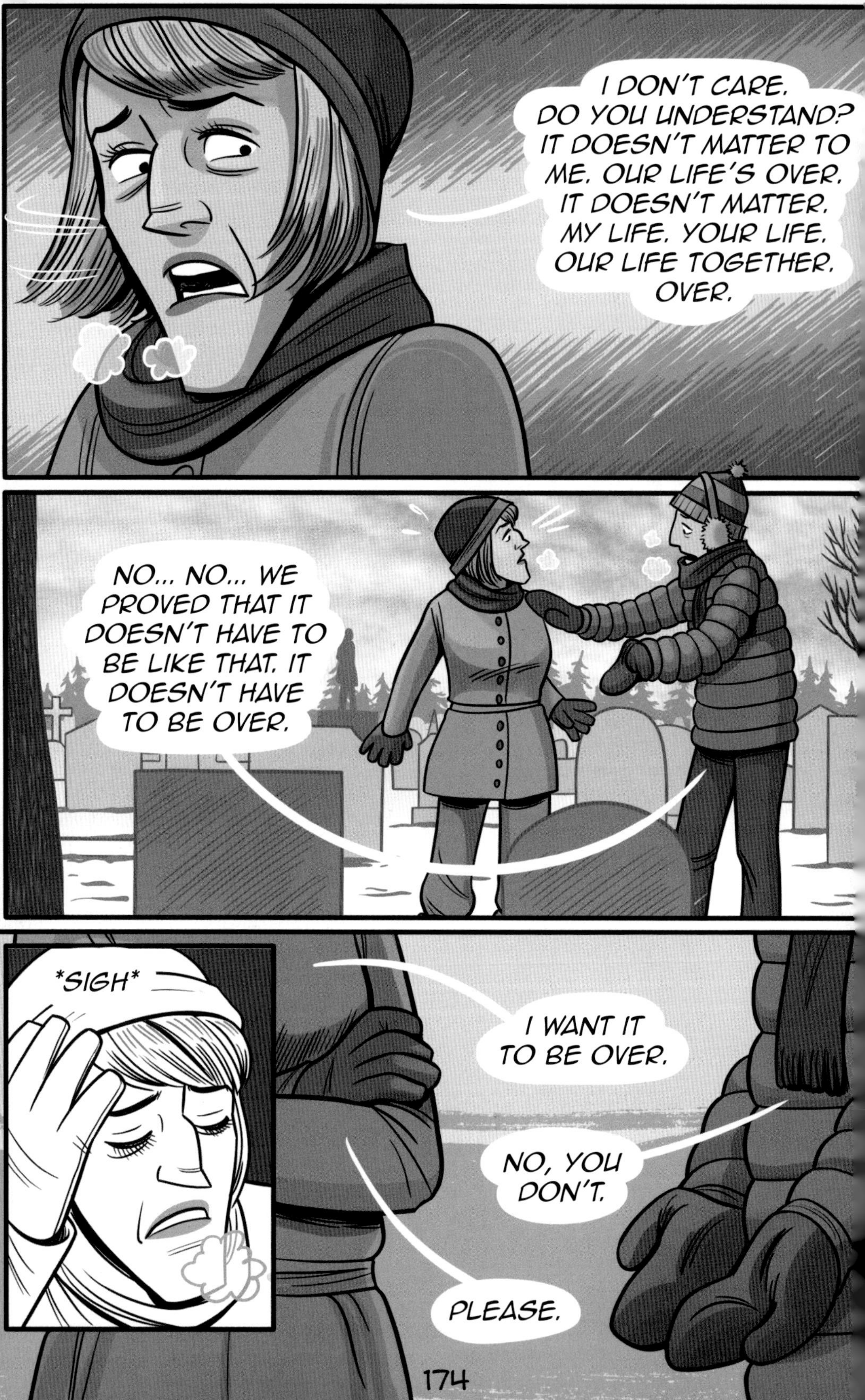
I DON'T CARE. DO YOU UNDERSTAND? IT DOESN'T MATTER TO ME. OUR LIFE'S OVER. IT DOESN'T MATTER. MY LIFE. YOUR LIFE. OUR LIFE TOGETHER. OVER.
NO... NO... WE PROVED THAT IT DOESN'T HAVE TO BE LIKE THAT. IT DOESN'T HAVE TO BE OVER.
SIGH
I WANT IT TO BE OVER.
NO, YOU DON'T.
PLEASE.

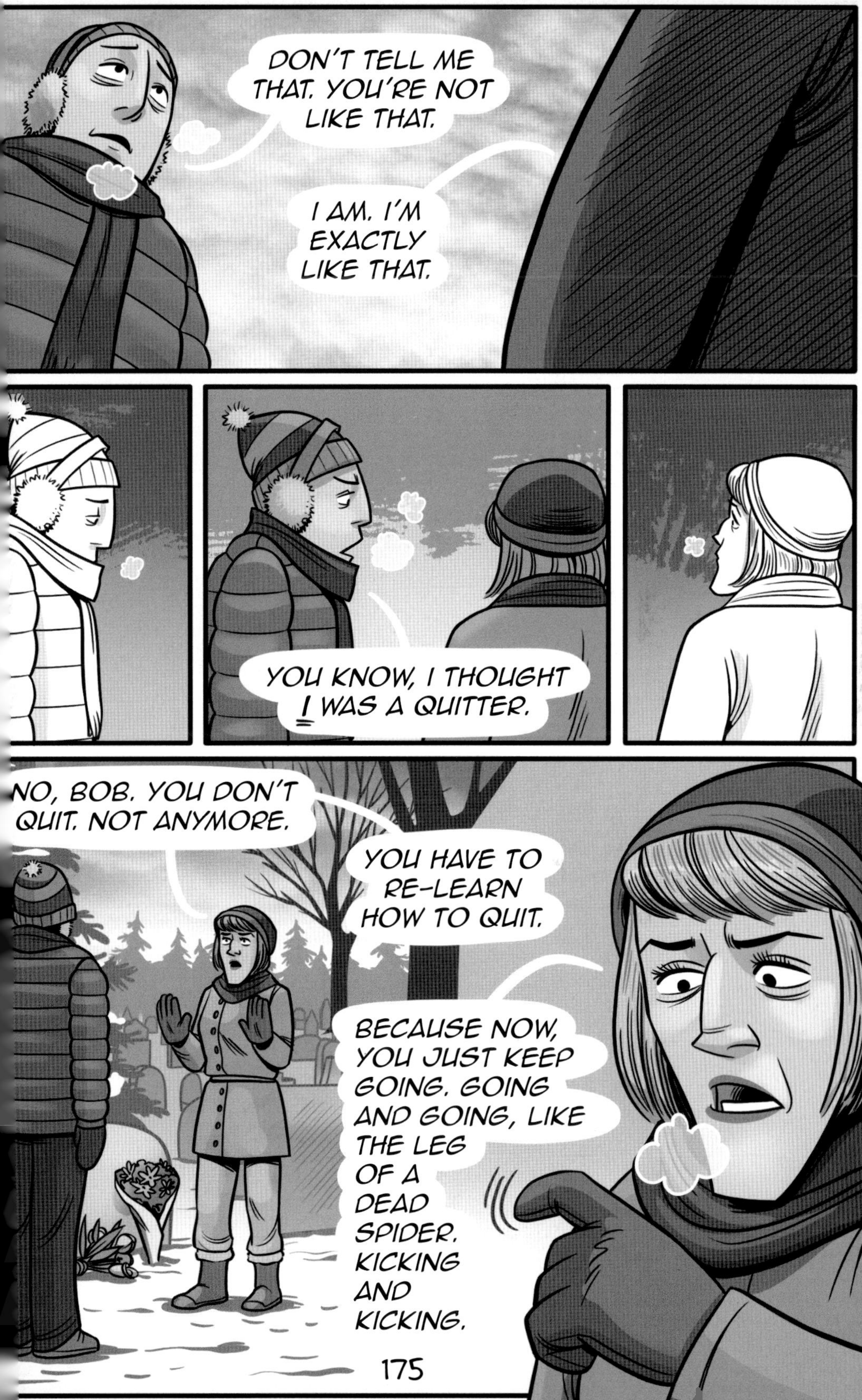
DON'T TELL ME THAT. YOU'RE NOT LIKE THAT.
I AM. I'M EXACTLY LIKE THAT.
YOU KNOW, I THOUGHT I WAS A QUITTER.
NO, BOB. YOU DON'T QUIT. NOT ANYMORE.
YOU HAVE TO RE-LEARN HOW TO QUIT.
BECAUSE NOW, YOU JUST KEEP GOING. GOING AND GOING, LIKE THE LEG OF A DEAD SPIDER. KICKING AND KICKING.

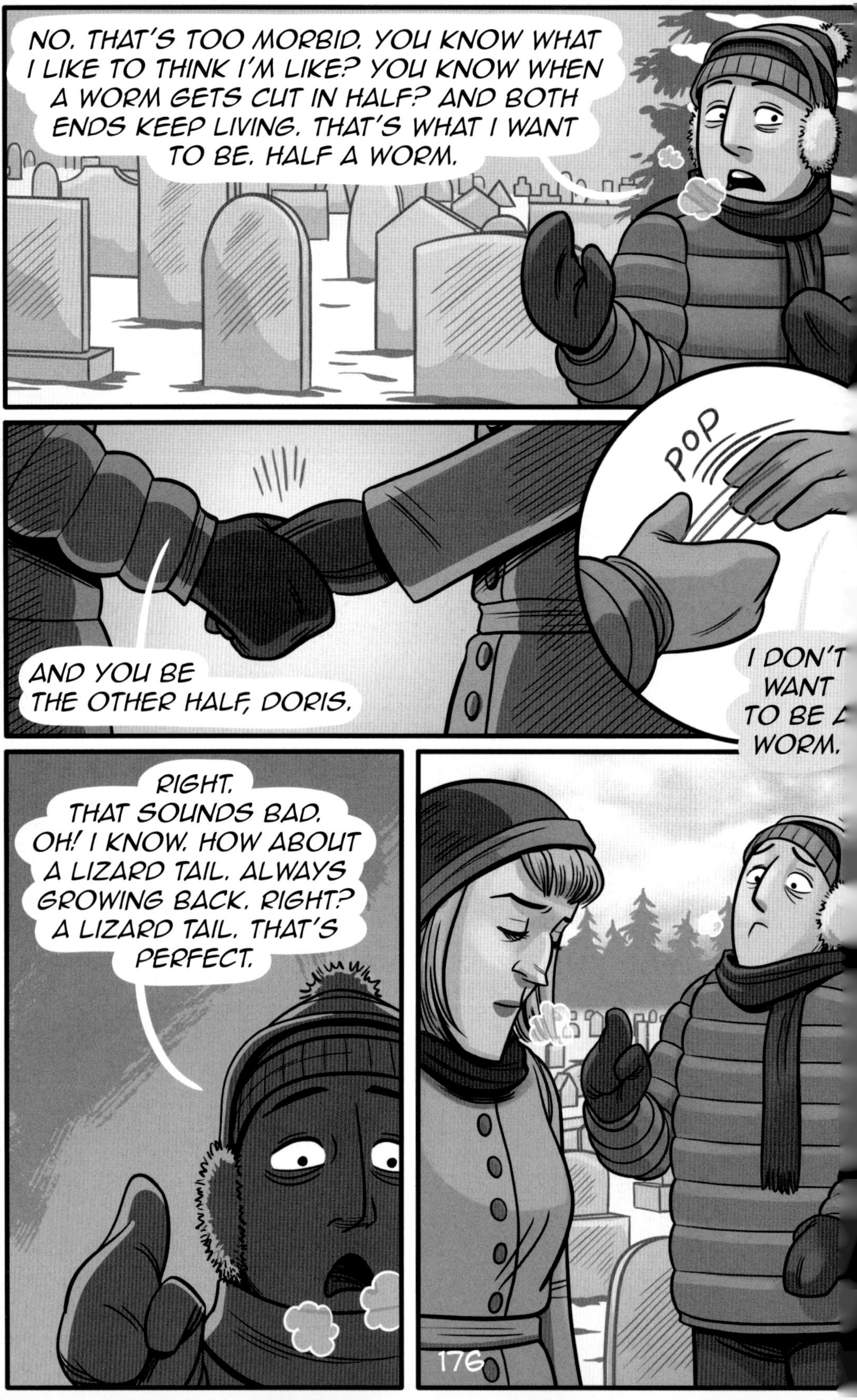
NO. THAT'S TOO MORBID. YOU KNOW WHAT I LIKE TO THINK I'M LIKE? YOU KNOW WHEN A WORM GETS CUT IN HALF? AND BOTH ENDS KEEP LIVING. THAT'S WHAT I WANT TO BE. HALF A WORM.
POP
AND YOU BE THE OTHER HALF, DORIS.
I DON'T WANT TO BE A WORM.
RIGHT. THAT SOUNDS BAD. OH! I KNOW. HOW ABOUT A LIZARD TAIL. ALWAYS GROWING BACK. RIGHT? A LIZARD TAIL. THAT'S PERFECT.

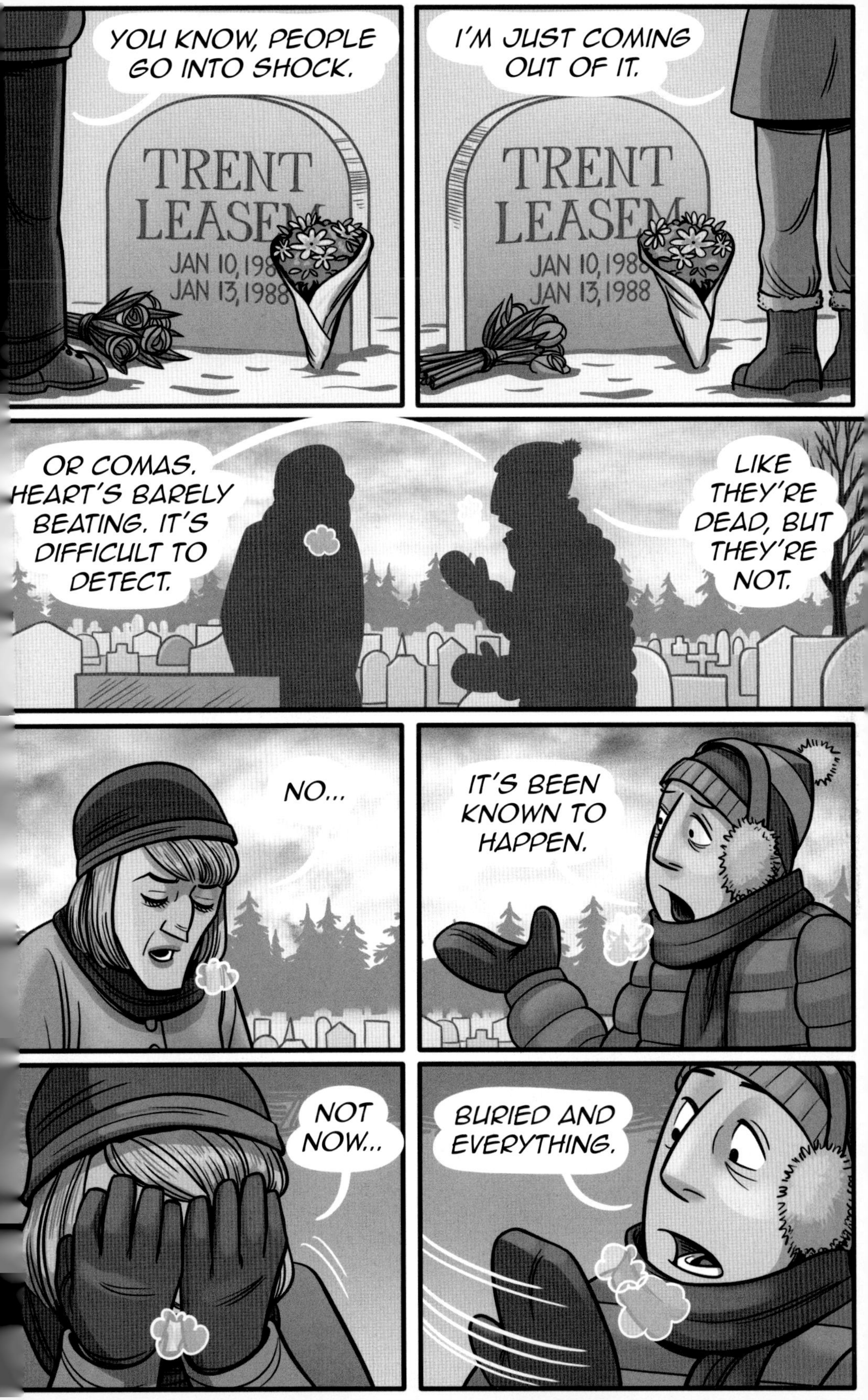
YOU KNOW, PEOPLE GO INTO SHOCK.
TRENT LEASEM JAN 10, 198 JAN 13, 1988
I'M JUST COMING OUT OF IT.
TRENT LEASEM JAN 10, 1988 JAN 13, 1988
OR COMAS. HEART'S BARELY BEATING. IT'S DIFFICULT TO DETECT.
LIKE THEY'RE DEAD, BUT THEY'RE NOT.
NO...
IT'S BEEN KNOWN TO HAPPEN.
NOT NOW...
BURIED AND EVERYTHING.

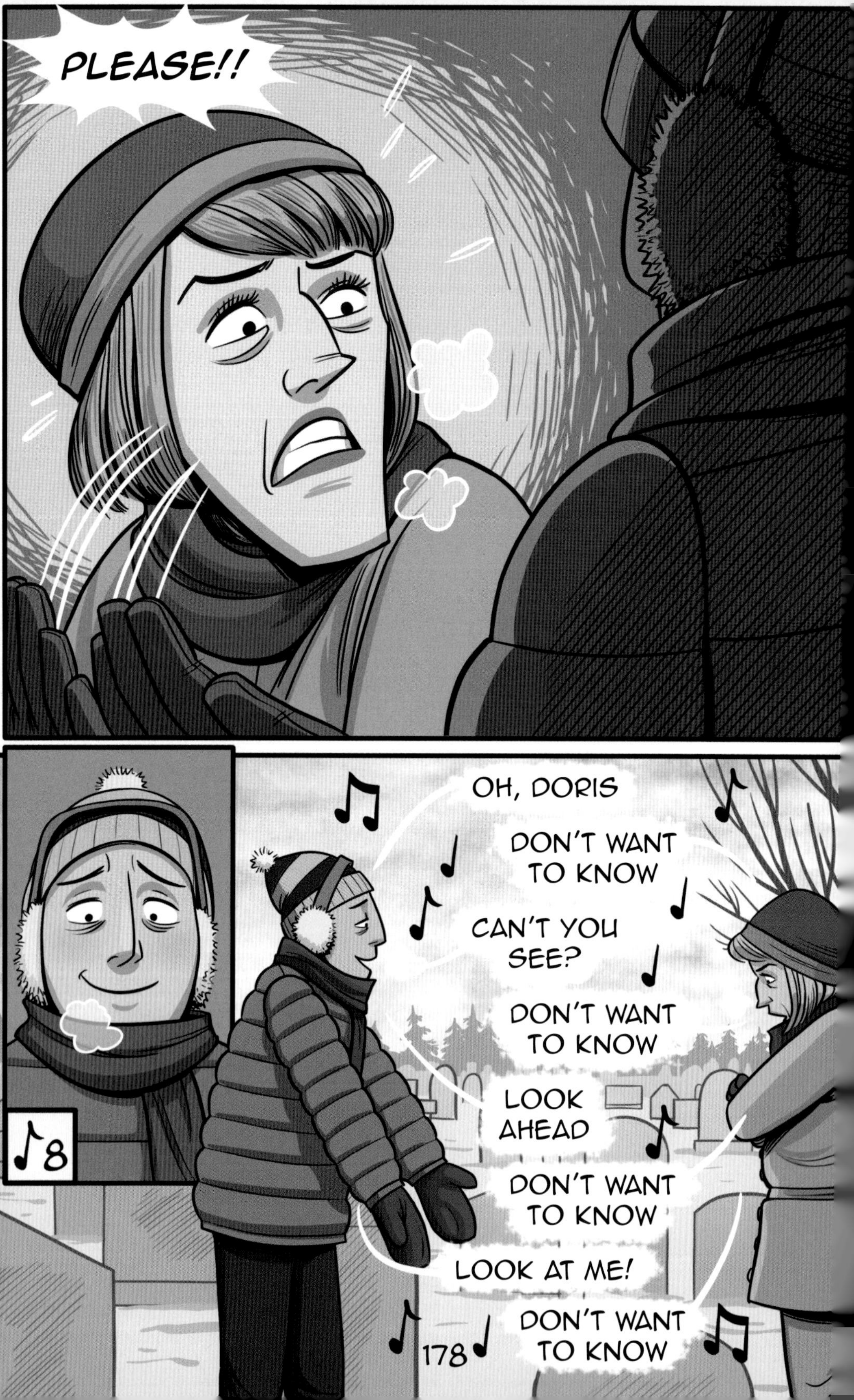
PLEASE!!
♪8
OH, DORIS
DON'T WANT TO KNOW
CAN'T YOU SEE?
DON'T WANT TO KNOW
LOOK AHEAD
DON'T WANT TO KNOW
LOOK AT ME!
DON'T WANT TO KNOW

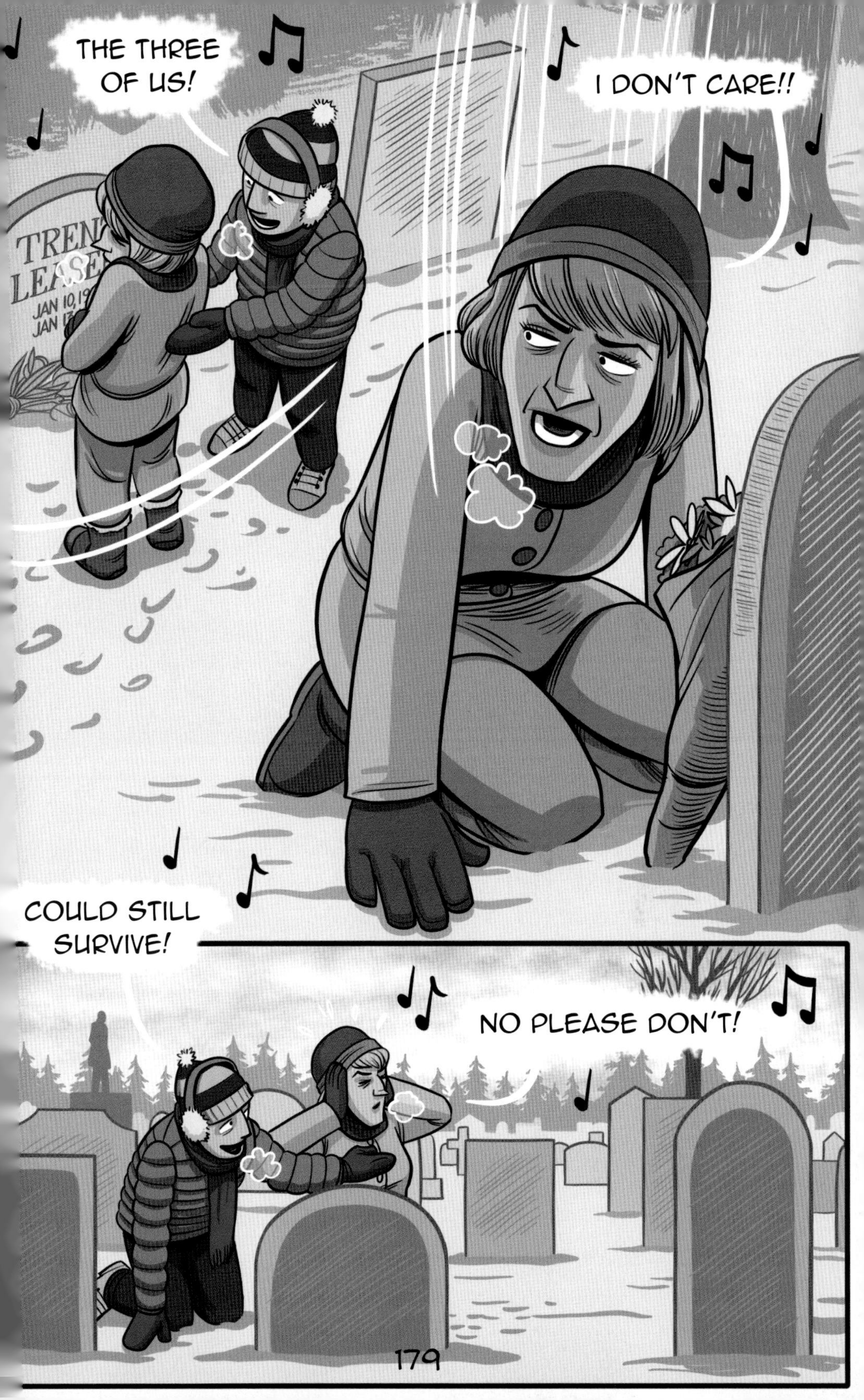
THE THREE OF US!
I DON'T CARE!!
TRENT LEASE
JAN 10, 19
JAN 1
COULD STILL SURVIVE!
NO PLEASE DON'T!

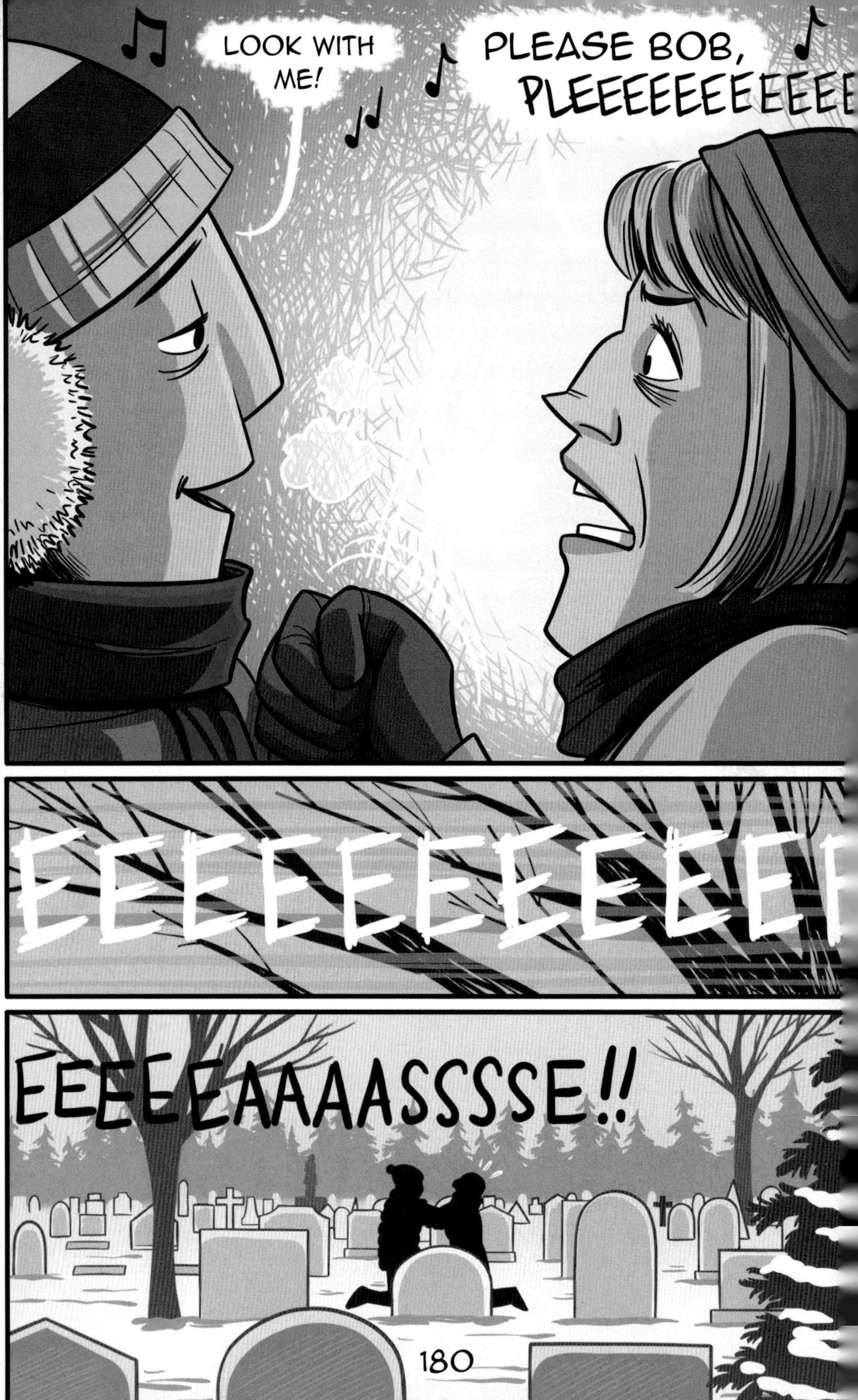
LOOK WITH ME!
PLEASE BOB, PLEEEEEEEEEEEE
EEEEEEEEEEEEEEE
EEEEEAAAAASSSSE!!

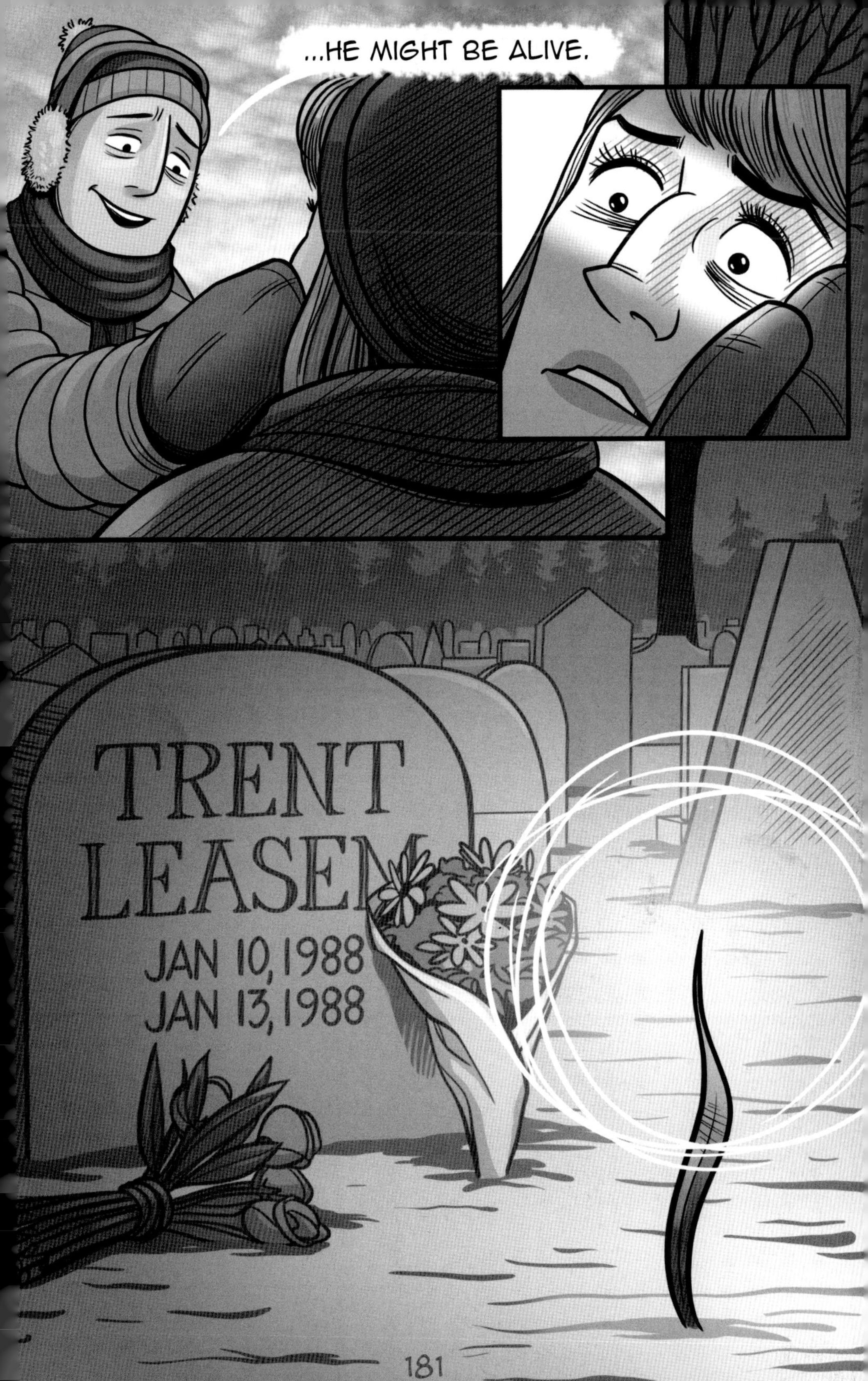
...HE MIGHT BE ALIVE.
TRENT LEASEM
JAN 10, 1988
JAN 13, 1988

afterword

by Dino Stamatopoulos

I wrote TRENT about twenty—six years ago. When I was twenty—six. Half my fucking life ago. The boring half. Oh it wasn't that I personally was bored during it. But if you witnessed me living those twenty—six years you would be bored. I was trying SO HARD.

TRENT started off as a comedy sketch. A guy taking a baby out for a walk on the coldest day of the year and it dies. Hardee har har.

Soon after I wrote that, Mick Napier said he'd give me a spot at his ANNOYANCE THEATER if I had something to put up. So I took that sketch and wrote it out in both directions. Made it a play. Then I added songs and made it a musical. Kind of. I wrote most of it on the Chicago "el train". Probably took me about a week. Before I knew it I had something to put up.

I'm not a smart writer. I'm what you might call a "dumb writer". Or if you're nicer than that you can call me an "instinctual writer". I always let the subconscious take over in my writing. TRENT for better or for worse is my ultimate example of that. But as the subconscious is wont to do: it connects things for the writer long after the fact.

I wrote this when I didn't know anything about relationships. Let alone having a baby. Ironic that I wrote this particular piece. Not only because I really had no idea what it was like to be involved with a wife or even a girlfriend at that point. But also because I had the balls to write something and put it up without knowing what it really was about.

What I gather now is that TRENT is ultimately about insecurity. A lack of confidence on an epic scale. That's what makes Bob sing the words "I just say love gets you too attached to things." It's not insensitivity. It's ultra—sensitivity. It's about a man not done with himself. Starting on someone else. Scary. And yet we all do it. He just was very sensitive to it.

Then later Bob sings forgiveness to his son. And I think he's really singing it to himself. To the same musical chords as BAA BAA BLACK SHEEP. But it's also a song about punishing the naughty boy crying in the lane. What I realize now —— twenty—six years later —— is that Bob was the Black Sheep and the naughty boy. Both. At least that's why I think my subconscious wrote it that way. Or maybe my subconscious is just as dumb as I am. I don't know.

But ultimately if you enjoy TRENT I really can't take much credit for it. AND... if you hate it. I can confidently take full blame. Because I'm like Bob and I like punishing myself.

thanks

Dino

I'll start out by thanking two people who are already credited in this book. Leah Tiscione whose wonderful artwork brought this story to life. And Simon Oré, who has been an unending font of energy, inspiration, and encouragement.

A big THANK YOU must go Mick Napier and his Annoyance Theater for playing a major part in springboarding this project. If Mick hadn't offered me dates at his space, I never would have written this.

Also, long-deserved "thank yous" to the original cast members in that early 90s production: Beth Kathan (Doris), Eric Hoffman (Bob), Brian McCann (Arnie), Audrey Kissel (Lisa, called Chelsea here), Jimmy Carrane (Doris' Dad), and Michelle Levitt (Doris' Mom).

And for guiding me in non-hacky directions all through my writing career: thank you very much, Norm Holly.

Specifically in the "birth" of TRENT, I thank Marty Duffy, who suggested a moment alone between each parent and Trent. This idea eventually became the TRENT/BAA BAA BLACK SHEEP song. And also thank you to Peter Blood who further suggested a monologue from Trent himself which –– finally, after years of head scratching –– turned into TRENT'S BALLAD and debuts here in this specific incarnation.

General "thank yous" of support to my immediate family: my father, Tom Stamatopoulos. I'll always miss you. And to my mother, Toula Stamatopoulos who probably passed her sense of humor on to me genetically. And my brother, Jerry Stamatopoulos, who was there right next to me when we first started joking around.

And finally: an eternal "thank you" to my daughter, Tigger, who proved beyond a shadow of a doubt that this story came solely from my head and not my heart; as I discovered that my love for her not only began well before her emergence into this world, but has been growing ever since, no matter how ill-equipped I feel ultimately as a father.

thanks

LEAH

I drew this in 11 cities and 5 countries over 3 and a half years: New York City, Los Angeles, Boston, Seattle, Bozeman and Livingston Montana, Acapulco Mexico, Dublin and Galway Ireland, Bangor Northern Ireland, and Montréal Canada.

To my "host" friends that put up with my schizophrenic working during TRENT: George Ouzounian and Jess Blum, Alix Kivlin and Grant Christman, Simon Oré, Brooks and Greg Simsar, Erin McGathy and Andréa Farrell, Jim and Josephine, Aisling and David, Sharai and Chris, Malori Doerfler. Thank you for letting me draw in your living rooms. And Theo Caviness, Amber Tozer, Elizabeth Messick, Jenny Fine, Cody Heller and Brenna Mahon, thanks for listening. I love you all!

MASSIVE THANK YOU to Marissa Louise, shade collaborator! We worked on shading a majority of the black and white pages together and I cherish your input. Without you the book would have taken an extra 3–4 months!

Thanks to my mom Christine Tiscione, for being the first person I went to for a varied spectrum of emotional support while working so hard on this. I'd be in the fetal position in a gutter without you.
Thanks to my dad James Tiscione, for listening to me, for all the business advice, for all the encouragement to keep going as long as I was happy doing it. I love you both endlessly.
And so much love and thank you to my stupid parasitic twin brother James and sister Christina.

I'm overwhelmed with the honor of visually adapting Dino's genius, provocative writing. Dino, Simon Oré and I combined efforts for years and made this very alive dead baby. You're like a drunk uncle and li'l brother high on candy to me. I unrequited love you guys a lot.

THANK YOU STARBURNS!

And thank you for changing my entire life with one small gesture, Louis.

bios

DINO STAMATOPOULOS has been writing comedy for the greater part of his life. You know the term "failed upwards"? Well, Dino has succeeded downwards. He has worked on some of the most influential comedy shows of the last two decades; The Ben Stiller Show, The Dana Carvey Show, Mr. Show. He was one of the original writers on NBC's Late Night with Conan O'Brien. He has even created three of his own shows: Moral Orel, Mary Shelley's Frankenhole, High School USA!. And yet, what has he got to show for all of this? This bio, that's what!

LEAH TISCIONE works (and worked) as an illustrator and Graphic Artist at the New York Post, Sky and Telescope magazine and other publications, illustrated for clients from Tom Green to Charlie Sheen, published a couple comic books, turned a car into a dragon, had fleas once, it's all on the website: www.leahtiscione.com

Now go write your own stupid bio!